Making Enterprise Information Management (EIM) Work for Business

Making Enterprise Information Management (EIM) Work for Business

A Guide to Understanding Information as an Asset

John Ladley

AMSTERDAM • BOSTON • HEIDELBERG • LONDON
NEW YORK • OXFORD • PARIS • SAN DIEGO
SAN FRANCISCO • SINGAPORE • SYDNEY • TOKYO

Morgan Kaufmann is an imprint of Elsevier

Acquiring Editor: Rick Adams
Development Editor: Heather Scherer
Production Manager: Paul Gottehrer
Designer: Joanne Blank

Morgan Kaufmann is an imprint of Elsevier
30 Corporate Drive, Suite 400, Burlington, MA 01803, USA

Library of Congress Cataloging-in-Publication Data
Application submitted

British Library Cataloguing-in-Publication Data
A catalogue record for this book is available from the British Library.

ISBN: 978-0-12-375695-4

Printed and bound by CPI Group (UK) Ltd, Croydon, CR0 4YY

Working together to grow
libraries in developing countries

www.elsevier.com | www.bookaid.org | www.sabre.org

ELSEVIER   BOOK AID International   Sabre Foundation

For information on all MK publications visit our website at www.mkp.com

Pam,
I could not have done this without you

Journeys cross and join,
Spirits become intertwined,
You've completed me.

Contents

Preface

I arrived at writing this book from two perspectives. My early career was as a yeoman corporate IT guy. I was a coder and a project manager. I will spare the details, but along the way it became evident to me that the more we focused on and were motivated to deliver software, the harder the projects became in subsequent years. And when we did point out a long-term problem in the making, we were told "we will get it later." Of course, later never arrived. My entry point into the process resulting in this book happened when I was designing a large application to help a financial services organization improve internal processes. All of my software skills could not find the answer. We could not design an operational system to allow the organization to shorten its cycle times within the confines of its operational systems. So I blended some techniques I had learned while doing data collection and reporting systems for a small defense contractor and teaching database design at Washington University in St Louis. But my approach was new, seemed risky, and our client needed justification. The only answer I could give was "because it will work." Luckily Bill Inmon came by, looked things over, and said "he built a data warehouse, he just didn't know it."

My second path to this book started when I was an industry analyst at the Meta Group, now absorbed into Gartner. I was there during the data warehouse and dot-com boom. I covered business intelligence and followed all of the trends. The mantra repeated by all of the consultants and vendors during that era was "make better decisions" and "get to the data quicker." Everyone had to "manage" their data. There was a "beer and diapers" story for everyone.[1] At the end of the day, our justification for all of the whiz-bang technology was not too different than what I told my financial company client. The solutions providers and technology vendors had the same business reason I gave to the financial client. "Well, because it is better and more useful."

So I began to look very hard into the dilemma. The tipping point was during a conversation with the head of a bank, a really large bank. He had to sign off on a multimillion dollar data analysis effort. He asked me point blank, "What is the return on this investment?" The stock answer of "doing good reports and analysis" did not make it very far. He said, "I can hire 20 MBAs out of school, give them spreadsheet programs, and get the same analysis and reports for the same money. So why should I do it your way?" I had no solid answer. I went away and developed a business case that proved satisfactory, but both of us observed and agreed there was more research to be done. He knew that rooms full of cheerful MBAs was not a long-term solution. I knew that if information was to move from the realm of ugly relative or occasional miracle I had to develop a better story.

This book has been actually been written three times. The more we (my companies, partners, and fellow consultants) did enterprise information management "stuff," the more we learned. The more we presented and evaluated, the more we knew we were on to something. Our IT peers said we were "too esoteric." But more and more of our projects entered into organizations via business area sponsors, not IT. In the two years preceding this book's publication, I have had numerous calls and conversations with business area leaders, and they all say that information management is a business issue. They want IT to manage data more holistically, as they sense that the departmental information management process is not viable over the long term.

Reference

1. If you do not remember, the "beer and diapers" story was given by numerous Business Intelligence software sales people, relating how a chain store had determined, via powerful data analysis, when sleepy fathers came in late at night to buy diapers, they also bought beer. So the beer was co-located with the diapers in an end cap and sales skyrocketed. This story has since proven to be a total fabrication. Plus, I had a young one in diapers then and I *never* saw beer next to diapers.

Acknowledgment

I cannot move onto the rest of the book without thanking the people who contributed to the lineage of this book. First, much thanks to the group who participated in the editing and finishing: Pam Thomas, Doug Laney, Loretta Mahon-Smith, Valerie Torstenson, and Danette McGilvray. I wish we had 28-hour days and could jam in more ideas. Second, I need to thank those who inspired me to finish the book. This was done either by providing forums to debate concepts, just listening to me, or irritating me by playing devil's advocate: Claudia Imhoff, W. H. Inmon, Ken Orr, Len Silverston, and John Zachman. We have had customers over the years that were awesome in letting us try things while we did the "day job": Terry Cavanaugh, Mike Zavasky, George Lucore, Eric Miller, Felix Orzechowski Jim Viveralli, Karen Forcht, and the rest of the gang at you-know-where; Jim Davis, James Farley, Evelyn Follet, Bill Prentice, Kim Stanick.

Lastly, and alphabetically, to the folks I have worked with or for and learned so much: Norm Beachum, Sandy Beard, Dr. Tom Browdy, Joe Buckel, Ken Dunn, Wayne Eckerson, Larry English, Roger Fisher, Eric Franzon, John Geiger, Jeremy Hall, Jim Hankemeyer, Tim Hendrickson, Don Kaskowitz, Ellen Levin, Dr. Wolfgang Martin, Rich Massa, Larry Michael, David Newman, Darin Purintin, Charles Robinson, Alec Sharp, Tony Shaw, Jeff Siefert, John Singer, Ed Tenholder, Gwen Thomas, Donn Vucovich, Paul Welch, Barry Wilderman, Wilbur and Orville Wright, and Steve Zoppi.

About the Author

John Ladley is a Business Technology Thought Leader with 30 years experience improving IT organizations and businesses. John Ladley is widely known as a data warehouse pioneer and a recognized authority in the use and implementation of business intelligence and Enterprise Information Management (EIM). He frequently writes and speaks on a variety of technology and EIM topics. He is currently one of the editors of the *Data Strategy Journal*, a web-based publication on all topics related to data and EIM. His information management approach and experience is balanced between strategic technology planning, project management, and practical application of information technology to business problems.

THE ILLUSTRATOR

Chris Ladley is a free-lance illustrator/graphic designer from St Louis, MO, and provided the original cartoons for this book. When not doing EIM material, Chris draws his inspiration from music, fashion, and hot-rod and tattoo culture. He is known for his "real world" art work. As the owner and sole employee of CWB Designs, LLC, Chris can also be found spending his downtime running a nightclub/concert venue. To experience more of Chris' work check out www.myspace.com/cwbdesigns.

Introduction

There are three reasons this book is necessary. First and foremost, you are already doing enterprise information management. You have customers, suppliers, ledgers, e-mails, memos, manuals, web sites, orders, and contracts. You sell stuff, build stuff, litigate, or legislate. And the fuel for all of it is information. If you are reading this book you already suspect you are not managing information very well, if at all. This book will teach you how to manage your information better.

Second, this book is an apology. Throughout my 30 plus year career in information technology, I have known in my heart of hearts that we must address data and information as an asset. That said, my peers and I have absolutely done a terrible job making a business case for this. We are even worse at explaining what we mean. We have asked the business to understand *us*. The organizations that pay our bills are repeatedly asked to change their processes or models to accommodate IT or guru-speak. Sometimes change truly is required, but most of the time we send our business sponsors out of the room muttering to themselves. We have applied tools and tricks and TLAs (Three Letter Acronyms) and most organizations will tell you they still cannot get to the data, or feel they are exposed in some way. This book is geared for business understanding.

Third, this book offers counsel, perhaps even forewarning. Business attitudes toward data and content are stuck in a "quick-fix, I can do it myself and Information Technology are idiots" mode. The average business area leader is always looking for a way to obtain information, or better mange the information resources required for day-to-day functions. This is certainly understandable, but the pursuit of "end-user information" mastery has created serious problems. The Vice President who authorizes his/her area to buy or build departmental databases and spends 50% of his/her FTE budget on scraping data together to do reports is the same person who goes through the mail at home and complains mightily about duplicate credit card offers and an incorrect bill from the hospital. Most business area leaders do not grasp the risks, costs, or accountability that goes with managing your own data empire. Many business areas outright abuse a vital asset, put the organization at risk, and still collect their bonuses at the end of the year because they were able to squeeze out a sexy report. This book will cover risks and challenges that can only be addressed by a different view of data and content.[1]

This book has to answer a question—What makes information management *valuable*? Not *useful*, but *valuable*. How do we recognize value from the billions spent on business intelligence, content and data management technology? What does the asset metaphor really mean? We easily recognize we can use data to do valuable things. But we still manage this treasure poorly. Perhaps if we treat information the same way we treat something we measure and track, the treatment will improve.

To be clear, I am not proposing sweeping organization upheaval like business reengineering or Information Engineering. Whatever the motivator, this book is intended to make Enterprise Information Management less abstract and more real. This book endeavors to explain Information Asset Management and place it into a pragmatic, focused, and relevant light. The concept is the management of your information as an asset. The pragmatic part is explaining what this means, why it is important, and how to build a program that adds value to your organization.

The two most important terms in the book are "EIM" and "IAM." We evolve a larger definition of these in Chapter 1. However, Table I.1 presents these terms and two others so I can review the contents of the book.

The assets covered in this book are called data, information, or content at various times. For the most part, these terms can be used interchangeably for the purpose of labeling the asset we are learning to manage. We will point out if there is the need to focus on data vs. information as two differing concepts.

Part 1 will provide the material required to sell, understand, and validate the EIM program. It is written for executive audiences, and is presented in business terms.

Chapters 1 and 2 present the concepts of treating Information, Data, and Content as true assets, and what that means. We establish a vision of EIM as a program, and then review current challenges and scenarios that can benefit from the IAM philosophy.

Chapter 3 presents the very important concept of Information Management Maturity. An executive cannot snap a finger and make an enterprise change the embedded behaviors around data. Understanding Information Management Maturity is fundamental to determining how to alter data behavior.

Chapters 4 and 5 describe what EIM looks like and how it affects organizations. Then Chapters 6 and 7 provide background and concepts for the EIM business case. Chapter 8 extends the business case, but delves into what can be described as notional concepts of information assets. We take a quick look at the ramifications of actually placing information on the balance sheet.

Chapters 9–12 review the actual steps and activity in the EIM program. We review the basic process that builds and maintains an EIM program. Since many EIM programs start out fine, but then die from lack of care, we focus a bit on the finer points of sustaining EIM. We address cultural issues and on-going adjustments to the program.

There are several reasons for the failure to take information and make it more valuable to an organization, so Chapter 13 reviews several organizations and offers examples from two case studies to provide a bird's-eye view of the products of the EIM program.

Chapter 14 is the final chapter in Part 1. The reader can stop here, and hopefully has acquired background and understanding enough to interact with or sponsor an EIM effort.

Part 2 will dive into the methods and artifacts necessary to maintain EIM and have the business manage information. Often it is tempting to get caught up in the technology, the new project, or the philosophical examination of "what is a customer?" Part 2 tries to avoid these distractions and

Table I.1 Terminology Guide to this Book	
Information Asset Management (IAM) The philosophy of managing enterprise data, information, and content as an asset in a business and accounting sense	
Enterprise Information Management (EIM) The discipline that manages and implements IAM	
Building Blocks The major aspects of EIM which a business person will see and interacts	**Elements** The framework, functions, and architectural structures that are used to operate and manage the EIM environment

sort out the details required to bring substantive results to managers and others responsible for EIM deployment.

Chapters 15 and 16 provide overviews of Information Asset concepts and the EIM process, but at a lower level of detail, and from the perspective of the manager charged with delivery of EIM. Chapter 17 covers how to get the EIM program initiated. Chapter 18 is a brief chapter that explains how to read Chapters 19–27, which present the activities and work products required to support EIM.

Chapters 19–27 review the necessary building blocks to manage the changes to managed data and content. Throughout these chapters, we will review how business personnel should assist the EIM program to develop deliverables that describe specific initiatives and processes that will result in healthier business performance, lowered risk, and more frequent exploitation of opportunities. There are a lot of artifacts that go with this, and these are described as part of the methods and techniques for building an EIM program. The artifacts of interest to business people are kept *separate* from the artifacts that will be produced by the IT folks to get the components of EIM designed, and up and running. We will cover what deliverables are truly the end products, and what other artifacts are necessary working products.

We also emphasize process, technique, and work products that are unique to the EIM program and of business interest. We will address designing these "information value chains" to be efficient and relevant to any business model. Certain technical work products like data models, databases, and application designs are necessary but we only mention them. There are many other books that cover these in detail.

Finally, after business artifacts like principles, policies, architecture, and frameworks are developed, and a sensible, pragmatic road map is produced to incrementally implement the various pieces of EIM, we cover the sustaining aspects in detail. We wrap up this treatment of EIM (the program) with a look at various means to measure the success of IAM (the philosophy), and we even take a crack at what the balance sheet might look like if we *could* assign a number to information value.

We will use two case studies in this book. They are amalgams. No one company has their EIM information presented. The main reason for this is I present failures as well as successes. However, all samples are real output, and have only been revised to conceal real financial numbers or guard corporate strategy.

There is a lot of ground to cover in the following pages. In fact, there is probably a Part 3 or revised Part 2 with more details waiting in the wings, but at some point you have to get something out there. There are web addresses at the end of each part where any ideas or feedback can be posted so that we can continue to provide better material. This book also approaches the topics at hand with, hopefully, a professional mix of humor and philosophy. This can be very dry material. It isn't that I do not take my profession seriously. I just insist on smiling during the journey.

Reference

1. Content means anything you cannot envision as rows and columns. Memos, manuals, media, and web sites are content. It carries the same issues as the Access database or mission critical spreadsheet.

The Asset Called Information

CONTENTS

Making Enterprise Information Management (EIM) Work for Business. DOI: 10.1016/B978-0-12-375695-4.00001-1

If you are not a CEO, pretend you are for a moment. If you are a CEO, then thanks for reading. As a CEO or Chairperson, imagine receipt of the following letter from an auditor sometime in the near future. While the following may seem trite, it sets the context.

Dear Sir/Madam:

You are well aware that as your auditor, it is incumbent on our firm to bring matters to your attention that, while seemingly under control, may threaten financial progress, or at worst, contain sufficient risk to cause irreversible harm to your organization.

In that context, we need to discuss your enterprise's treatment of an asset we believe is at risk:

- This asset is costing your organization millions per year, and while we have documented expenses, credits, and amortization in relation to creating this asset, we cannot find it on the balance sheet.
- Regulators and compliance may soon require us to report liabilities inherent in that asset.
- Nobody can tell us where the asset sits, how much we have, or where it came from.
- In spite of this lack of control, this asset is repurposed thousands of times a day.
- Many managers claim to own this asset, but an equal number try to absolve themselves of any accountability at all.
- Those that do claim ownership deny all accountability.
- For every request from compliance to destroy this asset once it offers more risk than usefulness, there are four requests to keep this asset available and "take a chance" with the risks.

Please schedule a meeting with us at your earliest convenience to review your action plan to mitigate these risk areas.

Since you know the title of this book, you know the asset is information. The sample note presented earlier is appearing in some form at many companies. But the note is not from auditors of information assets. There are no such positions (yet). The message in the note is swelling up from middle managers, external regulators, and customers.

This fictional memorandum contains good news and bad news. The good news is that there truly is genuine interest in Data Strategy/Information Management (IM) at the enterprise level. But that good news is being delivered in the form of reports and documentation of the cost of poor data and content quality. Part of the interest comes from the "new ROI." As a client recently put it, ROI is the abbreviation for "Risk of Incarceration." In short, the legal and regulatory ramifications to the presentation and accuracy of data are beginning to materialize. As this book was written, a global recession was under way, fueled in part by poor information and failure to recognize risk.

The bad news is that those who are close to hands-on management of information still really stink (and I use that word with deliberation) at explaining what this means to business people. Even if the explanation of data value and the need for good data is presented well (via Davenport & Harris, 2007; Redman, 2008; and others), someone still needs to make it *real* for the business. If the CEO gets a note from the financial auditor, he/she goes to the CFO. If there is an operations issue, he/she goes to the COO. Where does the CEO go for Information Asset Management (IAM)? Can he/she go to the CIO or not?

This chapter sets the stage for the remainder of this book. We are going to talk about managing an asset called information. Some of this material will be basic and familiar, but with a twist. Some of it will be new. All of it is wrapped around a holistic approach to managing "that which cannot be counted," i.e., data, information, e-mails, web content, catalogs, memos, and the list goes on.

Is there an executive who will say "information is not an asset—it is a burden?" Is there an executive who does not want to "exploit" information? Probably not; if there is, give them a copy of this book. But take any businessperson who states information is an asset and make them explain it in realistic, comprehensible terms. Are there formal standards and policies deployed for creating, using, and disposing of all data and content? Not written down and ignored—but deployed. Does his/her company or division have a formal program to reduce or manage inherent risk in data? Does the CFO or CEO sign the Sarbanes–Oxley form every quarter with unabashed confidence? Ask him/her to explain the difference in accounting or balance sheets if information is treated like an asset, or it is not. This isn't easily done. But if the asset metaphor is more than metaphor, these questions require better answers.

Information as an asset is the main theme of this book. Until data, information, and content are managed as other assets are managed, neither information nor data nor content has a chance to fulfill its potential or its role within organizations. There can be billions more spent on "exploiting" data. Buying Business Intelligence (BI) tools and replicating data and content many times in many places just increases the costs with little perceptible gain. It is wasted money unless you know what to exploit, where it comes from, and what it is worth to your enterprise. If you are going to do business or operate any organization in the twenty-first century, the asset metaphor needs to become the asset *policy*.

FORMAL ASSET TREATMENT

There is a lot of proof that data is valuable. But formalizing the management of data to make it more efficient and add value has been elusive. There are frameworks and guidelines and still, solid IM remains elusive. "An increasing amount of money is being spent on new technologies that will deliver even more information. Yet, neither the information nor the technology dollars are being consistently translated into business value."[1] We manage entire Information Technology (IT) portfolios as programs, we look for earned value and strive to find (ROI) on IT. But we totally miss the boat on the "stuff" that IT and all of the technology manages.

There are scores of "tools" to move and look at data, yet few businesspeople know how to truly handle data. There is access, literally, to more content than a human being can possibly comprehend, yet we still miss findings or fail to communicate critical conclusions. I believe the basic root of this problem is twofold:

1. We focus too much on the ROI and contribution of IT in general. However, IT is a label for a myriad of functions. We do not focus on what IT has to manage; i.e., data, content, information. All of the rules and tools are for the processes, not the product.
2. Organizations are too hung up on parables and metaphors as a technique to explain the real value proposition of IM. One of the core reasons for this book is to bypass metaphor and present a *real foundation for value*.

"Information Is an Asset" is an extremely common statement, and probably the most common information principle published within organizations. The subsequent explanation is that assets are *managed*, so *information* has to be managed. While this makes eminent sense, it does not sell or get IM efforts funded. Leadership is not impressed. The metaphor certainly starts the explanation process, but does not complete it. There have been several excellent books printed in the last few years that delve into the definition and explanation of the asset metaphor and offer a somewhat focused business justification. But the justification is anecdotal, and quantifiable results are scarce. We have plenty of examples of cool things that happened AFTER an organization took the risk to exploit data in some way. We have few examples where organizations embarked on a formal business-altering program that treats data and other content as a formally managed asset. There are also many books on the "value of IT," or the return on technology investments. The emphasis is on program or portfolio management. This is a great start, but the raw material that is being handled, used, abused, and replicated has no formal oversight. The bottom line is we do not have a guide (hopefully until now) that instructs the business on creating and operating a formal program to create the opportunities to improve the value of your organization through information and content management.

Often CEOs will demand a precise business case. This can be done, and I will address the topic in a few chapters. But they also may want the business case to *predict* valuable usage—in effect, promise analytical "aha" moments. This is not unreasonable, but there is no way this can be done unless the care, feeding, and use of all enterprise content are understood as *business* issues.

EIM AND IAM EXPLAINED

Enterprise Information Management (EIM) is a program to treat data and all other types of enterprise information as assets. This book calls out the asset management concepts separately, and I will use the label IAM to separate these concepts from the EIM program. IAM represents the fundamental asset management concepts and processes to manage an asset—in this case, the asset of information vs. cash or a physical facility.

The program we have labeled EIM shows a company how to best weave those asset management concepts and best practices most effectively and efficiently into their core corporate business model. IAM represents the concepts and EIM is the program that implements those concepts.

We need to know what an EIM program, or the concept of IAM, does for us on a daily basis, what its value is, and what impact it would have on the balance sheet. We can always look at a financial statement and say "My, didn't we do well!" If we get an "aha," that's great. But we cannot *guarantee* the "aha." We also certainly cannot tie that financial result or "aha" moment to the data or content that we used to generate the result or have the flash of inspiration. How can we increase the chances of the "aha" moment? Right now it seems we can only justify and program the scenario to make the "aha" possible.

Does that make data and information mundane? No. I contend that when we weave EIM into the day-to-day fabric of a company, we see that the IAM concept can have value and assist us in managing the value of our content. A company does not want to flat out grab and store every single tidbit of data and hope for the "aha." It is too expensive. We want the right amount of content and detail to use data to our advantage. So we need to not only acknowledge the asset metaphor, but also *apply it*.

AN EXAMPLE

Managing information at the enterprise level must be pragmatic. There is too much "shelf-ware technology" where long-term development of applications like data warehouse fails to align with the needs of shorter-term business cycles. Managing information assets must also be efficient. We will point out how and why an EIM program should not result in higher costs. But managing information is, in itself, strategic. Finished goods inventory, supply chains, and customer retention are all strategic processes. Information is in the same league, but it does not receive the same treatment. If EIM is to add value, and if the asset is real, then data and content must move into the strategic league.

To further understand the implications of information "inventory" asset management, we should "track" a "piece" of information inventory. We can contrast this with a "piece" of hard inventory, like an aluminum billet. (I chose an aluminum billet because many years ago, aluminum billets created great career angst for me.) A billet is a large chunk of something—in this case, aluminum— and we made doors, window frames, and the aluminum frames that go on the outside of buildings to hold glass and building-climbers.

The hard asset/soft asset comparison is given in Table 1.1.

We can beat this example up ad nauseam. For example, if the aluminum billet is of lower quality alloy, perhaps it is qualified. If the data is from a source that is less than reputable, perhaps it is also tagged as to its level of reliability. If the billet can be heated and improved, then the data can also be enhanced or changed to improve its usefulness.

Of course, any use of the billet is recorded. Eventually, it is melted down and made into appliances, door frames, or baseball bats. The data is also used. It is read, updated, and enriched. The one, and *really irrelevant difference*, is the data isn't "used up." Some experts will declare that this aspect of data means that information cannot be tracked along a value chain like other consumable items. However, this difference is insignificant. The billet is turned into valuable goods. The data is used to create value as well (business decisions, documents, and reports). The key to asset management of the nonfungible item (like data) is measuring its usage vs. value. Other than that, both accrue value to the organization through *usage*, *enhancement*, and *consumption*. I can look at the billet and see the potential value in its usage. The same goes for information and data.

Table 1.1 Inventory vs. Information Asset	
Aluminum Billet	**Information Assets**
Billet received, inventory amount and record created.	Inventory receipt transaction creates data and stores content (paper) on the billet.
Billet tagged for quality and usage.	Inventory data sits there, we do not tag it nor asses it for usability (we should). Under IAM, we need to "tag" data.
Billet is assigned to a job or process, billet inventory decremented, work in process incremented.	We know the billet was assigned, and we know the accounting data. What was the impetus to use that billet? Who authorized it? Data is enhanced, as work in process data is collected. Shop forms are filled out. We are adding more and more data. Do we tag this data?
Billet is processed into a final product that is shipped and sold. We know who touched the billet, and where it went. We know who bought the aluminum door or other products. There is a paper or data trail.	The data for the process is collected via forms, keystrokes, or scans. Who touched the data after entry? Who read the work in process or finished good records? Who accepted the inventory data so that it eventually showed up in a financial statement? Who adjusted this data before it was posted?

TIPS FOR SUCCESS

The philosophical discussion around data being the only asset that is not "used up" or "decremented" is frivolous. Many words have been written around this, and I suppose it makes for good discussion after hours. When you start to do EIM or address IAM, there will be challenges based on the "intangibility" of data and content. However, goodwill is intangible, appears on the balance sheet, and can certainly be "used up." There are many other business products and components that are intangible. We review this later in the book; for now it suffices that this particular discussion is in the league with angels and pins, and does not have any business impact.

CONTENT AS LUBRICANT

The reason any institution using data and content must become more formal about managing these assets has to do with the changing role of information. During the 1950s, data and information were used as a *lubricant*. We removed friction from processes, like oil does for a car engine. We used data to speedup processes, eliminate some back-office jobs, and drive a few easy dollars to the bottom line through efficiencies. The first large-scale IT systems (back then they were called Data Processing Systems) were dedicated to the back office; e.g., payroll and general ledger. Afterward came back-office support for sales and inventory, but the applications still greased processes.

This created an arrangement where business drove requirements for IT, or IT became the "enabler" for business. The relationship has always been a linear one. But this practical need for separation has evolved into a "we" and "they" view of business use of technology. When I play cards with my father, he makes two columns to keep score. They are labeled "we" and "they." The first time you see this, it is amusing. However, there is a simple, diplomatic, but adversarial implication in this. There was "we"—our side, the good guys, and "they"—the other team. *The competition.*

Sadly, this same mind-set has plagued IT for quite a while. From Grace Hopper's time to today, there seems to be the innate need to separate business functions and technology functions. There are "users," usually the "they" team. There are the IT people—the "we" team. We have mountains of methodologies designed to make sure what one is saying the other understands. Certainly some of this is necessary. We can't understand everyone else's professions in detail. And IT is engineering of a sort, so specifications and requirements are mandatory. However, the implication of two sides has resulted in an adversarial mind-set. The net result is an elaborate mix of technology and business methodologies, techniques, checks and balances that accommodates the differences rather than remove them. The EIM program in this book takes a large step toward aligning business drivers, needs, and IT along a more natural, collaborative path vs. an environment where heritage-processing philosophies cannot deliver timely solutions.

The data environment has become focused solely on the distribution of information. The most common requirement I have heard from businesspeople over the last 20 years is "Just give me all of my data. I know what to do with it."

To go out on a limb, Mr. Business Person, you *do not* know what to do with it. If data is an asset there must be more to managing it than just looking at a report. That is the easy part. The business person perceives an analysis result, but has no idea of how to position the asset properly. Ms. Business Person has no idea that for every positive action taken to use the data, you might be inducing enormous liability. In addition, this is not efficient use of information. We do not gain any

> **OBSERVATION**
>
> Over the years, my teams have kept track of the ratio of spending on data movement and positioning vs. spending on doing a report or analysis to make the big decision. For nearly 20 years, the ratio has remained relatively close: organizations spend *four times more* to move, clean up, and position data than they spend on accessing it.

additional value or insight as a company or even retention of the knowledge gained from information over time. IT departments can be compared to grocery distributors—customers select from a list of items for "push" delivery, or go get what they need at the source. This mind-set does nothing to address "knowledge" or collaboration. This mind-set does nothing to ensure that information is used efficiently. There is no incentive to really know where all the information is and what it means. As for the grocery distributors, unless they have precise control of their supply chain, they are second-class citizens in their markets. The same for IT shops—they can be "push or pull" distributors, or supply chain managers.

EIM/IAM acknowledges that this relationship is changing. EIM programs move companies away from the "we"/"they" or demand–pull model. We will also see later in the book how EIM offers to remove business silos without breaking them. IAM sets a mentality of a common asset vs. "my data." IAM sets the tone for collaboration.

CONTENT AS FUEL

Twenty-first century competition requires creation of *new business models*—models based on cultural, political, technological, and competitive realities. Separation of IM from business processes must become historical artifact. Technology is not the challenge to growing (or ruining) a company. The challenge is in identifying new processes and assuring there is real value being created, all while managing the implementation of ensuing cultural shifts, and managing content and new communities toward a common benefit. Linear, two-dimensional approaches and traditional structured communication processes are inadequate for new business models. Many new business models will have nothing to do with IT, but will require well-managed information. IAM positions your organization for this new mind-set.

A great thinker in the area of IM, specifically, information quality, is Larry English. He has a view that merits some consideration; we need to act and design systems as though information flows along a supply chain.[2] If we do not do this we attain a linear view that creates isolated efforts. This is also a fundamental precept of supply chain management. Supply chain may imply a sequence, but supply chains are really complex, multidimensional structures that are not based on flows, they are based on networks. The same illustration stands for information. On its own, there is no intrinsic value in the data or content sitting on the disk, it only has cost. It must be used to discern value. This does not mean a supply or value chain simile is ineffective. It is a crucial component to creating sustainable value.

The twenty-first century business features information as the *fuel*. We don't replace processes; we enable operators in existing processes. We assume that there is "data" processing. We now demand

---

OBSERVATION

I occasionally offer a wager with a client that I will find data that puts the company at risk. The IT department will state all is under control, and Finance will say all data is secure. But I can always find at least one or two social security numbers on a desktop or thumb drive in a context where privacy could be compromised. Would your organization take the bet?

"information." We also demand "knowledge" management. And since the late 1990s we demand "web content" management. We also *sell* our data, so that it is a product (with all of the liabilities that go along with products), and go through extraordinary steps to make sure privacy is maintained. At the same time we are trying to sell our data and focus on privacy, we seek to identify households and individuals and new prospects in new market segments. We seek out more opportunities of risk so we can exploit new opportunities to gain market share.

This is *fuel*. We are driving the engine of our companies and agencies with data and knowledge. The lubricant phase is over.

This concept of data as fuel comes with baggage. There are risks and liabilities:

- In not knowing where data is, or liability in knowing where data is and allowing improper access.
- (At minimum embarrassment) when one executive vice president states we have added 5,000 new customers, and another says we have lost 5,000.
- In being unable to prove a number on a report is THE number and is accurate.
- If the SEC requests documents and you cannot provide them or have inadvertently destroyed them too soon.
- If you destroy documents too late, as overzealous attorney generals will strive to find anything improper. And in a large company with a lot of content, they *will*.
- If one area gets really, really excellent at analyzing data and fails to share that expertise, or in fact, hoards the findings to attain political advantage. (I know it would NEVER happen in your organization.)

These are not trivial challenges. But the bottom line is: if information is fuel—then improper treatment is risky. Fuel can be volatile. Fuel can explode.

CHANGE

The aforementioned move away from adversarial relations to more collaboration also creates cultural tension and business model alteration. When EIM becomes a program, you will discover that business culture will be challenged. Moving beyond the mind-set of individual or departmental projects and applications and into IAM will require setting aside embedded mind-sets. For example, try convincing a division head that giving him "all his data" is too risky. This will not work even if it can be accomplished. Think of it this way—during the writing of this book my team had a client where the various business functions all explicitly believed they could acquire, store, process, and report on all the data their function required. They felt no obligation to share or learn with any other function, even when 80% of the business data used by one function was used by two other areas! In effect, each area had its own IT department, data analysts, software tools, even hardware, and storage. The inefficiencies to an outside observer were stunning. Moving an organization away from this mind-set is a huge challenge. Over the last 20 years, an approach known as "data warehouse" tried to address this challenge by offering to store all the common data in one place. Early results were mixed at best due in part to cultural challenges. EIM programs formalize the effort required to shift the culture.

It is crucial for upper and middle managers to understand what EIM really is and what it means to organizational success. Your number one obstacle will be these very same managers who nod their heads when you talk about IAM making sense.

Is information (or data, or knowledge) an asset to your business? The obvious answer *seems* to be yes. Again, few executives would say "no—it is not an asset and not needed for my business." But accepting the concept and making it real mean moving from the lubricant phase of history to the fuel view of data, as well as accepting that there will be some changes in your organization—and the IT changes are the trivial ones. Accepting the definition of information as fuel and an asset means you agree to track it. Inventory it. Assign rigid and at times unmerciful accountability for its accuracy and use.

DEFINITIONS TO GO FORWARD

Many definitions from other authors around EIM or IAM focus intently on data quality or the nuts and bolts of data management from an IT context. This is not without reason. Data quality is usually the most likely manifestation of the need for EIM. But this falls short of an enterprise definition. Granted a data quality program will get an enterprise a long way toward benefits. Data quality can account for enormous costs.[2] But the definition also has to mention proper activity that applies the content toward the needs of the business. In other words, we also need to manage the *use* of data. That means it cannot cost too much for the benefit we obtain, and we need to ensure that the right content is delivered to the right people for the right reason—that's *all*. Consequently, EIM/Data Strategy (or some combination thereof) can usually be defined along the following lines:

> *EIM is the program that manages enterprise information asset to support the business and improve value. EIM manages the plans, policies, principles, frameworks, technologies, organizations, people, and processes in an enterprise toward the goal of maximizing the investment in data and content.*

The definition in this book does something the others do not—it avoids the "asset" metaphor as a part of the definition. Real assets are tangible. There are numerous books on IM, and they all end up talking about abstractions of data modeling and templates. Information is certainly an asset but is an abstract concept, and abstractions just do not sell well. Another key word in the definition is "program." This implies that EIM is ongoing and must be sustainable. "Projects" have beginnings and ends. Programs are forever.

For a businessperson, the key concept here is "*managing* the asset." Managing implies setting goals, planning, directing, and supervising the execution of a plan. Managing implies governance to make sure we manage the asset in a uniform manner across the enterprise. It means being aware of compliance and risk management. To the businessperson, this is entirely palatable. The act of managing the people, processes, and technology that touch data then becomes easy to understand. This is the mind-set we label as IAM.

> *IAM describes philosophies to ensure that data, information, and content are all treated as assets in the true business and accounting sense, avoiding increased risk and cost due to data and content misuse, poor handling, or exposure to regulatory scrutiny.*

Business leaders need to clearly understand the information value proposition. Alignment of IT with business drivers, integration issues, and regulatory problems are just the beginning. So there needs to be a strong focus on promoting IAM and educating upper management. This book will spend time with this by looking at EIM/IAM through the lens of managing the assets of the business: Managing a metaphor is nice for understanding, but managing an asset requires discipline and commitment.

Clearly, this is a different meaning for IM than has been used historically. EIM is the program that deploys IAM. In other words, *EIM is the management of all enterprise information content, be it structured (rows and columns, files, and records) or unstructured (memos, e-mails, web sites, audio, and video).*

In the twenty-first century, the difference between unstructured and structured data is blurred. In addition, the line between IT and business functions is also blurred. An enormous amount of money and effort has been poured into rows' and columns' content—aka information. This investment has not been in vain; however, the amount of unstructured information in an organization that must also be managed is an order of magnitude larger than the structured information. It is doubtful there is an order of magnitude of money left in corporate coffers to spend again getting unstructured data to the point of structured data. EIM is the means to avoid having to spend enormous amounts of money to get value from unstructured data.

VALUE PROPOSITION PLEASE

It is easy to advocate that there is value in information and knowledge. It is quite difficult to calculate and *deliver* that perceived value efficiently and accurately. Data, information, and content are considered abstract concepts. Knowledge is perceived to live only between people's ears. Information is data with meaning, but the meaning is difficult to quantify, and few organizations have managed to place the value of their information on a balance sheet. In spite of the abstractions, twenty-first century organizations that "manage" their intellectual capital will succeed where others will fail (Davenport & Harris, 2007). Intellectual capital management will differentiate companies, as their other technologies become commodities (ERP, SCM, and CRM packages).

Any savvy executive will hear these definitions and words about data, and then follow up with some elegant question along the lines of "So what?" This is not a discouraging sign, merely an indication of interest. Therefore the next step is to have a very clear two-level statement of EIM's value for an organization.

The first level of a value proposition comes from alignment with pragmatic business initiatives. For example, many Customer Relationship Management (CRM) projects of the past 10 years have ended up becoming "oh shoot, we don't really know who a customer is" projects. The governance and semantic management that accompanies EIM certainly supports projects such as this. Another practical initiative that has worked for many of our clients is the cost of data quality and "dis-integration." It is relatively easy to calculate, and usually presents some serious numbers for consideration. Lastly, the aforementioned risk considerations are easily associated with EIM practices. A good actuary can develop a financial model on risk inherent in an information portfolio.

So EIM has value because it manages data and information so that it costs less for the same anticipated set of results. Most companies have many of the elements of EIM in place and funded. They are not managed together and with the same philosophy. EIM consolidates and manages these elements.

The second level of the value proposition is the elevator speech. These are the 50–100 words that drive home the value proposition. Anyone associated with EIM efforts, business, or IT side should commit this to memory. Everyone involved with the program should say something along the lines of:

> *Over a 2-year period, the EIM program will directly increase cash flow by supporting customer retention and cross-selling, while reducing the overhead and risk associated with spreading too much data around the enterprise.*

The key words here are "cash flow" and "overhead." If the EIM effort cannot supply support for a positive change in business value, then it's not structured correctly and is not sustainable. The business case portions of this book will delve more deeply into the nuts and bolts of determining what that elevator speech and value proposition should be for your organization.

EIM VISION

Any effective program must produce deliverables that address some of the abstract concepts required when doing architecture and business alignment (like visions and models) but avoid obfuscating technical jargon and use business terms.

The technical tangible results of IAM take the form of measurable changes in infrastructure, data usage patterns, data quality, and redundancy. We connect business results to the statement that we will improve data quality nn%.

A set of metrics must be put into place to reinforce the benefits and usage and adherence to the programs and governance. We must measure the effectiveness of EIM *alongside* the effectiveness of the business activities supported by EIM.

SUMMARY

The EIM program provides an effective platform for creating flexibility.

The bottom line for an EIM program, which must be reinforced from time-to-time, is supporting the business with clear, documented, and effective data and information. The business user wants this as badly as anyone in IT.

Remember, we need to move past the metaphor and make IAM "real." The expression of this will vary from organization to organization. At the end of the day, we must get better at managing the material we spend billions on annually. We need to treat this so-called asset as an asset. That means examining other disciplines like accounting and supply chain management. It means acknowledging and implementing a new philosophy without disrupting day-to-day operations. This is not trivial, but it is also not unheard of.

EIM is a program that will allow us to measure the contribution against the costs incurred to handle and distribute the information assets.

If you are looking for a silver bullet to deliver projects to the business without the discipline of alignment or the challenges of governance, you may want to pass on this book. If you are serious about getting more value from information without little or no incremental increase in spending, or even have a slight notion that there must be a better way to deal with information, then read on. You will find something here. If you feel like you build excessive cost and risk into your company by allowing current IM practices to continue, or what you spend on data is not commensurate with the returns you see, read on.

Thanks in advance for your time and attention.

References

1. Thorp, J., & Fujitsu Consulting's Center for Strategic Leadership. (2003). Introduction. In: The Information Paradox, Revised Edition. Ryerson, Canada: McGraw-Hill.

2. Redman, T.C. (2008). The (Often Hidden) Costs of Poor Data and Information. Data Driven: Profiting from Your Most Important Business Asset. Boston, MA: Harvard Business School Press.

Exploring the Challenges

You can't put lipstick on a pig.
Numerous

CONTENTS

Businesspeople thrive on challenges. Rather than the information century, the twenty-first century therefore could be called the business century, because there is great fodder for thriving. This chapter will address how new challenges are asking for new applications of information and content and review how EIM can address them. We will also reflect on past treatment of data and point out how EIM could have improved some sample business scenarios.

GLOOMY SCENARIOS, TIPPING POINTS, AND FLAT WORLDS

What drives us to focus so hard on data and content? For that matter, what makes this discussion and focus on "information as an asset relevant?" The challenges of the twenty-first century almost mandate IAM. Besides some contemporary but common scenarios, we need to look at the regulatory "tipping points" and global trends affecting IM.

Gloomy Scenarios

There are many examples that bring to light the current and rising issues facing organizations in terms of this topic. Here are a few:[1]

Scenario One

A large retail bank realizes that the merger of its finance products and a newly acquired insurance company potentially creates new opportunities for dealing with customers. A large consulting firm is called in and leaves behind a hefty document explaining the need for CRM systems. The document is really a specification for a data warehouse, a database that "sucks in" nonintegrated data (like from a bank and an insurance company) and makes it available for analysis. The data warehouse is built (cost US$10 million or so), and a handful of savvy branch managers and marketing professionals do some cross-selling. Victory is declared.

Five years later, a new CEO is examining budgets. He/she spies a US$3 million per year item for "operating the data warehouse." A few queries are made, and the CEO is told that there are five branch managers and two marketing professionals using reports from the data warehouse. The CEO divides 7 into 3 million, and decides that $428,000 per year (and change) is a bit much, and requests that the data warehouse justify its existence, or be shut down. After some scurrying, here is what the data warehouse support team has to work with in terms of a business case:

Nowhere in the original document were there any metrics or accountabilities for the business to accomplish something once the information was delivered.

The EVP of Marketing has been rewarded handsomely for creativity and innovation by somehow developing product packages that attract high return clients. However, any access to data on the financial impact on the bank or if the data warehouse was used to support product development is denied.

Three former branch managers are now EVPs in the bank.

There are eight branch managers *not* using the data warehouse. They have been very vocal that the information in it is inaccurate and "they can't run their business with it."

Should the data warehouse survive? Does it?

Scenario Two

A discount retailer is losing market share to a juggernaut competitor. Without a great deal of research, the retailer decides the answer is "to do e-commerce" like its competitors. It hires a mid-size firm to develop order entry and shipping applications to run over its web site. The company continues to lose market share and experiences minimal hits on the web site. The web site, while accurate in content and processing, simply shows a thumbnail photo of the products the merchandising department determined to be worthy of e-commerce. The VP of Sales writes a memo asking for the web site to be closed down, but the CEO is afraid of market perceptions. Another consultant is hired to analyze market share and web site effectiveness, and after a six-month effort brings the following findings to the table:

- Very few site visitors actually order products.
- Even the listed products on the site have out-of-date pictures and descriptions. At times the prices are old.
- Products that are ordered through the web sites were rarely in stock at stores located near the home of the purchaser.
- Analysis of the "out-of-stock" issues reveals gross inconsistencies in the inventory of certain product classes.
- A recommendation that the company close down or radically overhaul the web site, develop applications to track merchandising issues, and manage product data more effectively.

Were these recommendations followed? Did the retailer survive?

Scenario Three

A health care company has a BI application that was intended for managing medical costs and disease management. While this application has been historically successful, business user interest is waning, as current company issues take on an operational flavor (provider payment, prescription effectiveness, reducing medical costs, regulatory issues brought on by HIPAA and Sarbanes–Oxley). The BI application now requires extensive reengineering to make the data more operational to meet these new requirements.

Should these investments be made in the current BI system, should a new one be built, or does the needed managerial reporting have to come out of the new operational processes that are garnering attention?

Scenario Four

A Manufacturing VP of Human Resource (HR) determines that the tight job market is causing too much knowledge to walk out the door. All employees are encouraged to do internal resumes to establish a "repository" of this intellectual capital. They are placed into a blind repository and can be viewed on the company intranet, where all managers can review what talents lay at their disposal. All seems well for six months and then turnover increases. Analysis reveals nonmanagement employees are reviewing other resumes and are able to assess their market value in even clearer terms than before.

Does the HR VP still work there?

Obviously, these scenarios involve data, information, and content management. Certain symptoms, such as poor data quality, can be placed in a long-term history bucket. We have been neglecting that for decades. Other issues, like managing content to appear on the web, have more recent history, but are equally aggravating and costly. The scenarios expressed earlier reveal that for many organizations, information and data management have evolved from a necessary inconvenience to a firmer mandate for a more holistic approach. IT has some kind of strategic role to play here. This may seem in direct contradiction to the now famous, and grossly misinterpreted 2003 *Harvard Business Review* article, IT Doesn't Matter.[2] If we need to manage the "stuff" that IT handles, then IT must matter. IT is unfocused, not irrelevant. Based on the definitions in Chapter 1, we can surmise that if strong attention had been paid to business and IT, treating data the same as an inventory of hard goods, you would not be reading this book, and I would be writing a science fiction novel.

What makes the need for a program like EIM? Often I hear "we don't need EIM…. better execution is the answer." There is certainly no commonality in basic technology in our scenarios. There is little commonality within the business disciplines that delivered these aforementioned "solutions." Maybe IT needs to get over its whining and just get the job done? I would almost agree with this except for one profound common thread from the scenarios presented here. None of the above aligned the business with the business use of IT. The lack of business alignment grew obstinately pervasive in the 1990s as technology whizbang could not match up with business models. Business alignment is a pothole for data and IM. One of the highest ranking issues stated by CIOs is the need for better business alignment. Executives hear this all the time but here is what it really means:

A business program or project will start, and discover they need data to actually make the effort work. We built the machine and forgot the lubricant, so a system is slammed into place. An application is purchased or hammered together or an older application is modified in a crude fashion. All at the directive to "get it done."

If it is done on time, then everyone is rewarded for hard work and dedication. In many cases, tools like Excel or Access play a leading role in managing the required data, and voila—an unsupervised volume of data liability is created. Alignment means someone should have told the data people much earlier this business direction was intended and allowed for some basic preparation.

Even projects that are executed with great leadership and business alignment miss. For example, large implementations and projects are typically managed closely. After all, there is usually a seven- or eight-figure investment. That tends to garner executive attention. Yet months or years after the large investments, CxOs often still complain of poor access to vital data, or inconsistent data.

EIM is required because none of the scenarios had a reasonable strategy to deal with the business aspects of the technology and measure its success. The lack of a reasonable strategy happens when IT initiatives get funded via squeaky wheel methods vs. a planned set of initiatives that support a business strategy.

None of these scenarios indicated a long-term view on the accurate use or the accuracy of their content. Many fellow executives can recall the promises of BI projects in the last 20 years that failed to meet expectations. Repeatedly, many companies remained with their "mission critical" spreadsheets because the usefulness of the data gathered up and presented via an exotic tool was found to be inadequate.

Lastly, none of the scenario problems were with traditional transaction-oriented applications—they were information/content centric. The so-called "operational" systems work—but they are useless for reporting, analysis, and decision making. Rather than a footnote, this writer is very comfortable saying that at least 20 times he has heard a business person say "just dump all my orders and/or claims into a database—we can certainly use it to make great decisions." And this fails *every single time*. Operational data, mostly due to data quality issues, is often inadequate for timely reporting, business measurement, or making complex analysis-based decisions.

Tipping Points

Many regulated organizations now have downstream areas that desperately "shine up" the data and hope that regulators are pleased or the data is "close enough" to be defensible. And just as this downstream data liability rears its ugly head, we discover our internal e-mails are also repositories of liability. Our web content is not timely or flat-out wrong. Then we find out content can be dangerous. For example, a corporate intranet is poorly maintained and stores outdated safety directions for maintaining complex machinery. Enterprise risk management, from liability and regulation, has been the "tipping point" for IAM.

All of the companies in the scenarios were faced with changing fundamental business processes, regulations, and cultures. In the 1990s, a spate of regulations created an *intense* interest in managing data for many organizations. This was due to the sense of nervousness created by regulations. So EIM moved from lip service to at least a concern in the boardroom or corporate compliance department. In the European Union (EU), privacy rules and Basel Accords started the tipping. Gramm–Leach–Bliley, HIPAA, and others created a regulatory push to ensure privacy of personal information. Sarbanes–Oxley was actually the icing on the cake, with its mandate to present "correct" numbers. Unfortunately, heroic efforts were put into shining up the spreadsheets rather than going through the pain to actually manage the root causes of the regulatory risk (Table 2.1).

TIP FOR SUCCESS

Data or content to run the company does not equal data or content suitable for analysis. *Did I say every single time?* It does not take a year of strategic planning to align information needs with the business. It takes what I call the three C's—communication, content, and collaboration. Convey what is coming, what content is required, and make sure there is transparency of the content. This will be apparent when we examine the processes to start managing information as an asset.

In short, these organizations embarked on their projects without the mind-set of managing the asset they were slinging around. The tipping points were the large investments in well-managed projects, and the painful regulatory scrutiny that, in essence, demands better management of data and content.

The head of a corporate compliance organization explained it to me this way: "We have fire alarms in our buildings, we have cameras in the parking lot. We know where each employee is at all times. But we have no idea what that employee has on a thumb drive as they walk across the parking lot to their car. We have no alarm that goes off if our data is sabotaged. *But the damage potential is as high as any risk of fire.*"

Flat Worlds and Other New Challenges

We need to move to formal content and data management. We need to move to the philosophy of IAM. The need to move to the IAM vision also means understanding upcoming challenges as well as historical ones. We have looked at some of the bad experiences and tipping points that are urging us to embody IAM in a formal corporate function called EIM. There seems to be new games afoot as well. New challenges are rearing their heads, and these have the flavor of adding enormous amounts of capital spending to the stew of missed expectations.

Table 2.1 Regulatory Summary

Regulation	Impact on EIM	Short Description
HIPAA	Forces encryption, rigid rules on individual record keeping	Regulates privacy of Personal Health Information (PHI)
Gramm–Leach–Bliley Act	Requires accurate name, address, and opt-out processes	Title V—Privacy and disclosure of private data policies, opt-out provisions
SEC Rule 17A-4	Forces policies for structured and unstructured data	Electronic storage of all financial and trading data
Sarbanes–Oxley		
Section 302	Pressures company's chief financial officer and chief executive to ensure data is correct, and no one can "game the system" via reporting	Periodic statutory financial reports are to be certified as accurate by executives
Section 404	Forces controls for data movement and traceability of usage	The scope and adequacy of the internal control structure and procedures for financial reporting
Section 409	Forces greater awareness of business status and lowers latency of reporting	Discloses information on material changes in financial condition or operations on a timely basis, in terms that are easy to understand supported by trend and qualitative information of graphic presentations as appropriate
FISMA	Justification for government bodies to improve information management	Forces government agencies to define information life cycles
BASEL II	Forced reporting and accuracy standards on large banks	Defines the minimum capital requirements for internationally active banks. Pillar 3 covers transparency and the obligation of banks to disclose meaningful information to all stakeholders

New Ways—Old Sins

Has your company purchased a massive chunk of operational software for tens of millions of dollars and placed it into service? Also known as ERP applications (SAP, Oracle, PeopleSoft, J. D. Edwards, etc.), these products dominate organization applications solutions.[3] They promised integrated data—because they were, well, integrated. Many companies easily spent and are spending eight figures. There is a story in my hometown of a CEO who asked what the total spend was for an ERP project. He asked for the number because he still perceived a lack of information to run the company any better than he had prior to the huge spend. The vendor had assured the executive team that buying all the modules would get them integrated data. Of course, the consultants and the internal middle managers knew that the culture had no desire to integrate, nor was there any kind of discipline in handling data.

The urban myth goes along these lines: When informed the final budget was $60 million he fired the CIO on the spot with the comment "I could have built a new plant for that."

The current issue with ERP is that it is implemented the *same way* as its predecessors—as transactional business event machines. Remember the scenario where we said that operational data is not analytical data. While the vendors supposedly provide the architecture and components to develop integrated data, we end up with the same mess. They build a suitable factory to produce the data assets, but we never install any good quality control or inventory systems. The vendors actually do provide the correct platform. They do not provide your corporate willpower to treat the data correctly, so you end up "trashing" perfectly good database containers with the same overrides and errors that have always been there.

We did work at a client two years after a massive ERP project was completed. Our task was to develop an EIM program. The main driver was lack of synchronization of data across various departments, inability to report accurate results, and failure to realize the benefits from the ERP investment. The root cause of all the drivers turned out to be modifications to the ERP software that allowed entry of items, customers, and orders to be done *as they had been done before*. This meant vendor identifier numbers that were all "nines" and work order assignments that still went to retired employees.

Why? Because the emphasis was not on managing the information asset; it was on expediency of process. Lubricant is applied when fuel is needed. Without better treatment of information and content, we have ended up with the same tangled mess of product codes, vendor numbers, duplicated customers, and questionable integration with other applications.

Mission Critical Spreadsheets and Shadow IT

Another looming black cloud that has attracted attention and urged us toward EIM is the spread of end-user capability to do analysis and reporting. While this is a good idea in concept (IT provides the data, the business user does the analysis), the reality is that IT usually dumps a file to a business department and that file gets massaged, appended, and repurposed a dozen times to other desktops, laptops, or, heaven forbid, leaves the company on a thumb drive.[4] IT has "passed" the buck on data management. And the business areas fail to realize the inherent risks.

There is a fine line between empowering the business to use data more effectively by making it accessible and smearing data to an extent that the organization bears exorbitant costs. Maintaining the technology to sustain data redundancy is costly, while all the time the data represents *huge* risk if it gets into the wrong hands.

There are also the costs of maintaining the technology for reporting and analysis in the business user's hinterlands. During one study done by my firm, we discovered the investment in BI technology outside IT to be *twice* the investments within IT, and the quality of decision making or leverage of the data was no better, if not worse, than their competitors. Table 2.2 is a "genericized" recap of that study.

A New Twist on Data Quality

Within the few years prior to this publication, a concept of developing a "master copy" of critical data shared by many has been refined. The development of so-called "master data" stores has great merit. We used to call them master files. And we created a lot of them. Unfortunately, without EIM, and its data governance cornerstone, many of these projects are becoming Band-Aids to

Table 2.2 BI TCO Chart Sample

	BI TCO Results	Company A	Company B	Industry Benchmark
People (not in 000's)	People % using BI tools	15%	12%	12%
	Total labor support cost per BI user	$25,200	$21,000	
	Total BI/DW cost per knowledge worker, excluding salary	$46,385	$42,000	
Process and information	Number of files sent downstream	764	54	
	DW files, cubes, and marts	182	483	
	MS Access databases in production	19,545	3,200	8,000–12,000
	Cost per non-DW interface	$18,062	$23,000	$12,000–15,000
Technology	S/W licenses	7 tools	5 tools	3–5 tools
	DW infrastructure budget (000's)	$3,200	$1,200	
Business results	Business benefits realized from current BI	None	None	9–12 months
	Three-year trends financial results (000's)			
	Units sold	−6%	2%	
	Gross income	−5%	1%	
	Net income	−6%	1%	

integrate or clean up more operational data. Sins of the past are being repeated when companies build a "golden copy" of customer data, for example. The source system or ancient operational application creating the original problems is not corrected. Old business processes that create the problem data are not corrected, and any new (additional) elements of data do not fit. So then we implement cleanup software in the hope we can "put lipstick on the pig." After millions of dollars, it becomes obvious that the real solution was to go to the source applications, prevent the data entry problems, and implement better controls.

Flat World

Are you managing an organization with international connections? Do you use any outsourcing or insourcing? Is intellectual property (IP) a major competitive advantage? If the answer is "Yes" then EIM is in your future. The flattening world[5] we do business within creates new challenges for data and IM. Some common data and content challenges of a flat world are:

- Conflicting regulations exist in multiple countries. Moving personal information between countries means complying with privacy rules for *both* countries.

- There is risk in shipping raw materials out and receiving finished goods to sell. Poor specification management and measurement can create liability if the offshore assembler improperly handles your products.
- IP laws can be quite loose. There may be no governmental protection for your IP once it leaves your borders.

THE DOMINANT ISSUES

EIM addresses the deficiencies and challenges presented here. As we move forward, remember the below summarized list of major issues from the past as well as the newer versions that are looming.

- *Alignment with the business*—Many information projects are initiated departmentally, thereby failing to honor the inevitable enterprise nature of all information projects. OR projects are initiated with the "build it and they will come" mentality. Either way, misalignment creates long-term costs. Subsequent chapters will present the business case and techniques for ensuring proper alignment of information initiatives by ignoring departmental requests and developing unified business "needs."
- *Achievement of tangible returns*—Most information and content projects offer weak business cases. Hence we have solutions that could not help the business, even if they were correctly executed. And we do not track data usage after the fact to reveal this problem. EIM develops business targets and business metrics to measure progress.
- *Failure to demonstrate value*—There are many technologies with great promise, but all are guaranteed failures unless business can see benefits. And many content and data projects are implemented in a vacuum. EIM will provide the processes and techniques to oversee value and progress.
- *Drawn-out and inefficient techniques*—Many information projects are developed based on beliefs and techniques that are obsolete in light of current technology capabilities. EIM leverages techniques for IM to achieve business results, and does not depend on deployment of only the latest technology as a success criteria.
- *Poor data quality*—The number one obstacle to information projects has been data quality, or data usefulness. While many texts have already been developed in this area, I will fold those concepts into the holistic view of IAM.
- *Lack of buy-in*—It seems there is never any technology where failed projects do not complain about the "lack" of business involvement. This is how the issue is stated, anyway. The real issue is managing the business culture. There is no buy-in because there is no incentive to participate or stated accountability for information project success or failure.
- *Excessive expectations of technology*—There is a tendency to focus on how to get a "data warehouse," "document management," or a "data mart" to solve a problem. There is rarely a holistic view. EIM focuses on the overarching culture, strategies, and techniques required to successfully implement ALL of the various information and knowledge processes.
- *Shadow IT or excessive application of business units "doing IT"*—This theme reviews the costs and risks of IT "dishing" the management of data to the business area. EIM means working smarter to ensure proper balance of IT vs. business area usage of data and content.

HOW DOES ASSET TREATMENT DEAL WITH THESE?

EIM has usually been approached in a reactive manner. The scenarios presented earlier in this chapter impart a case for formal management of information as an asset. Formal management, of course, means an emphasis on proactive vs. reactive. It also means policies and procedures to avoid mismanagement of data and content, including data quality and distribution.

First, we are *not* just creating a strategic plan. Regardless of the intent, very few "strategic plans" result in a flexible approach that is responsive to business changes and easy to roll out. Granted, EIM uses strategic planning techniques, but the outcome is not a plan—because if you accept the premise of asset management of content and data, then *you don't need a strategy to convince you* to do it. You need to build the programs. The business has its strategic business plan. That is enough.

In fact, strategic plan is a misnomer—and a bad approach. Plans have a tendency to sit on the shelf. IAM means invoking a program (called EIM) that creates a vision, and deals with issues both tactically and strategically.

EIM in this context is a strategic function, like marketing or budgeting. EIM is its own strategic area and like others (marketing, sales, R&D) contributes and coordinates toward reaching organization goals. Are there marketing plans that are done in a vacuum? Of course not.

IAM/EIM may also offer a different approach than expected; we will focus on moving IT *toward* the business side, in fact, urge elimination of the IT/business distinction altogether under this program.

A DAY IN THE LIFE

An organization that has an EIM program will exhibit an understanding of data as the fuel of the enterprise. Whereas other organizations might view data as a lubricant, making local processes better, or targeting specific business targets, the EIM enterprise makes sure that the data asset is recognized as a key component for success.

Asset treatment for information also means that the evaluation of risk in data will be very evident. Massive data downloads and mission critical spreadsheets will be prohibited or closely governed.

The lineage of a particular chunk of data will be able to be tracked from its entry into the enterprise to its ultimate retirement and destruction. From a compliance standpoint, it will be simple to see who has looked at data and how it has been used. The same technology that allows for data lineage will also allow companies to build a value model for data and be able to adjust investment in technology accordingly. Figure 2.1 shows how the various aspects of EIM operate. At the center of the figure is the information life cycle, supporting business events and the various types of content EIM will manage. However, it is surrounded by business-driven discipline and standards.

AVOIDING THE SCENARIOS

Creating a program that expresses the EIM vision means understanding the contemporary ins and outs of IAM as a corporate priority and strategy. There are three views to help the businessperson understand the context of information and content management and show us how we can avoid the scenarios mentioned in the beginning of the chapter. These are convergence, principles, and value. Later in the book, we apply these views to building the program. For now we need to understand their importance.

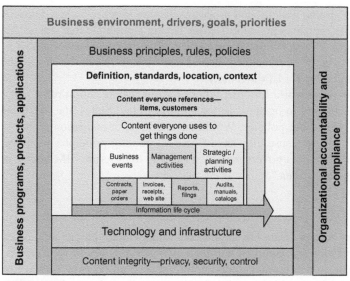

FIGURE 2.1

A bird's eye view of EIM

Convergence

Managing information as an asset starts with accepting this concept:

There is no "we" and "they" in the field of IAM.

"Convergence" has been an overused term in these early years of the twenty-first century. But convergence is the first principle to understand in EIM/IAM. Current descriptions and boundaries of information projects offer little hard ROI. This is because of the historical separation of IT and business. But in an environment where regulatory and market concerns demand closer relationships, convergence becomes a goal. Remember in Chapter 1, I talked a bit about history. The engineering aspect was necessary to get us started in this data processing field. Solid engineering is necessary, but that is not the end game.

A converged EIM environment will create a different portfolio. The aforementioned bifurcation of IT and the business created silos of technology. A converged portfolio will (should?) ignore functional silos and focus more on communities and cross-functional initiatives. Opportunities for collaboration between business units and IT can be exploited. The separation of church and state does not apply to content. Assets are cross-functional. Recall that a balance sheet does not list assets by department. Why support information assets by department? If it is content (be it rows, columns, or e-mails), asset treatment views these together and avoids pitfalls of conflicting initiatives, "squeaky wheel" prioritization, and reactive applications.

Principles

In the context of asset management of data, "Principle" is a statement of belief or direction that guides the organization. When applied to EIM, principles regarding the asset treatment of data become adopted by the entire organization, and frame policies and processes that are triggered when data and content are touched. So our data quality scenarios are addressed by having a principle that states "All content entering our organization is edited and verified for accuracy, effectiveness, and context." A CEO once expressed to my team that if a set of principles such as this were followed, he/she would have 50% fewer meetings and that would pay for EIM. (It did.)

Similar principles exist in the accounting world for other types of assets. Depreciation rules, capitalization rules, etc., are all principles applied to business actions. In the United States, the Financial Accounting Standards Board (FASB) sets these policies. Would anyone in an organization write off a US$50 million factory in one year? No—because they have FASB accounting principles to apply. EIM principles establish the foundation for data governance. A good way to describe EIM briefly is what a COO told me—"This is FASB for my data."

Value

Does data have value? If your answer means "Data has an abstract value," then you cannot answer the next logical question. The next question is, "Can you tell me how much it means to your organization?" Later we will actually propose some notional valuation techniques, but for now we have to be clear there is no formal treatment of data and information for the corporate balance sheet, unless under special circumstances.[6] But treating information as an asset means the following happens:

- The *cost* of managing information is tracked and managed to an expected percentage of sales, earning, or some other metric. This means that the CIO moves from being an order taker and takes on a partner or governance role.
- The *culture* of the organization embraces data and information with the same fervor it treats products and services. Departments do not sell separate products, there is commonality. This means that "shadow IT" starts to shrink as the organization starts to look for commonality vs. separation.
- The *value* of your data and content portfolio, while not reported on a balance sheet, is still tracked and investments in information and content are considered in light of the value added to the enterprise vs. the risk incurred. This means that the CFO should take an active role in information portfolio management.
- You understand, in terms of market, reputation, and financial exposure, the *risk* buried in your content, reports, and hardware. This means that corporate legal and compliance staff are involved with the healthy use of data and content. You also avoid dropping US$60 million on ERP with no data benefits.

Avoiding the earlier issues, or getting your organization to exploit its data, as opposed to exploiting technology, is part of the vision of a firm maturing and deploying EIM. The other parts of the vision that usually appear are uniform metrics, agreement on a single source of the truth, a healthy respect for the usefulness of all content (i.e., data quality), and consistency across major content and subject areas (master data management (MDM) and content management). Organizations can even approach modifications to workflow and collaboration as part of EIM.

A firm that has embraced EIM understands that all the investments in technology are naught if the data, information, IP, and content are not used to achieve the goals of the organization.

SUMMARY

To be sure, EIM means a change in the data/content business environment. The change in environment can be likened to the difference between football and soccer.[7] Football is structured and planned, with bursts of activity interspersed among long periods of inactivity. There is offense and defense, and the two never coexist on the field. Soccer is an empowered group of individuals working with a set of rules, principles, and boundaries, but free to execute and respond as needed. There is no separate defense and offense. The game flows back and forth.

Most businesses and other types of organizations currently operate IT and IM under a general football mind-set. The techniques and methods of IT are based on the perceived need for reconciliation and negotiation. Business users are the offense, IT is defense. They communicate, but never play together. Each team may score, but never together. And great practice and discipline is required *separately* for each squad to get it right. Most of the processes in place in the current information environments in organizations are to get the two teams to communicate, but by definition, they don't want to. EIM is the step beyond that.

References

1. The scenarios presented here are based on actual clients and assessments performed by the author and his staff. Some of the situations have been modified to avoid identification of the hard-working parties struggling with these situations.
2. Carr, N. (2003, May). IT doesn't matter. *Harvard Business Review*.
3. Gartner Research Note, ID Number G00169615, September 2009.
4. Eckerson, W. (2008, October). TDWI of St. Louis, Myth of end-user business intelligence, *Presentation*.
5. Friedman, T. (2003). *The World is Flat: A Brief History of the Twenty-First Century*. New York, NY: Farrar, Straus and Giroux.
6. FASB Codification, copyright, September, 2009.
7. Many thanks to Toby Younis of the former META Group for the soccer metaphor.

Information Management Maturity

3

How does your organization exploit data and content now? If you had to place a grade on this, would you give yourself an A or an F? And what would you measure to assign this grade? If we are going to manage information, we need to measure it. You cannot manage what you do not measure.

Excerpt from Business Case for EIM

CONTENTS

This chapter will examine one of the key shapers and metrics of the EIM program—IMM. It is assessed early in any effort to create an EIM program. It is also assessed frequently after the program goes into operation. The actual process of IMM assessment is addressed later, but the concept of information maturity is key to understanding the results of any assessment that you may execute or have executed for you. That is why this chapter appears early in this book.

OBSERVATION

IT managers will wring their hands and cry that "no one understands" when they try and implement projects or programs that require some aspect of managing data, and the business customer claims no effect, or missed expectations. "We can't measure the value of this stuff, you tell us if it is working," will be at the post-implementation review. When this happens, someone gave up on defining a way to measure success. Information Management Maturity (IMM) develops the foundation for these measures.

Making Enterprise Information Management (EIM) Work for Business. DOI: 10.1016/B978-0-12-375695-4.00003-5

IMM shapes your EIM program, as it will influence the nature of ongoing governance, the size and characteristics of projects, and even the types of technology to be acquired. Lastly, if you are going to tie organizational value to IAM, you will need to know the level of IMM your organization requires.

The means and nature of how an organization uses data and content is expressed as a measure of its IMM. IMM is a relative measurement, not a scorecard. It is a statement of relative ability. Obviously, some companies do more with data and content.[1] But one company appearing with a different maturity than another does not mean it is "better."

The concept of organizational maturity in the context of data may seem superfluous or a synonym for "current state." After all, EIM by definition is an acknowledgment that you are not where you need to be. Why dwell on where you are in great detail? There are two reasons:

1. Maturity is not a "score." There are not universally *good* or *bad* levels. Every organization has an *appropriate* level of maturity. You need to understand what levels work with your business model. You may be at or have defined the level of information maturity required to be effective in your market. If so, your EIM program would address other aspects of EIM to help accomplish your goal. Or you may be many levels away from where you need to be. Then the EIM program must emphasize improving information maturity as a major goal.

2. Knowing where you are and the level you need to be means an *appropriate* program vs. a whiz-bang technology push with hazy objectives. But a "current state" examination is usually a collection of facts regarding "what is not right." To say that data quality is "bad" may be an appropriate finding, but there are numerous other criteria, such as the regulatory environment, where an objective evaluation of what "bad" actually means is important. Since information and content is everywhere, a current-state inventory without a root-cause analysis or a blending and presentation of all findings is simply a pile of facts without relevance to setting future direction.

Maturity, however, has some more dimensions than how exotic your analysis and interpretation of data is. The assessments early in an EIM program also need to accommodate the culture, the business environment, the current state of IT (in terms of capability and infrastructure), the usefulness of existing content, the effectiveness of leadership in providing business vision, and the potential for communication and collaboration within the organization. Table 3.1 presents a summary of the EIM assessments and how IMM factors in.

It is essential that these assessments take place. Situations may dictate emphasizing one over the other, but at minimum there has to be an anecdotal understanding of where the organization sits in relation to the spectrum of IM. The EIM program cannot succeed without determining a target maturity level and an organizational vision of how it wants to use and exploit information assets. A key point to remember here: it is not enough to tell business units to go "do better data." This can be interpreted as analysis, quicker transactions, or more spreadsheets! A more precise statement of how content is to be used is required. And you cannot produce that statement without knowing where you are.

Table 3.1 EIM Assessment Areas

Assessment Areas for IMM	Sample Factors Affecting IMM
Capacity to change	How does the culture view the use of data and content currently? How numerous are the silos? Is there incentive to move to a more integrated picture of data and content?
Business alignment	Is the organization a leader or follower? Are there urgent business issues creating pressure to act immediately? Is the business regulated? If so, how highly charged is the relationship with regulators? Is this business ready for EIM?
Technology readiness	How is IT regarded by other areas? Is the "plumbing" adequate to meet a future vision where more data and content is moving around? How much "shadow IT" is there? Is the IT staff ready for EIM?
Data and content usefulness	Is the quality of the existing content portfolio considered accurate? Is there the need for external data? Have privacy and security been a concern?
Awareness of risk	Is management aware or able to quantify risk inherent in data and content? Are risk management or mitigation strategies considered when doing IT planning?
Enterprise boundaries	Is there an EIM aspect to outsourcing? Are there regulations for data movements between countries? What is the awareness and tactics for dealing with these and other globalization issues?
Leadership	Do the business leaders convey strategic and tactical plans well? Is there a business strategy that can be reviewed? Do executives care about data?
Collaborative potential	Based on culture and other factors discussed earlier, how well can this organization use managed content if it existed? Can we wring all the benefits out of EIM?
Information and content usage	Does the business exploit data using analytics? Is content managed formally? Can we support workflow? What standards are there? Is the organization immersed in producing reports?

TIP FOR SUCCESS

Consultants are useful for assessments, as experience in surveying many organizations always leads to a better survey. If consultants are not on the radar, there is a maturity template in the Appendixes you can copy. However, it is recommended to get external help with interpretation of the results, given the implied objectivity a consultant brings.

Most of the time IMM is reported as a relative number, like a location on a scale or a scorecard-type metric. Most CxOs are interested in the scorecard-type metric, so they can see how they compare within their market. Others are interested in discerning what it will take to move to a different state of maturity if so desired.

One thing that you should not see is a statement that you are "good" or "bad." It is most likely that few organizations will ever appear to be the most mature. In fact some organizations, based on the nature of what they do, may have no need to be at the high end of whatever scale is used.

We assessed a consumer products company information area that was created by merging two large organizations. The nature of the post-merger information environment was such that the acquired company was deemed to have "better" IT, so the acquiring company was told to move toward the acquired company's platforms and BI applications. The IMM assessment confirmed the reality was that neither company's mid-management really wanted to go through the changes, and were doing their best to hide their respective projects. The internal strife ultimately led to a political battle, where the acquiring company shut down the "acquiree's" IT area, moved it across the country, and still tried to fit the acquired company's BI applications into the old culture. Eight years after our EIM strategy was delivered, they still cannot implement a uniform view of their organization. In a large organization, there will be disparate capabilities in staff, technology, and capability. Given EIM, by definition, is cross-organizational, a move up the maturity scale will require intimate knowledge of where the current differences and strengths lie.

IMM—BASIC WAY TO LOOK AT USAGE

Some education is necessary at this point. If you mention the term capability maturity, or CMM to anyone connected with IT, chances are they will understand, or at least be aware, that the CMM represents a relative scale of capability for development and management of software. The entire concept of the CMM was originated at Carnegie Mellon University in the 1980s under the oversight of a U.S. Air Force funded contract.[2]

This concept is what we are applying to the information and content spectrum. Naturally, with the maturing of technologies for dealing with data and content, BI, and knowledge management, there is now discussion related to a maturity spectrum for IM and BI, an Information Management Maturity Model (IMMM) (sorry).

A significant aspect of any discussion around maturity is that business and other types of organizations, at a grassroots level, are beginning to see that there is a predictable curve of information and content production and usage that can be climbed. After the current and desired states of maturity are known, an enterprise must then develop principles, guidelines, and governance that affect all aspects of IT to drive it up the curve. A survey of the current thinking reveals it to be more focused on increasing levels of sophistication of information usage and embraces more of a business tone.

PERSPECTIVES ON MATURITY

There are as many IMM scales as there are consultants offering the service. Some of them will emphasize the speed of using and exploiting data, i.e., moving from a once-a-month report to real-time indicators. Others focus on the organization (people, process, and culture) and avoid underlying technology. Others base the score on effective usage of content, basing the score on business usage contrasted against business effectiveness. Rather than declare one or two correct, it is better for the executive to see and understand how we can measure maturity, and therefore measure EIM progress. Furthermore, the IMM is NOT a measure of IT effectiveness, but reflective of the entire enterprise.

TIP FOR SUCCESS

You must understand these perspectives if you are to assume a leadership role of any sort in EIM. Remember, the IMM not only offers a glimpse of where you are, but can be used to present very clearly where you want to be. You carry the banner of corporate image, business vision, and mission. Information maturity is an important part of that banner.

Tables 3.2–3.4 explain maturity levels for the four perspectives shown in Figure 3.1. Each perspective, again, emphasizes an aspect of the business. It may be effective to present two perspectives, develop your own hybrid, or pick the one that is most representative of your organization. Later, Part 2 will get into details around each perspective, but here they are now for comparison purposes.

Table 3.2 IMM Usage and Content Basis

Content Basis	Usage Basis	Description
Events	Make it happen	An organization is primitive, using forms and process-level data gathering. Consider a start-up business or small family-owned business.
Transactions	Make it happen faster	Data is a lubricant. Business events become transactions that are captured. For example, a Point of Sale (POS) system at each outlet for a retail chain.
Reporting	What happened?	Transactions are gathered and summarized to inform the organization of what has happened. This is the most common use of structured data. However, you are still at the lubricant stage.
Analyzing	Why did it happen?	This level is where most organizations believe they are. Transactions (business events) are collected and evaluated post facto. Trends, correlations, and statistics enter into data use. At this point, a company may actually base business actions on the result of historical analysis. Executives may now believe they are entering the "Fuel" stage for information use.
Predictive	What will happen?	Organizations extend their historical analysis into predicting events, then compare the actual result to the predicted. This is really the entry point for the "fuel" stage of data management. Note that, most likely, nothing is done with documents or workflow-related content except print it, use it, and file it. Analysis of unstructured data is still manual.
Operationalize	Make it happen by itself	An organization becomes confident enough in its patterns and behavior where some events (think MRP systems) are understood enough to be triggered automatically. At this stage, we also see unstructured content (e-mails, documents, paper work orders) generated, and a new level of content management and data is born. Some semblance of compliance or governance will appear from outside of IT.
Closed loop	What do I want to happen?	The operations and event creation are based on triggers derived from analysis. Where in the operationalize phase we create events based on a threshold that was defined, this phase defines new thresholds based on desired results. The organization is getting intelligent with its structured data. This is truly a fuel stage. In addition, e-mails, memos, and other internal content are recognized as areas of value and risk, and we start to govern and define an expected level of business behavior.

(Continued)

Table 3.2 (Continued)

Content Basis	Usage Basis	Description
Collaborative	How do I make it happen better?	We start to blend the structured and unstructured content. Even if the organization has functional silos or distinct business areas, content and data are made available together, and functions cooperate with data, vs. hoard it.
Foresight	What should we do next?	The organization has data that measures its data and content; we reach a "meta" stage where we can, in effect, have the organization learn and remember, based on collaborative patterns, workflow, analytics, etc., store these learned behaviors, and react accordingly.

Table 3.3 IMM Capability Basis

Stage	Description
Initial	The organization is entrepreneurial; individuals have authority over data, so processing is fragmented. Chaotic and idiosyncratic are common adjectives. There are few users, any business rules or criteria for behavior are nonexistent. Obviously, data quality is far from integrated, and data handling is costly.
Repeatable	Departmental data becomes the norm. Processes for consolidation and reconciliation may exist to improve the context of data. All data and content are defined internally (vs. using industry standards). Usage is still reactive. Any cleanup or sophistication in usage, such as analysis, is departmental, specialized, and costly.
Defined	The organization starts to consider an enterprise view, and looks for some sort of integration across applications and silos. A desire for data accountability evolves. Strategic alignment to the business becomes an activity in IT. Standards are developed, and sharing and reuse become watchwords. Data quality becomes formal and may centralize. Data usage becomes more common, less specialized. Facilities to track usage, meaning, and maintain data assets evolve. Efficiency of data management improves, costs decrease.
Managed	Data and content assets are tracked, lineage of all content is understood and documented. Analytical results are used to close process loops. Availability for use may become real time vs. monthly or weekly reporting. Personnel can be interactive and collaborate on content and data. E-mails, documents, and web content are also managed, and can be called up alongside "rows and columns." Data quality is built into processes vs. corrected post facto. Data and content management is integrated into the companies' culture and value chain.
Optimized	There is no need to determine if information assets are managed effectively—they are woven into the fabric of the organization. Real-time innovative use of content is ubiquitous. There are effective measures in place, so allow IM to be continuously improved to support business innovation. The organization can place a value statement on its content, if not the balance sheet. Knowledge bases exist, and the distinction between structured data handling and unstructured data handling dissolves.

Table 3.4 IMM Organization Basis

Style	Description
Operate	Skills combined with charisma win Power of information mavericks Information processes and tools are individual and informal Individual agendas drive competitiveness
Consolidate	Teamwork within functional units Streamlined and measured processes Functional agendas Multiple versions of the truth Departments implement applications
Integrate	Workers think enterprise-wide Workers understand their impact Enterprise agenda IM formalized Collaboration among peer group
Optimize	Constant market alignment Incremental improvement Capture tacit knowledge Focus on edge-cases Infrastructure provides context
Innovate	Innovative mentality Diversity of experience New business models Risk management Change is expected

Information management maturity spectrums

Usage basis	Make it happen	Make it happen faster	What happened?	Why did it happen?	What will happen?	Make it happen by itself	What do I want to happen?	How do we make it happen better?	What should we do next?
Content basis	Events	Transactions	Reporting	Analyzing	Predictive	Operationalize	Closed loop	Collaborative	Foresight
Capability basis	Initial	Repeatable		Defined	Managed			Optimized	
Organization basis	Operate		Consolidate		Integrate		Optimize		Innovate
Scale	0	1	2	3	4	5	6	7	8
Capacity to change		X							
Business alignment			X						
Technology readiness				X					
Data and content usefulness			X						
Leadership					X				
Collaborative potential				X					
Information management		X							

The Xs show the relative IMM scores of a surveyed enterprise

FIGURE 3.1

IMM Perspectives

Usage and Content Basis

Usage basis emphasizes how information is used. Content basis emphasizes the type of content used. These are used by my firm, and we use both simultaneously. Note that the first two columns are two views with similar descriptions, one is content based, the other is usage based.

Capability Basis

This next scale is based on the same levels of maturity used in IT to manage internal process maturity for software development. Capability basis focuses on the nature of interaction with information. I insert it in this book because the terms may be familiar, and many areas of your company may understand them. The stages are a little less distinct, but may be applicable or more acceptable to your organization. They tend to lean more toward your processes and handling of data and content.

Organization Basis

The last example is in the context of organization evolution and behavior, with a focus more on the people and process personality of an enterprise. Thanks to SAS Institute, Cary, NC, for their permission to work on this and use it in this book.[3] SAS has a set of criteria to assess organizations and assist them in evaluating their current investment in IT for their current maturity level. Note that the emphasis is not necessarily to force an evolution, rather understand where you are and maximize that level of understanding before moving forward.

Figure 3.1 is provided to contrast how each view (all have strengths and weaknesses) might map if aligned with a set of sample scores from an assessment.

Assessment Instruments

A few notes on how to oversee this exercise to make it effective and relatively painless. A business leader cannot burden busy staff with hours of interviews to assess current EIM capability. It will seem repetitious, for one thing. "We have been saying this for years. Why repeat it?" is a refrain commonly heard. This is a data point for IMM. It means for sure that there are some silos because they are being vocal. Granted there have been complaints about data and content. But no one has complained about the lack of enterprise governance over data. The complaints have been local in context. So interviews only reinforce isolation. Again, IMM is an enterprise metric. Departmental IMM will not contribute much to the baseline you are trying to identify. Interviews and meetings will occur after the assessments when results are presented, verified, and you start to develop a consistent view of current capacity and ability to manage information and content on a formal basis.

TIP FOR SUCCESS

Consider this technique. Do not have *any* interviews to assess the current level of maturity. Use other methods and then present results. You will get much higher engagement when managers see all the results in an enterprise context. You need to force business staff to think holistically. In my practice, we only interview the highest placed executive we can get to, usually the CEO or business unit leader. If we cannot get their perspective, we usually "dumb down" EIM to more of a business alignment exercise, and we use quantitative data and benchmarks to do the IMM assessment.

A committed management team can complete this assessment rapidly, usually within one to two weeks after design and approval. The most efficient approach has been a focused online survey. These are not casual lists of questions; they are engineered instruments, limited to what can be done within 15 minutes. In addition, we use demographic categories to be able to differentiate responses across multiple levels of management and the organization. In this manner, we are able to monitor response rates (middle management ALWAYS drags its feet) by audience. There are examples of survey instruments in the Appendices.

SUMMARY

The maturity of the organization in the context of data and content usage, quality, alignment to the business, and other factors is a crucial concept to understand if you are serious about EIM. Everyone (even within the same industry) will most likely have or desire a different type or flavor of maturity in terms of using data. Company A makes widgets but wants to be most innovative, so it may require more capability in the areas to enable R&D. Company B makes widgets and desires to be the most customer intimate. Therefore, they may need to master the management of their basic reference data, like customer and sales records. Understanding the gap between your needs and capabilities permits a more efficient and measurable EIM program. If you do not know where you are, you cannot develop a plan to get where you want to be. But IMM goes beyond a current-state analysis. IMM sets the metrics for measuring the amount of convergence. IMM means institutionalizing IAM principles. Using the sports analogy from Chapter 2, IMM measures the distance to traverse from playing "football" to playing "soccer." The nature of the IMM assessment creates baseline attributes for future measurement of EIM success.

References

1. Davenport, T. H., & Harris, J. G. (2007). The nature of analytical competition. In: *Competing on Analytics*. Boston, MA: Harvard Business School Press.
2. Specification 2167A, CMU/USAF.
3. Copyright © 2006; SAS Institute, Inc. All rights reserved. Reproduced with permission of SAS Institute, Inc., Cary, NC, USA.

The Business Model

But out of all the secrets of the river he today only saw one....this water ran and ran, incessantly it ran, and was nevertheless always there, was always at all times the same, and yet new in every moment!
Siddhartha

CONTENTS

We have already made a case that data, information, and content are organizational "fuel" in the twenty-first century. And even if you want to stay with data and content as a high-powered lubricant of the business, you still have to understand what that means and what makes EIM a business program.

In Chapter 2, we got a high-level view of EIM as a program, and what some of the bits and pieces are called and where they fit. So how do these become a business program? Where does EIM fit into your business model? If you want to elevate managing content and data out of the realm of an IT project (with the aforementioned dubious outcomes) and into the realm of running the business, some components have to be assembled and organized into an effective mechanism. Enabling the business, managing costs, and supporting staff are all important business vision concepts. The EIM program needs to do the same things, and be structured accordingly. This chapter will look into EIM as a business component.

Making Enterprise Information Management (EIM) Work for Business. DOI: 10.1016/B978-0-12-375695-4.00004-7

EIM—THE BUSINESS MODEL

Remember EIM is a program not unlike marketing or R&D. There is ongoing value. But the program (EIM) is the medium within which the activity (IAM) happens. Where would the ink for these words you are reading (assuming you aren't reading this in digital form) be without the paper? So what is the utility of the data without the EIM backdrop?

Enterprise information assets are not unlike a river. Yes they flow—but the flow just allows things to happen. Many times your CIO will focus entirely on the "flow" of data urging the enterprise to have a "back plane," or "interface bus," or "services layer," or other technical terms. These just describe the river as plumbing, but not its purpose.

TIP FOR SUCCESS

Frankly, EIM can be carried off with 1970s technology almost as well as twenty-first century. So forget the whole "wiring up a back plane"; that's engineering, not business. The engineering has to be done but it is not the end product and is not really the job of EIM. It is necessary at some point, but not in setting up EIM as a business program. The IT infrastructure is sometimes a part of EIM, more often the enterprise plumbing is defined separately and EIM contributes requirements. Infrastructure should never be a driver for EIM.

The business aspect of EIM answers this: what is the river for—do you cross it or go down it? Do you have to go upstream? Do you have a business model with multiple rivers? EIM manages those rivers of "stuff" that course through your organization (see Figure 4.1).

The river of content has to provide data to report on events. You have to get managerial reports from the river. Documents and forms are used and moved around within a value chain of content events. You have to analyze the river to see where you have been and maybe predict where you can go. You can even have the river tell you what you need to do.

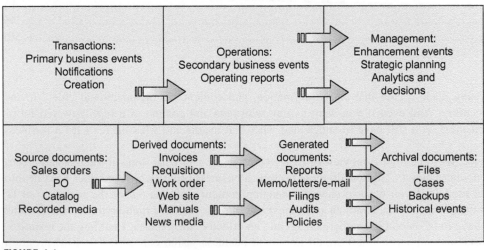

FIGURE 4.1

EIM value chain

This is not rocket science. Once you understand that you will need to delve into all the main currents and backwater eddies, it becomes an engineering exercise. So EIM is river management of a sort. What components do we need: Boats? Dams? Locks? Paddles? What are the basic building blocks?

EIM BUILDING BLOCKS

An EIM program that will keep you out of trouble, as well as allow leverage of other data and content for your business, requires several layers of interacting components. The illustration below lists these components and describes how they fit. The ultimate goal, of course, is management of information, data, and content to the needs of the business (building block Number 11). The entire framework of business EIM has to exist in a business environment. Clearly, the unique intersection of the business environment and your organization will impact how business is accomplished. EIM in a small company or in a developing nation is not going to require the same component makeup as EIM in a highly regulated advanced corporation. Hard economic times will require different component interaction than good economic times. In general, these are the fundamental components to which a businessperson must pay attention to be successful.

1. *Business model*—This layer represents how your organization operates to achieve its goals. Are you bureaucratic? Lean and mean? Decentralized or federated? Government or not-for-profit? The manner in which you get things accomplished is your business model. EIM requires an understanding of the business model for a few key reasons:
   a. An organization that is highly regulated will require a different EIM structure than one that is not as regulated. Data risks will be different.
   b. A governmental body (or not-for-profit) will usually have a different EIM model depending on accountabilities than a for-profit entity. Often budget cycles and budgetary limitations drastically affect what can be done. Cultural obstacles can be much more intense in government areas.
2. *Information handling and use*—Part of EIM is making sure that data and content are handled properly and efficiently, and benefits the business without extra risk. How much redundancy are you comfortable with?
   a. We have stated earlier that there can be too much handling of data and that can be as harmful as too little movement of data.
   b. Proper handling means keeping data and content around as long as it is useful, then getting rid of it when contingent liability exceeds the value of the data.
3. *Information life cycle*—All data and content have life cycles. They enter the enterprise, are used, changed, read, and analyzed but then at some point must go away. EIM balances the conflict of retiring data vs. the cost and risk of keeping data for too long.
4. *Applications*—How data is used reflects directly on its value. If you are managing the data as an asset, then the only way to know if that asset has value is to understand how and where it is used.
5. *Technology*—Granted, I promised a "low-tech" book. However, the extent to which organizations deploy various technologies is also a component of EIM. (But take a look at your BI maintenance and support budgets, divide by the number of knowledge workers, and get back to me when you see the size of the number.)

6. *Organization*—When you do EIM, some organizational changes may be in order. For one thing, you will need to implement positions and accountabilities for the information being managed. You cannot manage inventory without a manager, you cannot do IM without someone with accountability for accuracy and availability. When in doubt, pretend the data in your organization is the same as the raw material.

7. *Compliance*—You have a compliance department. It may be one lawyer, a liaison to a regulator, or an entire building of high-strung audit types. EIM requires you to consider the regulatory and other risks that go with data, with the business lens provided by your compliance area.

8. *Enterprise "DNA"*—"Where is the data we need to analyze this issue?" "What does this piece of content mean?" "Where is it used?" These are common questions. A significant component of EIM is tracking where data came from, who touched it, and where and when it should go away. As an executive reading this, you may be surprised to realize that your IT organization has most likely cut this feature from the budget of every data project done since 1990. EIM means that you need to know *full lineage*, plus the definition and rules that go with each class of data. Are there rules and tracking of employees? Complicated machinery? Of course. Why not track the data?

9. *Culture*—Every organization has a culture. When you engage in EIM, you put stress on that culture. People have to act differently. Accountabilities change. Sadly, organizations will believe that the new program or solution is so self-evident that managing this pressure during a period of change is not required. There is the perception in many organizations that utilizing good change management practices is fluffy soft stuff that takes too much money, time, and energy. However, it's one of the most critical things to which you need to pay attention. In fact, culture change management is probably the number one contributor to success in EIM.

10. *Governance*—When processes change due to EIM, there is the need to see that the new guidelines and policies remain in place. Like compliance, governance is primarily a means to manage risk, in this case, risk of returning to the point you started. In addition, most information programs tend to run out of the feeling of newness, the "new car smell." When they do, governance ensures that the new roles and data standards continue to be used. The number one area that will bypass these new policies is the IT department. Governance is one mechanism to manage the inevitable areas of resistance that will arise.

11. *Managed content*—What is being managed in EIM? Simply ALL enterprise content—reports, forms, memos, catalogs, web pages, databases, spreadsheets—and the list goes on. All enterprise content can be valuable; all enterprise content can contain risk. It is an asset. Do you only manage the cash or finance in certain areas and not others? No. Why then allow row-and-column data to be managed and other content to be untouched?

As you can see, these fundamental building blocks for EIM must interact with each other. To be sure, EIM requires a commitment to doing things differently as far as data and content is concerned.

Figure 4.2 may seem daunting—it seems like a lot, and may seem like another one of those consultant-driven guru models, like process reengineering or CRM. However, it is NOT a program that is a sinkhole for money. It is not a program without a business case. More importantly, it is not a program that has to be based on monolithic projects, huge staffs, and budgets. Honestly, while there is the potential or even desire for large projects in EIM—small incremental efforts work best.

Many organizations can start with EIM and have *no incremental increase* in spending. Nearly, all organizations can generate a huge return on the investment in EIM. I'll cover the development of a business case in Chapter 8.

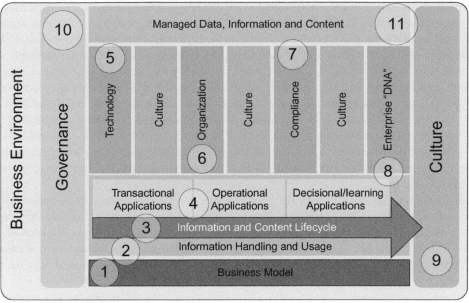

Managed Data, Information and Content

10   11

Business Environment

Governance

Technology   5

Culture

Organization   6

Culture

Compliance   7

Culture

Enterprise "DNA"   8

Culture

Transactional Applications   4   Operational Applications   Decisional/learning Applications

3   Information and Content Lifecycle

2   Information Handling and Usage

1   Business Model   9

© IMCue Solutions, 2008

FIGURE 4.2

EIM building blocks[1]

EIM PROGRAM FUNDAMENTALS

We cover organization charts in detail in Part 2. For now we will cover the basic actions that occur within the various components. We have to show visually where EIM and IAM fit into organizations. Boxes and arrows do not convey everything to assimilate EIM into a business model, but we will start there.

EIM creates an environment where information is managed as a business within a business. A reasonable way to keep this in perspective is to consider what "being a business" means. The EIM business area, like any other, is:

- *Self-sustaining*—It shows how it benefits the business.
- *Proactive*—It does not bring problems to the CEO, rather delivers opportunities.
- *Efficient*—It spends only what it needs to, and invests wisely.
- *Supports the business goals*—The EIM program is aligned with business needs, not acting as an order taker delivering one-off business wants.

EIM functions are aligned along the roles required to manage an asset, similar to an inventory function.

1. *Structured data management*—This function, in essence, "tracks" where the rows and columns' data is. This function knows the meaning of the data, where it came from and where it needs to go, and ensures that storage occurs in the most efficient manner, even if that means multiple copies, one copy, or some combination thereof. Typical assets managed are databases, spreadsheets, Access databases, and data for transaction systems. While other activities will also deal with these assets, this area deals with the actual values and occurrences. The actual value to the organization (in terms of risk, cost, and benefit) would be calculated here if the organization attempts to generate a notional value statement.

2. *Unstructured data management*—This function "tracks" the data that is text based or in a form other than rows and columns: memos, web content, documents, and any other content. It knows where this type of data is residing and is used. It needs to know meaning, origin, and destination. This function ensures that storage occurs in the most efficient manner, even if that means multiple copies, one copy, or some combination thereof. Typical assets managed are e-mails, memos, web content, and documents. While other activities will also deal with these assets, this area deals with the actual occurrences and use of the content. Therefore any unstructured content management processes will be found here.

3. *Lineage*—This function may coexist with the hands-on management, but needs to be called out as a separate duty. This concerns the actual ability to report and analyze where data and content originates, who touched it, when it was touched, what it was used for, and how it was disposed of.

4. *Data quality*—This function assesses, identifies, and remediates the usefulness and accuracy of data and content. Since data quality, as we have discussed, is the number one manifestation of poor data management, this is a mandatory function. It is essential to formally measure data quality.

5. *Business processes*—There needs to be an activity to correlate and cross-reference the key content elements with business processes. Processes alter, use, and create data. Therefore, they need to be understood. Examining for potential improvement in processes will ensure successful lineage.

6. *Data governance*—This is the most important function, so important it appears as a component of EIM as well. Other areas will set standards or invoke policy. However, EIM means rules that require enforcing. Governance is the auditor and the enforcer of the principles, policies, and processes required to manage the data asset. No different than an internal auditor, governance does not make the rules, but they make sure they are being applied appropriately and adhered to.

7. *Architecture*—Also called modeling, data administration, information resource management, or something similar, this area designs the standards, the models (blueprints), and the definitions required for uniform management of content and data.

The Combined View—"A Day-in-the-Life"

A picture of "a day-in-the-life" of EIM appears when you look at the building blocks through the lens of the program fundamentals. Table 4.1 can be used to recap this "day-in-the-life" on one page.

EIM ORGANIZATION

With a functional model in hand, an executive will likely wonder "if we have components to put in place, and these components execute and support certain functions, where does the organization accommodate the people and processes to execute the program?" There are two basic models for EIM program organizations. EIM organizations will adapt to these models over time, as few are able to start out with the ultimate organization—meaning you will evolve. You will require some formal

Table 4.1 Basic EIM "Day-in-the-Life" Program Overview

Building Blocks	What Does EIM Look Like? — A Day-in-the-Life Overview Sample EIM Functions						
	Structured Data/Content Management	Unstructured Data/Content Management	Lineage	Data Quality	Business Processes	Governance	Architecture
Business model	EIM will ensure the data and content supports business directions and programs. The various types of projects and applications that occur within EIM need to be driven by and supportive of the business.						
Information handling and use	There are many touch points between constituents within and external to the life cycles of content and business activity. These touch points require regulation in terms of who, what, when, and where interactions with content and data occur.						
Information life cycle	The various types of content all have a life cycle of birth, use, and death. You do not want to keep content any longer than it is useful, or the risk in the content providing bad results outweighs good results.						
Applications	The application is where the enterprise builds and uses information to handle, manage, and track data and content. Examples of applications in this context are ERP systems, data warehouse, computer systems, business intelligence, reporting, content management, and web portals.						
Technology	There are many layers of technology to support EIM. These range from the obvious—i.e., the servers and networks—to the subtle, i.e., security applications and disaster recovery. There is also software, ranging from the actual code installed to operate applications, to databases, to layers of software that manage communications between applications, such as middleware or web services.						
Organization	Organization is affected in two ways by EIM—first, an EIM organization is needed to manage the program. Second, many other departments within an enterprise will experience subtle changes in responsibility and accountability related to IM.						
Compliance	Compliance is listed as a major component of EIM because of regulations. Historically, IT has not proactively interfaced with compliance. In an EIM world, they are partners, and in many cases, EIM may even report to compliance depending on the business model in force.						
Enterprise "DNA"	All organizations need to understand their "DNA," which in the case of information is definition, navigation, and administration. In other words, what does the information mean in the enterprise's context, where is it located, and how do we take care of that content?						
Culture	Culture describes how an enterprise does what it needs to do, i.e., the style and characteristics that make it unique, even within the same industry. Culture is very difficult to change, but often EIM will require a business culture to shift perspective and roles. Government and non-profit entities are the most resistant to change; however, most for-profit entities require significant considerations of their cultures as well for EIM deployment.						
Governance	Governance is a mandatory component of EIM that ensures policies, procedures, and standards related to the management of information are followed.						
Managed content	This is what it is all about—managed content represents the managed assets called information. Managed content refers to the ability to know what, where, and why information is used. Very advanced organizations will evolve the ability to place a value on their managed information assets.						

organizational development activity. You do permit an organization chart based on a few minutes discussion in front of a white board.

Both of the basic models offer a baseline template for designing the EIM organization. Again, in Part 2 we will dive into the details, but here is a bird's eye view (Figures 4.3 and 4.4).

Do Right Things—The Things—Do Things Right

This is a functionally ordered organization. In essence, it takes the basic components of EIM and creates a managed area based on the function. The philosophy behind this organization is threefold:

1. You need to oversee HOW content and data is to be managed. (Are we doing the right things?)
2. You need to MANAGE the actual content. (Are the things getting done?)
3. You need to ensure that the management is occurring the right way. (Are we doing things right?)

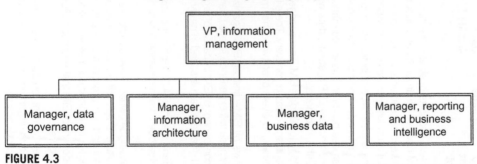

FIGURE 4.3

EIM organization chart—right things basis

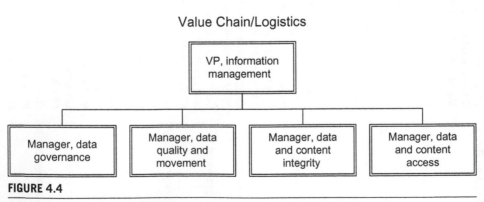

FIGURE 4.4

EIM organization chart—IVC basis

This is not unlike the configuration of a typical finance organization:

1. Determining what things need to happen may come from compliance or the CFO.
2. Actual manipulation and use of "stuff" occurs in the controller area.
3. Audit makes sure that things are done right.

This EIM organization was built around the basic model given in Figure 4.4.

Logistics

The second basic style is based on the logistics of moving data and content around in the organization. This is called an Information Value Chain (IVC) or data logistics basis.[2]

In essence you organize around the information's perceived movement through the organization (remember it is a river, not a linear process—so this is where the bizarre reference to philosophy makes some sense). For example, part of EIM manages the content coming in—so data quality and controls are applied as though inventory were being received. Another function manages the content "in situ"—making sure that the environment takes care of the content until it is used. Think of this as managing the plumbing. The last step would be distribution; this function makes sure the content inventory is accessed and distributed or circulated properly. This organization is built around the model shown in Figure 4.4.

Nearly all organizations that execute or oversee EIM will feature aspects of both models.

Note that we have not stated anything about the EIM organization existing within the IT area. As this book was developed the evolving best practice was for EIM to be distinct from IT. At minimum, governance should be distinct from IT. Since many CEOs view IT as an annoying necessity, this may be a difficult view to implement. But if information is considered a business asset, there needs to be consideration of the principle of separation of duties.

SUMMARY

If a business user or customer or other constituent question the source or relevance of the data or content being presented, they will hesitate to take effective action. They will create or acquire their own, or come to their own conclusions. This is information *mis*management. However, society and pervasive technology are forcing organizations into taking some formal stance on their information assets. A reasonable first step is to begin to incorporate data quality and formal IM into all projects that create or rely on data to enable business actions and decisions. The devil is in the details of the EIM program. There are basic required components and functions that must be designed into the organization. These components and functions are not very different than the basic building blocks of any other strategic area within an organization.

References

1. Ladley, J. *EIM Series*. Information management review 2008 and 2009.
2. First coined (to my knowledge) by Meta Group's Dr. Wolfgang Martin and Thomas H. Davenport at almost the same time.

EIM Alignment

CONTENTS

Making Enterprise Information Management (EIM) Work for Business. DOI: 10.1016/B978-0-12-375695-4.00005-9

Business alignment is a crucial component in managing information. It is also one of the most often stated obstacles to effective IT (Gartner, Forrester, et al.). The two concepts are related. If information is handled and used without regard to an overarching business perspective, then you get what we have been talking about the past few chapters: quality issues, lack of accuracy, and chaos around data. Hence, IT is historically considered ineffective by business leaders. When CIOs are asked why they have trouble keeping the business side satisfied, they say "we do not know what the business needs, only what they want." So IT tends to deliver data and information on a "squeaky wheel basis" that is unaligned to real business needs and fragmented. The joke goes that CIO stands for Career Is Over. This dark humor has roots in the lack of alignment between IT and business direction. This chapter will cover why business alignment is so important to IAM, and review the essentials of the EIM processes for alignment.

Efforts to link business directions to information and content needs are often not effective. Organizations try alignment exercises, but successful efforts that demonstrate linkage with IT—and especially with EIM—are rare. Often the alignment exercise is done against an entire portfolio. This exercise is valuable and focuses increasing business value on the ROI of achieving business change with IT.[1] But such an exercise falls short in terms of asset management because information is relegated to a kind of application to be managed vs. a business asset that IT is interacting with.

Too often the shortcoming is that business goals are aligned with one-off projects, or focus on short-term activity. (The famous "low-hanging fruit.") This is not to say that short-term needs are not met by EIM. On the contrary, we will show in this chapter they are actually met more readily. We will also see how deriving the correct business drivers and aligning the EIM effort with them is a key step in managing information as an asset.

HOW DO EIM OBJECTIVES TIE TO BUSINESS GOALS?

There are many needs to be met by an organization that understands that data and content are fuel. There is also a balancing act that has to occur. Goals requiring some sort of data or content enablement cannot all be met simultaneously. We have to understand the nature of the business needs, and present a picture of what the data and content can make possible. Alongside the satisfaction of business needs, we have to blend in the formalizing of information as an asset so the meeting of business needs is sustainable.

Figure 5.1 represents the intersection types of business drivers and managed information. When data and content are considered in support of the business, we need to understand there are three distinct benefit areas:

- *Business benefits that stem from efficiencies*—Organizations can drive numbers to the balance sheet or bottom line by getting leaner. We can do things faster. In the information arena, we have promised data efficiencies via reuse or low redundancy, but these tend to be squishy, and rarely drive a hard dollar to a financial statement.
- *Direct support of business initiatives*—These are hard dollar benefits that have eluded being attributed to IM efforts. However, information certainly does support new business projects. The benefits are there, but aligning them with the information project in terms of contribution, cost, and benefit does not happen often.

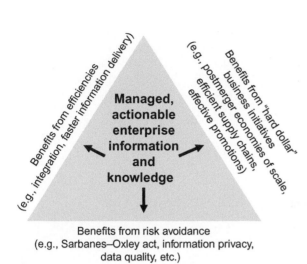

FIGURE 5.1

EIM benefits and drivers

- *Risk avoidance*—This category of benefit has been remote from EIM-type efforts until recently. Risk can stem from traditional fiduciary risk, or risk from noncompliance, civil suits, or fraud. However, using and managing information to avoid risk has become more prominent in recent years as regulations requiring advanced IM (privacy law and regulations like Sarbanes–Oxley) come into play. (Review Table 2.1.)

As we view these benefit categories from an asset management standpoint, we want a balance point where information adds the most value to the organization. We will expand on this in Chapter 7. We may be able to justify and reap benefits simply from the efficiency context. We have done this with IT for years. Occasionally, we deploy new technology that supplies huge business benefits. But after the initial rush of benefits, we always seem to end up with a dénouement where the data supplied by the radical new technology does not stand the test of time. The large returns initially experienced are not sustained.

So let us add the asset management view. What combination of benefits will not only supply early payback (i.e., improve the income statement), but also improve our balance sheet? To improve a balance sheet means improving assets or equity, or reducing risk.

Assets must be used or they have no value. An empty factory is written off. Machinery that is depreciated and no longer supporting required capacity needs is replaced. So the assets must contribute to a financial benefit. Figure 5.2 shows that IAM must display a decidedly deliberate drift AWAY from the IT efficiency play to align EIM with business activity and direction. The efficiency side covers benefits generated from "making better decisions" and "getting reports faster." Granted they are legitimate benefits, but they do not align to the business at all. The business improvement (increase equity and assets) and risk management (reduce liabilities) sides move us closer to benefits that change financial statements and better justification to handle content as an asset.

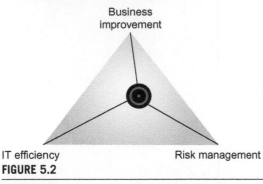

Business-balanced business case emphasis for information management projects

FIGURE 5.2

EIM benefits

The initial step to achieving IAM success is a thorough understanding of business needs in terms of applying data and content to achieve business goals. This happens in two steps.

1. Business objectives/plans are developed or gathered.
2. A formal technique is applied to identify business needs or opportunities where information and content create leverage or enable attainment of business goals.

TRANSPARENCY AND PLANNING

There are two scenarios that play out when gathering business needs for EIM alignment.

1. The first scenario develops where the business is cooperative. Detailed business objectives are available in strategic planning documents. There is enough transparency, so the EIM function can review these, and through an aligned EIM program manage information assets for maximum value in light of business needs. The organization usually will have a plan that ties business programs back to a taxonomy of business goals and objectives. When this happens, creating the EIM program business picture is a relatively straightforward exercise. When there is transparency, there is usually a nice list of corporate strategies or directions. The strategies are decomposed into programs with measurable goals and objectives and a clearly defined use of information to achieve objectives. Figure 5.3 shows the decomposition of a typical goal for a transportation company and highlights where we must use content of some sort to achieve the goal and objectives. The origin of all these columns is addressed at a later point in the book, but it is best to see the appearance of the end product of the gathering of objectives before reviewing any techniques. Columns 1 and 2 of Figure 5.3 are gathered, the next columns are derived. Once these are reviewed with management, it is easy to place them into the business alignment exercise to be covered shortly. You can see that one goal can decompose into a large set of requirements that shape EIM.
2. In scenario two, the business is not forthcoming. Sadly, the experiences of IT and EIM areas have been more along these lines. At times, organizations do not have business plans that are easily reviewed or even found. Often the organization *has no plan reflecting any kind of targets*. Additionally, personal experience shows that at least 60–70% of large organizations do not possess

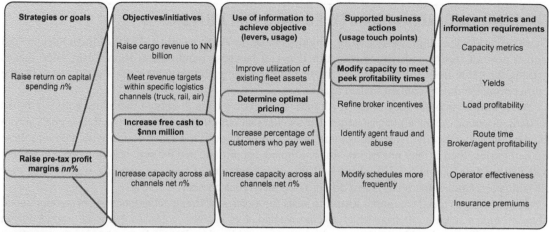

Strategies or goals	Objectives/initiatives	Use of information to achieve objective (levers, usage)	Supported business actions (usage touch points)	Relevant metrics and information requirements
	Raise cargo revenue to NN billion			Capacity metrics
Raise return on capital spending n%	Meet revenue targets within specific logistics channels (truck, rail, air)	Improve utilization of existing fleet assets	Modify capacity to meet peek profitability times	Yields
		Determine optimal pricing	Refine broker incentives	Load profitability
	Increase free cash to $nnn million	Increase percentage of customers who pay well	Identify agent fraud and abuse	Route time Broker/agent profitability
Raise pre-tax profit margins nn%	Increase capacity across all channels net n%	Increase capacity across all channels net n%	Modify schedules more frequently	Operator effectiveness
				Insurance premiums

FIGURE 5.3

Business goal decomposition chart

a culture that is transparent enough to allow IT to see a clear vision of business direction. In this situation, IT is considered an order taker. That's when the EIM "wannabe" team needs to get creative.

TIP FOR SUCCESS

If IT is "kept in the dark," then why continue with EIM? Well, EIM in the sense of IAM may not be plausible, but there is a principle of due diligence that requires information professionals to make an attempt at alignment *anyway*. Assume information has some kind of asset status, even the metaphorical version we talked over earlier. Then those closest to the information must follow some type of due diligence even if it cannot be done in an ideal method. Your content is a fuel and represents a liability. Regardless of how IT is regarded, and whether you are outsourced or insourced, a CIO or EIM lead needs to do some kind of alignment effort. Most employment agreements and contracts mention "safeguarding of company assets." This is where the due diligence needs to enter the picture. I often have IT staffs do "brown bag" alignment sessions in lieu of business transparency.

In the context of scenario two, EIM has *no executive support*. There may be a desire to support EIM, but someone does not "get it." A business area leader, even a CEO, may want to manage data and tighten up content and is willing to spend millions to do so. However, without the alignment and transparency, there is no support from within the business. Moral support is nice, but clear organizational support will get data and content assets managed. Remember, EIM is a business program. As such, you must allow it to participate as any other strategic function.

Assuming no clear business support or visible plan, the EIM team, or its equivalent, will do the alignment exercise in a guerilla mode or as a means to sell the idea of EIM. The team has two options:

1. Derive a high-level business "plan" from existing documents to the extent it supports further development of the EIM program.
2. Reduce EIM to an exercise to develop a rough blueprint of an EIM program based on what it *does know*. Benefits will stem from avoiding costly data mistakes and regulatory and compliance risks. The EIM program will be aligned at a level that will enable improved handling of data and content, but perhaps without a precise road map aligned with the business.

TURNING BUSINESS OBJECTIVES INTO EIM DRIVERS

There are many techniques for ensuring alignment and moving toward IAM. All of them have to start with a desired business direction and turn it into a business requirement. Remember, IAM means striving for value from the content you create and use, so any alignment exercise should recognize the connection of value to content or data usage.

After almost two decades of doing alignment work, we have discerned there are really six broad classifications or means an organization can use data and content to improve or achieve goals. From the executive perspective, keep things simple—if you cannot fit the stated action with data into these six categories, then it may not be a business-aligned use of data, and for sure it is not a data asset that will drive value. Table 5.1 lists these and provides examples. I have an ongoing wager—if a new classification can be uncovered, then dinner is on me—your choice.

These "usage value" categories form the basis for a series of simple techniques to ensure alignment. They provide a stable view from which to contrast and align business goals. Any artifact produced from a business strategy should contain something that resembles this. Remember, value is in usage. So it has to be acknowledged in the alignment exercises. Business leadership cannot track the EIM program and EIM effectiveness unless EIM functions and activity can be tied to results. That is the direct tie.

For example, Figure 5.4 takes a high-level strategic view of organizational value. Part of the view is from a groundbreaking book by Karl Sveiby, *New Organizational Wealth*. He states that organization value can be viewed from several perspectives. In Figure 5.4 it is internal, external, and staff. If we align these against the six categories of usage, we can see how it is not a major concern to come up with statements to align business direction with a statement of information asset usage value.

Take heart if you are not publicly traded, or cannot base your business strategy on brands and market position. The Sveiby lens is best for EIM scenarios where there is a lot of content involved

Table 5.1 EIM Benefits and Drivers Comparison

Usage Value Category	Data, Information, and Content Used to Improve or Achieve Goals Through	Explanation/Examples
Processes	Improve cycle time, lower cost, improve quality	We analyze events to look for efficiency gains; we examine feedback from clients to improve quality; we improve forms, interfaces, or workflow
Competitive position	Capture competitive intelligence and differentiate yourself	We find out what our competitors are doing; we develop new messages and brands that attract market share
Product	Create, package, and market unique, higher margin products and services	We develop new products and services, or we make existing products more profitable
Asset/intellectual capital	Prolong leadership, embed knowledge into products and services	We sell what we know, or we incorporate lessons learned into our services; we present the customer with intimate knowledge of them
Enabler	Foster employee growth and empowerment	We empower employees with data at the point of contact; we provide better service or facilities to be more productive
Risk	Manage risks of various types that threaten value by increasing liability	We reduce regulatory fiduciary and civil risk; we manage our reserves and portfolios; we do not break laws while doing business

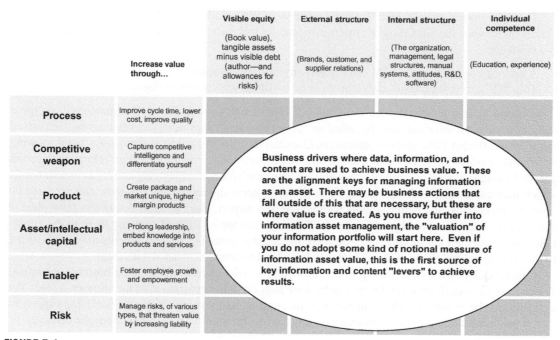

	Increase value through...	Visible equity (Book value), tangible assets minus visible debt (author—and allowances for risks)	External structure (Brands, customer, and supplier relations)	Internal structure (The organization, management, legal structures, manual systems, attitudes, R&D, software)	Individual competence (Education, experience)
Process	Improve cycle time, lower cost, improve quality				
Competitive weapon	Capture competitive intelligence and differentiate yourself				
Product	Create package and market unique, higher margin products				
Asset/intellectual capital	Prolong leadership, embed knowledge into products and services				
Enabler	Foster employee growth and empowerment				
Risk	Manage risks, of various types, that threaten value by increasing liability				

Business drivers where data, information, and content are used to achieve business value. These are the alignment keys for managing information as an asset. There may be business actions that fall outside of this that are necessary, but these are where value is created. As you move further into information asset management, the "valuation" of your information portfolio will start here. Even if you do not adopt some kind of notional measure of information asset value, this is the first source of key information and content "levers" to achieve results.

FIGURE 5.4

Content and information leverage

that can leave the organization or is unstructured. It is just as useful to replace the columns with other traditional strategic context, such as market leader categories (e.g., product, customer, efficiency would replace external, internal, and enabler in Figure 5.4—not shown in the chart earlier). If you are nonprofit or government, a slight adjustment of that model would result in columns saying services, funding, and efficiency.

We will fill out matrices like these in Part 2. We will get a list of business actions, or value levers, that form the basis for what an organization will do with data and content to fulfill its business vision.

ALIGNING EIM PROGRAM OBJECTIVES

The alignment exercise provides a pure business representation of what data can do for an enterprise. Data can be tied to direct business benefits—if the business achieves its objectives, what are the anticipated effects on balance sheets and income statements? Executing this technique at dozens of companies has given very pure and reliable indications of what is important to organizations.

The objectives of EIM programs, both initial and ongoing, are rooted in the Alignment activity. The EIM program will be positioned to support the execution of the statements in these matrices. If the data or content cannot support the statements, then it may not be a vital content subject to management.

Occasionally, a business strategy will appear in a column and there is nothing to say. This most likely means that the business driver or goal is not data intensive, nor does it require extensive content. This is not a concern; it is just a business direction that is not concerned with EIM.

There is another view to take that may supplement the business value levers exercise in Figure 5.4. This is done when the EIM program meets resistance at this early stage. Typical reasons for resistance at this point are:

- A lack of confidence that EIM can support any business programs.
- This "IT" effort should not lay claim to or be involved with business alignment.

It becomes easy to see why an "order taking" IT area will have problems. Encountering this type of resistance calls for what can best be called an "urban planning" approach. The value levers are derived, but from a different view of the organization. Consider the case of a medium-sized town that is growing. It becomes evident the town needs a larger airport. Airports tend to be infrastructure efforts, with certain parties having to cough up money (the users aka taxpayers) for something they know has benefit but for which they cannot find a direct reason. Even if it is apparent the region will not grow and get more tax revenue, more jobs, and better schools without the new airport, there is vocal resistance. How, then, is the funding sold? It is sold by adding up the benefits from the region and applying them to the airport. Does the airport get the money? No. Are there measurable benefits? Yes. So benefits may not be direct in the ROI sense, but they are there. And they have hard numbers associated with them.

Often, a CEO will prefer this approach to a controversial exercise for gaining business alignment. A business case–derived set of levers can be done later on in the program after the concept is sold. You can support the business actions but without the ensuing business case (Chapter 6). Using Figure 5.4 you would replace the internal, external categories with community, government body, or taxpayer.

SUMMARY

Regardless of the technique or presentation, creating a clear vision of the role of data and content in achieving business direction is vital in getting EIM designed and adding value to an enterprise. Assets are used to further organization goals. This business usage must be defined if EIM will be based on IAM.

The alignment activity within EIM should be revisited annually. Alignment is a formal exercise and while the first iteration will be visible, it needs to become a scheduled function. We have seen that it is not hard to create a view of how information assets can support the business. The hard part is acknowledging and executing this critical activity if earlier efforts or culture has left IT or IM in a poor light. In an ideal world, the exercise of alignment is a *business* exercise. If there is an "order taking" culture where the CIO just receives work orders for reports and systems, the alignment exercises will require creativity. Formal IAM is impossible in these kinds of organization, regardless of the inevitable and dire consequences. In those situations, it is best that the IT department perform a guerilla alignment exercise, just from a standpoint of due diligence. It is like the commercial for oil filters, pay now or pay later. Business alignment *will occur*. Do you want the alignment to information assets to be reactive or proactive?

Reference

1. Thorp, J., and Fujitsu Consulting's Center for Strategic Leadership (2003). *The Information Paradox* (Rev. Ed.). Canada: McGraw-Hill, Ryerson.

A Case for the Case

It usually takes more than three weeks to prepare a good impromptu speech.
Mark Twain

CONTENTS

Once it is understood, via some type of alignment exercise as suggested in Chapter 5, that there is a business connection between EIM, IAM, and business actions, then it is time to think about a business case. This chapter is not about building the business case. It is about understanding why a more formal business case is required, even if it seems to be unnecessary.

Maybe at this juncture you, the reader, feel a business case is not required. Full speed ahead! After all, we now know at some instinctive level that EIM is good. We understand that asset treatment of information leads us to tightly connected business and information value. But we need to be resourceful for a while yet. Due to the abstract attributes of information and data, there are some challenges in bridging those good feelings over to a business case.

There are two reasons we need to invest in the effort to build a formal business case:

1. There are still many naysayers out there in organization land. They need to be convinced that a holistic EIM program is better than any one-off effort. It is easy for a department head to state that

there is no time to participate in a squishy information project. After all, there is a business to be run. It is much harder to say you are not in support of a program with a goal of making $MMM for the organization.

2. You cannot succeed with IAM if you cannot measure it. And the success measures of EIM/IAM need to come from a business-oriented set of metrics.

Essentially, the EIM team is in selling mode at this point. We have not really started the program. Later on we will cover the process to initiate and deploy EIM, but for now we are still explaining why it needs to proceed and how EIM is positioned. Often you might be tempted to go forward without the business case. This may be due to overwhelming data quality issues or strong pressure from regulators. It is perceived that the business case is self-defining. Often the EIM program is then launched via focusing on a subdiscipline—usually in the form of a data quality effort. This is all well and good, except you may create a weaker program in the long run. You end up with not one EIM program, but a set of sub-programs that have some business value and certainly express some business vision if done properly. The various elements and components of EIM can be deployed separately. But while there is value here, success will be hard to measure because you will not be able to track the asset nature of information. Any resistance to the data governance required for data quality effort will be harder to overcome because there will be no business justification.

TIP FOR SUCCESS

If there are immediate needs, or incremental steps are your cultural means of accomplishing things, fear not. Label the tactical efforts as part of EIM, but *in parallel*, continue with the formal program development. Truly, if there is no oversight of the projects that all manage data and content in some way, you end up exactly where you are now—still painted into a corner.

The rub is you do not get a *sustainable* program. EIM becomes a data quality "project." Or the IT department deploys a batch of technology to move and track data, but has no REAL data worth tracking and using. Next to poor sponsorship the number one reason EIM fails is it is "dumbed" down from a business program to a business interest that is passed to IT and becomes a project. Table 6.1 shows the typical series of events.

Strangely, another persistent obstacle for EIM programs has been the insistence in many organizations on developing a hard and fast business case with "real" benefits and strong financial return, based on traditional benefits like headcount reduction or reduced costs. In this event, a business case with tangible returns seems impossible because managed data and content is "intangible." So again—the business case is de-emphasized, even though we will soon see that the "hard" benefits can be derived.

Table 6.1 An EIM Tragedy in One Act

Business program without a formal case
A tragedy in one brief act
Sponsor: Wahoo, yippee, slam dunk. I love this EIM stuff!
Middle manager: There was no sustainable business change seen last time we tried something like this—what is the big deal?
Sponsor: Don't worry—everyone is doing it, government says we gotta do it!
Executive: Proceed—I read about it in a magazine, too.
Middle manager: Well, OK, but I'm busy, so I'll send Bill instead.

Table 6.1 (Continued)
Chorus: "Here we go again. Demoralization. Lack of interest."
Executive: I am spending a lot of money—I need to see something.
Sponsor: OK—Let's do *something.* Let's do a (INSERT YOUR VERSION OF A LOW-HANGING FRUIT PROJECT HERE).
Chorus: "Here we go again. Demoralization. Lack of interest."
Sponsor: The (LOW-HANGING FRUIT PROJECT) is done—ta daaaa.
Middle manager: See—it still doesn't do all the wonderful stuff we were promised! I told you it was a bad idea. You can't even use Bill anymore. We will do it ourselves with a spreadsheet.
Sponsor: Why didn't they understand—where did I go wrong?

COMPLEMENTING BUSINESS ALIGNMENT

The business alignment exercise showed us why business and information/content usage is connected. Now we need to position the organization for a formal business case. This means taking the business alignment material that you have already prepared and starting to use it.

It is at this point that organizations that have not done business alignment stop, hire a consultant, and then do an alignment exercise. Let us then reinforce the importance of business alignment—it will be done—the issue is to do it early on and in fully understanding the relationship of EIM as a business program within your enterprise.

We mentioned earlier that many companies do a horrible job disseminating their business plans, and that assumes they actually has one. My company(s) has executed dozens of EIM-like engagements over the past 20 years. Few of these companies had business vision or strategy that was readily available to the very people whose job was to ensure those plans could be measured. Often the EIM effort would trigger an embarrassing fumbling in a cabinet during an interview and a strategic plan would be produced. Organizations that do publicize their strategies and push this information to all levels tend to have much less challenging information and content needs. This is not a coincidence. If business drivers and goals are endemic, how hard is it really to match up the applications portfolio and business intelligence efforts with the business direction?

The typical scenario is that once the business plan has been developed, it is considered "top secret." This is also misdirection from management. Obviously, you can have secret strategies and still give middle and lower management enough to discern business alignment. It's already in their performance objectives, isn't it?

OBSERVATION
The plain and simple fact is this—if everyone knew where the business was headed, many of the IM issues we have covered would be minimized or eliminated. The business alignment has produced a view of usage from a strategic level. Now we need to look at *what* is being used, and start to look at the *IVC* that produces the information to be used. We can then drive toward more detail that removes the intangible aspects and presents a solid set of benefits for each component of the EIM program.

THE IVC—LET'S BEAT UP ANOTHER METAPHOR!

Earlier we mentioned the IVC. Again, we have a concept that is easy to understand as a metaphor. But like IAM, we can direct the metaphor toward real business needs. The IVC immediately presents an image of data and information movement through the organization, but at the same time, it is "something" that requires understanding and management. We caught a glimpse of this in Chapter 2.

Specifically, any content in our value chain does not simply move through the enterprise. This is illustrated in Figure 6.1. The content and data around claims is always "there." The IAM goal is to make sure that the accumulated cost and risk never exceed the value of the content. That means we manage data and content across a life cycle. And when we no longer need the data, we get rid of it. The enterprise IVC is made up of hundreds of these smaller series of events, where data and content gets added to, re-purposed, and used to alter and improve the organization. These events are all common in several regards:

1. The content is initiated or created at some point. This is a major event, for if the content is wrong or incomplete at this point, *every other action taken from this point forward increases cost*. Often data is entered with the caution "we need to finish later." This may be the timely action to take, but the enterprise must acknowledge that right here and now, they are agreeing to handle higher costs of data and content.
2. Once the content is added, it may also change. Again, this is an opportunity to manage the asset correctly. Again, "catching it later" embeds a higher cost of ownership of the asset. Can the higher cost of handling be offset by operational advantages gained by quick entry of data, or shabby data editing, or poor content screening? We have discovered that over the long run the answer is a resounding *no*.
3. As data "moves" through the chain, it is exploited for a variety of purposes. A report is produced, an action is taken. Beyond poor quality, if the data cannot be reported accurately, analyzed competitively, or confirmed to be in compliance with regulation, the IVC is not helping to manage the information assets.

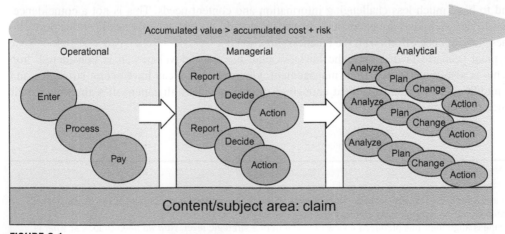

FIGURE 6.1

IVC

4. The content means different things to different constituents. There is no end consumer or raw material in this value chain. One person's data is another person's information. One person's content is another person's hit on a search engine. There are interesting debates about information being data in context and so forth. This is all superfluous philosophy. The fact is ALL of it requires managing. This is why this book has not separated out a difference between data, information, knowledge, and content. Extending our asset discipline, would a manufacturer take inventory of the finished product but not the raw materials before doing a balance sheet? No. Might there be an interest in the state of the material? Yes. Same with content—it is of interest to know what content or data is used in which manner. But to say you manage "information" and not data as part of EIM is to abrogate responsibility for the big picture. The IVC manages the changes in data usage. Content can be more robust, polished, less structured, or more structured. The changes in state occur in a nonlinear fashion and must be managed.

The IVC is touched at different points and content is used in many different ways. The value of the content comes from how well it is, and can be, used. This is where the IVC and the alignment exercise done earlier come together. When you produce what the business wants to do and present it in a form of *where* it is to be done, you get a very clear picture of how the IVC needs to work. The added benefit of the IVC approach is that the information life cycles within an enterprise are identified. Data is born, used, and eventually "dies." Regulatory scrutiny has made compliance to data retention and destruction rules an important issue to organizations. A well-documented information life cycle supports data retention policy.

The value of information increases as it moves (or appears to move) through an organization's processes. The value increases when the usage of information makes an economic contribution to the business. Even though information is not consumable as are tangible assets, information, when used, adds value to the operation and accomplishments of an enterprise. In Figure 6.2, it is evident that many processes will touch a key subject or information component. There is a cycle of value. In other words, as the information content is used, the organization accrues benefit and the value of the information increases. Changes are made; analysis done to maintain the client relationship. Similar life cycles may be drawn for any subject area in any organization.

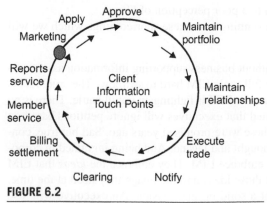

FIGURE 6.2

IVC—cycle view

In Figure 6.2, we have reproduced an IVC looking at processes to identify the inherent needs of a particular business model to efficiently create, increment, and use information. This is no different from management of a "customer" (also an abstract concept from a valuation standpoint, by the way), or "goodwill," or intellectual capital (human experience, patents, and copyrights). All represent areas of increased value in an organization and few appear consistently on the balance sheet.

Since the value of the content increases as it moves through the IVC, and we can describe the various touch points for it, we can now connect the business alignment to a program vision. Then we will have a set of circumstances that facilitates the development of a business case that will allow us to measure progress and manage expectations.

The asset and value chain metaphors provide a foundation for a solid business case that will focus and direct the entire enterprise, making IAM a philosophical keystone vs. a one-off program that delivers a "chunk" of IM.

If this reason is not enough, there is another excellent reason to formally develop this "case for the case."

OTHER ASPECTS OF THE "SELL"

Let us first acknowledge that EIM is a program similar to other information-related programs that have been proposed over the past three decades. As such, you will quite likely find within your organizations the following:

- Prior efforts at managing data
- Politics of data—the data czars
- Short-term focus—"we need it now—so we have to build this Access database"
- Silos—managing data means integrating across silos—often a political challenge
- Perceptions of IT or another IT "project"—this is characterized by the following:
  - A belief that data initiatives such as CRM and data quality fail all the time
  - A perception that any "pure" IM projects are wasteful spending
  - Outspoken criticism of the IT area
  - Ongoing complaints that the IT data is not "correct"—so business areas need to create "correct" data
  - A growth of "stealth" or shadow IT in reaction to a poor perception of IT
  - Plentiful evidence of projects where we "get it running with these shortcomings which we will fix later"—of course later never happens.

Face it—IT has been identified with IM efforts. Without business supporting information asset treatment, the track record of IT projects makes embracing full-scale EIM hard to swallow. The cruel fact is that without a good, solid, money-in-the-bank business case, EIM is fighting an uphill battle. There is no motivation or basis to proceed. History has demonstrated that executives will ignore petitions based on "better access to data" or "single versions of truth." These were promised years ago. Sad but true, concepts like these are now part and parcel of corporate thought and legend. And being ingrained in corporate thought does not mean that a business leader will embrace EIM. They embrace the *ideas* that EIM represents. Barring any other influence, they will craft those ideas into the image they need at the time. So we need to make sure that image is in the form of a solid business vision. An executive will also need to rely on the business case along with the vision to overcome the inevitable negative momentum.

KEY IT AND BUSINESS CONSIDERATIONS

The business case must address the aforementioned IT failures and the perceptions of the IT organization. While the perceptions may or may not be grounded in truth, they exist. A long-standing perception that IT does not deliver will poison EIM. EIM is for the entire business to deliver. Causality for success is spread evenly between the business and technology camps. The IT perceptions have the following origin:

1. It is easy to blame IT. Information projects are sold with inflated expectations. Therefore, an EIM effort needs to develop a business case with realistic expectations. In addition, the case must also align with the business, and reflect the direction required by the business within its current and planned environment. Even if the component parts are "plumbing," they need to be kept in the context of a larger mission.

2. EIM projects deal with abstract concepts that obfuscate the entire effort and that IT professionals are happy to present. However, abstractions do not make money. The road to EIM is littered with projects where EIM staffs have locked businesspeople up in rooms to draw models and define "dimensions." To be realistic and accepted, the EIM effort must not be based on the abstractions that business rules and models will lead to the nirvana of business success. EIM teams have been selling their techniques and tools as final products. *This is wrong. The business case cannot be about the acquisition of tools.* The final product of EIM is a business or organization that accomplishes what it sets out to accomplish.

3. IT projects are all soft benefits, right? Not so. The reality is that when IT projects are successful, IT does not get credit for the benefits. If there had never been any money made off of an IT project, *we would still be closing the books with an abacus.* The business department cannot be the sole claimant of benefits. Nearly all initiatives require data of some sort. There can be no such thing as a business unit claiming all the benefits from an initiative if that initiative uses *any* data or information to accomplish objectives. Even if the data is not from IT, it is still corporate data, and as such cannot be claimed by a department. Benefits from data usage are global. But that is how real assets work, right?

TIP FOR SUCCESS

I remember an exasperated vice president at an insurance company tell me, "if you even dare to say the term 'star schema' in any conversation you are fired." If you don't know what a star schema is, that's OK—her point was that her IM people and consultants had spent two years burying her in technobabble and had totally ignored the business needs.

We have already stated even if a business leader really wants "better data," and is willing to push hard and use up political capital to get it, you do not go forth without a business case. The risk is falling into the waste can of failed initiatives. Therefore, there are some business considerations for the business case as well:

1. The business case will feature accountability—if the goals are not met, who is responsible? Historically, it has been very easy to blame IT for failure to communicate or insist on business terminology. The business will share in the accountability for the project where IT is involved.

2. Business leaders are poorly incented to do well at EIM projects. Often we hear that a "good business sponsor" is the key to the success of an EIM effort. This is only partially true. The business sponsor can be as excited and supportive as can be imagined. But if, at the end of the year, their bonus or compensation is not tied to EIM-related goals, forget it. The excitement is political and amorphous. Often it is merely lip service. It will not hold up to stress or business changes. When you hear that a project has "lost" a sponsor, it is more likely *that it never really had one in the first place*. The business case requires business accountability be built into sponsors' objectives and personal targets.

3. Once IT projects "happen" there is a tendency for interest to wane, even return to the old alternative. Business areas need to understand that the investment continues beyond deployment, and some effort and will is required to sustain the project's goals. The business case must accommodate the costs and benefits of sustaining the effort, and ensuring changes are fully adopted and integrated into the fabric of the culture.

At this point (hopefully), you are convinced that some homework is required leading into the business case, and the business case has to be a powerful document. Now what does this "precase" look like?

COMPONENTS OF THE CASE FOR THE CASE

There are several basic components to build the "case for a case."

Vision

Vision is perhaps the most abused term in business, but there is an important concept here—the "big picture" phenomenon. When you do EIM, you will be asking the organization to change. Change does not happen among humans without some view of the big picture. This is your goal for the vision. What will a day in the life look like when EIM is in place? What will you see in the organization? What business goals will be more achievable?

Do not ever say "better decisions or "better data quality" as business vision statements. These are not business statements because:

- They have no relevance from a vision standpoint.
- They are not measurable in terms of business value.
- They improperly position expectations.

Risk Statements

You may as well address risks now. A business case is also a vehicle to present how a venture will overcome risks and result in a return. If you do not talk about risks now you are not positioning yourself for the detailed case. Risks come in three flavors for EIM:

1. Business risk—EIM fails to do its part to prevent loss of market share, reputation, failure to hit targets, or avoid fraud.

2. Regulatory risk—EIM needs to ensure the organization is in compliance and not violating statutes around privacy or security.
3. Cultural risk—The organization will fail to engage with EIM.

Business Alignment

State the various value levers, actions, and/or scenarios EIM will enable. These can be stated as supporting the business' strategies or scenarios. When you actually do the case, you will be looking for some hard dollars in these areas. So it is best to present the benefit areas now to ensure that the business is in line with EIM thinking.

Costs of Data Quality

Part of risks is dealing with data quality. Many books have addressed this component of EIM, so we are not going to delve into the topic deeply. However, the business case will undoubtedly incorporate improving data quality, so it is advisable to position the organization. Data quality consumes an enormous amount of cost (English, 1999).

Costs of Missed Opportunities

There is always the need to highlight what will happen (or continue) if you do not do EIM. Usually, you will highlight existing issues with data, reporting, poor content management, scary compliance issues, or high cost of ownership due to shadow IT. There may be business actions and scenarios; however, that cannot happen unless EIM happens or may happen but not fulfill all expectations without EIM. Opportunity cost and the urban planning-type case will be supported by this line of thinking.

Obstacles, Impacts, and Changes

It is fair to tell the organization before diving into a business case what may occur as EIM rolls out. This means covering the cultural and other organizational issues. If there is the possibility of technology changes, these can be mentioned (you do not need details, those come later). Any obstacles that are known need to be presented as well. It is possible that an organization may not have an appetite for EIM and will have to settle for a reduced version of IAM.

Presentation of the Case

When the case for the case, or sales pitch, is presented, there are a few basic considerations.

First of all, it must be presented as a business document. This means there should not be three letter acronyms, technobabble, and exotic and abstract pictures. I had a CEO tell me point blank one time, "I am busy, and while it sounds silly, I want to see simple pictures and primary colors. If I want more detail, I will ask. This does not mean to be abstract, just clear." (Think of it as writing for *USA Today*, only with PowerPoint.)

A few themes have to dominate the entire deliverable so the executive can reach understanding:

- EIM is not a deliverable; it is a program. It is forever.
- The various components you are hearing or will hear about are not the end products; EIM is a means, IAM is the end.
- Governance and change is mandatory. Often there will be a regulatory driver behind this. If not, it is still mandatory as a success factor.

At the highest level, a short concise presentation is required. My guideline for a CEO-level briefing should be 10 slides or less. If the presentation is done well, the EIM team will expect an expression of interest, commitment to proceed, and feedback. The feedback must be acknowledgment or correction of the business alignment items, as well as conveying an understanding of the risks and impacts. If this precase material is presented at lower levels, add details around impacts, business benefits, and risks. Present a uniform business view.

SUMMARY

The quotation at the beginning of this chapter sums it up. The EIM team needs to prepare to sell, so they can go and officially sell. This means examining the business alignment material, merging in some concepts that reinforce the relevance of the IAM philosophy, and recognizing that the long-term animosity between IT and business areas must be addressed with a business program.

Reference

1. English, L. P. (1999). *Improving Data Warehouse and Business Information Quality*. New York: Wiley Computer Publishing; John Wiley & Sons, Inc.

The EIM Business Case

CONTENTS

Making Enterprise Information Management (EIM) Work for Business. DOI: 10.1016/B978-0-12-375695-4.00007-2

Implementing the components of EIM requires more than starting a few projects. The business will, and should, require a financial business case of some type. The business case exists so accountabilities can exist, progress can be measured, and buy-in sustained over the long term. Additionally, asset management means that there needs to be an ongoing appraisal of value.

Is there really explicit business return (not "soft benefits") in EIM? There has to be if an asset generates a useful return from its usage. There are three specific elements of the business cases for IAM: alignment, ROI, and asset value. This chapter starts to peel back the layers of business alignment, and presents the details a businessperson needs to know to recognize a solid business case for EIM and IAM. We will delve into valuation (think balance sheet) in Chapters 8. This chapter delves into the business case in terms of ROI (think income statement).

Alignment

As stated previously, an alignment refers to the direct linkage of IAM efforts to business strategies, and measuring information projects against the anticipated benefits. Alignment is also an objective of the EIM program— aligned means that business needs are directly filled by EIM. Alignment is the ability to tie a project to a specific business objective, and measure against that objective. We started the alignment discussion in Chapter 5. Now we will add some necessary details.

Most methodologies and analysis systems have a hierarchy of goals and objectives to tie the various layers of alignment together. For this text, as well as our templates and examples, the hierarchy is as follows:

- Drivers/strategies are industry- or market-inspired trends, usually stated in terms of a direction. These tend to be categories of business goals.
- Business goals are refinements of drivers, expressing the general trend in terms that indicate desired accomplishments within a time frame. Business drivers and goals state how an organization is trying to improve itself, and are stated in terms relevant to the business area being described.
- Objectives are the specified, measurable criteria for achieving the goals and drivers.
- An example of a driver is customer intimacy. A goal would be improve customer retention, and the objective would be increase customer retention to 97% by a point in time. Table 7.1 shows a more complete example.

The EIM alignment team should start with business drivers or strategies. This gives the team the big picture. In the event a business strategy is not clear, we would substitute industry trends. Business drivers at this point *do not* include examples such as these:

- Inability to share information across the organization.
- Multiple, inconsistent sources of data.
- Lack of ability to generate reconcilable financial reports.

These items are not business drivers or business objectives. They cannot be measured and are really requirements of the EIM program. Setting these up as objectives is unfocusing. The EIM team might say that the goals or objectives are too hard to connect IM to translate or align with, or too difficult to gather.

Most organizations have goals and objectives, or strategies. There are many layers to corporate and organizational strategies. A great deal of the time, goals, objectives, and/or drivers can be discerned by the EIM team from corporate documents. (There should be no need for exhaustive

Table 7.1 Sample Driver Decomposition

Driver—General Business Influence, Direction	Goal—General Strategy	Documented Objectives—Measurable Target
Customer loyalty	Reward customer loyalty	Target high value customers to increase market share to 3 points
	Be consistent across product divisions	Increased speed of case resolution to average of three days
	Improve service representative efficiency	Respond within 8 hours—90% of time
	Improve effectiveness of each customer "Touch"	Enable employees to use customer data effectively
Profitability	Grow the business	Increase new client sales by 15%; increase renewals by 5%
	Maximize investment in customer programs	Customer-related spending YTD
	Increase marketing campaign effectiveness	Reduced mailing costs
Market loyalty	Maintain a consistent view of company products and services	80% of customers express intent to renew
	Make customer experience a competitive advantage	Increased sales growth year-over-year, 15%
	Develop passion for product	Increase customer satisfaction via survey
Service capability	Increase ability to keep up with sales volumes	POS information collection
	Empower service reps to understand the customer	Service rep retention increase to 90%
	Consistent experience at every touch point	Increased customer satisfaction, more accurate information
	Single point of contact for all interactions	Increased customer satisfaction, quicker resolution

interviews, just confirmation.) The key is to make material available that lists or implies measurable goals and objectives. There are several fundamental reasons to take this perspective:

- The EIM team needs to understand the ability to manage data and perform information projects is not of prime interest to executives. It is lower costs, more revenue. Period.
- Business metrics are objective, and supply the same level of information to an information architect that exhaustive interviews provide.

After business drivers are confirmed, business goals and objectives are nested within the drivers. A brief example is shown in Table 7.1.

A consequence of the alignment exercise is the ability to plan and monitor the return on the IAM investment (ROI). ROI has been one of the most significant obstacles to IM projects of any sort. The reason (excuse) for minimal ROI on projects and poor business case development is that information supposedly can't be tied to a single business benefit. Or the business areas refuse to share the "credit" and apply some benefits to the IT investment. Alignment is the key that opens the door to the ROI calculation.

ROI

Managing information as an asset means an assessment and audit of current content holdings and risk (regulatory and others). It requires applying the basics of financial management to the information realm. The business case must be developed to create a picture of current information value, and present the current and future information value in a financial context.

Most or any business financial model entails examining the Internal Rate of Return (IRR) and the Present Value (PV) of information projects. We use these financial concepts to give us a consistent benchmark to judge the benefits of a particular IM effort, or ROI. Calculating these requires factoring in two views of value:

- The cost of production, or the investment in getting and providing data and content, usually represents a baseline number we need to exceed. In other words, if we can't come up with a future value that exceeds our cost, why do the project in the first place?
- The future value is the second view, where any future value is represented by the increased market value of the enterprise, a series of cash flows or incomes, or accumulative increase in wealth gained from multiple applications that benefit the business. The rate of return represented by the difference in future and present value is an effective means to judge the fitness of a business case.

Cost of production and future value represents two conventional means to view information value. A third means, subjective value, is an assessment of value "as if" the information portfolio was an entry on a balance sheet, and is covered in Chapter 9.

The cost *not* to do IAM must also be addressed as a valid part of the business case. This is where risk, regulations, and competitive pressures are considered. Conducting a risk assessment as part of the EIM business case is a critical step.

Admittedly, it is difficult to extract specific benefits from cross-functional data initiatives, but failure to discern benefits results in reduced buy-in, loss of momentum, and long-term disdain for information managed as an asset. Without a good business case, measuring success is difficult, and accountabilities become hard to identify. Without a good business case, IT takes the heat if the project fails. But if the project was looked at from an objective business sense, it would have been deemed a poor idea in the first place.

Earlier, we discussed that IM and regular business initiatives are no longer separate. At minimum, it is counterproductive to view them that way. Convergence of technology and business is a reality in competitive twenty-first century companies and organizations. Therefore, to avoid a business case because it seems abstract, or the business function is hesitant to commit benefits against the IT investment, is narrow-minded. What if the IT organization cannot convince its business partners to pony up a clear set of goals and objectives? In this situation, the onus falls on IT to still develop the business case.

There is a basic principle of IAM that must always be applied:

Information provides no increase in value until it is used.

For instance, if our EIM strategy calls for an information delivery mechanism (a business intelligence or data warehouse application, for example), we can assume no future value or ROI potential until we know how it will be used by the business to accomplish business goals. The benefit from the use of that data needs to exceed the cost of creating, maintaining, and accessing it, as well as the risks that might be built into it.

The business case for IAM is based on how and for what the data is used. Benefits will stem from business processes that are recognized by the business and, ideally, are approved. This promotes buy-in, of course. In addition, the business process emphasis focuses the delivery team on the desired results and should produce explicit, measurable goals. The respective accountabilities of the business users and IT team will be unmistakable.

Remember there are three benefit areas that can appear in an EIM business case:

1. *IT efficiency*—This is the traditional area where organizations justify IM projects by the "cost avoidance" approach. This approach looks at what it would cost us if we did not manage information better. Another common benefit is *reuse* of technology elements, e.g., if we know where all the application code is, we can reuse it vs. reinvent the wheel. The metrics achieved in this area are related to lower costs of information gathering, storage and processing efficiencies, and lower development costs. This is a good start, but history supports that if program measurement stops here, it will not sustain any EIM program or subdiscipline. IT seldom measures whether the declared efficiencies are achieved, or generates effective metrics on areas where costs were incurred due to poor IM.

2. *Business benefit*—The areas of most interest and the focus of all good business cases are the positive cash flows, increased profits, or lowered costs resulting from business units embracing information solutions to business problems.

3. *Risk management*—Government regulations (e.g., Sarbanes–Oxley, HIPAA) have created a highly motivating set of business benefits—those of avoiding the costs an organization incurs by failing to comply with a law or guideline. Large fines and jail terms are proving to be significant IM incentives for executives who realize that their information is not verifiable. The benefit to these types of projects is manifested in goodwill and equity valuations. Risk management also covers risk from fraud committed on the enterprise, risk from civil actions resulting from lawsuits from employees and constituents, and financial risk inherent in assets and investments.

The definitive business case would almost certainly contain elements of all three of these benefit areas. However, the historical application of benefits of EIM projects usually ends up looking like Figure 7.1.

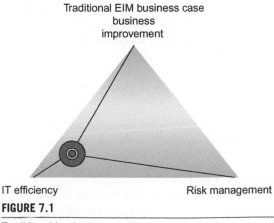

FIGURE 7.1

Traditional business case view

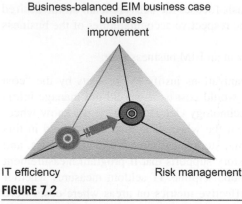

Business-balanced EIM business case
business
improvement

IT efficiency   Risk management

FIGURE 7.2

Balanced business case

In Chapter 5 we stated that efficiency is not a good alignment reason. Justification of an information project (such as a data warehouse) with this emphasis *may* get the project going; however, the ability to sustain it longer term is a risk at best. Why? You still have no business skin in the game.

In fact, the traditional business case presents a few items to be *avoided*. Most of these situations take the pure efficiency view of the information solution. But they are not quantifiable. These typical reasons to do EIM, but NOT to have in the business case, are:

- *Faster access to information (access is too abstract)*—If there is a process that will be spedup, then grab *that* benefit.
- *Better quality data*—Unless there is a formal measurement of data quality, data quality is relative. So a project with this justification has no focus.
- *Faster decision making*—Again, if cycle times are decreasing due to data usage, then that is the benefit, not the faster decisions.
- *Better decisions*—Since 80% of any business decision is made up of experiences and context in addition to the raw data, this is no way to determine if decisions have improved.

The ideal business case will look at *all* aspects of the benefit equation. Ideally, the benefits should push more to business benefits and risk management, and de-emphasize the IT aspect, as in Figure 7.2. This promotes better buy-in over time, and establishes a firmer basis on which to sustain an IM program. It's important to review the detailed benefit potential from each of these areas.

NUTS AND BOLTS—BUSINESS AREA

The business case emphasis for IM will apply basic financial and material management concepts to derive a cash flow or income stream from a project. This happens in a series of steps:

1. Discern the core business objective.
2. Quantify the financial results for achieving this business objective.
3. Identify processes or touch points where the managed data or content will be used to achieve or enable the objective. There must be a link from the business action to be taken (more, better, less, and so forth) with the information usage. Should business users refuse to credit information usage

with specific benefits, the EIM program will be able to call upon the processes that were identified when the business case was developed.

4. Confirm the business opportunities created by the new processes that arise from the managed information, reduced cycle times, increased revenue, and reduced inventories.
5. Identify any cash flow or income associated with these processes. When using present value calculations, a cash flow is better than income, but an income stream will suffice.
6. Determine the costs to create, deliver, and access the content for this business action (remember the cost of creation and delivery is going to be shared with many other business processes).
7. Impute a cost for risk, or add a risk avoidance benefit, as appropriate for the content being managed.
8. Develop ROI calculations based on a simple ROI (benefit over cost or a "flat benefit"), Net Present Value (NPV), and IRR. This gets you started but do not rely too heavily on a flat benefit over cost percentage. Unless you take into account the business' internal financial constraints (which is built into the acceptable IRR), and the time value of money, the EIM team is not speaking in an enterprise context. The so-called "flat benefit" ROI requires very high returns that business financial people find hard to grasp. See Table 7.2 for the flat benefit ROI.

The business case then, contains:

- A vision of what will be done in the future with managed information assets
- What the cash flows are from the refined or new processes and
- The IRR and NPV of EIM efforts as mapped to the anticipated development costs.

Therefore, the business case for IAM will determine a ROI.

Semantically, ROI is but ONE equation, but the entire category of measuring benefits has taken on the label of "ROI." The ROI for IAM is made up of three types of calculations:

1. *Flat benefit*—The returned benefit divided by the initial cost is the traditional IT view of ROI. I call this a "flat" benefit because it does not take into account the time value of money or variable cash flows from the benefit stream. As we said earlier, this is useful for an initial view of business relevance. Table 8.1 shows a fairly incredible ROI, and this is not at all uncommon. (In fact, when an EIM project really delivers, it *really* delivers.)
2. NPV—This is a method to analyze the cash flow over time, resulting from an information investment applied to a business problem. This requires knowledge of an organization's cost of money, investments, etc. NPV compares the investment in the EIM program to investing the equivalent amount of cash at the rate the company gets for its money. In other words, if it is more economical to put the money in the bank than spend it on IAM, the business case is weak. Conversely, an absurd NPV would also raise eyebrows. Table 7.2 shows a set of numbers more palatable to a business leader.
3. The final useful metric is IRR. This number reflects the ROI in an annuitized fashion vs. the simple calculation of ROI. The key to IRR is to know the net cash flow or net income stream resulting from EIM. "Net" means the benefits after applying costs of doing EIM and delivering the content. Table 7.2 shows reasonable IRR for IT projects.

The specific items that result in return to the business originate in the business objectives drawn from the IAM processes. As I stated earlier, the business participants may not readily attribute

Table 7.2 EIM Return Comparisons

Flat return basis	Business benefit Cash benefit	3,150% 62%	Obviously, a good return, but not reasonable. We did not account for the irregular flow of benefits or the time involved.
NPV basis (6% annual discount rate)	Business benefit Cash benefit	$58,245,015 $246,660	Much more relevant—we can stash away US$58 million at 6% and get the same return, although the business would be no better off in terms of data leverage. A more detailed approach would be to try and contrast supporting the business directions both with and without EIM. We would need to incorporate the higher costs of business areas doing their own data management.
IRR basis	Business benefit Cash benefit	277% 19%	The business IRR is still a bit high, although threefold return on EIM-related projects is not unheard of. The more relevant number, and it seems to work most of the time, is the IRR from cash flow (after taxes). By using cash, we factor out any other overhead areas or intangibles that can muddy the final income numbers. There is some finance theory at work here, but that is for the experts to work out.

business accomplishments to an information project. The business/EIM team must understand that if information is a managed asset, then to avoid measuring its benefit is tantamount to management saying they will ignore their inventory turns, or cash flow numbers. Even when recent regulatory events make it difficult for an enterprise to ignore financial benefit or cost around IAM (e.g., privacy legislation), there is often a reluctance to accept the statements of return. The EIM teams need to take the following steps if the benefits are hard to come by:

1. *Take a contrarian approach*—Produce IRR, NPV for the company if the information projects do *not* occur and existing processes are used. (Negative numbers, but numbers nonetheless.) Even a conservative estimate of risk produces frightening numbers.
2. *Present these analyses*—If there is still no willingness to "spread the credit" for meeting the business targets, or use the numbers to justify EIM/IAM, then the EIM team needs to reexamine the drivers and sources of benefits. In a worse-case scenario where no one upstairs wants to hear about the benefits of IAM, retrench and focus on the costs of poor data quality and the risks of poor data governance.

NUTS AND BOLTS—IT EFFICIENCY AREA

The efficiency justification for EIM is best represented in an article by Bill Inmon. "A more direct approach to the cost justification of the data warehouse is the approach of looking at the lowered cost of data in the face of a data warehouse."

In other words, an EIM environment properly architected costs less than the alternatives.

The efficiencies come from many directions. Some companies have even gone as far as estimating the cost of an average "interface" to data. If a user requests data, a metric is applied that reflects the cost to develop and support the new interface to the source of the data. An organization with which I am familiar, priced an interface at $11,000 per request. So a business request with four sources costs $44,000. If the same information was gathered out of the corporate data warehouse—a *managed* environment—it would cost only $5,000. Therefore, business users would have to prove that EIM could not meet their requirements (and also pony up the $44,000).

Efficiency also takes the form of quicker delivery of answers or lowering latency of information required for analysis. In theory, the executive getting information sooner means the decisions are more timely and accurate. This flavor of business case places a time value on information, but the benefits are realized from execution of the business decision, *not* the decision itself.

EIM has an interesting effect on business processes. As various silos start to use managed data, or collaborate with managed content, traditional silo barriers weaken. The enterprise view of information as an asset and the resulting governance and accountability tends to weaken traditional silo barriers. EIM is not business reengineering and the silos still exist, but an IAM environment can have this pleasant side effect.

NUTS AND BOLTS—RISK MANAGEMENT AREA

The final type of business case is related to risk management. These benefits can come from obvious sources, such as preventing fraud, avoiding fines, or reducing insurance premiums. In fact, these could also be considered business benefits with large direct cash flows.

The newest aspect of risk management relates to regulatory risks. The reform-minded climate of the early twenty-first century has created a set of rules that places corporate executives, and more importantly, shareholder value, at risk. Gramm–Leach–Bliley and HIPAA designate harsh penalties for companies that do not manage information privacy. Sarbanes–Oxley specifically mentions the need to manage data movement, implement firm controls, and assure that calculations are correct. Review Table 2.1 for a recap of sample regulations.

SUMMARY

Developers of the EIM business case must understand what needs to be put in place or changed to achieve stated business objectives, compared to the current way of doing business. An effective business case requires alignment to business strategies and understanding of business requirements. Once alignment is understood, an examination of the three areas where benefits appear can be applied to the alignment findings.

Achieving business alignment and developing solid business cases is supposedly the greatest challenge facing IT. A mind-set that blends business needs into a business case based on information usage can address this challenge.

The Economic Conundrum
of Information

He had discovered a great law of human action, without knowing it—namely,
that in order to make a man or a boy covet a thing, it is only necessary
to make the thing difficult to obtain.
Mark Twain

CONTENTS

"Data may be the dark matter that permeates the economy, but that shouldn't stop us from trying to measure it. Second, in a universe of copious mergers and acquisitions, how is an information-centric enterprise expected to receive a fair valuation if accounting only for its people, material assets, financial assets, and goodwill?"[1]

That is a fair question. In this chapter, we will be looking at a method to develop a valuation for information and help complete a business case. The only real barrier to the EIM business case is where the ROI or benefits are applied, not where they are created. However, as an executive, you need to understand a few more aspects around the economics of IAM. This chapter will look into the *valuation* of information assets. The perspective of the business case is to influence the income statement via looking for our cash flow or income from EIM. This chapter looks into the balance sheet, or long-term valuation.

The genesis of IAM valuation stems not only from examining 30 years or so of "data processing" and "information management," but also from some basic economic work done early in the twentieth century. A particular school of economists tackled some long-standing arguments over the value of labor, capital, interest, and the derivation of prices in a free market. Known as the Austrian School of Economics, their theories and principles offer much insight into some of the issues in this chapter. At the peak of the industrial revolution, Austrian economists sought to understand why the cost of production is only part of the "value" or "price" of an item. The other aspect of price or value is the *subjective* component. In other words, where does the item fit in a complex scheme of microeconomic priorities? A simple example illustrates this issue. Why will I part with $100 for a winter coat in the middle of January in Green Bay, but not even pay $50 in August? Obviously, because I need the coat in the dead of winter. My subjective value of a coat is higher in winter.[2] However, the cost of production for the coat is identical no matter when it was purchased.

The same question can be asked of information. Why do we strive to value information only at the cost of production? That is the conundrum: how do we view, value, and truly account for information? How do we begin to account for subjective factors?

What is the relevance of valuing and measuring information? In simple terms, information (and knowledge) is *fungible*. Put more plainly, it has become a commoditized means of exchange. There are information dealers (Dun & Bradstreet, Dow Jones, Axiom, Trans Union). There is an entire branch of the legal profession dedicated to intellectual property. Information is also powerful—the right information at the right time has created that juggernaut of retailing, WalMart. The wrong information at the wrong time (think Enron or WorldCom) can ruin a company and devastate its people. A global financial crisis occurred, in part, because of lack of information as to the extent of risk. Lastly, anyone who is on Facebook™ or other social network actively trades personal information for access to the community's features. These are all examples of the value of information.

Remember there is not a single CEO who will tell you information is NOT a critical asset to his/her organization. The overall investment in moving and storing information is astronomical—in the hundreds of millions of dollars (billions?). It would seem then, that information valued as an ASSET means that it has to appear somewhere on a balance sheet on an ongoing basis vs. only as a result of a merger or calculation of goodwill.[3] Most work to date on valuing information has been related to these intangible classifications. But we have seen that the quality of information within an organization affects the value of that organization. It affects the stock price. The valuation shows up somewhere.

Companies do amortize software and hardware. These calculations rely heavily on the investment in infrastructure that creates, moves, and stores the information. But the infrastructure only handles data. Information has no *value* unless it is used. As long as the data sits in a database, the capital invested in placing it there has no return. Like the winter coat, it is not valuable until needed. Once the data is needed, I can create value by applying the data to business decisions, or improving processes, or even reselling the information.

Given its prominence, do you value information by its cost of production or its market price? Do we place footnotes on statements? Or do we stick with Sarbanes–Oxley's subjective declarations of information accuracy and relevance?

The cost of production is the cost of the software that produces information or literally, the cost of production from the capital required to enter, move, read, and store the information. But given that usage is key to information having value, should we not utilize a scheme like that done with marketable assets: the market price of an item at a given point in time? Or perhaps show both (a "basis" as well as "market value")?

What of the time aspect of information? To one information consumer, relevance means the information must be recent, and as accurate as possible, such as a current address for a customer. For another consumer, the current address is irrelevant, such as an actuarial calculation that wants to know only if the address has changed. Other aspects of the value of information (as defined by usage) are characteristics such as availability, accuracy, latency, and history.

Information appears nowhere on regular financial statements (excluding mergers and acquisitions) because no one can figure out or has agreed upon how to calculate it. Maybe a different means of valuation is required, one that considers the various related aspects of information usage. But given that information has no value unless it is used, and once used, can be reused, it follows that demand for information must be considered. Like the Austrian economists, we need to apply some intellectual consideration of subjective value and usage.

The opinions and scenarios of how information is used are all that we currently have available to present a balance sheet image of information. It is doubtful that these calculations will find their way onto a corporate balance sheet any time soon, given the accounting profession's incredibly conservative response to this "knowledge-driven" century we live in.

RELATIVE METHODS

When we measure subjectively, we need to understand what the subjective criteria are. As an executive who may be striving to determine the relative or subjective value of information in an enterprise, the first step is to understand what makes data and content important within our organization. These are the characteristics that business users of content are predisposed to apply to value their information assets. Most of the time, the main criteria are:

- Accuracy
- Relevance
- Completeness
- Availability.

So if a set of content meets expectations in these areas, it can be surmised the content has value. It makes sense then that assessing these characteristics in light of a business user's lens gives us at least a subjective value of an organization's information.

At one time, my firm embarked upon a small research project. My former associate, Doug Laney, and I were very interested in information valuation. (Doug has since obtained a real job.)

We sent simple surveys to executives within our various client companies. We used a straightforward scale (Table 8.1), and had them rate information subject areas on a relative basis. We did not specify if the usage of the information was operational or managerial. Nor did we differentiate structure or nonstructure. We merely asked how all the content and data in the named subject area met their particular expectations across a set of characteristics.

We generated a weighted value based on responses (Table 8.2). The weighted value is the easy part. Now, what do you apply the weighted scores to? After reviewing many industries, we looked at three balance sheet numbers. One was free cash, a number unencumbered by depreciating assets. It's also a number that reflects healthy activity. In addition, we used current assets. This was almost

Table 8.1 Scale for Relative Valuation Criteria

1	2	3	4	5
This content has no value for this criteria	Some value, but I can be happy if it is not perfect	It is of some value but no more important than other areas, it is a "nice to have" criteria	I am inconvenienced or endure higher costs if this criteria is not met, or poorly executed	This criteria has mission critical value—we suffer if this condition is not fully met

Table 8.2 Relative Valuation Example

	Relevance	Importance	Accuracy	Completeness	History	Volume	Volatility	Latency	Value Total	Weighted Value (%)	Weighted Amount ($)
Pro Forma Valuation of Data—Subjective Method											
Top 10 Highest Values Content Areas—Goodwill Basis											
Subject area of content or data	Relative importance to your job	Relative contribution to overall business success	Relative importance of accuracy of data to business success	Relative importance of all elements of this content being available	Relative importance of keeping history	Relative amount of events or transactions required to provide useful analysis	Relative effect of changing of values or instances	Relative importance of making this data or content available	Total of all scores	Content value total divided by total all values	Weighted value times the chosen asset basis (goodwill) (000's)
Claim	5	5	5	4	5	4	4	5	37	7.505	157,606
Coverage	4	4	4	4	4	3	2	4	29	5.882	123,529
Household	4	3	4	3	4	4	3	4	29	5.882	123,529
Loss	4	4	4	4	5	4	4	4	33	6.694	140,568
Payment	4	4	4	4	5	4	4	3	32	6.491	136,308
Policy	5	5	5	5	4	3	5	4	36	7.302	153,347
Policyholder	4	3	4	4	4	3	4	4	30	6.085	127,789
Property	3	3	3	4	4	2	4	3	26	5.274	110,751
Underwriting	4	4	4	4	4	4	5	3	32	6.491	136,308
Reserves	3	3	4	4	5	2	5	3	29	5.882	123,529
Criteria totals	61	64	61	60	71	54	60	62	493	100	21,00,000
Subjective value basis (000's)	Organization goodwill	2,100,000									

as good, allowing for the very different views certain industries have of a "current" asset. Lastly, we used goodwill, given that there are criteria expressed by FASB to incorporate information "value" into goodwill.

Did the results turn heads and create whirlwinds of activity? Not really. However, every executive who saw the findings expressed some degree of surprise. The net results showed that most organizations had a different emphasis, or subjective value, than they initially perceived they had.

Is the survey a valid means to justify placing information on a balance sheet? No, given it provides no quantitative basis for doing so. Is it a good opener for a business case? Absolutely. Table 28.3 shows a more detailed, refined version with more criteria and valuations if you want to take a look.

SUMMARY

The essence of this chapter and the previous three or four is this: EIM is a business program and must be treated as such. It can be positioned to financially justify implementing IAM, EIM economics can reveal financial justification, or at least measurable targets. The real issue is not whether there is value in managing information. The real issue is the association of the benefits of exploiting and leveraging information to the actual program that enables the leverage: *EIM*.

References

1. Laney, D. (2006). Information accounting and asset management. *Submitted White Paper for Publication.*
2. von Bohm-Bawerk, E. (1973). Value and price. In: *Capital and Interest Extract.* Grove City, PA: Libertarian Press.
3. FASB Codification, copyright, September, 2009.

An Overview of the Process

Always be wary of any helpful item that weighs less than its operating manual.
Terry Pratchett

CONTENTS

Chapter 7 reviewed aligning business drivers and goals to information content and usage in order to develop a solid business case for EIM. Business case development anchors the rest of the development process to establish and operate an EIM program. There are many process-related disciplines in the business world. Movements like reengineering and CRM have had their share of material explaining the steps to follow to make such a program successful. This chapter presents an overview of the steps required to start and sustain EIM. We will also cover some of the *how*. The level of detail presented here is for the executive and is not a field guide or manual. It sets expectations and establishes the role of the business executive in ensuring the success of EIM.

The format taken in this chapter is to review each major step and its activities, and describe what the business leader will see if the activities are going well. We will also cover how to adjust the step if it is not going well, and how the business can leverage the output from each step (Figure 9.1). Each major step will be covered as follows:

- Definition—The business purpose and description of the step and its activities.
- Visibility to business—A description of what the business will see occurring during this step.
- Success factors and metrics—A list of occurrences that ensure success and how to measure them.
- Adjustments—What options may be available to make changes if the step is not going well.

Making Enterprise Information Management (EIM) Work for Business. DOI: 10.1016/B978-0-12-375695-4.00009-6

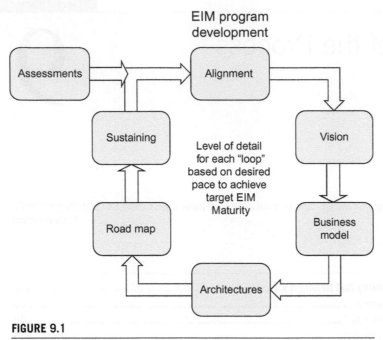

FIGURE 9.1

The generic EIM process

- Leverage points—Each step is designed to add value to the business, such that if the EIM efforts were to be suspended at any point, an individual step in the EIM process will still contribute to the business.

ASSESSMENTS—UNDERSTANDING CAPABILITY AND READINESS

As the basis for an effective EIM program, the organization must assess two areas. Information maturity measures how capable an organization is in actually using the information it produces. Cultural change readiness determines how well the business culture is positioned to use information assuming it can be delivered more effectively and accurately.

Note the word "must." This step is not optional. Candidly, early on in our EIM days we presented this as an optional step. We soon learned that even if we did not actually assess culture and maturity, we ended up reviewing or referring to these at some point, but without any hard data to back up our position. (Consultants are very good at saying how things "should" be without a lot of "why," and you will need to explain the "why" in an auditable fashion as EIM progresses.)

So we must develop a baseline that permits establishing a future state and then a means to close the gaps between current and future state. It's interesting to note that nearly every client we have assessed with formal instruments has been surprised at the findings. For example, a financial services company knew there was a rift between the IT and the business areas (not a big surprise there). When we assessed the culture, however, the client was surprised to find out how enormous the rift was. We had to tell this company that this rift was probably going to contribute to a failure of any sort of initiative from the IT area.

Definition—The assessment step gathers data about the perceptions and means an organization deploys to use data, and how the organization is positioned to carry out its day-to-day work.

Visibility to business—These activities are entirely visible to the business. In fact, there may be resistance to EIM even at this early period. It may come from a "here we go again" attitude, or from insecurity and fear.

Success factors and metrics—The surveys are successful if you get statistically relevant returns. The more the merrier, but usually you need to exceed 50% response rates. Middle management and above is surveyed.

Adjustments—In the event there is resistance to the surveys, you *already* have a finding that the organization has no stomach for IAM. In the event there is no approval to do a survey, then an anecdotal review like interviews across middle management can be used as a substitute. To be clear, we do not like interviews, but they are an effective alternative to surveys. Just make sure the questions are similar to the survey questions. Remember this step is mandatory. Without it there is no baseline for managing the organization going forward.

Leverage points—The value add here is an awareness of resistance, lack of knowledge, or failure to communicate that goes within an organization. Often organizations find that if perfect data and content were to magically appear, they cannot explicitly say what will be different.

ALIGNMENT—ALIGNING EIM TO THE BUSINESS

Actually, we have already taken a peek at this, when we reviewed how business drivers create scenarios where information is used, and we looked at examples. Clearly, this is a required step. In addition to what was explained in Chapter 7, there are a number of other activities:

- Create information levers/usage scenarios
- Set businesses priorities
- Identify high-level business data and content requirements.

Lack of business alignment is the most frequently mentioned obstacle to IT success in organizations. Sometimes the business does not like what IT does, so it goes alone. Conversely, IT believes it knows what is better and charges ahead. Lastly, IT is positioned as an "order taker," and succumbs to the demands of the loudest requestor.

It cannot be sugarcoated—if you will not do a formal alignment of IAM philosophy to the business, even if it is to improve data quality or improve BI, then please hand this book to a subordinate so he or she can take the later techniques and do better one-off projects. But your EIM effort has failed. This book is not a bully pulpit for IT strategy. However, it needs to be restated—EIM is a business program, not an IT project.

Definition—This step develops the business view of how information will be used by the business to accomplish its goals. This step requires access to business plans and business leadership.

Visibility to business—This step is highly visible by definition. It is foundational for business understanding and dissemination of the "big picture."

Success factors and metrics—This step is successful once the executive team has agreed to a set of scenarios that represent the business application of information. This step should take no longer than a few weeks (elapsed time), and most of that is getting the executive team into one room for a review session.

Adjustments—Very few adjustments are required if these activities take place. There may be a few executives who start to flex political strength, perceiving a threat to their areas. Accommodate them by a reminder of their role as manager of an enterprise, not the head of a specific function.

Leverage points—This is an excellent exercise even if EIM is not a "for sure" project. It can act as a powerful add-on to periodic planning exercises, since business leadership is forced to break down information requirements into how the business will operate.

VISION—CREATE THE VISION "DAY IN THE LIFE"

After a business statement of actions around content and data is available, develop a vision. In this case, vision means what a "day in the life" looks like at some future point. A stated period for fulfilling the vision is nice, but is often unrealistic at this juncture, and frankly alienates middle management who perceives such statements as arbitrary (best to put a schedule together with middle management involvement).

Definition—This step puts forth and maintains a "day in the life" of the organization when EIM and IAM are deployed. What is different about the organization and the way it operates? What is occurring of benefits achieved? What hazards and risks are we avoiding?

Visibility to business—This effort is primarily intended for an executive team or any other stakeholder where EIM will create significant opportunity or changes.

Success factors and metrics—Buy-in and approval are entirely dependent on the executive team's comprehension of what EIM means to the enterprise. The success factors here are simplicity and clarity. Convey the concepts of IAM and the future state as briefly as possible. If this activity starts to take more than a few weeks there are problems. A drawn out vision step may indicate lack of serious sponsorship, poor business understanding, or there is too much detail being built into the vision.

Adjustments—Any problem requiring an adjustment to the vision or the EIM program design will be from comprehension of IAM concepts or a historical precedent that will work against the vision, like the "I've seen this before" type of resistance. Please take extra time if you need to clarify the vision and educate the leadership team.

Leverage points—The vision itself is not a value add if EIM does not go forward. The value add (again using our scenario that the EIM effort stops at this point) is the communication and education among the executive team. They will understand that they are doing EIM anyway, just choosing to do so poorly. Or that continuing the siloed information programs will not gain as much benefit over the long term as they may have initially thought.

BUSINESS MODEL—EIM AND BUSINESS IMPACT

Once the discovery and alignment is done, the resulting blueprint needs to be placed back against the existing business model to determine any changes to business practices or to the business model itself. Often EIM will suggest that a business revise its approach to its external business partners such as suppliers or distribution channels. For example, our case study insurance company (UBETCHA Insurance) has a problem with data quality from its field operation. If it is discovered that this data is poor because its independent sales agents are entering junk, UBETCHA may have to change its agency compensation agreements to change the behavior and fix its data quality issues. Any business-person can readily envision the possibility that required changes may create major issues. It is best to identify these issues now so they can be anticipated and dealt with proactively rather than reactively. In the real-life situation, UBETCHA is based on the organization was confronted with a huge problem. Their agents were asked to revise their treatment of data (via significant process changes) at the same time a major push was on to process policies faster. The outcomes were mixed signals delivered from two different functions, resulting in a hostile agent force.

Definition—This step defines how the business will operate after EIM is established. The result is either acceptance of the implied changes or an adjustment to the EIM business vision. Going back to the inventory metaphor, we are taking the vision to build a new warehouse and making sure it fits business demand, can be built on the intended land, and won't irritate the neighbors.

Visibility to business—The intent is high visibility to the business. In essence, the EIM team is "floating a balloon." They are displaying future impacts for proactive consideration and adjustments. After these steps, any impacts to the enterprise will be handled as culture changes and business process changes. This is the point at which the business can draw a line around specific areas to control changes. In return, the EIM team must feed back to the executive team the consequences of "walling off" business processes from EIM.

Success factors and metrics—There should be a healthy list of business processes that are subject to change, or where the EIM/process interface is adjusted. If the number of adjustments to the EIM architecture exceeds the processes changing, then step back—there is a problem in the organization's view, understanding, or commitment to EIM. This is why we do this step AFTER discovery and alignment. The ideal EIM picture (via the architecture) permits a clear gap analysis. If business processes were reviewed and exempted before the architecture, there would be a compromise to the enterprise benefits of EIM at an early stage.

Adjustments—If the EIM team needs to step back because too many processes are being exempted, prepare an analysis of the impact of a nonenterprise view of IAM. There will be obvious and glaring issues. For example, exempting the UBETCHA agents from worrying about data quality could result in a never-ending stream of bad data into the EIM architecture or a massive (and expensive) infrastructure having to be built to clean up after their poor performance. Allow the executive team to make a call; then acknowledge the impact and consequences in writing.

Leverage points—If the EIM effort is stopped at this point, the organization has benefitted from a deep understanding of what needs to change to reach a future state capable of supporting business direction. Perhaps the EIM effort should be suspended pending some business redesign or emphasize near-term projects to deliver immediate assistance to a struggling functional area.

ARCHITECTURES—THE BLUEPRINT FOR EIM

All IAM solutions, deliverables, policies, and standards must originate somewhere in the business driver/goal/objective framework.

The basic process is to decompose business drivers, or goals, into qualitative and quantitative-based requirements. These in turn are used to create data or parameters that suggest the type of infrastructure and project required to meet business needs. The driver/objectives hierarchy developed earlier is applied to standard uses of information, and we can derive new processes models and detailed information requirements. The net result is the architecture, defining the elements and efforts required to establish EIM. The elements efforts are tied to an overall philosophy and governance program. The asset management philosophy ensures business needs are met, and the risks and cost of information are managed.

For example, in Chapter 7, we used an example of an objective—increase customer retention to 97%. Decomposing this objective gives us a set of requirements:

- We need a metric to measure customer retention.
- We will need the data that makes up the calculation of customer retention. If this data is of poor quality, we now know we need to remediate the deficiencies in the data.
- We will discern usage requirements of how often this metric is to be calculated, analyzed, accessed, and stored, which in turn tells us something about the technology required to meet use requirements.
- We will explore any new or refined business processes that may result from the ability to know and apply decisions based on customer retention.
- We can design specific policies to ensure proper governance of the creation, movement, treatment, and disposition of the customer retention data.

In short, generating business requirements aligned with business needs allows us to build an aligned architecture.

Once the EIM architecture is clear, the various elements that will carry forward into the EIM program must be defined. At this point, the CEO or executive sponsor will meet with the EIM team leadership to ensure there is momentum and business benefit. From an executive view, this is where the architect designs the building. Most of the details for deployment of EIM begin here, so these activities are for the EIM team to carry out. All of the components, required materials, and responsibilities are described and positioned for implementation. The processes, people, and technology required to treat data as an asset are defined. At this point, there will be names given to some of the elements of the overall architecture. Some of the more common ones are listed and defined in Table 9.1.[1]

Definition—Create the blueprints for the various component elements that will eventually deliver EIM. This blueprint is the expression of what EIM requires to support the business. It will include processes, functions, frameworks, roles, organizations, and technology items. There are several activities in this phase that will create new business functions, most notably data governance. There will also be interfaces or liaisons with other support functions, such as audit and compliance.

Visibility to business—This step requires significant participation from organizational leadership. It's one of those areas where delegating to a lieutenant is not a good idea unless the lieutenant can set policy. If this is done correctly, the level of involvement can be compacted into a few facilitated sessions and a review. Moreover, if an organization has clear published business plans and strategies, this effort can be done with only feedback and review sessions.

Success factors and metrics—Metrics for this are simple—did everyone show up for the meetings? Was there visible support for the process? If not, there is a problem, and the EIM program is in danger of losing focus. Success factors are also simple—observable executive-level representation

Table 9.1 Architectural Elements of EIM

Architecture Elements	Short Descriptions
Analytics	Features that allow sophisticated "drilling" and application of algorithms to rows and columns data
Applications	Collections of functionality with a common business purpose
Business intelligence	Common label that applies to all types of reporting, scorecards, and data analysis capability
Collaborative technology	Class of products and functions that permit sharing, common updating, and joint use of content and data without regard to department silos
Collaborative intelligence	An offshoot of business intelligence where an organization can measure, analyze, and manage workflow and collaboration
Content management	Technology that creates and maintains "unstructured" content, web pages, documents, forms, etc.
Document management	Technology and processes that ensure integrity, viability, and manage the risk involved with unstructured content
Data governance	The organization and implementation of policies, procedures, structure, roles, and responsibilities which outline and enforce rules of engagement, decision rights, and accountabilities for the effective management of information assets
Data models	Representations of the business in an abstract form
Data quality	A discipline that strives to ensure quality, integrity, and effectiveness of data and content
Information management infrastructure	The technology used to manage information assets
Information management tools	Technology used to manipulate, track, and develop information assets
Information management organizations	Departments, units, and teams arranged to support IAM
Master data management	Authoritative, reliable foundation for data used across many constituencies managed to provide single view of truth
Metrics	Measurements of organization, market, or business performance
Portals	Internet-based software to access multiple functions or applications
Privacy	The protection of personal or confidential data for customers or other key business parties
Reference/code management	The control over common values that describe specific domains, including standardized terms, code values, and other unique identifiers, definitions for each value … and the consistent shared use of accurate timely and relevant reference data values
Reporting	The reading, organizing, and display or printing of data
Security	The functions and rules that manages and ensures content is accessed and updated by authorized parties
Social networks	Internet-based facilities where groups/or individuals share data, thoughts, or content of common interest to others
Standards	Policies that specify appearance, handling, access, and use of data or content

(Continued)

Table 9.1 (Continued)

Architecture Elements	Short Descriptions
Taxonomy	A hierarchical description of an item, topic, or any other topic information is retained about
Tools	Nickname for the various software products that can be used to assist in EIM
Workflow	A discipline that manages and maintains efficient business processes

and a clear articulation of where the enterprise needs to go. Without these, the EIM team is not conducting an EIM effort, it's conducting a technology planning effort, and a poorly guided one at that.

Adjustments—As referenced in the Vision section, adjustments will stem from lack of comprehension or apprehension of repeating similar, but failed, efforts. If resistance is encountered (key players do not show up or have more pressing priorities), then the sponsor needs to verify the commitment to an EIM program. Many times during my work with these types of initiatives, I've witnessed a CEO leaning toward an executive VP and reminding them of the importance of the effort.

Leverage points—If the EIM effort stopped at this point, there would still be a significant document that aligns information with business direction. This can be used to guide technology direction, even without the increased levels of detailed activities that are developed later.

ROAD MAP—THE ROLL-OUT STRATEGY TO ACHIEVE IAM

The most common question asked of me by EIM practitioners is "where do we start?" This is how the personnel responsible for implementing EIM or one of its components (like a data warehouse) see the program. "We all get the concepts, now how do we make it happen?" The devil is always in the details, and the road map is where the details are addressed. Any depiction of a road map for EIM is much more than a Gantt chart with a few bars representing phases. Figure 9.2 is a typical example.

Road maps are multidimensional depictions of the means by which all of the EIM components will come together. There are many parallel events occurring with an EIM program. This is no different than any other program, but often is interpreted as being too complicated to attempt (because it is only data). The most important aspect of any road map is to show the entire journey, and the alternative routes, all on one (admittedly large) page/poster.

Definition—The EIM road map depicts the interaction of the EIM elements, the intended sequence of implementation, and the relationship between those elements in an understandable form. The road map deliverable also contains the details that were developed to produce the high-level depiction. The detailed contents for a road map are explained in Part 2, but the executive-level outline of a road map deliverable is as follows:

1. Scope—enterprise definition of EIM, the role of IAM, and the extent of the "enterprise" that is addressed by EIM.
2. Business objectives—what will EIM accomplish *as indicated on a balance sheet, income statement, or other financial report?*

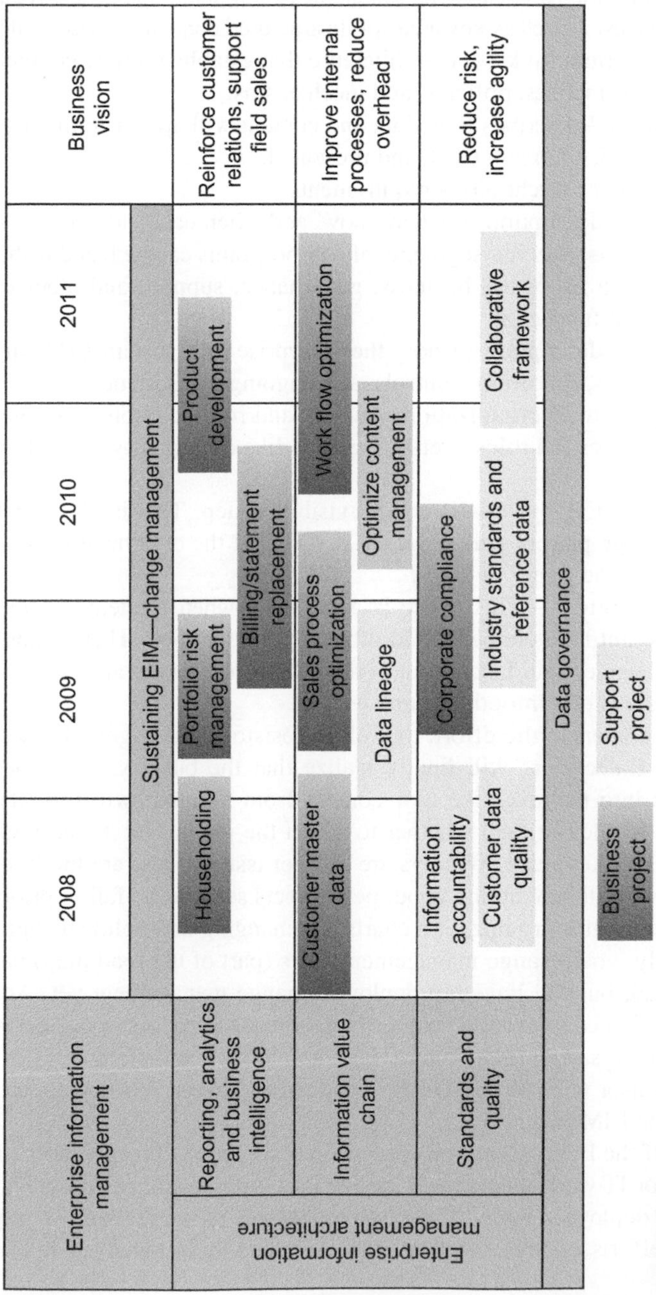

FIGURE 9.2

Road map examples

3. Information Value Chain (IVC)—picture depicting how content and data will appear to flow through an organization and add value.
4. Business model—details on how the business model will look at a functional level once EIM is implemented. It outlines the KPIs, financial statements, compliance audits, and regulatory reports that will be supported by EIM as well as key areas of unstructured content such as catalogs or web sites.
5. Content management framework—the architecture that establishes how content and information will be managed: the principles, policies, and mechanisms.
6. Data access framework—describes how data and content will appear to the organization, that is, how it will be navigated, accessed, used, and presented.
7. Technology—a short list of technology requirements.
8. Business alignment—a description of where, how, and when data and content will help the organization achieve its goals. Specific segments of sub-programs can be listed if these are relevant.
9. Incremental projects—a list of the business, governance, support, and other efforts required to make the EIM program functional.
10. Sustaining plan—brief description of how the enterprise will sustain EIM; in other words, the culture change programs, education, controls, and ongoing measurement.
11. Organization—impacts to IT organization structure and roles, and other business areas affected, as well as the new entities and roles overseeing areas like data quality and data governance.

Visibility to business—Clearly, this is a high visibility step. This is also where business areas that to date have been fringe players will suddenly realize that the organization is serious. There will inevitably be some "late to the game" activity.

Success factors and metrics—This phase is going well when the team is not asking for additional business guidance until the elements and projects are identified. That means you have done a good job of providing business guidance. Quick review of documents and timely determination of priorities are also good signs of a smooth running team.

Adjustments—Latecomers to the effort, as well as resistors, will signal the need to address barriers to moving ahead. Latecomers will finally realize that the business is serious and will throw additional requirements into the mix, like new content from an unknown web site. The reaction is simple—determine if it is relevant, and whether to adjust the plan or let it wait until next year when the annual review of EIM takes place. Whiners are another issue—these are the first resistance points you will encounter. There will be whining about pet projects seeming to fall in priority. There will be whining abut the realization that organization charts are changing and political capital is perceived as lost or wasted. Hopefully, your change management tasks (part of the road map) have addressed this possibility down the road, but you have not deployed change management yet. At this juncture, the sponsoring executive will need to exercise authority to address concerns or tell the whining parties to stand down. It goes without saying that we have seen situations grow pretty contentious at this point. Often the executive sponsor (CEO/COO/CFO) will need to have a face-to-face conversation about what priorities are for the EIM program.

Leverage points—If the EIM program were to stop here, the road map would still serve as a strategic and tactical plan for IT work. In essence, the EIM program would exist, but be manifested in the project segments being deployed. So the material produced here is excellent for supporting budgets, enterprise architecture efforts, business strategic planning, and impact analysis in the event of a major business change.

SUSTAINING—KEEP EIM ADDING VALUE, CHANGE YOUR BEHAVIOR, AND MANAGE BEHAVIOR

The prior step mentioned change management and sustaining change. This area of activity requires separate treatment. The number one obstacle to EIM efforts (and its various components) is the inability to change behavior. Your culture *will be a barrier*. If it were not, you would not be deploying an EIM program.

(This is why Chapter 10 is dedicated to change management—this chapter will only focus on the activities as part of the EIM planning.)

It is easy to comprehend and acknowledge that your culture is a function of the business environment, its history, and the people within the business. It is hard for most EIM leaders to fully recognize the extent of the challenge.

Culture change issues are why a strong sponsor is required. This is why business alignment is required. This is why a solid road map is required. All of this provides information to present to the resistance points that will help address concerns, demonstrate the value and rationale for proceeding, and serve to develop incentives to change. The road map also provides a baseline for metrics that can be applied to manage resistance. There may be soft techniques to adjust behavior, such as orientation and training. There may be harsher techniques, where adjusting an individual's career may be required.

Definition—This phase defines and develops activities to *sustain* EIM and ensure IAM "sticks" over the long term. A plan is built to address the various obstacles to execution that come with our natural tendency to resist change.

Visibility to business—This step must be highly visible. There can be no impression of stealth. At this juncture, the organization needs to know that change is coming and must understand how the new EIM vision will affect the business and its day-to-day activities.

Success factors and metrics—Perhaps the best indicator of how well the development of a sustaining plan is going is watching for early resistance. For example—analyzing stakeholders is often questioned. The whole executive team appears to be on board—so why examine the issue? Well, the fact is if there are 10 stakeholders, most likely there are at least two who are not on board. Unless enrolled in the process, they will figure out a way to sabotage the effort.

Leverage points—Any change management program is of value to an enterprise. This is simply because, as stated before, most companies do not think this is a necessary activity. "If we tell them to get on board, they will" is often heard. Again—this is not true; this is simplistic thinking. If EIM were to cease at this point, at least the framework developed here can be deployed in support of the various isolated efforts that are under the EIM umbrella: data warehouse, MDM, data governance, and so on.

Adjustments—None can be made—the development of a sustaining plan needs to occur. There are tactics to deploy that can garner better acceptance of the need for the plan, such as developing a business case for change management. This, of course, requires additional time, but may be needed.

SUMMARY

The EIM program is accomplished through a set of activities that use techniques and methods to produce auditable, incremental steps, and components to manage information assets. The activities specified are not just executed one time. They represent ongoing processes required to adjust and sustain EIM.

During these activities, the philosophy of IAM is manifested through business alignment to a vision and subsequent architecture elements. Business processes are refined and the protocol for managing information is specified. Finally, a detailed road map that expresses business needs in the form of projects is delivered and the activities to sustain EIM are specified.

Reference

1. Most elements are summarized from the description in the DMBOK (2008).

Sustaining EIM and Culture Change

Change is inevitable—except from a vending machine.
Robert C. Gallagher

CONTENTS

EIM strategies abound. Rather, they are often bound books ... and sit on shelves ... and are never heard from again. We touched on sustaining EIM as a part of the overall program. This chapter will delve into the details of sustaining EIM and culture change. We are descending into detail here for one critical reason—this is one of the foremost, if not the main reason, EIM flounders. This chapter suggests key factors to keep an EIM program going over the years and make it an integral part of your organization's business culture.

COMMON EIM SCENARIOS

The following scenarios are extracted from actual EIM efforts. We changed the names and blended some results to avoid embarrassment. Suffice it to say, none of the organizations represented below are tiny and you would recognize their names.

Industry A—Energy

The EIM effort started strongly at this organization. The strategy effort went well, with well-defined principles, policies, organizations, and a solid road map. One would think that visible support echoed through the hallways. The CEO fully embraced an IAM mind-set. After defining the road map, a PMO set out to execute projects and a formal change management team was deployed. The first item of business was orientation and training. And this was where the wheels came off.

The CIO was new and ran into a middle management phenomenon called "the clay layer." This layer in a company filters what goes up to leadership as well as what is heard below. In an energy company, the generation plant manager symbolizes this. Due to political factors, the CIO did not push orientation and training out to the plants. This in turn gave tacit permission for other business areas to resist. The CIO reduced the change management program from two years to two weeks of training for upper and middle management on all aspects of EIM, IAM, and data governance. Besides having these personnel "drink from a fire hose" in terms of training, it smacked of "just another IT project"—a little training and "see you later." This gave the appearance of a project vs. a program. The result—EIM was summarily ignored. The CEO, who was initially a strong sponsor, permitted this to occur as he/she never understood the importance of change management and thought the CIO was responding properly to a change in the business environment.

Industry B—Retail

The CIO of a large retail company started out with a requirement to reduce the operating costs of the data center. Analysis determined the data center was benchmarked as too expensive because of a profound amount of business user computing—thousands of spreadsheets and over 40,000 Access databases. Some tactical cleanup efforts led to a request for an EIM effort. The executive team gave full support, but refused to appoint a business head for EIM, and the CIO was named sponsor. As the EIM program unfolded, a political struggle between the Director of Applications Development and the CIO intensified. A change management program was defined, but members of the change team were only made available part time. This lack of focus allowed the Application Development Director to build a large base of opposition. Every attempt to implement standards or methods met with open resistance. Without business sponsorship, the entire effort became an internal IT battle. Large components of the EIM programs eventually were not funded and the effort died.

Industry C—Government Agency

The CIO of a government agency saw EIM as a career enhancer. While the organization embraced the technical aspects of EIM fully, the areas where functional units would have to deal with new processes or procedures were ignored, in fact, prohibited. The EIM strategy developed within a vacuum. During the effort, the assistant CIO pointed this out and was terminated. The strategy was delivered, the CIO promoted out of IT, and the effort closed down. Any mention of formal change management was dismissed as unnecessary, as it was assumed that government employees would always change if the rules and policies changed.

OBSERVATION

An earlier form of IAM was known as information engineering (IE). It was very much the "next big thing" in the 1980s. At one point, I actually encountered a shop that really did implement IE all the way, with accompanying tools, standards, methods—all the bells and whistles. While the entire global business community spent billions on the Y2K mess, they accomplished Y2K remediation in a few weeks by regenerating all their COBOL code. Even though the conversation had nothing to do with EIM, I had to ask what their "secret" was. The net was they followed IE by the book. It took *10 years*. And all code came from the IE tools, no exceptions. The "secret" was they were a very old, established manufacturer in Europe. Their product line and market had not changed in *200 years*. They had the time, market, and discipline. But the reality is few companies have a 200-year-old product line and 10 years to develop applications. And they really made no fundamental changes to their business—only a few people in IT had to change.

ROOT CAUSES

Obviously, there are some lessons to be learned from the above examples. At first glance, an analysis might conclude that lack of the right sponsorship and unmanaged resistance were key factors. My belief, however, is that these are only symptoms of a greater underlying cause: no understanding or acceptance of the fact that having to change the culture and effectively *manage* that change are core aspects of EIM success.

Human Behavior

Given the amount of writing and "leadership development" that's been done about the success factors in driving and sustaining change, and about the role of human behavior in undermining change, it continues to amaze me that organizations pay so little attention to this as a serious factor in *really* making change happen. There are reasons why the terms like "buy-in," "strong sponsor," and "resistance management" came about. They've come from dozens of documented instances of poor understanding and execution of effective change management. These terms all express the *symptoms* of a situation, however, not the illness. For decades, IT departments have struggled to find strong sponsors. The most often asked questions when I present a class on anything EIM-related are "How do I get buy-in?" and "How do I get a good sponsor?" Frankly, until we began to look for a broader cause, the answers given by me and my peers were less than satisfactory.

To change behavior, whether for EIM or a different shift in the business, you must address the need to *formally* manage that change and put in place the appropriate mechanisms to sustain it. So what are those factors that you must consider to be successful?

Human Dynamics

People dislike change. And everyone reacts differently to change. Seagal addressed this issue in *Human Dynamics*.[1] There are literally hundreds of other authors and organizations that can be referenced: Bridges, Kotter, Connor, LaMarsh and Associates, and Prosci are some of the well-known ones. Each of them emphatically point out, in a situation like EIM where the change in day-to-day habits has the potential of being viewed as disruptive, people's reactions to that change must be considered if the effort is to be successful.

Any change has two sides: situational (who, what, when, where) and psychological. The situational aspect is why you use plans to manage the steps in rolling out an EIM program. The psychological reorientation that each individual goes through is purely personal. People resist change because of fear: fear of failure or loss in the new environment. To get people through that fear to make the necessary behavior changes, you must have a strong executive sponsorship from the business, a formal program of communication, training in new skills when required, and very clear expectations about what needs to be different. For EIM, this means that you must explain to your organization why things must change, what that means in terms of everyday behavior and the "what's in it for me" factor—the "WIIFM."

Information Maturity

If IAM is a goal, then the EIM program was developed because the organization was NOT doing IAM. Our earlier discussion of information maturity pointed out the various levels and capabilities that can exist in relation to successful use of data and content. Changing an organization's information maturity level requires altering behavior. Understanding IMM allows the change management process to accurately describe what is wrong *now* and offer a future state that the affected parties can comprehend.

Governance

The last factor and most profound aspect of EIM requiring change management is data governance. An immature origination (like the one with 40,000 Access databases) cannot be educated and incented away from the addiction. Formal intervention is required. Downstream enforcement is required. Personnel who believe they are far too busy to address new processes never openly embrace adding a new layer of rules or oversight. Making change happen here requires significant and ongoing executive sponsorship and support, willingness on the part of management to address resistance, and realignment and enforcement of accountabilities.

FORMAL CHANGE MANAGEMENT

A preferred definition for change management is from Gartner Group: "The transforming of the organization so it is aligned with the execution of a chosen corporate business strategy. It is the management of the **human** element in a large-scale change project...." I like to add an enhancement more focused on EIM: "Change Management is the bridge between implementing EIM and its components, and the organization embracing the benefits associated with the change."

As stated earlier, change management is a *formal* effort. It cannot be handled as a part-time endeavor. There is a strong correlation between a project supported by effective change management and that project's ability to meet or exceed its objectives.

In the 2009 Best Practices in Change Management study conducted by Prosci, 95% of those who rated their change management program as excellent met or exceeded their project objectives as opposed to only 16% who rated their change management program as poor or nonexistent.

In that same study, there is a significant correlation between the quality of the change management program and the project's ability to stay on or ahead of schedule. Seventy-one percent of those respondents with excellent change management programs had projects that were on or ahead of schedule.[2]

A LITTLE MORE ABOUT RESISTANCE

As an executive embarking on EIM (or even implementing one of its subdisciplines like a data warehouse or a customer master database), you will encounter change management issues daily. Many forms of resistance become evident. Here are some things to watch for:

- Attempts to outlast the changes, and bargaining for exemption from new policies or processes
- A reduction in productivity and missed deadlines (foot dragging)
- Going back to the old way of doing things
- A lack of attendance in project status meetings and events or training
- Higher absenteeism
- Open expression of negative emotion
- From executives and peers, resistance could be:
  - No visible sponsorship of the changes; no open endorsements
  - Refusal or reluctance to provide needed resources and/or information
  - Repeatedly canceling or refusing to attend critical meetings
  - Development of whitepapers or external consultants conveying a contrary opinion.

Before you fire them all, first understand that initial resistance is *normal*. There are reasons humans resist. Some more common ones are:

- Loss of identity and their familiar world
- Individual human dynamics difference (introvert, extrovert)
- Individual capacity to embrace change
- Disorienting experience of the transition between the old and the new
- Overloaded with current responsibilities
- No answer to WIIFM
- No involvement in crafting the solution
- Other work and personal issues
- How well an organization has handled changes in the past.

Mitigating the resistance and leveraging the EIM program as an executive will require activities to counter it. The list below will sound familiar—it is really the list of critical success factors you will find associated with *any* corporate change effort, EIM, or otherwise.

- Clear vision for the change and a plan to drive it
- Clear presentation of the current problems and need to move away from the current state
- Strong and visible leadership of the initiative
- Early (and often) communication to affected stakeholders to educate and engage them in the process
- Opportunities for and responsiveness to feedback
- Effective education when needed
- Measurement of results
- Aligned policies/practices, rewards and recognition, organization, and jobs.

TIP FOR SUCCESS

In very large organizations, or in cultures that are deeply entrenched, an executive needs to occasionally reach into the same bag of tricks used when he/she was brought into the enterprise. Time should be allotted to build relationships as the EIM program is being designed. Evaluations of friends and enemies need to take place. And often, if the need to move to EIM is severe (e.g., severe regulatory issues or data quality issues that cause loss of business), the CEO or sponsoring executive will need to provide an example to the organization by removing disruptive opponents.

A BASIC CHANGE MANAGEMENT PROCESS

There is no magic to a change management process. A lot of it derives from common sense. At minimum, here's a summary of what you as an executive should expect to see happening. Look for and demand these key activities.

Build the Change Team

Your organization needs a dedicated team. It can be temporary or a part of HR, but it must be able to *focus* on EIM change. It does not have to be large—even the largest organizations we have worked with have had a core team of no more than 6–8 people. It is key that the members have the necessary skills, knowledge, expertise, and, most important, influence. Most likely some training will be required as these are not typical resources that organizations have waiting in the wings.

Conduct an Analysis of the Project's Potential Impact on the Organization

EIM and the related disciplines of governance and standards will affect organizations differently depending on their culture and maturity level. The changes that data governance will bring need to be crystal clear. Surveys or interviews with various stakeholders' groups provide insight into potential reactions and issues with the proposed changes.

Build a Strong Sponsorship Coalition in Support of EIM

The right sponsor for EIM is one of the most significant critical success factors for any change effort. In the 2009 Prosci study of 5,575 participating organizations in 65 countries, the number one cited reason for success was a strong executive sponsor.[3] If you have not designated yourself as the executive sponsor, make sure you pick the right one—someone who has the power and influence to make EIM a success. And make sure he/she is building support among the organization's leadership as one of their key activities. Make time to meet with those who champion EIM and show your support for their efforts.

Plan and Execute a Comprehensive Change Strategy

The team will be determining what actions need to occur to prepare the organization for the changes, e.g., communication, training, orientation. Also, it is important to set a schedule and milestones. There will be resource and priority issues to resolve. Certain levels of change must be measured and anticipated according to a schedule or the effort will wander. Make sure that the change team has a solid grasp of the differences EIM will create; it may entail some training if the change team has no EIM background. Once the plan for change is being carried out, you should demand regularly scheduled updates that include metrics for change (see later). If any issues crop up, resolve them as soon as possible.

COMMUNICATIONS—A FEW THOUGHTS

Most likely communications will hold the key to successful deployment of an IAM philosophy. The EIM program will touch (or may touch) anyone who uses or creates data or content. The change significance is not to be taken lightly, and the communications aspects are critical. It is important for an executive to understand a few of the finer points of communications for EIM.

First of all, if the EIM team is just doing presentations or telling the staff to "please change and do it this way" will not work. The communication must be adjusted to address two dimensions. The first dimension addresses the need to raise stakeholder awareness to the appropriate level. These levels are:

1. The stakeholder group has no real knowledge of the initiative and related projects. For example, certain executives may be remote enough from the EIM effort that they only require a degree of awareness.
2. The majority of people at this level are aware of some of the initiative's "basics," such as scope and timing, but do not necessarily understand the program's strategic and/or competitive rationale. They are aware of EIM but are not impacted to an extent they require more than awareness.
3. The majority of people in the stakeholder group are aware of the initiative's "basics" and understand the initiative's strategic and/or competitive rationale, but are concerned about the initiative's impact on the way the organization is structured and operates today and the initiative's impact on individuals' jobs and careers. This group has "bought in," but is still reserved, and is always weighing risks against perceived benefits. Surprisingly, these groups are not as risky to the EIM effort as they may seem, and if educated and informed will not impede the effort.

4. Key stakeholder groups are aware of the initiative, understand the benefits and impacts, and are committed to implementing the solution. This group is fully engaged, and have internalized the EIM vision and strive for its fulfillment.

Based on the type of awareness required, the communication plan needs to reflect the different audiences and their requirements. Communication efforts and techniques need to vary in intensity, with lukewarm communication like an e-mail or memo being perfectly adequate for stage one staff. But obviously if stage three or four is required, the communication plan needs to be more intense. Other stakeholders may be crucial to success, and require extensive education and even one-on-one counseling to achieve the required level of acceptance and ability.

The second dimension that influences communications relates to the human dynamics at play. Briefly, the differences in people need to be considered. Introverts will require different treatment than extroverts. Engineers will require more details than marketing staff. Often an organization may want to conduct an assessment like Meyers Briggs to better adapt communications to the nature of the various audiences.

To summarize, the communications plan is something that requires thoughtful planning. If you have a communications area, they will be invaluable in assisting with the effort. Otherwise, please understand that cranking out a list of orientation sessions and some training probably will not satisfy the communication needs of EIM.

BUSINESS CASE FOR CHANGE MANAGEMENT

Often there will be a push to avoid culture and change management as it is "soft;" that a formal program is too hard to manage, too hard to measure, and has no tangible return. There may be a push to do a business case (this is a form of resistance by the by) to prove it is too "squishy." However, the sustaining activities have a bottom-line impact. As an executive, it can be your choice whether there is a positive or negative impact.

Change management (or the lack thereof) has a significant hard-dollar impact on an organization. Leaders are generally unaware of, or dismiss, the impact of poorly managed change on the bottom line. Consider this client experience: on a teleconference to the entire organization, the CEO of a financial services company, unaware that the speaker phone was on, casually announced the consolidation of one of its regional offices into another office. No one had communicated anything in advance to said office: There were no "heads-up" and no rationale for the consolidation. The result was days of complete and utter chaos as the staff spun themselves into the ground around what they had heard and their resumes flooded the street. How much work was accomplished during this time? What was the cost in terms of pure dollars and broken trust? How much productivity and loyalty do you think that company will get from that office as it tries to salvage the key players and go through an orderly consolidation?"[4]

Be prepared to request information if there is the need to translate the "soft stuff" into the potential hard-dollar impacts of change management. Research past efforts in your organization where similar IM efforts took place. If this is the first time you are trying it (doubtful), use what other organizations may have spent trying to implement something multiple times. Why did those efforts fail? Chances are change management factors like communication and sponsorship were involved.

"Available research on the impact of poorly managed change shows organizations experience an increase in turnover, benefits claims filed, absenteeism, and missed deadlines. There are hard dollars attached to all of those. Engage your finance and HR people to help develop your assumptions about possible impact to those cost drivers using (or developing) current baselines for each. For example, what is a reasonable increase in turnover to expect if the change is not well handled? If your usual turnover rate is 10% and it suddenly shoots up to 20%, what does that additional 10% turnover cost you? As a simple example: to an organization of 1,000 that has a usual annualized turnover rate of 10% (100 people per year), an additional 10% per year means another 100 people to find, hire, train, and get fully productive. If your usual cost of turnover is an equivalent of $5.0 million (an average of $50,000 per person—internal and external recruiting costs, compensation, orientation, training, etc.), you will spend the equivalent of another $5.0 million to replace the additional 100 staff who left."[5]

Examples like those above can demonstrate what kind of dollars can be wasted when managing change is absent or ineffective. In turn, you have a basis for a case, as well as a basis to measure success going forward.

The choice is to manage change for a positive financial result, or neglect it (as a soft issue) and suffer the consequence of investing in EIM program design and specification and then allowing that investment to fade away.

Perhaps the most common mistake seen at this point is when the executive sponsor says "we know how to make our folks go where we want." Often there will be talk of mandating change. Or we will "power through" and order things to happen. Sadly, this management-machismo just creates an opening for resistance. Ordering change gives the appearance of lack of planning. Lack of planning means that other efforts with better presentations will garner more attention. It will be much easier for resistors to point out their higher priorities.

ORGANIZATION CHARTS, ROLES, AND RESPONSIBILITIES

There will not be implementation of EIM without the modification of organization charts, and the identification of accountable parties, including individuals and groups.

During the EIM program design a lot of terms like "data steward" or "data custodian" will be bandied about. There are terms derived from the struggles of IT staff to get business personnel to accept a role in data quality and integrity. Often, however, these terms are assigned as a matter of course, and there is little thought as to the role of the newly named "steward." And more often than not, there is inadequate training.

Developing and identifying the organization changes associated with EIM require the assistance of HR or internal organizational development (OD) staff. Remember there will be a new slate of accountabilities and new duties for many personnel. In addition, the data governance function will deploy new policies and present new standards. This means new job descriptions and performance objectives.

The bottom line is plain—like the communications plan, some thinking is in order. Often the EIM program organization, identification of new accountabilities, appointment of governance bodies, and revision of performance criteria is done via an HR program. Several times we have had to engage in formal organization design, using RACI charts and other techniques to build EIM into an enterprise.

SUMMARY

The essence of sustaining EIM is to manage the required change. Remember you are moving from an era where the accountability of keeping data and content clean, correct, and efficient is an afterthought. This has to be new stuff, or you would not be reading this book.

The target vision is an era where individuals accept and bear accountability for data quality, accuracy, and efficient use. More accountability is never popular. A perceived loss of control of "my" data is never popular. But if no one is held accountable, EIM becomes a passive IT project. If IAM is deemed a necessary cause, then the organization's leadership must accept that IAM usually equates with change.

References

1. *Human Dynamics* (1987).
2. Information courtesy of Prosci (2007), Best Practices in Change Management. Benchmarking Report.
3. Ibid.
4. Thomas, Pamela, *Business Case for Change Management* (2008).
5. Ibid.

Sustain EIM and Business Alignment

Preachers err ... by trying to "talk people into belief; better they reveal the radiance of their own discovery."
Joseph Campbell

CONTENTS

Businesspeople meet and assess the effectiveness of the marketing program, the sales campaign, or the cost-reduction imperative. Businesses revisit their programs frequently. EIM should be no different. And again, while the statement makes perfect sense, IT departments rarely formally revisit the effectiveness of the EIM-type efforts they already have, a classic example being the BI/data warehouse project two years after implementation. Usually, the assessment is along the lines of this conversation:

> Executive: "Are we getting what we need from the investment in data?"
> CIO: "I believe so. No complaints."
> Executive: "OK, thanks."

Making Enterprise Information Management (EIM) Work for Business. DOI: 10.1016/B978-0-12-375695-4.00011-4

Earlier we established that EIM is a business program. Reiterating, EIM strives to manage the content and data in an organization with the same philosophy and structure as a formal accounted asset is managed. Therefore, it stands to reason that once the program is established, we need to determine if it is truly adding value as time goes on. The prior chapter presented the need to sustain EIM with a process to manage the shift in thinking EIM creates. This chapter will briefly visit what needs measuring, what to revisit, and what needs to happen if the business environment changes.

MEASURING EIM AND IAM

There are two broad areas where we need to establish and monitor metrics around EIM. We need to measure business results through a lens of EIM. We also need to measure the EIM program itself. There is a third area where some organizations can examine additional means to measure if IAM results in a change in the enterprise financial view. This third area consists of a pro forma financial statement of information value.

Measuring Business Results

The first area is to provide for measuring business results. Of course, any enterprise measures its performance to a degree. However, we need to take these performance metrics and view them through the lens of information usage; in other words, did the leverage of content and data enable the achievement of a business goal? This means taking existing business measures and evaluating them with several new dimensions.

Key Performance Indicators (KPIs)

Most types of business have significant performance indicators. An insurance company like our case study of UIC would use *policies in force*, *loss ratio*, and *earned premium* as three of a handful of KPIs. In the course of business they would want to slice these by product lines, regions, or other subsets of the organization. For Farfel, same-store-sales and inventory turns represent these types of KPIs. The success of IAM through an EIM effort can be measured in part by using the same type of indicators, but slicing the data differently. In Table 11.1, columns two and three would be after the word "by" on a report.

Column two, typical dimension, is a mean by which data is "sliced" in a BI environment. Once IAM is in place, the EIM program will need to monitor whether the business is benefiting from EIM, for example, by looking at financial results by those leveraging the data (knowledge workers).

Other examples are:

- Operating income for year divided by the number of knowledge workers.
- Percentage of the cost of knowledge workers within the total overhead or direct costs of specific functions.
- Direct cost of information—Cross-functional collection of all shadow IT, central IT costs vs. burying them within department budgets.

Table 11.1 KPI and EIM Dimensions

KPI	Typical Dimension	Dimension to Measure IAM
Policies in force	Product line, coverage, geography, distribution channel	Knowledge worker, types of content, error type, control discrepancies
Written premium	Year over year, product, demographic	Knowledge worker, types of content, control discrepancies
Loss ratio	Product line, coverage, geography, claim size, item type covered	Knowledge worker, types of content, control discrepancies
Same-store-sales	Product line, region, promotions	Knowledge worker, source application, control discrepancies, data error
Inventory turns	Item type, time period, facility	Knowledge worker, source application, managed "master" data, control discrepancies

Pro Forma or Potential Risk Metrics

Other business metrics, while not as common, may also be used to set the context for the usefulness of EIM. A prime example is the compliance area. Very often, regulatory compliance provides a driver for more effective information management. If regulatory risk is reduced via EIM, then a metric should be made available to demonstrate the reduced risk. Such a metric might be a pro forma of penalties per area of data content or subject, to show reduced exposure. Over time, changes in reserves or budgets for litigation can also be aligned with improved compliance and IM.

Some other equally informative metrics are the following.

- The pro forma statement of:
  - Possible legal fees arising from dealing with bad information
  - Legal fees to defend privacy issues
  - Lost funding for government entities or contractors
  - "What if" vision assuming penalties and prosecution
  - Calling out specific shifts in reserves, retained earnings, and goodwill.

Broad indicators, such as market share or shareholder value, are often overlooked. Again, viewing these through a slightly different lens produces a correlation potential between governance and IAM and company value. Looking at market share by the number of knowledge workers year over year will assist in determining if use of content and data has an effect. In many organizations this can be an implied relationship, in others an obvious relationship. If shareholder equity is $1,000,000, and there are 200 individuals using data and making decisions, then the equity per knowledge worker is $5,000. If we invest in BI, train 50 new knowledge workers, but equity declines to $900,000, then we have $3,600 per knowledge worker. Granted there may be no tie to knowledge workers and equity, but all things being equal, I would look into how the new BI elements of EIM were being used.

MEASURING EIM SUCCESS

There are other EIM metrics that may help confirm the relationship between EIM and business progress. These other metrics are those that focus on the actual performance of EIM and IAM programs.

Part 2 of this book details these metrics and provides examples. The list below is provided mainly to prove a point—measuring the effectiveness of EIM and IAM is not difficult.

Data Quality

Obviously, accuracy is an issue in organizations. We reviewed data quality previously. Measuring ongoing data quality and its related costs are excellent indicators of EIM success. Examples of basic data quality metrics are:

- Counts of data occurrences that are in error, both gross number of errors and errors per number of total occurrences
- Percentages of accuracy (e.g., numerical values are not correct but are within some percentage)
- Specific samples of fields in error and the financial errors contained (e.g., total premium at risk is $$$$$ because nn% of policies contain bad information)
- Percentage of e-mails that should have been deleted or contain potentially damaging information
- Cost of bad catalog entries and poor content management due to lost online orders or returned product
- Data quality profile results—percentage of completion, accuracy, relevance
- The year-over-year delta of data quality metrics combined as an index.

EIM/IAM Efficiency Metrics

This category is similar to the business metrics listed earlier because they are based on data we can find on an income statement or balance sheet. However, they are focused more on actual costs of operating EIM.

- Total cost of IT/party (customer, member, etc.)
- Data governance/compliance cost divided by total income
- Data governance/compliance cost vs. risk reserves/premiums/financial reserves.

Data Governance Metrics for Sustaining

Governance is a core component of EIM and is not sustainable without effective monitoring. If you do not support and develop metrics for the effectiveness of data governance, the "nuisances" of change will overwhelm perceived subjective benefits. You are defenseless if there are complaints of longer cycle times or interference. Examples of these metrics are:

- Document and data life cycle times vs. regulatory requirements
- Compare application deployment to data governance approvals of deployments
- Feedback results from surveys of parties impacted by EIM
- Document and data life cycle times—is content available when it needs to be, is it deleted when no longer of benefit?
- Use of standard structures and major data subjects that are "certified," e.g., number of customers stored in a customer master database and certified as accurate as a percentage of all possible customers.

EIM Progress Metrics

Finally, as a sponsor or beneficiary of EIM and the changes it delivers, certain metrics need reporting as the EIM effort rolls out. It is easy to collect metrics on the nuisance of required change (count your e-mails). Countering these measures with ones indicating progress is essential. They fall into several categories.

Incentives and performance, to indicate use and effectiveness of tactics to ensure change occurs:

- Total count/amount of data governance or data quality incentive rewards
- Attendance at orientation and training
- Issues presented to steering committees
- Performance reviews done with EIM targets included
- Job descriptions revised with IAM accountability included
- Performance targets achieved related to IAM.

Usage, to indicate extent of the organization moving toward managed content vs. staying with departmental data:

- Number of users and access to single sources of truth
- Reduction in departmental Access databases and spreadsheets
- BI use by user log on ID to track who is doing what.

EIM success targets, to indicate progress toward objectives set by the EIM program:

- Counts of content by life cycle stages (e.g., transactional, operational, decisional)
- Total cost of IT/party (customer, member, etc.).

MEASURING THE PRO FORMA VALUE OF CONTENT

We avoid measuring the value of data because it is "abstract," but we manage to measure many other elusive abstract items. The example of an electric meter and billing for electricity comes to mind— electricity is in the wires, and somehow we manage to measure it and send out a bill. Energy companies maintain "inventories" of energy. They trade and sell kilowatts and megawatts. So accounting for abstract things is not a new discipline. We merely need to step back and look at the basic principles of asset accounting and apply them. When we do, we see that there are a few possible means to measure the value of enterprise content and information. Chapter 9 touched on the economics of information and relative value as a means to build a business case. This section will look into the ongoing accounting aspects of information value.

Generally Accepted Information Principles™

Much like FASB that maintains principles and guidelines for accounting, we base pro forma value statements on principles. FASB bases these standards on a set of Generally Accepted Accounting Principles. Our "accounting" is based on Generally Accepted Information Principles™. In Chapter 28 we map FASB to GAIP™ to illustrate how an accounting mind-set can be allied to information assets. Table 11.2 shows the basic GAIP™ principles we use.

Table 11.2 GAIP™—Principles for Information Asset Accounting

Principle Name	Description	Remarks
Asset principle	Data and content of all types are assets. Data and content assets have all the characteristics of any other asset. Therefore, they should be managed, secured, and accounted for as other material or financial assets.	There is the concept that data assets do not deplete when "used," e.g., when I read data, it is still there for someone else to read. But this characteristic (that other assets do not have) actually pushes data and content toward requiring even more rigorous accounting, given the risks and costs of duplication and incorrect use. In addition, the debate that "data is not information" is meaningless in this context since business context is the only determinant whether content stored in digital form is information, content, or data. All are *assets*.
Value principle	There is value in all data and content, based on their contribution to an organization's business/operational objectives, their intrinsic marketability, and/or their contribution to the organization's goodwill (balance sheet) valuation. The value of information is reflective of its contribution to the organization offset by the cost of maintenance and movement.	This principle acknowledges that there is value in the inventory of information and content within an organization that requires an accounting.
Going concern principle	Data and content are not viewed as a temporary means to achieve results (or merely as a business by-product), but are critical to successful, ongoing business operations and management.	This principle recognizes the role of information as *fuel*, as opposed to the concept of information as a lubricant for business processes.
Due diligence principle	If a risk is known, it must be reported. If a risk is possible, it must be confirmed.	Concealing a potential liability just because it has "always been there" is as bad as not reporting unethical interactions with suppliers or banks.
Risk principle	There is risk associated with data and content. This risk must be formally recognized, either as a liability or through incurring costs to manage and reduce the inherent risk.	Risk management is a normal business function. In IT we manage risk with back-up data sites. We do not recognize the risk associated with lost business or higher costs if we lose or mistreat data. We also overlook the considerable risk potential of content and data because of inaccuracy and unauthorized use.
Quality principle	The meaning, accuracy, and life cycle of data and content can affect the financial status of an organization.	This principle acknowledges that data quality is important to business success, and is recognized as a high-level principle vs. a requirement for a specific project or initiative.
Audit principle	The accuracy of data and content is subject to periodic audit by an independent body.	If data quality is an enterprise principle, it is therefore subject to verification.

(Continued)

Table 11.2 (Continued)

Principle Name	Description	Remarks
Accountability principle	An organization must identify individuals who are ultimately accountable for data and content of all types.	Accountability means ultimate responsibility. Every type and occurrence of content must have a party designated that is ultimately accountable for effective management and quality of the asset.
Liability principle	The risks in information means there is a financial liability inherent in all data or content that is based on regulatory and ethical misuse or mismanagement.	This principle recognizes the need to account for contingent risk buried in data and content if you have not invested in a means to eliminate the risk.

The actual valuation of the value of data and content assets is a function of looking at goodwill (if it is on the balance sheet) and determining a prorated portion related to information. If there is no goodwill, or the goodwill is not relevant to information, we do a calculation of subjective value based on the volume, relevance, quality, and effectiveness of the various categories of content and data. See Chapter 28 for a detailed presentation of this.

Revisiting Business Alignment

Rarely are metrics produced on a regular basis as presented in the earlier paragraphs. Most of the time they are produced on-demand to meet an ad hoc request ("does this stuff work?") or justify a new project within EIM. But it is advisable to revisit business alignment. The enterprise should map content exploitation to a business plan. At minimum, the EIM program should be scrutinized once per year in terms of its effect on the business. (The progress of EIM spawned projects and supporting efforts are evaluated all year, as is other projects.)

The real work of revisiting the alignment of EIM begins after the measures are reported, and the executive team determines how to respond. In addition to determining how to respond, the timing of *when* to do the review is important. While EIM is an umbrella program to manage projects, there will be funding changes in response to business changes. So EIM redirections tend to affect capital budgets. The process to do this is no different than the initial process of aligning EIM to the business, just shorter.

The ideal protocol for revisiting EIM effectiveness is as follows:

1. The executive team or EIM steering body initiates the review process.
2. If metrics are not regularly collected then the ad hoc process begins to gather agreed upon metrics for evaluation.
3. Once metrics are collected they need to be verified and checked for reasonableness. (Hence the notion the ideal approach is to collect them all the time anyway.)
4. The metrics are presented to the steering committee or executive team.
5. Metrics that present a poor picture, or lack progress, need to have a root cause analysis performed. For example, data quality metrics might be presented that indicate a lack of improvement in overall data quality. The root cause analysis would pinpoint if processing, entry, or external factors are

preventing an improvement in data quality. Perhaps income per knowledge worker did not increase even after investment in a BI project. The day-to-day usage of the BI solution needs to be reviewed to see if there are issues with the deployed application, usage, or ability to exploit the data.

6. Assuming root causes are determined, then a sub-team should recommend additional EIM oversight, project modifications, or organization programs.

7. The executive team also needs to review the progress of in stream projects in light of information levers. Remember, there was a formal effort to tie the HOW of content and data usage directly to business goals. The EIM team must report, either by lever, goal, or project, the specific business program or goal that was targeted by a particular component of EIM.

8. While EIM performance metrics are being complied or prepared, the EIM team must also meet with corporate governance or compliance. New regulations, imposed penalties, and any other risk area need to be reviewed in the context of how content or data is affected, or affecting organization risk. A notable example is the area of documentation of safety protocols around dangerous equipment. One of the most impactful projects my teams ever worked on was documentation management in an industrial environment where lost time and fatal accidents were a serious consideration. The liability to this particular business was enormous and required regular scrutiny of progress in this area. Financial services businesses can also exploit this exercise to verify effectiveness of risk exposure, and risk reporting, such as Basel II.

Another situation where the EIM program requires review is a change in business climate or model. The information levers and uses of information will typically require modest adjustments every year. But a sharp market change, regulatory upheaval (think Enron), or merger would require a visit to the EIM road map. There will more likely be more ad hoc metrics. It may also be necessary to realign the business plans with EIM, such as shifting priorities or funding between road map projects.

Lastly, the executive team needs to hear about the human capital side. Since we have stated several times the organizational change and a critical success factor, it makes sense to visit the progress of any activities intended to sustain the EIM effort.

ONGOING ACTIVITY

Sustaining EIM means periodic review of the value of the EIM program, and the ongoing value of the content being managed by EIM. If the business changes direction or EIM is falling short, making adjustments needs to be based on a quantitative method.

Maintaining alignment to the business means taking the metrics and holding them up to the scrutiny of normal business activity. Are we achieving our goals? Can we tie the use of data and content to these achievements? Many times this will be a pro forma, given that organizations are unwilling to allocate benefits to information-based IT projects.

Often IT departments will complain that it is too hard to measure information "stuff." This is a fallacy. What needs to be in place for effective EIM metrics are:

1. Willingness to collect the data.
2. Permission for the EIM effort to count business progress towards the relevance of the EIM program.

SUMMARY

Many of the metrics presented in this chapter are familiar, but add the dimension of information. In addition, there are new metrics to be considered. Essentially, the organization must be willing to invest in collecting the data and producing the metrics. EIM is about managing assets. You cannot manage what you do not measure.

Finally, all but the smallest companies should consider the value of their information in the light of the value of the entire organization. This means applying some of the concepts of intangible asset accounting. While not official this exercise forces the EIM area to examine the relevancy of information to the enterprise, and determine risks as well as value.

References

1. Sandra, S., & David, H. (1997). *Human Dynamics* (1st ed.). Waltham, MA: Pegasus Communications.
2. Prosci Benchmarking Report. (2009). Best Practices in Change Management; Creasey, Tim and Hiatt, Jeff; Prosci; page 15.
3. Prosci Benchmarking Report. (2009). Best Practices in Change Management; Creasey, T. and Hiatt, J.; Prosci; page 21.
4. Thomas, P. (2008). *Business Case for Change Management*. White Paper submitted for publication.
5. Ibid.

Sustaining EIM and the Organization

12

The hardest part about gaining any new idea is sweeping out the false idea occupying that niche. As long as that niche is occupied, evidence and proof and logical demonstration get nowhere. But once the niche is emptied of the wrong idea that has been filling it—once you can honestly say, I don't know, then it becomes possible to get at the truth.

Robert A. Heinlein

CONTENTS

EIM, while potentially of minimum impact in incremental cost or hiring, does create organizational changes and build new business processes. As such, organization design and development enter the picture. This chapter covers the organizational aspects surrounding EIM, what must be considered, and how the organization structures may affect current organization charts.

EXECUTIVE CONSIDERATIONS FOR EIM

There will be changes to organization charts under an EIM program. Larger, more information-savvy companies may not make many changes, while a company with a limited record of information projects may confront significant changes. These changes will occur both inside and outside of IT.

Accountability

The EIM team will need to focus on information accountability. A very important concept in relation to rolling out an EIM organization is that of accountability and ownership of information assets.

Without well-defined accountability, you are not serious about data governance or management of information assets. There needs to be accountability in the "care and feeding" of the content assets. This concept of accountability has been buried in the label "stewardship." It is possible your organization already has "data stewards" or attempted stewardship programs in the past. My guess is that the program did not meet expectations. There are three reasons for this:

1. People were "appointed" stewards without training.
2. There was no well-defined accountability for the role.
3. There was no prioritization of the role, i.e., being a steward takes a back seat to day-to-day activities, and eventually is ignored.

Most attempts at stewardship are deployed too literally and simply. IT departments have erred often here, and the EIM program will not be successful without accountability for the quality of the content assets and adherence to the standards surrounding IAM.

There cannot be a valid business process and/or program without accountability for execution. However, if you put this book down for a moment and consider if anyone has ever been fired in your organization for improper data handling, you may come up empty. Unless the data misuse is egregious and fraudulent, few companies even notice it. A classic example would be the need for a particular code in a new system that is used to segregate activity. Let us call it product type. Once in place and entered, this field could be used to segregate out various products to examine if a particular product line is profitable or not. At one time, a standard list of product types was specified and a memo sent out that stated "these are the legitimate product types." Fast forward a few years and you will find an application being done under duress—perhaps late, or under a regulatory deadline. The developer creates his/her own product-type field, being too lazy to embed the correct standard code. This seems minor but this is exactly how databases get out of synch over time, and why reports do not match. This egregious misuse of data is easy to see but our example is typical and has caused many issues. Imagine this example 10-fold—or a 100-fold. This is exactly what is sitting out in your applications and data as you read this. Disconnects galore.

So if you are to manage information as an asset, who ensures misuse does not happen? Obviously, we need an accountable party. This is where the stewardship idea entered the EIM literature in the 1990s. Someone needed to take ownership and ensure data quality. However, the concept, while noble, is too simple to work. For any given subject in an enterprise, there are many parties that touch and manipulate data. Each party has its own context and agenda. Yet if we accept that information is an asset, then it follows that all parties that touch content are, in effect, caretakers or stewards.

Think of it this way. We have already stated that usage makes it valuable. Usage also gives the data context; that is, the process that is using the data or content contributes meaning and value. But it is the context that prevents us from having ONE steward or accountable party for a piece of content.

Suppose the sales force in a company enters new customers into the "system" with an initial order. Obviously, we want the salesperson to be cognizant of the need for accuracy. But is sales the owner and steward? For sure we can say the salesperson is accountable for some degree of accuracy at entry point.

In the same organization, the product ordered is shipped and invoiced to the customer. Shipment information and other data pertinent to billing is entered. This is still "customer data." Should sales be accountable for this process? Hardly—and even if they (sales) were told to be owners they would tend to ignore the shipping context. Therefore, there are (in this scenario) *two* stewards that take care of the caretakers.

Table 12.1 Information Accountability

Role Activity	Caretaker	Accountable
Sell a policy	Sales channel: Ensures policy is entered correctly	Sales management; oversees all areas where policies are entered in terms of correctness
Revise policy rates	Policy administration makes sure rate changes are applied	Underwriting is accountable for accuracy and business compliance to regulators
Add a new underwriting code	IT may actually make sure the code appears in software	Actuaries or underwriting creates a need for new code and are accountable for seeing its correct application

We still have not addressed accountability. Who is the "throat to choke" if sales data is misused over time? Should a salesperson be held accountable for errors in shipping or even in IT? Again, this is doubtful. Yet at an enterprise level, we need an asset manager. So the greatest challenge of the EIM team in terms of organization is to find (not appoint) the proper asset management structure. It may not be one person. The accountability can be shared. But it must exist. Your EIM team should develop a formal analysis of where accountability lies. An example appears in Table 12.1.

Data Governance

The EIM organization has many functions. The most important function an executive will see is typically called "data governance."

"*Data governance* is the organization and implementation of policies, procedures, structure, roles, and responsibilities which outline and enforce rules of engagement, decision rights, and accountabilities for the effective management of information assets."[1]

Note that the definition of data governance describes a business function. You could remove the words "data governance" and "information" and substitute "inventory control" and "raw material."

The personnel accountable for information assets will be guided by the policies from a data governance area. Remember that data governance was called "FASB for data" in an earlier chapter. Data governance is akin to the audit function. Where data controls look for "content" things are "right," data governance is concerned with doing the right things. In a manufacturing setting, they would be similar to a quality assurance area (vs. quality control). In financial services think compliance.

Changes from data governance will cause the most resistance. The areas most impacted will be applications development in IT, and business areas where significant data handling and analysis occur.

Organization Charts

Because of the cross-functional effect EIM can have, building the actual EIM organization will require a formal organizational design effort. There are new responsibilities that various business areas will acquire (e.g., maintaining data quality or ensuring correct access to personal documents), there will be areas charged with oversight, and there will also be the new accountabilities. The net is there needs to be an agreed-upon list of EIM functions and duties, and a list of what new duties and activities are required across the business. A large matrix is developed based on the EIM function list, and a RACI analysis (Responsibility, Accountability, Consult, Inform) is performed for all EIM functions.

There are several of these new functions that require awareness at the executive level:

- Ongoing education on enterprise information principles and oversight for EIM policies.
- Interface with compliance and legal areas.
- Clear vision for the changes data governance and EIM will create.
- Engaging EIM stakeholders.

EIM requires executive oversight. This means some type of steering body or governance "uber-committee." Before heaving a deep sigh of "dang, another committee," review the following carefully. An EIM oversight committee will:

- Exist to ensure that EIM is starting and various efforts of resistance and hesitancy are addressed according to a change management plan.
- Step up to issues that other, lower levels of the EIM functions have not been able to address.
- Review project status of various deployments and redirect where required.
- Verify EIM progress, and make the final call if it is working or not.
- Appoint project steering bodies consisting of people with a genuine stake in the effort vs. those seeking executive visibility.
- Visibly demonstrate sponsorship and support for EIM.

Any executive who has been a sponsor of a large stand-alone project will see that the EIM oversight body will actually address many projects as one committee. In practice, the actual number of meetings related to information and content projects should *decrease*. Finally, consider that this particular committee has some very well-defined duties. Once EIM is up and running, it should not meet very often.

The location of EIM functions will be important. Use the mind-set of instituting any other management functions; rules of management apply. There must be clear performance expectations, separation of duties, and adequate controls in place. For this reason, do not place data governance within an IT department. CIO and IT directors cringe when this advice is given. However, years of IT development point to the fact that if someone is incented to do it *right* or do it *fast*, *fast* always wins. Business areas need the application *now*. So IT gets the marching orders and EIM is pushed aside. IT cannot possibly stay even-minded in that environment. Again, separation of duties is required. Failure to do so is another reason many earlier EIM-type efforts have failed. (This is the equivalent of having the person with the petty cash drawer balancing the petty cash drawer.)

A great place to locate all content governance is within compliance or legal. If these areas are not significant enough, then a separate organization within finance reporting to internal audit also works.

Who is Affected?

More often than not EIM touches many employees. If your enterprise is rife with data quality issues, tons of Access databases, and you have no idea how many customers you have, then plan on some organizational impact, and the subsequent need for some behavior change or change management. Keep this scenario in mind as your company considers EIM—somewhere in your organization is an hourly employee whose job is to enter a certain transaction as soon as possible. At some point in the past, a system glitch created a scenario where, rightly or wrongly, this operator can enter all 9's in lieu of the correct part number, serial number, vehicle number, whatever. Now EIM, besides obviously affecting IT developers and content managers, is going to change that job, and change that incentive.

Organization Chart Creativity

We have already pointed out that there does not have to be *one* steering body, or *one* accountable party for a particular area of content. Very large organizations will require some sort of information oversight by business unit, or even brands within business units. A scenario for a large global organization produced Figure 12.1.

Each broad area of content (customer, product, etc.) was given a central asset manager. Business units brands reported to the central asset manager. A corporate data strategist (I never liked that title, but . . .) was the enterprise asset manager. All of the individual data strategists were given accountabilities embedded in performance goals to manage their own segment of a particular type of content.

One thing to avoid if possible (even the example earlier has them) is the dreaded "dotted lines" for reporting. I had a client tell me that they despised dotted lines, because "it means the boss only hears every other word."

Controls and Compliance

Controls and compliance are critical areas that EIM can leverage. In turn, compliance can leverage EIM. The notable fact is you already have a compliance function. When we meet with compliance areas, they are delighted to discover another part of the company is also concerned about regulatory risk. Conversely, EIM teams often find it effective to ask compliance to draft a letter supporting a data

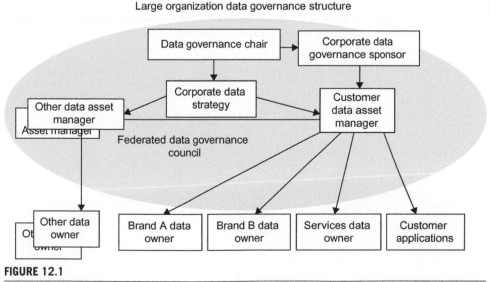

FIGURE 12.1

Large organization governance structure

policy, or assist in overcoming resistance. No matter what size or type of enterprise you have, there is some kind of legal compliance at work, and some kind of document and/or data controls in place, from neighborhood dentist to international megacorporations.

SUMMARY

While the process and concepts are familiar (organization design), the subject matter is new. This does not mean EIM requires different treatment. You are still looking for smooth communications lines. You are looking for the right people in the right places. You need to apply some intelligent engineering to the organizing of EIM, data governance, and affected business areas.

Creativity will be key—with the structure of your guiding bodies, stewards, and accountable managers being defined by the nature of the organization.

When planning for the EIM organization reaches the point of determining accountability and identifying the caretakers, a formal exercise for the organization is highly recommended. This would take place during the Road Map and Sustaining phases of the EIM program. Accountability means measurement and performance goals; incentives then come into play. So to declare someone a steward because it seems like he is the right person and to also make him an enterprise steward even if he has a narrow functional view is risking job confusion. Unfortunately, many organizations have caretakers or stewards who have not internalized accountability, or haven't even a vested interest in a business process of any sort. Frankly, if you want EIM but do not have the stomach to add accountability to the mix, then lower your expectations of the program. It will not succeed.

Reference

1. Ladley, J., McGilvray, D., Smith, A.-M., & Thomas, G. Common definition of data governance. Presented 2008–2009 by all four contributors at various venues to ensure common understanding.

Placing EIM into Real Context

13

Few things are harder to put up with than the annoyance of a good example.
Mark Twain

CONTENTS

Making Enterprise Information Management (EIM) Work for Business. DOI: 10.1016/B978-0-12-375695-4.00013-8

Part 1 of this book is focused on turning an accounting metaphor into a tangible program to support the need to manage information and content in a way that is different from what we have done historically. As we proceed into actually describing what this looks like and how to go about building out the program, we are going to use examples taken from actual experience. Setting EIM into real scenarios will provide context for understanding the potential value and impact of EIM on your organization. In this chapter we will go into some basic information about the components of EIM, consider what they might look like, and introduce two case studies for this book.

The case studies will help lock in relevant concepts, as well as provide an overview of how the programs were developed, what some of their artifacts contain, and what outcomes were achieved. Here we will provide examples of what the various work products from the case studies look like. While Part 2 of this book also contains sample outputs and appendices with templates, this chapter will provide the executive audience samples emphasizing business drivers, visual aids, and comparisons to best practices. Part 2 will also drive more into how to develop the products represented below.

CASE STUDIES

Throughout this book, I will use several case studies to illustrate the actual development of an EIM program, the issues that can surface, and how those can be addressed. They are amalgams of several past EIM projects conducted by me and my team. While carrying out the actual EIM work at these companies, we assessed their culture of using information, their capacity to change, and we looked at business alignment. Each of the companies also addressed most or all of the building blocks of EIM. Most of the companies proceeded with implementation of various elements of EIM.

CASE STUDY—UBETCHA INSURANCE

Ubetcha Insurance Company (UIC) is based on work at three diverse insurance companies. Each company arrived at the need for increased information oversight from different directions. Each went through an EIM refinement and strategy process, but with markedly different results.

Company A
- This enterprise had an existing IM department, an established business intelligence team, and widespread use of business areas performing their own analytics. Competitive pressures and lack of consistent analysis had resulted in loss of market share, and some very bad underwriting decisions resulting in several years of excessive claims payments. The current claims and policy applications were old, and there were multiple versions in production.
- Their assessment focused on Readiness and Business Alignment. We combined culture readiness with the Business Readiness survey.
- Over the two months after the assessment, the alignment and planning were done for EIM, with a focus on deploying the business intelligence elements first. Resistance from business areas was very strong, with statements like "the business area can do the job, just give them the data they need" commonly heard at status meetings with management. An additional assessment of the effectiveness of the business BI capabilities was requested to prove this point.
- The original assessment contained some strong recommendations to manage the organization's culture. We designed an incremental strategy to modify and enhance BI capability. A deeper

assessment of current BI readiness was an eye opener. The existing IM department was able to demonstrate that business areas currently provided, via direct download, 98% of the available data elements from all operational systems. The amount of departmental computing capability, in terms of hardware, software, *and staff*, exceeded the existing BI areas costs by a factor of three. The results were presented and taken under consideration by the steering committee.

- The BI strategy was adopted; but before the internal team could complete the initial steps of the new efforts, the management team had the CIO replace the BI director with a business unit head. The first step taken was to table all recommendations, and give business user areas direct access to production data. Our engagement was deemed "complete."
- Since this effort, the company has lost an additional 5% market share, and several states where it is licensed are examining the viability of the company.
- While culture was an obvious fact to this information disaster, the root cause of the data issues was that information was not viewed as having value. The various business leaders with access to all possible data could neither use the data nor analyze it properly. It was not culture or technology. Information was not an asset. It was a departmental tool.

Company B

- The company had a very effective distribution channel in the form of captive agents, affinity relationships with several nonprofit associations, and managed a client base that historically supported a profitable set of insurance products. However, growth was not unfolding as forecast, and product design seemed to lag behind the competition.
- The assessments showed a level of maturity that was not sufficient to support the various growth strategies that were on the table. There were serious data quality issues in the policy and sales applications, and a complete picture of their customer base was not possible.
- Within two to three months following the assessment, the alignment and planning were done for EIM, with a focus on deploying the business intelligence elements first. In addition to specific recommendations to bypass some politics that were inevitable due to the organization's culture, we designed an incremental strategy to modify and enhance BI capability. Further refinement of EIM through additional data governance and data quality efforts was recommended to follow the initial surge from the BI effort.
- The BI strategy was adopted; but the culture change effort was dismissed for "budget" reasons, and subsequent EIM work was tabled until the following fiscal year. Against advice, the data governance and data quality portions of the BI work were also dropped and the EIM team was told to "clean up" the bad data. Business areas went around the new BI team, and continued to gather their own data and get assistance from other areas in IT. The end result was an additional several million in BI development, no additional work on data governance, and a herculean effort to clean up the data for analytics vs. correct the issues through governance and data quality. This company still struggles with understanding its market and pricing its products. Their growth strategy has been tabled and replaced with a tactical strategy based on advertising and pricing, and they have failed to exploit their essentially captive customer base.

Company C

- A new CEO requested an assessment of the entire IT organization. He then followed up on a recommendation that the company address the IM findings from the IT assessment. The business environment at the time of these efforts was becoming increasingly complex, as new competition and a perceived change in the demographic composition of their historical customer base required changes in marketing, distribution channel management, and product pricing.

- The follow-on effort conducted Alignment, Data Quality, and Culture assessments, produced the structure for an EIM program, designed a data governance program, a road map of a series of BI applications to address immediate business needs, and a serious attempt to resolve a series of data quality issues that were affecting many aspects of the business.
- During the Data Quality activities, the CEO took an active interest in some of the findings, and found that the cost and risks of poor data were not acceptable. While the BI projects were important, the Sustaining strategy was focused on the data quality issues.
- During orientation to new policies, some anticipated resistance started to boil up. The EIM team was stretched between the data quality and BI efforts. A public statement of support by the CEO at a management meeting reduced resistance, but more arose as new data quality and usage policies became "real."
- This EIM program is still viable as of the writing of this book, and quantifiable metrics and benefits from EIM are being produced. A formal team has been formed to address behavior changes around data.

Background for UIC

UBETCHA (UIC) is a mid-sized standard personal and commercial lines property casualty insurance company located in the central portion of the United States. Market pressures are forcing the company to examine all aspects of its claims applications, customer relations, distribution channels, and underwriting processes. Enabling the analysis of product profitability is critical to their future success, but in their current environment, it's difficult and time-consuming. Rapid response to changes in the market is impossible and several promising new products never made it to market because competitors beat them to it. Several attempts have been made at implementing an IM strategy, but these were less than successful. Regulatory pressures are also forcing the company to examine its controls and data management policies. Many of its applications are more than 15 years old and are written in a variety of programming languages.

After a series of initial meetings, it's apparent that executives at UIC are beginning to hire their own data analysts and do not trust the IT department. Conversely, IT says that there is little executive sponsorship for new initiatives, but it is "still easy to complain."

The business itself is under great stress, as the aforementioned market pressures have created a decrease in premium revenue and policies in force. The specific causes are seemingly unknown, and there is dissension among management as to whether the revenue decline is a result of fewer policyholders, poor underwriting, or poor service.

The board removed the CEO and recently hired a new one. As the new CEO (Bob) gets to know his staff and the employees, he is besieged with many ideas as to how to fix the various issues confronted by UIC. A recent management meeting on the strategic plan presented Bob with two reports of growth projections as a result of new marketing and service programs. While the programs were solid, the initial number of current policyholders was presented as 6,500,000 by marketing, 5,900,000 by finance, and the chief actuary said there were really 5,373,201—approximately. Bob stopped the meeting and asked, "why three different numbers?"

At another meeting, the CIO states that the entire applications portfolio should be thrown out, and a new technology platform be selected based on a new generation of "off-the-shelf" software that is service based. Bob sort of understands what this means, it sounds like the object-oriented lingo he heard at his prior company.

The COO feels all IT should be outsourced, and external services used to provide reports and analytical capabilities.

The chief actuary feels that the actuarial area should take over all data reporting to reduce the potential risks arising from poor reporting and analysis, citing the customer count issue as an example.

The CFO feels that inaccurate data is the cause for many issues and urges the CEO to implement new mandates for cleaning up data. The VP of Sales is opposed to this as the mandates will require the direct sales force to change their entire process for submitting new policies, and the web-based sales software will require replacing. Right now the policy application on their web site is really a front end to the old underwriting system, and quotes must be e-mailed to the applicant.

Bob is looking for some common thread for a strategic response to these pressures, but must also look into some of the immediate problems.

As time progresses, UIC determines (with consultant assistance) that the mix of older technology, business and regulatory pressure, and reduced abilities to actually run the company mean a new look at technology is in order. So an Enterprise Architecture project is initiated. The goal is to discern the most crucial problems and deal with them soon from the standpoint of IT.

After the Enterprise Architecture effort, Bob feels no more comfortable. The final presentation presented a litany of three letter acronyms and a lot of talk about layers, services, and clouds, but how it would all help his immediate and long-term business issues remained foggy. One item that did catch his eye was that a great deal of data was being distributed to all major departments, and the Enterprise Technology Inventory from the study showed serious efforts being made at departmental levels to gather data and produce analysis.

He also had a copy of the *Harvard Business Review* article from 2003, "IT Doesn't Matter," left on his desk with an anonymous note attached—that simply said "outsource?"

A few months later, Bob attended an industry conference. He had given the head actuary the all-clear to address some immediate reporting needs, and look into why answers were so scarce. At the conference he heard a talk from an analyst on the concept of information assets, and how information needed to be managed as such. He decided he needed to look at information as a business issue, not a technology challenge. Bob went home feeling the need to craft a long-term strategy based on IM that would enable UIC to respond to market pressures better, and permit executives to communicate more effectively and access data to run the company.

UIC Case Approach

This brief introduction to UIC covered a series of business issues confronting the organization. Does EIM have a role? Would IAM help UIC accomplish its goals? There is an immediate need for data analysis (product profitability). But there are also some other drivers lurking—the slowness of getting new products to market, for example. Not to mention regulatory pressure. On the other hand, there have been attempts at IM. Finally, there is a push for departmental data management or business intelligence. All of these, of course, start us to at least assess UIC from an EIM perspective.

Facts from Data Collection

Annual premiums	$5,200,000,000
Policies in force	Approximately 6 million

Market environment
- Strong competition from larger companies with better rates and real-time quoting web sites.
- Market share—dropped from ninth to tenth in property and casualty market.
- Policies in force declined 5% in each of the last two years.

Stated issues
- Three claims systems—one legacy, one acquired in a merger, one to replace both of the others but supposedly cannot replace them, yet.
- Four policy administration applications—two from the acquired company, and two legacy applications, one for personal, and one for commercial business.
- Customer relations—claims processing and services are reported as good. Large percentage of policyholders seem to be very loyal.
- Distribution channels—direct sales force and licensed agents complaining of not enough support to get new clients. Web site users complain about no real-time quotes. New policies are submitted for underwriting and are rarely bound the same day.
- Products and underwriting—no one knows if pricing is competitive or product features are retaining business. Product features are hard to modify.
- Data warehouse—an effort to build a data warehouse failed when the policy and product data was found to be too disconnected to allow creating an integrated view of product and policy performance.

EIM Assessments

The UIC effort assessed Maturity, Readiness, Change Capacity, and Data Quality. Data quality was a formal profiling exercise and required a month to complete. The other assessments occurred over the same time period but took only one or two weeks, respectively (Figure 13.1).

EIM Alignment

We will follow the alignment items through vision on into where they appear on the Road Map. The example below shows a segment of one strategic area of UIC. In reality this type of artifact depicts a dozen or so initiatives with associated value uses. The UIC example was done with representatives of the executive leadership as a facilitated session (Table 13.1).

EIM Vision

Vision is a combination of graphic and preliminary requirements. Figure 13.2 is the UIC vision for how the business will view the EIM environment. The storefronts are entry points to subject content. Table 13.2 shows a high-level view of the business case. Note we added more detailed levers and started to examine the metrics.

EIM Business Model

The business model for UIC is a sample, as the real product is much longer. This sample includes the overall view of actions and metrics, and a sample list of defined metrics (Tables 13.3 and 13.4).

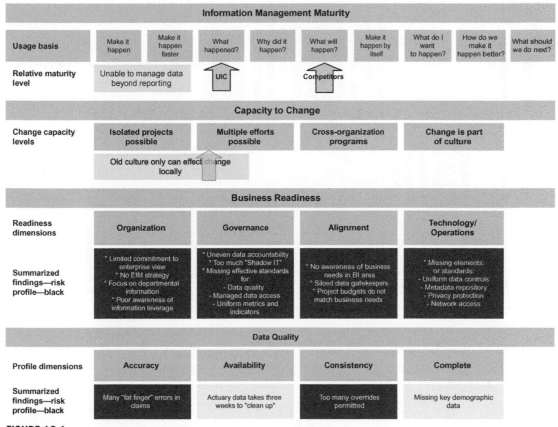

FIGURE 13.1

UIC Assessment summary

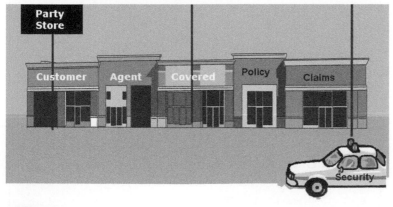

FIGURE 13.2

UIC Vision

Table 13.1 UIC Information Alignment Value

Increase Value Through	UIC Business Valuation Increase (Value Levers) Due to Information and Content Usage					
	Growth	Products	Pricing	Efficiency	Service	Marketing
Process: Improve cycle time, lower cost, improve quality		Remove obstacles to new products being sold on policies	Provide a common look and feel for underwriting support	Enable claims staff with access to consistent policy and insured data	Improved policyholder satisfaction from more accurate and timely answers to questions	Create marketing targeting families, e.g., school-age children preparing to drive
Competitive weapon: Capture competitive intelligence and differentiate yourself	Identify growth states and determine required investments			Determine more effective direct mail targets		Develop core product bundle; minimize price increases or target appropriately
Product: Create package and market unique, higher margin products	Work closely with marketing on household awareness	New product features determined				Increase brand cohesiveness across regions
Asset/intellectual capital: Prolong leadership, embed knowledge into products and services	Determine opportunities to improve Internet sales, direct sales, and customer service areas			Build integration into policy and claims data		
Enabler: Foster employee growth and empowerment	Develop new agency office model geared to growth		Implement common tools for underwriters/actuaries	Implement common tools for underwriters/actuaries		
Risk: Manage risk, of various types, that threatens value by increasing liability				Improved risk pricing with more timely information		

EIM Architecture

For this case, the executive summary of the Architecture is shown. More detailed versions of this are produced for technical support, applications, and the most affected business areas. Remember this phase produces a large amount of material. Other examples from this phase are shown in Part 2 (Figure 13.3).

EIM Road Map

Most executive presentations need to feature a sequenced Road Map, and it is of great value to show the Sustaining Requirements. The UIC Road Map was kept simple for the executive presentation—sequencing was a big issue with a lot of contention related to what was to be addressed first. As a result, the roll-out priorities were based on subjects vs. specific projects. The EIM strategy was able to address "something for everybody" during the first few iterations of projects (Figure 13.4).

Sometimes the presentation of the Sustaining plan has to show all aspects of change management. Other times there are specific areas of focus that need to be addressed. In the case of UIC, it was important to show what key stakeholders had to do and how the EIM team was intending to work with them (Table 13.5).

EIM Sustaining Plan

If the organization is very large or highly politicized, then reviewing some of the details of the Sustaining plan at an executive level is not a bad idea. This is where the rubber meets the road. The Communications plan is a keystone product of the Sustaining program (Table 13.6).

CASE STUDY—FARFEL EMPORIUM

The retail case study is an amalgam of two, retail and wholesale, organizations with similar distribution channels and market challenges. I picked these since they represent a different set of circumstances and content. However, there was strong emphasis on business cases and content other than rows and columns. The samples presented below highlight the variations in the two cases and offer an alternative method of presentation.

TIP FOR SUCCESS

Not every organization represented by Farfel did all of the assessments. For example, Company A flat-out said that any Culture assessment would have to be done underground—"IT" was not allowed to meddle with "HR" matters. If you hear comments like this around any EIM effort, there is either a serious disconnect in understanding what EIM is or the EIM effort is becoming an IT-only project.

As with UIC, the outputs are representative and summarized, intending only to establish a sense of what is happening to form the EIM program. The total duration of these efforts depicted later did not take more than 12 calendar weeks, from inception to rollout of the EIM program. EIM efforts should deliver *something* within a few months after starting assessments.

Table 13.2 UIC Business Case Summary

Support Corporate Strategy—Commitment to Measure EIM Support to Business Goals, Road Map Determines Exact Contribution					
Growth	Value areas for EIM	Identify growth states and determine required investments	Work closely with marketing on household awareness	Determine opportunities to improve Internet sales, direct sales, and customer service areas	Develop new agency office model geared to growth
	Associated financial targets	7% Growth	$104,000,000	Increase productivity to increase policies in force	$367,500,000
Products	Value areas for EIM	Remove obstacles to new products being sold on policies	New product features determined		
	Associated financial targets	12 New product features, market-size increase	$104,000,000		
Pricing	Value areas for EIM	Provide a common look and feel for underwriting support	Implement common tools for underwriters/actuaries	Improved risk pricing with more timely information	
	Associated financial targets	Reduction in loss adjustment expense	$84,000,000		
Efficiency	Value areas for EIM	Enable claims staff with access to consistent policy and insured data	Determine more effective direct mail targets	Build integration into policy and claims data	
	Associated financial targets	Decrease underwriting and overhead	$24,000,000		
Service	Value areas for EIM	Improved policyholder satisfaction	Increase customer retention to 95% renewal rate		
	Associated financial targets	Retention	$26,000,000		
Marketing	Value areas for EIM	Create marketing targeting families, e.g., school & age children preparing to drive	Develop core product bundle—minimize price increases or target appropriately	Increase brand cohesiveness across regions	
	Associated financial targets	Increase households to 1,200,000	$104,000,000		

Support intangible business area needs
Reduce data risk
Reduce training needs for tools
Exploit opportunity for operational improvement (operational data as important as analytics)
Reduce cost of purchasing external data
Reduce staff (perhaps as high as 12 FTEs)
Prevent shadow IT growth

Business case costs
Incremental increase in IT budget of $3,000,000 for two years to support program startup
A blend of external and internal staff
Incremental funding approach
Fixed budget amount per year based on labor ONLY
Allocation for capital (determined at end of Road Map project)
Estimates are level of effort—i.e., accomplish what is possible within budget constraint using fixed but DEDICATED team
Other factors to consider
Most DW and reporting applications can be capitalized

Table 13.3 UIC Metrics and Actions

Strategic Area	Business Strategy/Driver	Goal/Objectives	Objectives	BIR Requirement	Process	Competitive Weapon	Product	Asset/Intellectual Capital	Enabler	Risk	Metrics for Metrics Model
Growth	Growth leverage	Deliver continuous growth of 7% per year	Determine two new test markets by 20nn	Market size, activity		Identify new categories of customers		Target-specific products at new markets			Household demographic count; Individual demographic count; Percentage of households by demography; Percentage of individuals by demography
				Investment per outlet, state, revenue potential		Understand current customers, look for new regions with similar demographics				Identify profitable new markets, vs. new markets	Combined ratio—excluding management fee; Combined ratio—including management fee; Operating cost per feature; Product profitability; Product profitability; Pure premium
			Execute on UIC-wide cross-sell initiatives	Sales by product	Identify cross-sell processes in multiple channels						
Products	Deliver products and services that meet or exceed the needs of existing and prospective policyholders	Get new product features marketed within one month of regulatory approval	Reduce new product deployment to one month	Reduce product data update time	Review and adjust product business activity						Activity time; Operating cost per feature; Product profitability; Revenue generated per sales expense
Pricing	Maintain acceptable pricing returns to support growth in all channels	Improve underwriting efficiency	Reduce loss adjustment expense	Accurate loss adjustment expenses		Improve salvage agreements	Adjust product features	Understand value of customer of lifetime		Prequalify prospects and customers based on risk	Claim recovery ratio; Percentage of claimed amount recovered; Recovery amount—net; Recovery amount; Alias for recovery amount—gross

Table 13.4 UIC Metrics

Measurement Name	Definition
Outstanding claims amount Alias—reserve amount	The amount of all claim loss reserves outstanding.
Activity cost forecast	Forecasted cost for an activity. This measure is analyzed by a particular task/activity as defined by UIC such as: compliance monitoring, investment transaction, billing and collection, write-offs and terminations, vehicle appraisal, policy administration, etc.
Change in reserve	A measure of the amount of money that must be available to cover incurred losses.
Claim acceptance duration	The time expressed in days between the date when the claim has been reported and the date when the claim has been accepted based on the claim status.
Claim recovery outstanding balance	The outstanding incoming recovery payment amount. This is the salvage reserve.
Claim recovery ratio	Percentage of claims recovered.
Claim severity—incurred net of recoveries	Claim severity represents the size of the losses in dollars amount, including recoveries but not ALAE.
Claim severity—paid net of recoveries	Total amount of claim payments made for losses without recoveries.
Claimant count	The number of distinct individuals who are claimants against policy coverage.
Claims count—claimant	The number of distinct claimant demands against policy coverage.
Premium growth rate	The proportional indication of the growth (or decrease) of revenue for the current period in comparison with the previous period. $[((A \text{ at start of period}/A \text{ at end of period})-1) \times 100]$
Administration cost ratio	The total general expenses of the insurer as a percentage of premium written.

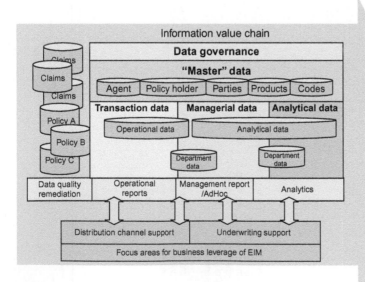

FIGURE 13.3

Executive summary of UIC EIM Architecture

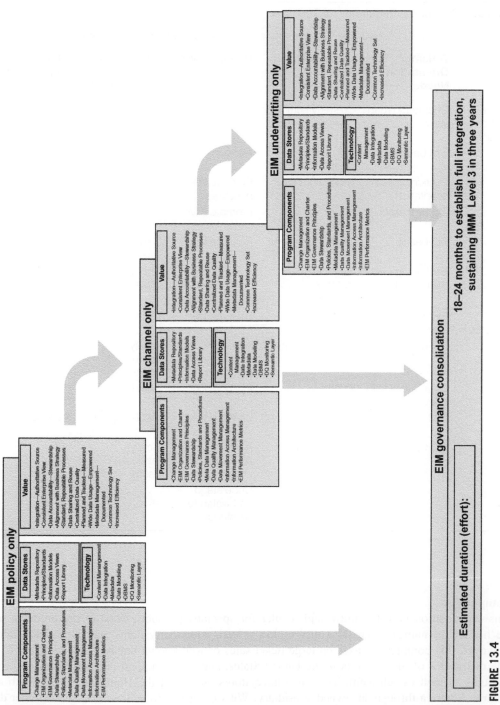

FIGURE 13.4

UIC Road Map

Table 13.5 Sustaining Requirements Summary

UIC EIM Change Management and Sustaining Requirements					
	Training/ Orientation Needs	Communication Needs	Notional Role	Requirements of Stakeholders	Interaction Requirements
Executive team and management	Orientation road show	Quarterly summary	Walk the talk	Walk the talk	Verify buy-in
	EIM basics	EIM metrics report	Back up CIO	Maintain priority of program	Brief, concise meetings
	Sustaining plan orientation	Issues summary	Promote EIM principles	Design incentives	Consultative approach
	DG processes	Sustaining updates	Promote EIM principles	Visible support	Consultative approach
	DQ basics	Issues summary	Promote DQ	Design incentives	Seek opinions
	Sustaining plan orientation	Sustaining updates		Codesign new processes	Proactively seek resistors
		DG metrics			
Data governance	EIM basics	Quarterly summary	Walk the talk	Visible support	Proactively seek resistors
	DQ basics	Issues summary	Allocate time for solid contribution	Timely resolution of issues	
	Orientation road show	Monthly summary	Promote DQ	Walk the talk	Proactively seek resistors
	EIM basics	EIM/DG metrics report	Walk the talk	Visible support	Seek opinions
	DQ basics	Issue status	Allocate time for solid contribution	Timely resolution of issues	
			Understand and watch for resistance		

Company A

- This organization is a distributor and retailer for specialty products. Most of the products sold are household names. There is a mix of low-priced, commodity items and large ticket items. However, this company focuses on large ticket sales of well-known brands. This company is the sole distributor of these brands in the United States, and has to support and service many of the products as well as sell them. They also have stores outside of the United States in South and Central America through an owned subsidiary. We were asked to address critical customer data

Table 13.6 UIC Summary Training/Communications Plan

Event	Target Audience	Objective	Timing	Vehicles	Sender	Feedback Mechanism
Executive steering committee meetings	Executive steering committee	Update committee members on project status Approve EIM projects/initiatives Set direction for EIM	Monthly	Meetings, status reports	Executive sponsor and sponsor	Immediate discussion and comments captured in meeting minutes
DG council meetings	Working steering committee	Update committee members on project status Resolve issues Confirm direction	Monthly	Meetings, status reports	Project management and sponsor	Comments captured in meeting minutes
DG committee meetings	Committee members	Allow the team to address issues relating to the quality of data and other data issues Provide direction and decision-making at the stall level Forum for escalating DG issues	As needed	Meetings	Committee lead	Immediate decision discussion and decisions
"Did you know"	All stakeholders	Promote tidbits and new information about DQ and DG	Weekly	Intranet	EIM team	Embed questions and opportunities to win prizes for those who visit the portal to review information
Monthly update	All stakeholders	What is complete and where EIM is with the transformation, update of the Road Map projects	Monthly	Newsletter (create list of EIM staff and key stakeholders)	EIM team	
Data accountability orientation	Data stewards	Allow the team to discuss tips and techniques for managing DQ Obtain direct input from forum lead on issues and concerns Information sharing	Quarterly	Meetings	EIM team	

issues. In the pursuit of seeking out new customers and servicing current ones, several data privacy issues had arisen. Many products sold were made in the European Union, and the difference in privacy laws across many countries were creating issues with marketing and product strategies. They wanted to leverage valuable information being collected about customers to sustain a competitive advantage and support higher value interaction with customers, but had to adhere to the United States and European Union privacy considerations.

- The EIM effort focused on Alignment, and developing sustainable business processes that would allow the company to manage and exploit customer data while remaining in compliance of privacy laws. There were significant data quality and governance issues to address as well.
- The EIM strategy resulted in a formal data governance program, and a series of closely managed projects that required BI, operational applications work, as well as business process changes.
- The global nature of this organization prevented formation of a centralized EIM area. However, a "virtual" EIM was put in place via the Data Governance organization, and the customer-centric EIM has expanded to other aspects of the business.

Company B
- This company is an international retailer. They found themselves squeezed by the mega-discount stores in product classes where prices were the main customer motivator, and the large "big box" specialty stores that also offered the same larger ticket items, but had more floor space. They used to qualify as a specialty retailer, but now must compete with general retail. In the flurry to find out what to sell, who their customers were now, and how to compete, many departmental databases were created. We were asked to initially develop a plan to reduce the expansion of end-user reporting and start to rationalize business reporting needs.
- After the assessments, it was obvious that there was more to do than consolidate departmental databases. There were profound issues with applications' delivery supplying any download or interface to any business area that asked, resulting in enormous data storage and management costs. The director of this area was incented based on a service model, so the more requests he fulfilled the more he was rewarded. However, the business areas were poorly educated as to how to do analytics. In addition, there were serious issues with catalogs, web sites, and other aspects of their merchandising business that affected everything from product availability to customer retention.
- An EIM program was designed and deployed. Product data "clean up" began, and the program improved data quality and streamlined analysis efforts. Even unstructured content around product merchandising was managed and improved. After two years, the only person not happy was the applications director. There was a change management effort, but the team was not permitted to use any firm techniques, and was basically an educational body. The CIO had run into some political battles and soft pedaled the aggressiveness of data governance.
- The lack of data governance created an opportunity for the applications director to build new alliances behind the scenes, and eventually was able to assume the CIO job after the current CIO retired. His/her first activity was to disband EIM. Many years later this shop was mostly outsourced. The retailer continues to struggle with its identity.

Farfel Emporiums Background

Ellen has a dilemma. As the new CIO of a major manufacturer/distributor and retailer, she inherited a mess. Farfel Emporiums is a retailer of specialty and novelty items. They have 82 stores sprinkled along the West Coast and southwest regions of the United States. Nearly all of its merchandise is imported and has long lead times. There are thousands of SKUs (stock keeping units), and Farfel has a tradition of having unique items such as exotic buttons. Farfel has always managed to identify fad items and is able to grab market presence before competitors.

Farfel as a company is almost 100 years old. The founder (C. W. Farfel) passed away but the family still sits on the board. Many employees at corporate offices started in the stores as stockers or checkout clerks. Average time of employment at Farfel is around 20 years.

Recently a series of events indicated the need to upgrade the company:

- A network issue caused a loss of stored data. It could not be recovered, and it took several days to reenter paper tickets. The quarterly statements to the SEC were late.
- The head of merchandising had retired the prior year, and Farfel found itself looking at competitors selling hot products while Farfel was not able to be stocked in time for the holiday shopping season. This individual was well respected and was able to coordinate product design, manufacturing, merchandising, and store operations. Her replacement was struggling to understand the 20–30 Excel spreadsheets left behind that were used to manage the merchandising area.
- Farfel has also found itself stuck with excessive amount of inventory of certain items that were historically steady sellers. There is a disagreement on the executive team over whether this is a result of over ordering, poor store performance, or a shift in consumer preferences. Respective VPs each brought their own supporting detailed analysis material to the meetings to prove they were correct.

While some major issues of connectivity and infrastructure have been addressed, Ellen has three major application packages (from three vendors) supporting most operations: replenishment, ERP for manufacturing, and warehouse management. The retail stores have a home-grown point-of-sale system (POS) that has a large backlog of requested updates and maintenance requests. A few years ago, Farfel's marketing area developed its own "data warehouse." The data contents are mildly satisfactory to the few marketing professionals who still use it. Annual maintenance on this product costs $1 million per year. Another "data warehouse" exists on an IBM mainframe, and it is used for some sales and store reporting, but the reports are tactical. None of the reports agrees with the general ledger or financial reports. Finally, finance recently created an analytical application for financial data analysis. It costs $4 million and is used by 10 financial analysts.

All of this would seem to be enough, but Ellen and her peer executives just found out that their once burgeoning company is rapidly losing market share to general merchandise companies. These new competitors are now selling products similar to the specialty lines offered by her company. Additionally, many of their unique items are now available on the Internet, and the Farfel web site was implemented in reaction to this challenge. The heat is on Ellen to come up with technology solutions to the market share and merchandising problems, and, of course, all the functional heads are crying for data to assist in the battle.

The last straw was a recent visit by Wall Street analysts who compared Ellen's operation to that of behemoths like WalMart and Target. While there were some justifiable differences, the Wall Street types felt that better IT should be a priority for Farfel, or the stock price would stay low. This was the first exposure of Farfel's executive team to a concept that information was somehow tied to the value of the company, in this case, equity.

1. There are currently four major information project requests and proposals on Ellen's desk. One is to reengineer the delivery of production reports. The justification and objectives are based on decreases in delivery times of operational reports, and the labor savings in operations for report distribution staff. The ROI is calculated at 8% on a $12 million project. This information was provided by the consulting firm bidding for the project. Data will be gathered from the packages and other operational applications, consolidated, and presented for operational and tactical reporting.
2. Marketing wants a system to develop customer segmentation and market-basket analysis. They have contacted an external data provider to clean up names and addresses.
3. There is a request for a major revision to the balanced score card—at this time it takes general ledger data and produces some high-level metrics. Management wants data that can be drilled down into, and reflects an operational view vs. a financial view. The project stems from a long-standing argument on what actual sales are, and what percentage of the market the company owns. Sales reports to upper management are from various sources, and are in consistent conflict with each other, depending on the source of the data, and the analyst developing the report.
4. The store managers want help in managing store layout and assisting customers to find what they need. Regular customers are also asking for features found on competing web sites and in-store kiosks.
5. Finally, and seemingly unrelated, there is a request to explore new content management software for the product development and catalog area. Apparently the company web site is not maintained well, and there have been customer complaints of different prices in stores vs. the web site, and also differences in product features.

Ellen realizes that she is on the horns of a dilemma. She has immediate needs for more information, but she cannot continue to propagate stand-alone solutions. She needs immediate help, and a long-term framework that has to be built bottom-up. Some of the issues stem from the old and new operational applications, in that they present incompatible models for reporting and data use. While she can't change the code of a package vendor, Ellen realizes that there has to be some consideration of the operational data and correcting it, or finding a way to make it more in alignment across the packages and legacy applications.

The fact that they already have "data warehouses" means that a new one or revisions to the current instantiations are going to be hard to sell.

The content management project is icing on the cake. There are enough problems with rows and columns type data being all over the place; now it seems crucial unstructured content is becoming unmanageable and the window of opportunity for a competitive web site is closing.

"Well, where there is chaos, there is opportunity," Ellen mumbled to herself. She thought, "There is an awful lot of overlap in these issues, I think there is business support, but there are enough differences to make it hard to find leverage … but there has to be a way."

Farfel Emporiums Case Approach

By now the cagey reader will grasp that there is a role for EIM in this case study. There are some twists. Farfel has some real "burning platform" issues, so perhaps change management won't be an issue? And there seems to be a consideration here for web sites, catalogs, and such areas that are not "rows and columns." On the other hand, there are some classic symptoms appearing—lost market share, uncertainty of consumer behavior, and retention of expertise. And the company has a lot of embedded experience that can be of use, or a huge obstacle.

Facts from Data Collection

Annual gross sales	$1,750,000,000
Stores	82
Customers	Average customer visits three times per year; would like to see that increase to four

Market environment
- Unique specialty products that were the core business are now being offered by "big box" retail outlets.
- Web site generates little revenue, less than $10 million per year, but an outside analysis shows most site users leave the site before entering an order.
- Market share—hard to tell, never really had to worry about it.

Stated issues
- Merchandising area—Farfel could not get last Christmas season's hot toy in time to meet demand, and was advertised in the catalog but Farfel issued rain checks.
- Operational applications are very diverse—the home-grown POS system has to interface with the ERP and distribution system, the warehouse system, and the financial systems. Most requests in the applications development area are to connect or interface applications to others, or consolidate data from various sources and provide a department with a report or file.
- Customer relations—the web site seems to be chasing away the younger demographic, but this is a supposition and not proved.
- Products—creating the catalogs and performing merchandising tasks are chaotic since the former VP left. There is no collaboration evident between product design, store operations, and merchandise procurement.

EIM Assessments

Farfel did two assessments: a combined Readiness and Change Capacity, and a Data Quality survey. Therefore, the summary shows highlights of the two surveys, with details as to the Culture or Information Maturity (Table 13.7).

Table 13.7 Assessment Summary Farfel

Farfel Emporiums EIM Assessment—Summary		
Findings	**Impact**	**Risk**
Business Readiness		
Reactive response to data issues has produced disjointed applications. Departmental computing costs are far above industry averages. 50,000 Access databases consume more storage than entire amount of data stored on applications and decision support systems.	False sense of security, lots of data are laying around. But there is excessive effort to get numbers right and get work done.	Severe—organization is already operating with excessive levels of overhead for data. Divisions are unable to respond to market changes or drivers anywhere near competitors' response times.
No evidence of any formal alignment of business to IT projects. Most projects start after a business area funds the effort and work is done "to order." IT department is geared for reaction, and little collaboration occurs between applications groups.	Regardless of return, lack of ROI allows "unfocusing" on goals, and risks incomplete information content. Accountability and vision are hard to see. Obvious lack of data integration.	Severe—no motivation or incentive to correct current bad data habits in business or IT area. Lack of accountability equals lack of enterprise focus.
Change Capacity		
The company relies heavily on embedded knowledge and experience. Longevity is a performance metric.	There is no retention of knowledge learned. Loss of staff equals risk of losing capability.	Serious—reliance on experience and failure to capture workflows or departmental knowledge can result in more issues.
Culture is "if it isn't broke, don't fix it." Changing how things are done (the definition of culture) is perceived as a threat to the evolved order of things. Most of the time persisting with the old actions (The Farfel Way) will be the strategy to deal with new challenges.	The culture does not recognize severity of issues and will resist any attempts to change.	Severe—any change to current habits will result in push back. EIM effort will need to clearly indicate what is working now and promote future state.
Data Quality		
Most core subject areas contain data that is unsuitable for decision-making. Some operational issues are also rooted in DQ problems.	There is a tangible cost to Farfel from DQ. IT affects ability to react and ability to perform as efficiently as possible. The good news is this can be captured and presented to management.	Serious—there is a great deal of remediation required for DQ. The good news is it most likely has a hard dollar return.
Areas where content needs to be managed and tracked are deficient, e.g., the web site and catalog areas. Product descriptions are out of date, and good performance is too dependent on information inside people's heads.	Obvious issues with web site, merchandising, and store operations. There is a clear cost to the business here.	Serious—Farfel is noncompetitive in this area. Market share is at stake, and the business case should take steps to include the cost of not correcting content management.

EIM Alignment

We will follow the alignment items through vision on into where they appear on the Road Map. The example later shows a portion of the strategic plan for Farfel. In reality, this type of artifact may depict a dozen or so enterprise initiatives with associated goals and objectives. Farfel did not conduct the "value uses" exercise. Resistance was too high from day one. So we managed available ties with executives very carefully, and performed a semi-underground analysis that went straight to levers, Business Information Requirements (BIRs), and actions. In addition, the lack of any solid workflows at all pushed this EIM effort into deeper areas of content and process design.

TIP FOR SUCCESS

While the examples show a decomposition, and derivation of metrics and requirements, let's face it—most industries are mature enough that 70–80% of the information and content needs can be derived from a standard model. In fact, this is what we do, especially after the fourth or fifth retailer or insurance company. A transparent strategy and decomposition into a solid baseline set of EIM/IAM requirements does not take very long. The EIM team should concentrate on that 30–20% of data and content needs where you are going to differentiate yourself (Table 13.8).

Table 13.8 Farfel Alignment Decomposition

Farfel Emporiums Summarized Goals

Driver	Goal	Documented Objectives	Measurable Attributes
Improve market share	Recover lead market share in category	Regain market share of 25%	Market share
	Increase top line sales across all categories and stores	Increase same store sales 15% over three years	Same store sales, forecasted vs. actual
Increase customer interactions	Improve customer experience	Increase visits per store from three to four per year	Store visits, market-basket return
		Improve service environment, highlight differences	Surveyed opinions
	Improve effectiveness of web site	Improve web site sales 15% without cannibalizing store sales	Percentage of sales from web site
		Integrate store and web site offerings	Frequency of assortment refresh. New products per season

(Continued)

Table 13.8 (Continued)

Farfel Emporium's Summarized Goals			
Driver	**Goal**	**Documented Objectives**	**Measurable Attributes**
	Increase repeat visits with more household awareness	Capture customer feedback, integrate findings into marketing	Store traffic
Product innovation	Offer a selection of products and services most profitable for target segments	Beat competitors to market on new products	Time to market averages for specified product
		Implement the most appropriate and profitable product mix, allowing for regional and local variations	Same-stores-sales, category product turns
	Maintain accurate merchandising processes	Improve procurement and store communications	Elimination of missed products or out of stocks
	Improve R&D to recognize new opportunities	Gain insight into Generation x, y buying patterns	Demographic, psychographic trends
Improve operational efficiency	Improve management of merchandise inventory assets	Reduce weeks of supply across appropriate product classes	Weeks of supply
		Improve cash flow and asset management to improve current ratios	Current ratio, inventory turns, and weeks of supply
	Identify business processes that can be improved to increase profits	Improve processes through more efficient collaboration	SG&A expenses, cycle times, division results
	Optimize store performance	Monitor and assist stores with declining performance of more than 3% gross sales decline	Same-store-sales, geographic, and demographic sales potential
		Eliminate/relocate bottom 5% of stores	Same-store-sales, geographic, and demographic sales potential
	Reduce SG&A	Reduce "shadow IT" to competitive or industry standard levels	Total cost of ownership for data usage, IT, and business areas

EIM Vision

Vision is a combination of graphic and preliminary requirements. Figure 13.5 is the Farfel vision for how the business will view the EIM environment. It is extremely conceptual, as the culture was not accustomed to any kind of presentation of integrated information. Table 13.9 shows a high-level view

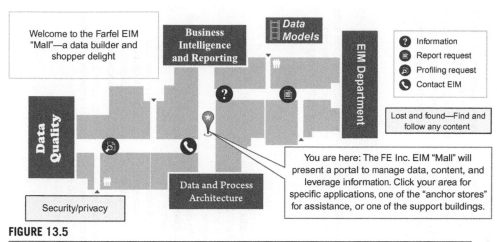

FIGURE 13.5

Farfel Vision

of the business case. Note we added more detailed levers and started to drive into measurable actions (remember, we needed to show the business something to get their attention and present the poor facts of the current situation).

Farfel management disclosed that a return to former market position and then keeping up with competitor growth would require a 25% increase in gross sales over three years. This was a large and unreasonable number to apply to the EIM program. There was an unwillingness to do a formal analysis of IRR and NPV, but the management team recognized the potential returns from using information after seeing the actions and levers derived by the EIM team. It was decided to base the EIM business targets (no business case was requested, but the EIM team asked to produce targets anyway) on the free cash flow available to go after the restoration of market share. This amount was $120,000,000, and the team based its benefits on $30 million (25%) of that amount. In other words, if the EIM project could help acquire a 25% bump in free cash, the business was amenable to seeing the rest of the EIM strategy. Benefits were prorated across the business actions. A subset is shown in Table 13.9, with the benefits from the process and product use of data staking a claim on prorating $20 million of the free cash.

EIM Business Model

The Farfel metrics are retail/wholesale metrics, and some of these are in Part 2. Farfel, however, had to take a close look at processes, so the Business Model phase drove into some details. The example of one area where the team drove into redoing business processes to achieve full-content leverage is given in Figure 13.6. If this resembles the value chain metaphor, you are correct. This is the beginning of refining business processes to maximize the IVC.

Table 13.9 UIC Business Case

Related Goal	Information Usage as a Product—Build into Offerings		Information Usage as a Process—Improve Cycle Times, Lower Costs		Benefit Potential (000's)
	Levers, Actions	Objectives	Levers, Actions	Objectives	
Improve customer experience	Determine level of attention (or avoid harassing) in-store shoppers; determine easier product location layout	Increase customer shopping satisfaction; increase revisits; improved customer satisfaction; increased sales	Explore use of self-checkout; develop online order, in-store pickup capability	Increase visits per store from three to four per year; improve service environment, highlight differences	$7,216
		Increase revisits; improved customer satisfaction; increased sales	Develop/supply customer profile/score at POS touch points to offer promotions affinity cards, repeat purchase ease	Increased promotional sales; more effective sales into more profitable segments	
Improve effectiveness of web site	Improve online ordering experience with access to order history	Improve web site sales 15% without cannibalizing store sales; integrate store and web site offerings	Store online information securely to avoid reentry	Increased promotional sales; more effective sales into more profitable segments	n/a
Offer a selection of products and services most profitable for target segments	Analyze Internet activity to adjust in-store inventory and products	Beat competitors to market on new products; decreased carrying costs; increased customer satisfaction; increased sales in targeted areas	n/a	n/a	
	Target-specific demographics based on product type/customer propensity	Implement the most appropriate and profitable product mix, allowing for regional and local variations	Offer products based on profiles and propensity ahead of time via e-mail notifications	Increased customer satisfaction	$2,887
Improve R&D to recognize new opportunities	Fine tune product offerings in store and web site sections	Gain insight into Generation x, y buying patterns	Order big demand items to grab market share before competitors	Increased sales in targeted segments	$1,443
Increase repeat visits with more household awareness	Capture customer feedback, integrate findings into marketing	Decreased mailing costs via target e-mails, or household mailings	Offer up-sell promotions at POS or web site to targeted households	Increased repeat customer purchases; increased product awareness; increased repeat visits	$7,216
Improve management of merchandise inventory assets	Provide better demand data to suppliers to reduce in-store stock levels	Decreased support and system costs; increased employee satisfaction (no longer have to go in circles to get the product info they need—regardless of department); wider product selection, increased store traffic and selling opportunities	Reduce weeks of supply across appropriate product classes through "just-in-time" restocking	Shorten cycle times to restock improved cash flow, balance sheet	$1,237
	Improve cash flow and asset management to improve current ratios	Improved current ratio, inventory turns, and weeks of supply	n/a	n/a	n/a

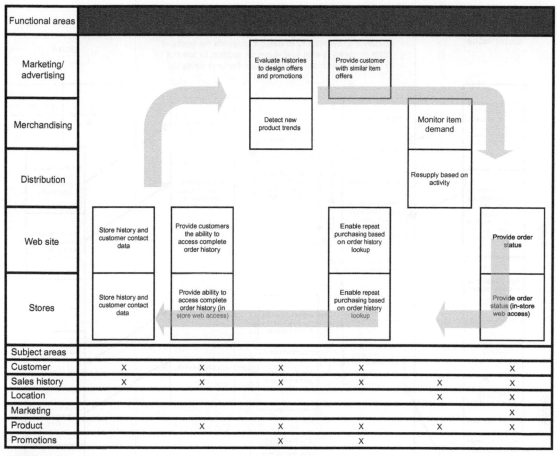

FIGURE 13.6

Farfel sample business action

EIM Architecture

Since we started presenting a small portion of refined processes, Figure 13.7 was included to show the end result. The various models are analyzed and the high-value processes are used to influence the data management and movement elements in the overall EIM architecture. The sample shows processes from the example in Figure 13.6 and one other merged and optimized for the customer area. Processes where using customer data adds value or contributes toward achieving goals are isolated and streamlined. This optimization step leverages process refinement and/or workflow design if you are doing work in those areas.

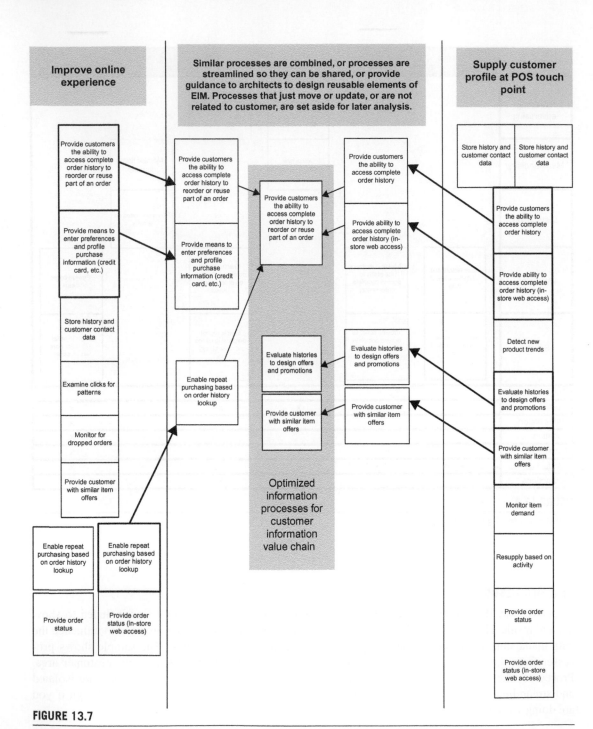

FIGURE 13.7

Farfel optimized IVC

Table 13.10 Farfel EIM Organization Principle

Information Is an Asset Principle

Description

The dictionary defines asset as "anything owned that has value." Information is an enterprise-wide asset that will be leveraged across Farfel to improve operational efficiency, enhance competitive advantage, and accelerate decision-making. It will be managed like other business assets, such as financial assets.

Rationale

- Successful delivery of achievement of corporate strategy depends on conclusions derived from accurate, well-maintained, timely, and secure information.
- Present a safe, accurate set of data to our customers and other stakeholders that adheres to privacy regulations.
- Farfel requires best-in-class enterprise information resource to be competitive.
- Many of Farfel's goals cannot be accomplished without well-managed information.
- All types of data, including data on forms and e-mails, present opportunity and risk that must be balanced by Farfel.

Implications

- The enterprise information resource must be managed from a formal organization, using an approach not unlike auditing. This function must be clearly responsible for the definition and application of data management policies and including software development, legal compliance, reporting, and operations. Asset treatment of data means governance over data modeling; data design; selection, implementation, and use of data management software; and performance of all responsibilities that comprise "data store life cycle management" (validation, configuration control, backup and recovery, privacy, security, etc.).
- Information resources will be designed and implemented with enterprise-wide management and use in mind.
- Information must be shared to maximize the effectiveness of business decision-making and maintain a competitive cost of data ownership.
- Information must be controlled, tracked, audited, and protected.
- Information must be assigned to parties who are designated and held accountable, and all stakeholders who handle or use data will have clearly defined responsibilities and accountability to ensure integrity and discipline.
- Formal information management principles and practices must be instituted to ensure prudent, effective, efficient, and secure use of enterprise data resources.

There are a plethora of architecture pictures in Parts 1 and 2. For Farfel, I included a look at one of their principles in detail, so the reader can see the implications of actually applying information principles to an enterprise (Table 13.10).

EIM Road Map

Given the cultural resistance and relative immaturity of Farfel, the Road Map focuses less on projects, and more on the activities that will be required to make the disciplined use of information "stick" (Figure 13.8).

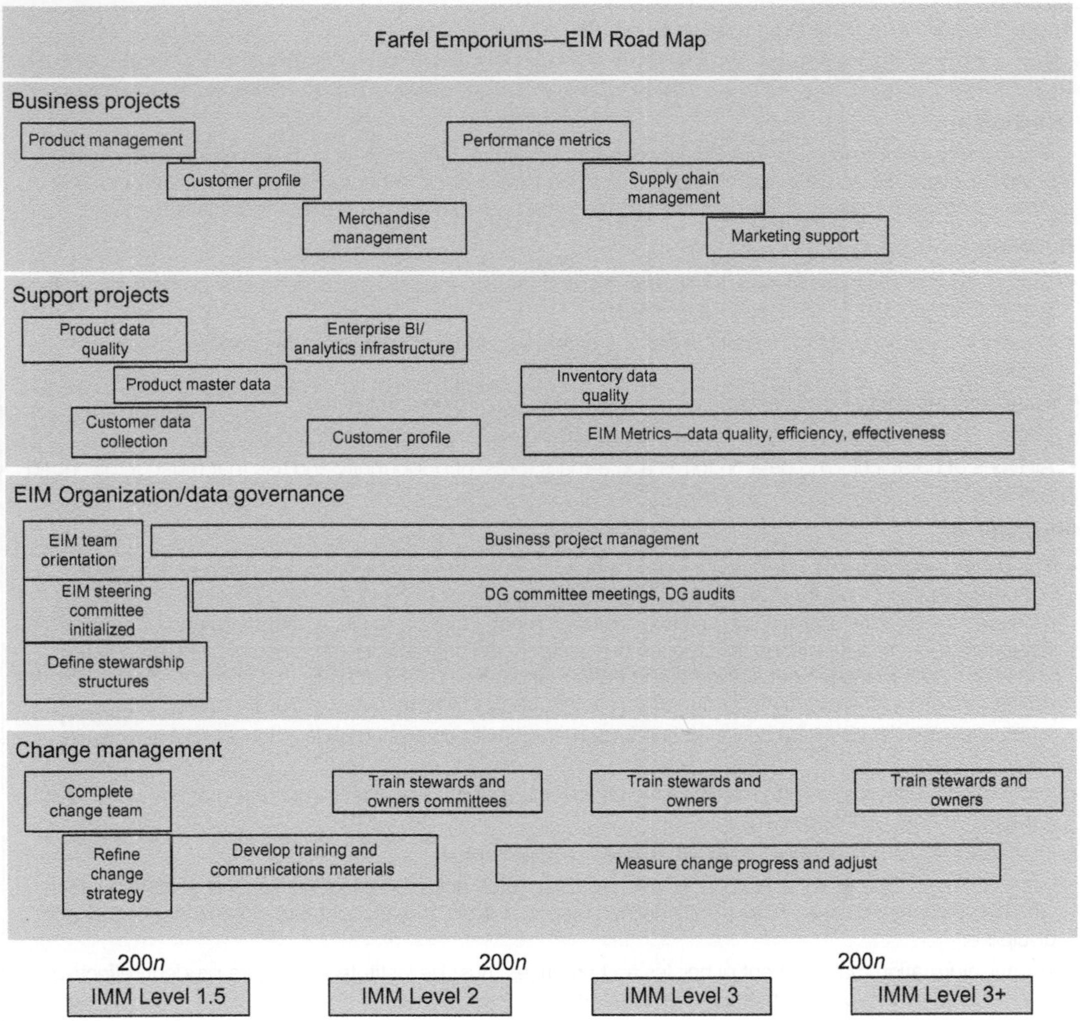

FIGURE 13.8

Farfel Road Map showing IMM

EIM Sustaining Plan

The Sustaining Plan presented to Management is a recap of the Change Management strategy, since most of the success at Farfel after the EIM program starts will revolve around change management (Figure 13.9).

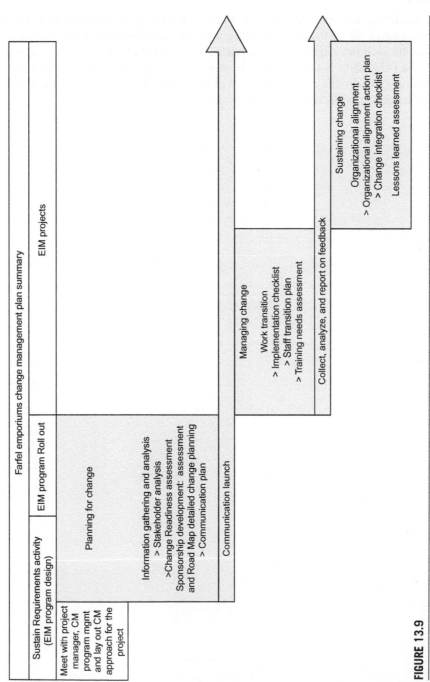

FIGURE 13.9

Farfel sustaining change management summary

SUMMARY

A business leader sponsoring, initiating, or leading an EIM program needs to make sure business alignment permeates all of the work. Starting with an understanding of business plans, the earlier examples emphasized the alignment of the business. The EIM program is launched with credibility. In addition, the EIM effort is sustainable; it is easy to revisit documented directions and make adjustments as business conditions change. Part 2 will cover the "How" in terms of activity and artifacts that actually define the projects and organizations.

Final Words for Part 1

14

It may be hard for an egg to turn into a bird: it would be a jolly sight harder for it to learn to fly while remaining an egg. We are like eggs at present. And you cannot go on indefinitely being just an ordinary, decent egg. We must be hatched or go bad.

C. S. Lewis

CONTENTS

An executive in a health insurance company once told me, "The guy with the best data wins." Automated and digital data, information, and content are all an integral part of any organization. Regardless of business size, model, for profit or nonprofit, government or private, there are desktops, laptops, filing cabinets, and recordings all sitting there waiting to help achieve the enterprise's goals, or suck up cost and incur liability. Hopefully, this book has made the point if you think of all of that content as an asset (or liability) you need to manage it. IAM is a philosophy and business discipline. EIM is the program whereby we apply that discipline. This chapter will summarize Part 1 by identifying the five most important EIM lessons and top three EIM success factors for an executive to take away.

The fact is, all organizations are managing information anyway. It can be done by default (as is the case with the majority) or by design. Someone is managing data or e-mail. Data is being entered, collected, processed, and manipulated. We have multitudes of data warehouses, MDM, content management systems, data analysts, and tools and tools and more tools. Since we keep spending money on this stuff, and since the level of satisfaction with most IT shops is poor, we are obviously still missing something. And we find at the base of all of the various initiatives a list of common success factors: Buy-in, sponsorship, data quality, and acceptance and support of standards and policy. If all of these initiatives have the same success factors, maybe we should reverse our perspective. Rather than apply them to each project, why not make them policy? Why not do EIM *by design*? The issue becomes how well you apply IAM. Without doubt, you are doing some form of EIM, but maybe you are not doing it well.

Managing information and managing information as an asset can seem to be two very different processes. Historically, we have managed data and information a number of ways, depending on

Making Enterprise Information Management (EIM) Work for Business. DOI: 10.1016/B978-0-12-375695-4.00014-X

where it was being used or created. Documents are managed differently than databases. The premise of this book has been if we manage information *as an asset*, any issues with different content or technology are subordinate to an overarching set of principles and policies that ensure increased value and reduced risk. EIM aims to strengthen balance sheets and income statements through accomplishing business goals.

Granted, that means accepting some new processes and policies. Some changes in behavior are in order, but deep down we have to admit we have been attempting these changes since the 1970s. Since it is always good to leave a reader with a "Top Three" list, let us start with the three most significant processes and policies within EIM that must be accepted. None of them is new to any corporate leader. They will sound familiar. EIM just implements them before they are pointed out as a "success factor" after the fact.

TOP THREE SUCCESS FACTORS FOR EIM

1. The need for Change Management is a fact. Deploying any initiative within the realm of EIM means, by definition, *someone has to do something differently tomorrow than they are doing it today,* and those kinds of changes must be managed. Would you implement a new sales process without training the sales force? Did you do Six Sigma or ISO 9000 without orientation and on-going measurement?
2. Data Governance must be an official process, and held in the same regard as internal audit, or corporate compliance. Remember, the reason you are considering *any* aspect of EIM or are curious about IAM is you are concerned about achieving business goals with your current IM processes. The root cause of 99% of your concern is a *failure to govern the development and use of data.*
3. Data Quality must be a mandate with accountability. Data quality is the function that must exist to ensure the content and data are usable and effective. *Mishandling content is as bad as mishandling inventory or customers.* If no one is held accountable for ensuring effectiveness and usability of data, then data quality will never be a priority.

There are also five core concepts that should be taken away from this book. They are truly lessons learned, and can be applied to EIM whether you need to implement IAM in small increments, or are addressing significant larger challenges.

TOP FIVE EIM CONCEPTS

1. *The "E" stands for Enterprise*—We must reinforce one more time that EIM is an enterprise effort. To allow the EIM program oversight, rules, standards, and functions to be localized is equivalent to saying we will have accounting controls, so everyone go make up your own. If you acknowledge information as an asset, then you accept the implication there is a balance sheet impact within your data and content. EIM is at minimum a federated approach with central policies defined and enforced. *You must think globally, but can act locally.* All efforts are aligned with, and justified by, business or organization needs. There is no request line: leadership determines strategy, strategy determines EIM.

2. *EIM is a business program*—The EIM sponsor needs to be a businessperson, with high enough position to speak for the enterprise in terms of strategy and business direction. The CIO is not a valid sponsor of EIM. He/she may be accountable to lead and deploy, but should never sponsor. The EIM program must have business support, so all of the various nuances of treating information as an asset can occur in a supportive (read *governed*) environment. This also means that EIM is accountable for predetermined, measurable goals. We expressed these as business projects. EIM is explicitly aligned with the business.

3. *The only way to eat an elephant is one bite at a time*—We made sure you understood that all the EIM elements are not needed in one big bang. In fact, it is not recommended. We recommend you roll out EIM incrementally, or focus on key subdisciplines, like data quality. The *oversight* is enterprise wide. The *benefits and measurements of success* are enterprise wide. For example, implement a product profitability project as part of a BI framework. Or implement by function, as in implementing data governance oversight as part of data quality, ERP, or a master data effort.

    EIM does not have to add much incremental cost. There are already existing information-type projects. Many companies have ERP software (like SAP, Oracle) that are not fulfilling the promised benefits. There are BI islands everywhere in almost every company and organization we have worked in. Consolidating and managing the information and content aspects of all these under one program is not costly and just makes plain good sense.

4. *EIM solves a logistics problem*—The ultimate goal for any IT project has been to get the correct content to the proper user at the proper time, with no more or no less than is needed. We stated earlier that this is a logistics problem. No matter if you are doing a subdiscipline, a pilot of a subdiscipline, initiating full-blown EIM, or revisiting the program in place, you are managing a value chain, which is most likely a concept already in place in your organization. Businesspeople tend to perceive a value chain as an assembly line, with a parade of consumed parts and materials marching by. But the information value chain is more of a river. The benefits come from the current, and interaction with the river. There is energy in the river, but the river is not energy. There is value in the data, but the data is not intrinsically valuable until it is used.

5. *EIM is not self-sustaining*—This means disciplined activities to manage from a current state (which has been stated as not desirable) to some future state (which we defined as desirable by aligning with the business). People accept the *need* for change readily. A person actually embracing and moving through a period of change is another story. We have acknowledged that formally managing change is a critical success factor. The concept of sustaining EIM is where we apply most of the change management. EIM will create resistance. The resistance can be sneaky as well as obvious. Three things can happen when an organization chooses to move from a current state to a new state:

    a. The resistance to change is not overcome, and there is reversion to the prior state.
    b. The pain of transition is too great, but the old state is unacceptable, so the organization "falls out," i.e., it stops working, or people leave.
    c. The organization reaches the future state.

EIM also requires measurement, oversight, and proactive management to ensure achieving *sustaining* the future state. EIM must prove it is contributing to the enterprise. Measurements and feedback must be collected and analyzed, and then EIM must adapt to what the measures and feedback have disclosed.

SUMMARY

There is something in this book to help you. Remember, even a few EIM elements (if done with the big picture in mind) will go a long way. Just approach with the following in mind:

Your information and content is an asset. Your organization already invests heavily in infrastructure, personnel, and time to deal with this asset. Most employment agreements mention "safeguarding company assets" or something to that effect. Aren't you really just doing your job by moving away from managing information by default to IAM? The reality is you are doing EIM *now*. You are merely choosing between the status quo and an IAM mind-set.

Thank you for your investment in this book. I hope it adds value through its use the same way your organization will increase value through use of its own data and content.

If there are any questions, thoughts, war stories, or feedback, let others know at www.imcue.com/EIM4BIZBLOG or www.EIMforbusiness.com/EIM4BIZBLOG.

If you have your own techniques, ideas, tips, or processes and would like to share them, add to our Wiki at www.imcue.com/EIM4BIZWIKI or www.EIMforbusiness.com/EIM4BIZWIKI.

Introduction to Part 2: EIM Overview for Managers

15

Make it so, number one.
Captain Jean Luc Piccard

CONTENTS

If you have decided to start this book here rather than at the beginning, go back and read Chapters 1–3. We will review the same concepts here from a middle management perspective, but understanding the information presented to the executives will help provide context for what is presented here.

While Part 2 of this book leans more toward details, it is still presenting EIM and its underlying philosophy of IAM from a *business perspective.*

If you are reading this book only to drive out a list of tools and technology, and sniff out a few vendors, contact the author. It is not in here. If you are looking for powerful details on subdisciplines of EIM, like data quality, data warehouse, or MDM, look at the bibliography. Granted, these items are important aspects of EIM. They may even be important within the context of the reader's role in an organization. But individual projects that manage information do not matter very much in terms of the success of EIM and IAM. (If you build a house, you will need to determine if you use steel or wood for the frame, but the actual design, construction, and using of the house goes on regardless of what is in the walls.) Sadly, there is a track record of most business projects setting the sole criterion for success as the successful deployment of a single project.

MAKE IT SO

Figure 15.1 is the deployment strategy most of us wish we had when we implemented a technology or program that, while offering great value, required an organization to revisit philosophy, process, and

FIGURE 15.1

Scan of make it so[1]

policy, and make some internal changes. Apologies in advance for the image—it has been duplicated hundreds of times.

The reality of EIM or any of its subdisciplines is it requires a lot more engineering, cultural hand-holding, and changes to staff and organizations than any of us ever realize. Anyone one who has dabbled in one of the subdisciplines (e.g., MDM, data warehouse, or content management) has discovered by now that it is not easy making a business change data habits, measure business results, and then sustain the necessary changes.

From Chapters 1–3, you should have at least gleaned the following:

- "Data as an Asset" is more than a metaphor. Treating data as an asset means changes to organizational models, within IT and the business.
- We can build a business case, and align EIM with business directions.
- EIM is a program, and requires incremental deployment.
- If you are doing a data warehouse or other subdiscipline, you are doing EIM. If you are doing a large ERP application to integrate your data, you are doing EIM. You are just choosing to proceed with less organization and forgoing long-term benefits.
- Over time, EIM does not incrementally cost a great deal more in terms of staff or even technology than what you are currently investing. The goal is to reduce long-term spending on IT and content handling technology.
- Information maturity is a goal, but it is not to be pursued blindly; many changes are required in day-to-day activities, and you have to seek the appropriate maturity level.

This chapter will cover the finer points of the IAM concepts, and more directly, how it affect those of us who have to "make it so." We will cover some definitions, frame EIM as a program, and make sure the components and the details of EIM are understood. From a high level, we will also present the process to develop the EIM program and set the stage for the remainder of this book.

INFORMATION ASSET MANAGEMENT

Chapters 1–3 delved into the executive view of IM. It is a business issue. I will stand firm that it is not a technology challenge, but a business challenge to manage content and data. Once it is made a business challenge, then the challenges of buy-in and justification become manageable. The technology or style of implementation is almost irrelevant.

What does it mean for middle management after the CEO says to "make it so?" IAM is defined as the philosophies, principles, policies, and technologies to ensure that data, information, and content are all treated as an asset in the true accounting sense, avoiding increased risk and cost due to data and content misuse, poor handling, or exposure to regulatory scrutiny. Your role is to translate this definition into more tangible requirements.

Philosophies and Principles

You cannot implement a philosophy. It can create a feeling or belief system, but an organization cannot just go "manage information." Some details are required. In the case of IAM, the principles generated by the philosophy provide the bridge for taking the belief in IAM and building it into the program for deployment. Principles are statements of belief designed to frame actions. They are applied every day as guidance for procedures and decision-making efforts. As you move toward an EIM program, you will need to discern principles that are business oriented and those that are more technology oriented. Business principles will be more challenging to get accepted than technology principles.

If an organization states, "We believe information is an asset," then they have expressed a philosophy. If they then say, "Our information and content will be treated as assets according to established policies," then the philosophy is a principle.

Policies are consistent, repeatable processes that implement the agreed-upon guiding principles. It can be said right up front that your management challenges will revolve around implementation of proactive policies, such as data quality and governance. Policies will create processes and standards.

In terms of scope, it is easy to see that IAM cannot be a "local" program. In our firm, my teams will often hear "we will implement EIM in one area." Or "we will do IAM on our business intelligence data, but not the production data." Neither one of these is an implementation of IAM. Nor is it EIM. Our client has described a project. This does not mean the project is bad, or of no value. But it does mean the organization has not addressed IAM as a philosophy. IAM may be a wish of a department head, and the ideal is lurking in the back of people's minds. A manager needs to be very honest about either adopting the philosophy or just being influenced by it. You can deploy the EIM program incrementally. But if there is not an enterprise "push," valuable cycles are wasted as staff start to look like Don Quixote going after those EIM windmills.

TIP FOR SUCCESS

Remember, you can implement the various components and frameworks that make up EIM/IAM, like data warehouse or MDM. You will be able to achieve value with diligence and hard work. But there will always be a disconnect somewhere. Most companies operate this way. They do an MDM project and ask me, "How do I get buy-in?" or "How do I get data governance to work with MDM?" Then they do a data quality project and ask the same questions. EIM answers these questions *first for all of the IM-related projects*. That is why IAM requires a business mind-set. As passionate an IT or business manager you are, you cannot do IAM unless your enterprise is convinced that the IAM philosophy will move the organization further along than simply implementing one-off projects that resemble it. One expert analyst in the information field has predicted "... enterprises without an overall, long-term MDM strategy run the ironic risk of building "MDM silos.[2]" The very efforts we take to fix data issues will create new data issues without EIM.

Data, information, and content are part of the IAM definition and are used interchangeably in this book. Usually, I say "data and content" to cover the spectrum. At other times, the word "information" is used to represent all types of enterprise content, whether it is in rows and columns, paper or digital, or streamed media or recorded voice. As a business leader, you can certainly choose to address one type of content before the others (usually rows and columns' content gets heavy treatment first) but IAM covers it all. Technologies will rapidly stop differentiating between documents and spreadsheets as the twenty-first century unwinds. As the distinction in content disappears, areas of your enterprise will start to interoperate, whereas historically they have been separate. The "document management" area will require management in the same manner as customer data.

Accounting treatment does not mean the CFO's office will take over the web sites or data controls. It means that data and content needs to be viewed differently than in the past. In Chapters 1–3 we mentioned the use of information as a lubricant, i.e., data makes corporate functions move more smoothly. We then contrasted the twenty-first century direction of data and content as the "fuel." Information provides the energy of commerce and forms the foundation to direct an organization's activities. The asset view also means that anyone who touches data or content cannot do so in isolation. "I am going to download data, tweak it because I know it is not exact, and then produce a financial report," are words that should never be heard. Many organizations have found themselves in a strange position; after promoting end-user BI for years, they are asking businesspeople to rein in the spread of data that is occurring.[3] We have departmental capabilities that, while appearing to produce excellent analysis and effectiveness of data, are causing risks and costs to escalate. It is not uncommon for a major function in a company to have developed data gathering, entry, and reporting capabilities over a period of years to such an extent that 50% of staff and budget is dedicated, in effect, to information handling. The redundancy alone is causing stunning cost issues in companies. A common scenario is one where a large company will have deployed analysis tools, Excel and Access to business areas, and these "downstream" data processing areas actually use more computing resources than all the other centralized applications and databases. One large company with which I spoke stopped counting at 500,000 *active* Access databases. The sheer cost of inefficiencies alone makes this an asset management issue.

Think of the risk of all of this content that can leave the company on a flash drive or a poorly constructed report. While this book was being written, I received two credit cards from different institutions which had lost or allowed social security and account numbers to get outside of their enterprise. In one case, the bank issued 2 million credit cards. This is not inexpensive. The *risk and cost due to data and content misuse, poor handling, or exposure to regulatory scrutiny* also requires a much different mind-set than is currently in place in many organizations.

The last aspect of the definition of IAM we will touch upon is **Technology**. The placement of this part of the definition of IAM is deliberately at the end of the discussion. IAM can be done with 1970s technology if need be. But IAM technology requires some capabilities that have been poorly addressed. If we apply the accounting lens, we require these capabilities to:

- Track discrete "pieces" of data or content, counting usage, as well as create, update, and delete
- Track and associate how the data is used with specific business targets
- Balance data assets across functions as well as applications
- Assess risk or exposure at will that may be embedded in information.

As you can see, IAM becomes a way of thinking. In fact, the IAM mind-set promises significantly easier data and content management once adopted, as we will see.

ENTERPRISE INFORMATION MANAGEMENT

EIM is the program that manages enterprise information assets to support the business and improve value. EIM manages the plans, policies, principles, frameworks, technologies, organizations, people, and processes in an enterprise toward the goal of maximizing the investment in data and content.

IAM is the underlying philosophy for EIM. EIM implements IAM. EIM wraps people and processes and investment around the IAM concept in the form of a strategic corporate program. As with the IAM definition, let's break it down to get an idea of what, as managers, we will need to build.

When we state that EIM manages **People**, we are addressing several aspects of human capital. Not only will we ask for acceptance of a new mind-set or priority (i.e., *our* data takes precedence over *my* data), we will also be affecting a number of other areas.

- *Behavior and culture*—Usually, a new mind-set requires a change in behavior. Adjusting individual behavior can be very difficult. However, when an organization must change its collective behavior, the sum of behavior change is even greater than the parts. EIM needs to be as aware of human capital issues as it is aware of technology or process issues. Remember, there is now substantial momentum for departments acting as mini-IT departments. At minimum, prying some of this capability away creates process issues, at maximum, political chaos.
- *Organization*—There will most likely be a few new titles or organization structures. Increased need for oversight, the required improvement in data quality and so forth, will require governance and more participation by business personnel in data matters. The new organizational structures need to be formally designed. Concepts such as ownership, custodial duty, and stewardship will create new roles and accountabilities.

We also affect **Process** with EIM. There are new processes, or perhaps modifications of similar processes. There are new means to get efforts started and completed as well. The process areas EIM affects are:

- *Governance/compliance*—The most obvious impact is in the area of ensuring standards, and policies for content handling are followed. In addition there will be a large tie-in with regulatory oversight, so the compliance areas are involved, and governance areas are enhanced or created. EIM program designers will need to consider process changes or new protocols for working with these areas.
- *Applications development*—The area that develops systems used by the business will most likely cause the greatest concern to the EIM team. There will be behavior changes and realigning performance objectives, but they will be initiated by changing development processes. Many organizations have formal processes defined to develop software. These methodologies must be modified to allow for governance and consider new standards and policies.
- *Key events and daily processes*—Critical business events, such as order entry, claims payment, approval cycles, underwriting, product development, all have one activity in common—they

Table 15.1 The "Algebra" of Information Value
Where C = Create, U = Update, D = Delete, R = Read
R represents Usage, i.e., we "read" content to take action and improve the organization, thereby creating an increase in Value, or V. Therefore the success of R depends on V. If Value = Usage, and Usage = R, then Value = $R_{benefit}$
If Value = $R_{benefit}$
Then Cost = $C_{cost} + U_{cost} + D_{cost} + R_{cost}$
We gain value from using content, but at a cost of investing in technology to Create, Update, Read, and Delete content, therefore, unless information is used (R) it has no value other than the sunk cost to produce the data (transactions and maintenance)
EIM Business Case: $R_{benefit} > C_{cost} + U_{cost} + D_{cost} + R_{cost}$

create instances of new data and content. Because of this, they are the "suppliers" of the information inventory we need to track. As such they have strong accountabilities for quality and accuracy. EIM has been likened to a logistics discipline, where what is really being managed is a supply chain of data (see Chapter 18).

- *Budgeting/planning*—If EIM is in place, the enterprise goals and objectives are passed through a filter of information and content impact, as well as the usual impact to markets, processes, and personnel. Budget approval for capital efforts are scrutinized for content management impact. Strategic projects like enterprise requirements planning software, or new product lines, are examined from the perspective of "How can data make this better?"

Technology, while mentioned as a part of IAM, is also a component of EIM. Where IAM needs to track and monitor (inventory functions) EIM also needs to *move* content, make it available. Also, EIM will most likely require technologies to alter data and content, interface with parties external to the enterprise, and provide capabilities to support collaboration and workflow.

EIM has the goal to **maximize value and leverage** of information assets. This means EIM needs to state what the value of information means to an organization and then measure how EIM is affecting that value. This also means that the EIM program constantly assesses the performance of data and content in terms of contribution to the business plan. The EIM manager must keep the "following formula" in mind (Table 15.1).

If EIM cannot manage information and *duly measure* its performance such that the benefits outweigh costs, the EIM program will falter.

WHAT DOES IT LOOK LIKE?

In Chapter 2 we presented a generic view of EIM in terms of the components the business sees. Table 15.2 gives a more detailed view. Each component has a brief explanation of the role it plays in fulfilling the functional requirements of EIM.

Table 15.2 Day in the Life of EIM Details

EIM Components—What Does a Day in the Life of EIM Look Like?				
	Sample Functions			
Components	Structured data/content management	Unstructured data/content management	Lineage	Data quality
Business model	Nature of business determines how much structured vs. unstructured content needs management	Nature of business determines how much structured vs. unstructured content needs management	Tracking and monitoring who and where content is touched is based directly on business need	Accuracy, and usefulness of content must be based on where and how business is used
Information handling and use	Define and manage rules and policies for moving, using, and accessing this content	Define and manage rules and policies for moving, using, and accessing this content	Determine mechanisms for tracking and monitoring the use and processing of content	Determine the "quality control" processes to maintain content relevance and accuracy
Information life cycle	Understand when content enters the enterprise, how long it is around, and when it must be removed	Understand when content enters the enterprise, how long it is around, and when it must be removed	Define and manage around a life cycle to provide a baseline for data lineage and compliance	Determine and oversee WHERE in the content life cycles DQ has the most relevance to the organization
Applications	Oversee development of applications to ensure proper DQ and handling	Oversee development of applications to ensure proper DQ and handling	Ensure information and content lineage is engineered into delivered work products	Ensure that adequate edits, policies, and rules are engineered into delivered work products
Technology	Monitor the types of technology and trends to ensure compatibility with business direction	Monitor the types of technology and trends to ensure compatibility with business direction	Oversee deployment of technology to support lineage	Oversee deployment of technology to improve and monitor DQ
Organization	Identify and facilitate changes in roles, responsibilities, and incentives	Identify and facilitate changes in roles, responsibilities, and incentives	Confirm where lineage is supervised and measured/ reported	Define the role and locations for DQ functions and processes
Compliance	Ensure IAM processes are deployed in accordance with regulatory limits	Ensure IAM processes are deployed in accordance with regulatory limits	Integrate compliance requirements with lineage design and deployment	Integrate compliance requirements with DQ design and deployment
Enterprise "DNA"	Implement applications to deploy definition, navigation, and administration requirements	Implement applications to deploy definition, navigation, and administration requirements	Ensure navigation and definition functions are integrated with lineage	Ensure definitions of data and content include rules for DQ
Culture	Oversee culture change management related to EIM	Oversee culture change management related to EIM	Ensure lineage becomes part of all content development and use	Facilitate DQ mindset through entire organization

(Continued)

Table 15.2 (Continued)

EIM Components—What Does a Day in the Life of EIM Look Like?				
Sample Functions				
Components	**Structured data/content management**	**Unstructured data/content management**	**Lineage**	**Data quality**
Governance	Provide required processes and rules to adhere to EIM principles	Provide processes, workflow, and rules to adhere to EIM principles	Ensure lineage data is maintained and used in accordance with policy	Ensure DQ rules and policies are followed and implemented
Managed content	Identify the elements and sources subject to EIM	Identify the elements and sources subject to EIM	Content and data are "labeled," tracked, and administered	Data and content has defined thresholds of accuracy and usefulness
Sample Functions (Continued)				
Components	**Business processes**	**Governance**	**Architecture**	
Business model	The interconnected events within a model form key drivers in how content is managed	While all EIM efforts require governance, the nature of the enterprise influences the nature of EIM governance	Develop frameworks and technology that support business philosophy	
Information handling and use	Define how and when business actions utilize content	Define principles and policies that will enforce information accuracy and handling	Create an efficient but responsive framework to access and move information	
Information life cycle	Manage the information life cycle so that processes have the data required and nothing more	Define the life cycle, especially in terms of balancing compliance vs. analytical needs	Accommodate the required information life cycle within the enterprise's architectures	
Applications	Ensure that application users understand how application supports and enhances processes	Develop the policies that applications will deliver products support of IAM	Ensure that delivered work products and systems concur with architecture guidelines	
Technology	Facilitate identification of technology opportunities for business processes	Deploy technology that supports governance requirements, e.g., DQ, Privacy, and so on	Ensure any EIM technology accommodates the business enterprise architecture	
Organization	Identify and facilitate changes in roles, responsibilities, and incentives	Ensure that governance impact or organization is conveyed to and transitioned effectively	Ensure that the EIM organization complies with enterprise architecture	
Compliance	Integrate compliance requirements with business process design and deployment	Facilitate communication and liaison between compliance and governance duties	Integrate compliance requirements with enterprise architecture	
Enterprise "DNA"	Evaluate business process needs to use and exploit the DNA "data about data"	Verify that applications and business area update and maintain DNA and lineage data	Liaison with architects to ensure enterprise technology supports "DNA" approach	

(Continued)

Table 15.2 (Continued)

	Sample Functions (Continued)		
Components	**Business processes**	**Governance**	**Architecture**
Culture	Identify changing processes and mechanisms to sustain revised processes	Educate and train organization on new governance processes	Ensure new architectures are communicated
Governance	Ensure processes adhere to new data management standards and guidelines	Governance is a stand-alone component in EIM, it is never embedded in other functions	Ensure architecture standards, frameworks, and guidelines are followed
Managed content	Identify adequate processes to comply with EIM policy	Associate managed content with required oversight policy	Ensure the architecture can handle content management and use processes

SUMMARY

The EIM program provides an effective platform for oversight of many different projects related to data and information. However, it is often easy to get caught up in the tool or package selection and implementation, or the philosophical examination of "what is a customer?" These activities are left over from the "we vs. they" generations. The bottom line for an EIM program, which must be reinforced from time to time, is supporting the business with clear, documented, and effective data and information. The business user wants this as badly as anyone in IT. The organization requires formal "asset treatment," or IAM. When this mind-set pervades the enterprise, a much smoother mechanism can be set in place to fully extract value from data and content, but in an efficient and low-risk manner. Only through focusing steadily on solid business cases, business alignment, and an effective practical road map will EIM succeed. The software, the dictionaries, the processes, the organization charts, the technologies, and the models are all tools to achieve what should be a well-documented and measurable business program.

The remaining chapters in this book are going to delve into the details of building an EIM program. It is as "how to" as we can make it and still fit into the allowable amount of pages in this book. We are going to follow a process, a methodology. The first half of the book presented a higher view of the process. We are going to embed a more detailed approach into the executive protocol and work through how to define, design, and deploy EIM. Chapters 16 and 17 will explain the ins and outs of getting started. Then we will develop each chapter based on the steps in the approach.

References

1. Source unknown, probably from the same place that the Ants at the Blackboard and the Tree Swing cartoons came from (look around, they are in a cubicle somewhere). If the images of these cartoons do not come to mind, find someone over age 50 in your office and ask them.
2. Zornes, A. (2009, August). *MDM Institute Presentation*.
3. Eckerson, W. (2008, October). TDWI of St. Louis; Myth of end-user business intelligence, *Presentation*.

EIM Program Design Overview

16

The trouble with the world is not that people know too little, but that they know so many things that ain't so.
Mark Twain

CONTENTS

Chapter 9 presented an overview of EIM program design from the executive view. I encourage you to go back and read it if you have not. This chapter may seem repetitive, but only in the sense we cover the same process. The purpose of this chapter and the several that follow is to present the big picture in the context of types of iterations and deliverable flow, so that the flow of work, the progressive iteration into details, and the types of artifacts generated are understood.

This chapter reviews the methodology this book uses to present the EIM program. The emphasis will be on those tasks that are unique to EIM. Activities such as status meetings or preparation of work environments are assumed. Designing and developing the EIM program has significant similarities to other strategic business programs. After all, it *is a business program.* Often, in actual practice, the business members of EIM teams adapt more quickly than IT staff. That said, there are also some significant differences in EIM from other business programs, and we will highlight those. We stay away from providing detailed estimates and staffing because EIM programs can vary greatly. Chapter 17 will present guidelines for staffing. When called for, I will point out minimal staff needs for certain techniques.

THE NATURE OF EIM DEVELOPMENT

The EIM design process is iterative. At each major stage, you will need to strive to provide real value to the organization. Enough detail needs to be presented to permit comprehension and continued buy-in. Additionally, each major step has to deliver enough detail to allow the organization to make strategic decisions in regards to EIM. You should be able to answer the following questions:

- Do we still see business value?
- Is the EIM vision consistently applied?
- Are all the EIM building blocks and required "day-in-the-life" aspects being addressed?
- If we stopped the EIM program's design at this point, can we discern a tactical effort that can still add business value without a full EIM effort?

It's important to be realistic. We have already touched upon the ugly truth that many organizations have tried EIM-type efforts and not sustained them. It is quite possible business or cultural conditions may affect any contemporary attempt to manage information. This is not the preferred course of action but stuff happens. For example, it may be pragmatic (but not more economical) to do a "piece" of an IM project to prove the concept. So we need to have enough detail to add value, but not so much that there is any need to revisit a prior step and cause disruption in progress. We need the proper level of detail to do EIM, but not generate superfluous material. More importantly, we need to base our approach on concepts that avoid typical pitfalls of strategic program development.

OUR EIM "METHODOLOGY" STRUCTURE

The context of the rest of Part 2 is that of a program manager or business manager who is part of or accountable for developing the EIM program. There is the need to understand what the executives must see, but there is also the need to develop a vision of a program into a plan that can be executed. Figure 16.1 presents the overview of the process.

Showing an iterative process means drawing a lot of spirals, or recursive loops on flow diagrams. For pragmatic reasons, I do not attempt that in this book. Instead, I show a taxonomy of activities. All of these are iterative within each major stage and its activities. The process moves from vision through conceptual and onto implementation, but it is not a waterfall. In essence, a solution is represented at each level. You iterate through lower layers of detail. We show them in a linear fashion because it aids in understanding the building blocks that are necessary to define a full function EIM program.

Each major stage is called a phase. This term looks the best on the project plan. In effect though, each phase is a reusable module, containing a series of steps we will call activities. Like any other defined method, these steps build on each other. Not all of them are mandatory. Our objective is not to define every single work step. It is to provide the business manager with a perspective of how work artifacts are related and the players must be coordinated. For example, during the Road Map phase there are activities called EIM Organization and Data Governance Roll Out. Upon review, these will seem to be redundant. But the first time through (as EIM is defined), they need to be done separately

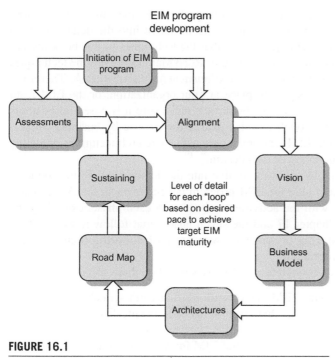

FIGURE 16.1

The EIM program process overview

for very precise reasons. Subsequent visits to the Road Map phase will most likely result in the EIM manager combining bits from both of these activities.

Modules imply flexibility and use, and that is a goal of the EIM program design. EIM efforts vary across organizations, and obviously some require differing areas of emphasis. For example, an enterprise with a long history of embedded BI projects will need to leverage these efforts vs. redesigning them. Therefore, the material presented can be viewed as Lego™ blocks—steps to be used or reused.

High-Level View of the EIM Design and Deployment Process

The activities are discrete steps that most likely produce a major deliverable. Within each activity are tasks. The tasks are discrete steps that produce work products, or interim deliverables. All tasks have either a work product or a deliverable as a result. A major deliverable is a work product that personnel outside of the EIM team will see; for example, the steering committee, CEO, or EVP. Again, each activity area could be peeled off "Lego-style" and adapted to a specific need.

Our EIM program design methodology will also address the other two disciplines of accomplishing work: tools and techniques. Tools are digital and automated devices to assist in performing analysis and producing deliverables, for example, Microsoft Project, Metis, Telelogic, and Erwin.

Techniques are specific approaches to creating deliverables, performing analysis, and executing tasks, e.g., affinity analysis, JAD, and measurement analysis. As we move into the details of these activities, we will review a sampling of the techniques. Note that the techniques in this book are not the only techniques available to produce a defined architecture or Road Map. However, the techniques presented here are designed and used to maintain a *very rigid alignment to business needs*. Therefore, I recommend if there are other techniques or styles in place at your organization, or the EIM team architects want to use a technique not appearing in this book, just make sure it is based on business alignment.[1] The techniques described in this book are also geared toward use by business Subject Matter Experts (SMEs) with assistance from EIM team members with some architecture or modeling skills. So they do not require training in modeling or data design.

There are task lists in each activity should you want to dive into the details required to produce a project plan. There is also a sample project plan for EIM program development in the Appendices. Figure 16.2 shows the process overview with the activities embedded in each phase, excluding the Initiation phase. We cover Initiation in Chapter 17 and the seven phases that follow it are iterative. The iterations will vary based on how far your organization wants to push toward formal IAM and how long you take to mature your EIM program.

Figure 16.3 shows that we might iterate through the EIM phases based on three scenarios:

1. You don't have anything at all resembling EIM, so you are starting from scratch. Strange as it may seem, there are a number of organizations that, even in the early twenty-first century, should take this perspective.
2. Your organization had earlier efforts and you have partial EIM functions, or your EIM effort is a year or so under way and it is time for periodic maintenance.
3. You have EIM, but it is stuck, or is under criticism for no value. You need to restore credibility to the effort.

EIM PROCESS CONCEPTS

Experience has shown that the largest obstacle to groups defining an EIM plan has been the interaction of work products, and the interpretation of findings. However, there are a hundred methodologies to do this. Just ask any firm that claims to do EIM—they will have a methodology. There are a hundred more techniques. It is most important that the program manager understands WHAT is being done, not necessarily how, and how the documents and data that are used to form and manage the EIM program come together.

There is some background understanding required before reviewing how these pieces of EIM come together. Treatment of information, data, and content as an asset requires the development of a distinct and specific set of artifacts. These artifacts work in concert to "tie together" all of the components and elements of EIM programs. They also provide the *quantitative foundation* for assessing the value of information. As we established earlier in the book, the value of information is based on usage, offset by any contingent risk buried within information assets. The usage of data and content has to improve business or organizational value, as expressed by a financial statement. Therefore, we need to know those scenarios or business actions that use the content or data to meet business goals, reduce expense, add customers, or sell more goods and services. A service or nonprofit organization will see

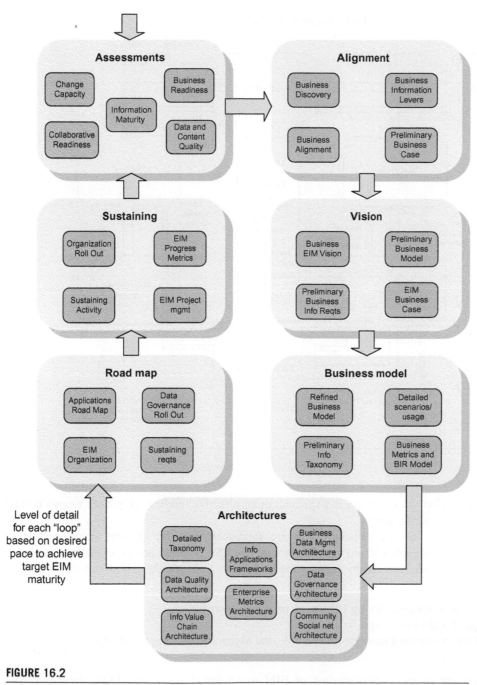

FIGURE 16.2

EIM process methodology

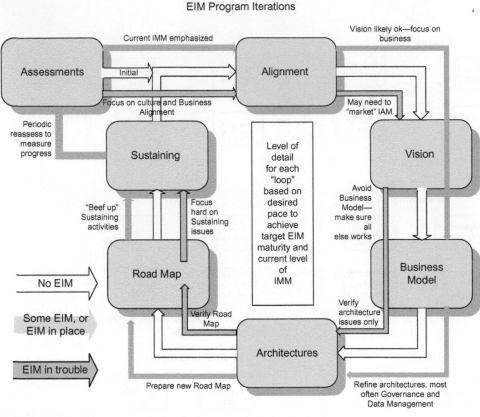

FIGURE 16.3

EIM iterations

information asset value via reduction in expenses, more effective funding, or greater recognition of contribution within its environment.

Specifically, there are two concepts that are fundamental to the process being presented. Understanding these concepts will aid in understanding the EIM program processes and how we build the foundation for value. This chapter covers these concepts and provides a few generic examples. The concepts are:

- The concept of cumulative, living EIM work products or artifacts.
- The concept of auditable design, via
  - aligned interconnected models, for example, the Metrics/Requirements Model
  - IVCs.

Even if you are doing a subdiscipline of EIM as an initial foray into IAM, these concepts apply. So consider these areas for BI, data quality, master data, document management, and other programs.

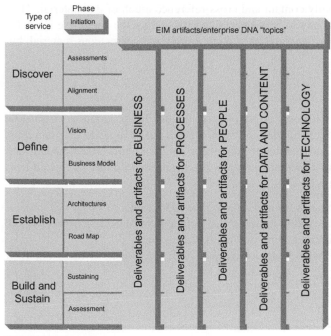

FIGURE 16.4

EIM artifacts flow overview

The Cumulative, Living Flow of EIM Work Products

Talk to anyone who has developed documentation to support a strategic program and they will have a common horror story. At some point, the strategic effort starts to suffer under its own weight. Documents become misplaced, or are used only for the purpose of a meeting, and are never visited again. The champions and sponsors move on, or manage to avoid blame, and the noble vision fades. This is, of course, expensive, inefficient, and not very good content management!

The EIM program as specified here endeavors to make sure all the artifacts are useful, and easily managed. They are "living" documents, in that they are always added to, or modified. There is not a need to re-create all of the artifacts when revisiting the EIM program plans.

At minimum you should arrange your deliverables by the taxonomy indicated in Figure 16.4. They will flow into each other, and you will only have to navigate four classifications of phases by five artifact topics. Granted, if you do not use a tool, you will have to manage documents and spreadsheets, but the cumulative flow built against this simple taxonomy reduces the navigation and maintenance of artifacts and documents to a manageable level.

As you move through your EIM program, remember you are also creating content to be managed. Do not be the "cobbler's children." It is a good example to walk the talk and manage your own content effectively. SharePoint, Lotus Notes, or other workflow products are useful, but first agree on the "taxonomy" of the artifacts and a management protocol, and set the environment up as soon as feasible. There are products that can actually contain and cross-reference much of the material. They are mentioned as appropriate. All of the material being generated is building the enterprise DNA for IAM. The processes described in the following chapters attempt to minimize extraneous material, but it can still seem voluminous.

The Concept of Auditable Design

Several times in upcoming chapters, we will mention that the results of EIM program work must be "auditable." This means any artifact, recommendation, or work product out of the EIM program must be justified on business-driven criteria. There can be no suggestion for an architectural element, tool, or product unless the EIM team can tie that recommendation to a business need and its related benefits. The advantages of this concept are to:

- Prevent vendors and product selection tasks from inundating the EIM team.
- Provide a continuous, convergent relationship between the technical and business aspects of the EIM program. Consequently, the institutionalizing of IAM is made easier.
- Avoid any potential "religious" wars that may arise from part of the EIM team favoring one EIM element design over another.

TIP FOR SUCCESS

The scariest phrase we hear when doing EIM work is "We chose direction X with tool Y because a consultant or vendor recommended it." The recommendation may have been solid and perfectly applicable, but without mentioning the business tie-in, the relevance of the direction or the value of the new tool is diminished considerably.

There are two techniques that are heavily used to enforce the concept of auditable design:

Metrics and Requirements Modeling

This is not a common technique, and I like to think we invented it. The essence is to define and develop an automatically aligned set of specific enterprise information and content requirements, and state them in both a qualitative and quantitative manner. The qualitative characteristics are extracted directly from business input via plans or documents or discussion. The quantitative characteristics are gathered via survey or research. The EIM team analyzes the qualities, models the quantitative characteristics, and identifies various EIM elements that meet the characteristics. There are similar approaches[2] elsewhere, so feel free to explore and combine the ideas. Table 16.1 shows a summary example of the types of characteristics collected, and more details are given in Chapter 23.

Much experience has shown that deriving a list of "information requirements" only gets you part of the way to the EIM Architecture. An "auditable design" requires the EIM team be able to justify the recommendations for delivery frameworks and Road Map applications. Metrics are isolated as an information requirement by design, not convenience. There are several reasons for using this or another rigid technique.

Table 16.1 Characteristics of Business Information Requirements (BIR) and Metrics

Characteristics	Characteristic Description
Measurement volume	The estimated occurrences of this measure in terms of data required to support, OR number of unique times this measure is generated over a specific time period.
Granularity	The level of detail of the data required to support this metric.
"Historicity"	The extent of historical requirements in the metric or requirement.
Distribution	The extent to which the information will be used across an enterprise.
Fact volatility or "periodicity"	The frequency that information or content is added to or updated for the purpose of use in this metric or requirement.
Dimensional complexity	The complexity of how we need to "slice" the metric, or index the document.
Access type	The means of access to the content or metric is important to managing the asset.
Latency	The time between when the data is available to and when is it required for placement into our managed environment
Source complexity	The relative complexity of gathering and moving data into the managed framework.
Frequency	Indicates how often the information is accessed for a particular measure or requirement. DIFFERENT from periodicity.
Response time	The desired time to respond to the production of the metric or requirement.
Follow-up time	The time desired to allocate to responding to a metric or requirement.
Persistency	The length of time data must be retained in the framework and be usable. Contrast this with historicity which relates to historical storage.
Availability	This indicates availability of the access mechanism, not how fast you want to see it (i.e., latency).
Data quality	This represents the degree of usefulness of the data BEFORE it is managed or received into the enterprise.

- If EIM sponsors get the impression you are basing the EIM recommendations and architecture on opinion vs. an auditable decision process, the EIM team's credibility suffers. Metrics provide nice quantitative characteristics that will shape and support the final EIM architecture.
- During an EIM program, there will always be debate about the meaning of a piece of information, or the semantics of naming a data element or document. When you hear your data architects joking about "What is a Customer?" they are speaking code for the fact that organizations cannot reach consensus on meaning because meaning depends on context. Metrics, however, do not have this issue. Once a metric is defined for a particular use, the context is set and meaning is known. The "auditable design" concept is supported because the metrics point to an agnostic answer, therefore, the EIM program is not constrained by semantics.

The Concept of Logistics and IVCs

The IVC serves an important role in understanding the value-added flow of information through an organization. The IVC represents how information is created, used, and disposed of throughout an enterprise.[3] It provides detail for the life cycle of data throughout and the business processes that directly affect information value. Since usage = value, we need to understand where content is used to improve value vs. where it is used to make things happen.

TIP FOR SUCCESS

A business leader of an EIM effort, or even an IT-trained leader, will need to avoid the hornet's nest of religious wars surrounding the design of EIM applications and delivery frameworks. Briefly, groups favoring one design philosophy over another have developed intense rivalries over the last few decades. Their passionate support for one approach over another results in the "hammer nail" dilemma. They are good with a hammer, and everything starts to look like a nail. It all started with data warehouse design, but there are EIM-jihadists for database design, development methods, and many other EIM elements. For the most part, data architects remain rational, but every so often, you may get a staff member or consultant who will consider one and only one way to design an EIM element. Move fast to intercept the debate, and rely on the data you are gathering to shape your solution. This is another reason we describe quantitative and qualitative criteria for metrics and BIRs. The design is supported by facts, not opinions.

A common definition of information is "data with relevance and usefulness added." Therefore something is necessary to provide relevance (a business context or need) and/or usefulness (we might need to add a number to another number). This applies to discrete rows and columns or documents or web content. For data or content to possess value as an asset, a business event or process must raise the "state" of data to a next level of "value." This is demonstrated in Figure 16.5. The original data or content rarely changes its own characteristics. The bits and bytes remain in the same arrangement within a computer.

Other than the fact that the original "raw material" does not become altered, this process resembles any other value chain. And that is OK—a river does its job in the same manner—moving goods or turning movement into electricity—and the water remains water. What will complicate matters is one area's IVC may create another's raw material, as in Figure 16.6. This requires more IAM as we will need to track the usefulness across several threads. Understanding the contextual changes of the data or content being used becomes important. Who or what touched it? Why? Were the results expected?

While the sense of movement is clear, information and data do not really *move*. In other words, data entering an organization does not move up and go over to the order entry department, then leap to the warehouse. Usually, it stays inside a transactional application, or its movement takes the form of extraction, being copied, transformed, or pushed as needed to other applications. To illustrate, electricity "flows" through wires in the same manner, but the copper does not move.

This philosophy of abstract "movement" vs. concrete requirements has made for good debate between business and IT professionals. Debating aside, those organizations that have effectively used information invariably have acknowledged a sense of logistics, or a view that "moving" data is another logistical challenge.[4] Granted, the data does not really move, but there are key features of logistics that make the application of the logistics metaphor appropriate. All of the above require a *PROCESS* to change the quiet state of information or data to a *VALUE* state. These processes have logistical characteristics.

- *Cycle times*—Usually a function of latency, availability, and business requirements (see Table 16.1), but data must be made available at certain times to certain functions.
- *Throughput*—There are volumetric concerns in providing information or knowledge to a function.
- *Protocol*—There are several ways data or content can trigger a process (see MART analysis in Chapter 23).

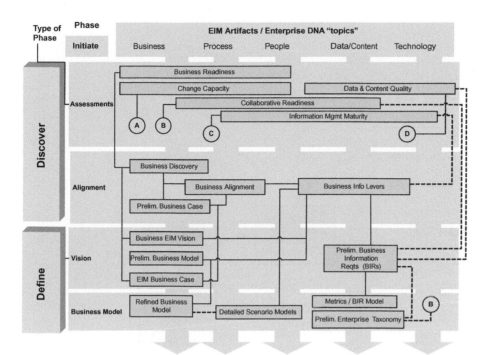

FIGURE 16.5

Simple IVC

- *Quality*—Information to be used must be useful. Poor content, in the form of errors, diminished integrity, accuracy, etc., makes information less useful.
- *Sequence*—One event must follow another.
- *Content*—What is the process supposed to do with the input and what is the output?

We get auditable design because we can connect high-value processes that use our newly managed data to exact business targets. In Figure 16.6, for example, we can promote a lagging product using some analysis. We can then use this new process as input to the Architecture and Road Map phases, determining how and when to implement the managed data that will fulfill the business goal.

A business leader of an EIM area immediately recognizes information and process are harder to manage if looked upon separately. However, many technology methods and software are based on separate treatment of the two. Only in the early twenty-first century have we been able to more easily address implementing process and data as one bundle. Terms like service-oriented architectures, object-oriented programming, semantic web, and XML reflect these trends. Once your team understands your ideal internal content logistics (your IVC), you are able to ensure that data and content management processes are defined to interoperate with and support business goals.

Information frameworks, information architectures, adaptive frameworks, and corporate information factories are all synonyms for managing information logistics—the creating of IVCs. Logistics is the science of efficient movement. Inventory management in the twenty-first century is rooted in logistics science. A logistics mind-set fits nicely with the IAM philosophy. During the various

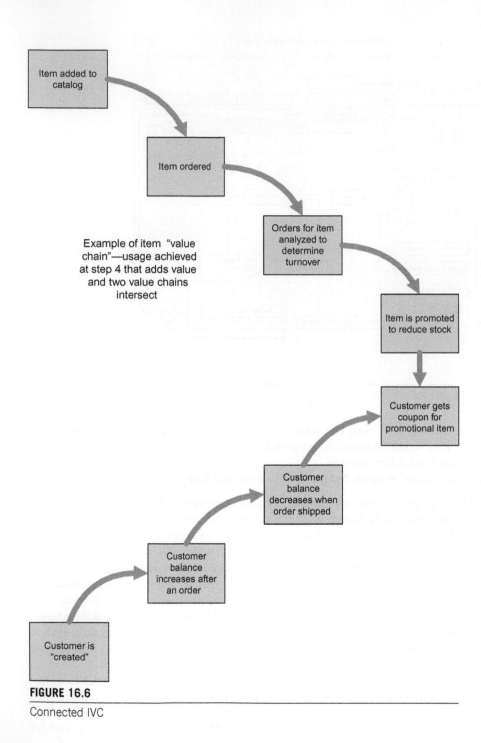

Item added to catalog

Item ordered

Orders for item analyzed to determine turnover

Example of item "value chain"—usage achieved at step 4 that adds value and two value chains intersect

Item is promoted to reduce stock

Customer gets coupon for promotional item

Customer balance decreases when order shipped

Customer balance increases after an order

Customer is "created"

FIGURE 16.6

Connected IVC

activities to define the EIM environment, there will be a series of process-related steps to determine and optimize the business activity taken with managed information. Sometime an EIM program requires only minimal consideration of an IVC; other times it becomes a significant effort. These conditions are pointed out in subsequent chapters.

EIM DELIVERABLES

Figures 16.7 and 16.8 show the general flow of deliverables across the phases, again organized by the recommended taxonomy. Deliverables connected by solid lines indicate they build on each other (cumulative and auditable design concepts). Dotted lines indicate they provide input to a subsequent deliverable (cumulative concept).

The EIM program is developed through an iterative set of processes that are based on living documents and express business alignment by design. The Assessment, Vision, Alignment, and Business Model phases provide the EIM business alignment foundation. Quantitative and qualitative analysis are applied to these work products to produce the EIM architecture. Business alignment and assessments are also applied to develop a pragmatic Road Map for rolling out EIM while supplying the business adequate data and content solutions. Finally, we can only accomplish the future state of a routine EIM area when we actively work to alter behaviors, enforce new standards, and measure the

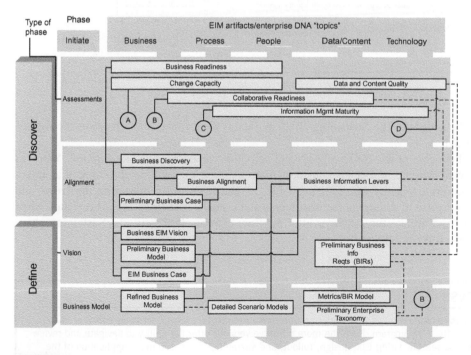

FIGURE16.7

Discover and define flow

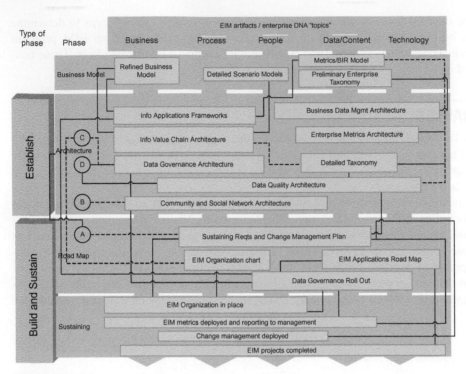

FIGURE 16.8

Establish and build flow

ongoing value of the program. The Sustaining phase maintains the artifacts and represents the day-to-day operation of EIM.

The entire EIM process or its various phases and activities can be revisited as required. You will always need to revisit Alignment, because business plans change. You will need to look at architecture as new technology capability becomes available, or you move from mastering the "rows and columns" of the enterprise to managing the documents and e-mails. The Road Map is revisited when business alignment and architecture changes alter the flow of projects. Lastly, the Sustaining phase actually never ends—it is always "on."

TIP FOR SUCCESS

If your enterprise has dabbled with, or is considering Enterprise Architecture tools,[5] seriously consider using them to also support the EIM program. Even the more primitive versions offer the ability to navigate and review critical data you will assemble during EIM design, rollout, and sustaining. They also make application of the auditable design concept much easier.

EIM Methodology Examples

We will supplement the major steps of our process with examples from the two case studies, Ubetcha Insurance (UIC) and Farfel Emporiums, Inc. (FEI). We will also highlight the tools and techniques that we have found to be effective.

I need to reinforce at this point that the process of developing an EIM program is not a cookbook. The sample outputs shown in the following chapters are intended to reinforce meaning and convey context. The Appendices provide a detailed table of all work products, deliverables, and tasks. You will also find templates for deliverables and a sample project plan in the Appendices. Combined with the phase and activity descriptions, you can start to build an approach to define or restore your EIM program.

SUMMARY

The design and deployment of the EIM program is focused on one overarching goal—make the philosophy of IAM part and parcel of an enterprise. To do this requires a process for business alignment to ensure long-term value, and engineering and management activity to ensure the EIM people and process frameworks are matched to your organization's culture and business model.

The EIM program will require many processes, techniques, and deliverables to define, convey, and implement IAM. Each of the subdisciplines has their own flavors and approaches. Regardless of the specific methodology or techniques, or mix of full-blown EIM or a portion via a subdiscipline, there must be two criteria met for all EIM activities to ensure success:

- All artifacts and recommendations need to tie to an expectation of supporting a valid business result.
- There must be acceptance that information assets are subject to the same basic logistics concepts as hard goods. We must manage for efficient flow and understand value-added processes vs. non–value-added processes.

In the information age, movement of information from one state of value to another is as crucial to an organization as movement of raw materials and merchandise. It is also an expression of the convergence of business and IT. We have to strive for auditable design and an easily connected set of EIM artifacts to express the EIM elements and building blocks.

This convergence is the basic driver for shifting to a new mind-set for IAM. Planning and implementing asset management is a logistics problem of tracking what is known, delivering what is known to the right people at the right time, based on the value and cost of the information and knowledge being tapped. Organizations that can filter, ascribe, and deliver data/information at the right times to the right people are executing EIM. We talked earlier about EIM having similarities in accounting concepts and other staff functions. Imagine an environment where information assets are boringly and routinely managed as efficiently as raw materials or personnel. This is the ultimate goal of IAM and the EIM program.

References

1. Significant collections of techniques are in the book by Ralph Kimball, *Data Warehouse Toolkit*; see bibliography as well as following links to articles by author: www.informatino-management.com.
2. Ibid.
3. English, L. P. (1999). *Improving Data Warehouse and Business Information Quality*. New York: Wiley Computer Publishing; John Wiley & Sons, Inc.
4. Davenport, T. H. (1997). *Information Ecology*. New York: Oxford University Press.
5. As of the writing of this book, two examples are *System Architect* from IBM and *Provision* from Metastorm.

Initiating the EIM Program Design

17

I'll be more enthusiastic about encouraging thinking outside the box when there's evidence of any thinking going on inside it.
Terry Pratchett

CONTENTS

The most difficult task in any large effort like EIM is the first step. This chapter addresses the question: "where do I start?" It focuses on getting EIM design and deployment started. Several foundational activities unique to EIM need to occur. First, however, there is the gray area of getting the OK to start. The EIM program may be initiated as a directive from the CEO or other executive. Often a CIO is asked to "make it so" and starts the EIM effort. More often than not, it is a "rank and file"–inspired effort, via the request for a "data warehouse" or "master data" file. Either way, a successful start is dependent on a few crucial initiation steps, as well as the usual project-type start-up tasks.[1]

Making Enterprise Information Management (EIM) Work for Business. DOI: 10.1016/B978-0-12-375695-4.00017-5

INITIATION

First, let's review the basic preparation and initiation of the EIM effort. Initiation will establish an expected execution plan and define the communications methods for the project along with the remaining detailed tasks, activities, and deliverables required to complete all other steps. At this point, you are most likely in a "pre-business case" mode—that is, you are permitted to explore the relevance and feasibility of EIM, and if everything works out then the program will be designed. Initiation may be a bit misleading: we are initiating the program design, but there is a checkpoint at the end of this step to ensure the enterprise possesses the will to proceed to the next step (or two).

Therefore there needs to be consensus that there is potential business value. We need to produce a prototype vision of what to expect from building an EIM program. The net result of Initiation is a thorough understanding among leadership that this will be a business program and there is an organizational expectation (aka constraint) for how long preparation of the EIM program will need to take.

We start by executing traditional project planning activities, e.g., scope, project objectives, schedule, and resources. Objectives, deliverables, and work plan are determined. The perspective is maintained that at the end of this effort the EIM program (if approved) will be in place and specific projects, such as BI or content management, will be under the auspices of the new program. There will be a framework for "data warehouse" and other elements at the end of the effort we are initiating.

Often upper management will demand to "see something." Legitimately, executives are tired of promises from technology projects, and EIM programs will seem like another IT program at first. It is most crucial that you begin the mind shift to enterprise program *now*. Do not get bullied into "show us low-hanging fruit first." These types of conversations mean that management has not grasped what EIM and IAM represent *yet*. If there are urgent issues around data and content (e.g., poor data quality is creating havoc in a new product line), then recognize this as a priority area of EIM, and build the business need into the program. You may even have to work on the urgent problem. But do not "trade" working on the problem "first" so you can then proceed with EIM. The problem solutions and EIM program development need to proceed in parallel. If not, EIM is DOA (dead on arrival). You are doing information projects, not EIM. Again, this is not horrible. I do not want it said that IAM is unrealistic and this book detached. However, your information assets *will remain unmanaged*. The urgent issue occurring now will be addressed and any messes will be tidied up in the *short term*. But without the IAM umbrella, you have set the stage for another urgent mess at some point in the future.

OBSERVATION

I did a seminar in 2009 where the audience deluged me with questions regarding "How to get buy-in?" and "What to do about political issues?" After my usual answers and emphasis on alignment, IMM, and cultural capacity, and being familiar with some of the organizations represented in the room, I also added the bits about guerilla alignment, and using brown-bag sessions in lieu of formal EIM activity. At last, one attendee asked me, "I understand this, but in my company they will not listen to anything from IT with the word "business" in a sentence. If I was caught having a lunch time talk with a business user I would be fired. I guess we are order takers, as you described, and our CIO believes that is our role, to deliver anything they ask for. What do we do?" My answer amused everybody, but was only partially tongue-in-cheek. After expressing my empathy I said, "You must be professional and exercise due diligence—write up your opinions, make your observations, file the memo away. Then give up. Cash your check every two weeks, … *and just take their money*. Buy more tools if they ask for them, get smarter, *then leave*. Your company is in for a major business crisis anyway. It is only a matter of time."

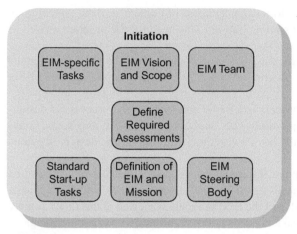

Initiation

- EIM-specific Tasks
- EIM Vision and Scope
- EIM Team
- Define Required Assessments
- Standard Start-up Tasks
- Definition of EIM and Mission
- EIM Steering Body

FIGURE 17.1

Initiation

Other traditional activities such as timelines, participants, project administration, and communication are also established. Also, review available relevant documents pertaining to business drivers and strategies. Gather them up or find out where they are, and get permission to access them, if permission is required. Like any other strategic effort, knowing what you have and what you need to dig up makes a large difference in estimates. Finally, this module develops or confirms a common understanding of the project's success measures. Figure 17.1 shows the details of the EIM Initiation "phase."

The following tasks are specific to EIM methodology:

1. *Define the enterprise*—How far-reaching is the EIM effort? If you are a megacorporation or huge government agency, the EIM effort is much different from a single product company, or local government. In addition, define the nature of the environment with which the internal EIM effort will interface.

2. *Define initial data and content asset types*—While I prefer that all content be part of EIM (remember you can *include it but not affect it* until a later time) many organizations choose to restrict EIM to "rows and columns" type data, or operational systems and BI. Others will add high risk areas, such as e-mail. Either way, any constraint of this nature needs revealing and discussion. A firm statement of what is in and out is required. Again, best practice says that ALL content is part of EIM. Prioritizing how it is managed is another topic. In reality it is silly to restrict content type at this point. The next steps will not incorporate critical business opportunities or challenges related to the content that's been left out. Again, you can implement asset management for one type of content before another, but it really is best practice to address all of it at this point.

3. *Determine and list the drivers for the EIM effort*—This is a fundamental task. Frankly, data quality is most often the primary driver of EIM. However, tackling data quality usually means tackling a host of other areas. Organizations trigger EIM efforts because of pain. It would be nice to say that a few companies proactively address the need for IAM but that is not the case. Often there is intense pain from data quality, poor support of business programs, or the organization has lost

reputation or suffered financial adversity due to mismanagement of content or data. Agreeing on this list of motivators can serve as a basis for gaining buy-in to the need for the program as well as determining success measures.

4. *Define the extent or constraints of altering the business model*—What can the business tolerate? Can the EIM program recommend blowing up core processes? Or is there a process area of Six Sigma structure with which to coordinate?

5. *Define how iterative the EIM development process will be*—Each stage in the process for designing EIM is iterative. But there is always the possibility of "analysis paralysis." It may sound counter intuitive, but successful EIM efforts usually have a very firm deadline for the design of a Road Map to implement IAM.

6. *Define a prototype vision of EIM*—At this point the initial drivers and awareness of IAM can be synthesized into a statement. The statement needs to supply the "elevator speech" or basic explanation, for the program. What is the intended value of the EIM program as viewed at this time? A more refined Vision is developed in its own phase, so this one is notional and subject to major refining.

7. *Determine the types of assessments required*—The next stage has several assessments that assist in understanding the nature of IAM in the current environment. Few organizations ever do all of them, some combine them; some only need to do one or two. A review of the business environment and the drivers for the effort usually reveals where the assessments need to focus.

MORE ON THE TYPE OF ASSESSMENT

Choosing from the various assessments can be challenging. Executive management may exhibit resistance to what will be perceived as more interviews and intrusion into daily operations. Executives in most large companies have been interviewed to the point of insanity. Somewhere, for certain, the CEO, CFO, etc., have told some employee or consultant their needs and priorities. The EIM team gains no early (and much needed) credibility pursuing a bunch of interviews. The assessments are structured to avoid this pitfall.

The two assessments that are absolutely necessary in my experience are the Information Management Maturity (IMM) and the Culture Capacity assessments. They are also the two that can be done very efficiently through online tools and are minimally invasive.

The IMM is the one assessment that is required as it provides an objective view of what the organization really does with information, and how the organization's leaders are viewed in the context of managing information and content. It provides an excellent baseline for a current state picture, and can be used to derive metrics that indicate EIM program progress.

The Culture Capacity assessment is necessary for similar reasons as the IMM. All organizations have a built-in resistance to change. As the EIM program is designed, and more and more business touch points are identified as potentially affected by EIM, it will become obvious that change is *required*. An objective baseline of the organization's ability to respond to change, and what I call "cultural momentum," is critical. Cultural momentum indicates how rigid the organization is in terms of willingness to change. Like an oil tanker, turning to a new direction may be very difficult. Some classic examples are:

- Large government agencies and programs, who are dying for EIM of some sort but cannot break out of decades-old processes. The blind adherence to political processes has come to overshadow benefits of cross-functional application of data.

- Closely held companies, or very old companies with executive staffs that have been there for decades. These environments create either "don't fix what is not broken" or "we will tell you what we need" cultures.

A MOMENT FOR CONSULTANTS

At this point, you need to consider if you want to go outside the company for assistance. You may already have consultants doing this step, so this section is not for you. But if you feel outside help is needed, there are some critical things to consider.

1. Many organizations have difficulty in procuring specific consultants due to government contracting mechanisms or preferred vendor lists. Others have a culture to rely only on certain large firms. However, many of the aforementioned firms are usually light on EIM capability from the context of a business program, and pursue EIM as an IT strategy.
2. When selecting outside help look for the following:
   a. The ability to explain EIM as a business program
   b. The ability to explain concepts of data management in business terms
   c. Experience doing EIM with your particular type of business
   d. Emphasis on business success versus deployment of a range of technological solutions.

Many firms possess these capabilities. If you have a list of preferred firms and none of them fits the bill, seek out one that does and make them subcontract to your preferred firm. The bottom line is you need to deploy assistance that has experience and is not distracted by a technology practice.

TIP FOR SUCCESS

At the risk of sounding self-serving, most consultancies with good EIM experience tend to be specialized. The larger firms, or vendor-based consultancies, tend to offer specialized aspects. With a larger firm you will buy a process and, most of the time, less experience. Smaller firms tend to have less formal processes but bring much higher levels of experience. If you are going to acquire a consultant, do not shut off access to the deep experience in the smaller firms.

SOMETIMES YOU HAVE TO SELL EIM TO SELL EIM

Chapter 6 started with a tongue-in-cheek title—Making a Case for the Case. The reference meant that getting the time to establish a solid EIM Business Case sometimes means doing, well, a business case.

Often the mention of a business case will start well before the EIM effort gets into any kind of a vision or design. If your EIM Initiation effort starts in the following manner, you need to allocate some resources to clarify the value proposition you will be driving toward.

- You are told to tackle urgent low-hanging fruit "first."
- You have an executive sponsor but no one else wants to join the steering committee or leadership group.
- The CIO is told to "be the sponsor of EIM *and* be accountable for other CIO duties."

Perhaps describing a response to these scenarios in a business case is overkill, but there is a clear need to communicate what is happening and why at least some of the initial stages of an EIM

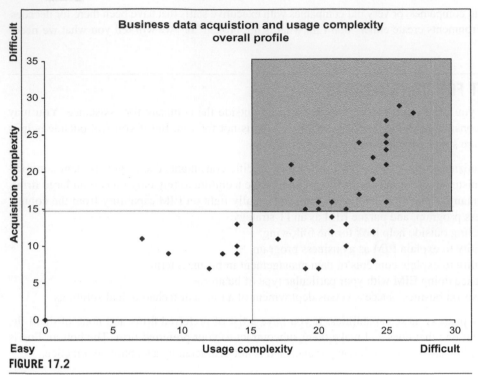

FIGURE 17.2

EIM requirement to manage complexity

program design add value. Luckily, there are some macro-level topics that can be used to convince management into at least "dipping a toe in the water."

Some Helpful Topics

The first connection to explain to your approving executive is the direct relationship between the sophistication of data use and the complexity of its acquisition. Figure 17.2 is based on data collected across several EIM design projects. We categorized requirements for information in two ways. The usage complexity was based on the combination of type of content, difficulty of delivery, and type of business issues being addressed. For example, a requirement to report daily sales would be of low usage complexity—we take transactions, add them up, and place the data on a report. The action taken is based on one data item on a report. Usage complexity is relatively low. It is important to the organization, but not complex. Acquisition complexity is a function of the timing for collecting content, the type of content, the risk if content were of poor quality, and the amount of technology that might need to be deployed to collect the data. For example, a portal that collected KPIs, news articles, and internal e-mails on quarterly earnings announcements, and had to generate alerts on a real-time basis and mash up the content, would rank very high in acquisition complexity.

It is not a surprise that companies want to do cool things with data and content, but the cooler the action, the harder it is to get to the content. Clearly the chart demonstrates that if you want to get sophisticated, you need to streamline the acquisition of the information.

FIGURE 17.3

EIM requirement to manage prioritizations

Another bit of high-level data you can show is to assemble a view of the various subjects or logical groups of content in your organization. Most of the time an exercise in prioritization of content would demonstrate (not surprisingly) that different areas have different priorities (Figure 17.3). For example, sales thinks customers are more important and engineering thinks drawings or items are more important. EIM can sort that out into an agreed-upon framework.

Lastly, it is important to clarify that you are dealing with a lot more than rows and columns. A clear description of the content challenges is essential. Figure 17.4 shows that a look at all of the possible classifications of content will indicate to any doubters that a modern enterprise has a data tiger by the tail.

More and more high-value business solutions require cutting across categories of content.

Factors in Customizing the Approach

As you look over the activities that will deliver the design of your EIM program (or its subparts), it may become apparent that you will not need every single task or artifact presented by the following chapters. You may also have time constraints, or be asked to go partway through and stop until a decision is made to proceed. Any of these factors will require a customized approach. Again, we're not dealing with a cookbook. It is OK to alter the approach, provided you still add value at each stage and manage expectations.

Can you do the entire program design and roll it out in two weeks? No. A full-blown approach, with no existing artifacts to leverage (this never happens, but it makes a good point) can take six

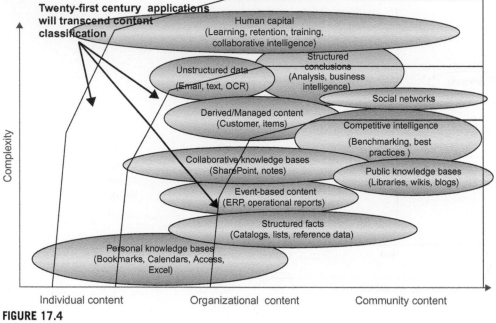

Diversity of content

FIGURE 17.4

Diversity of content

months. But you can get a company started on EIM program rollout in two months, and address any urgent data issues simultaneously.

What you can alter easily are the following components of the approach:

- Include all content, but develop the IAM principles and policies for only one class of content (like rows and columns), then make another pass through the EIM program phases for unstructured content.
- Place a "level of effort" constraint on program design. That is, allow only a given period of time for a specific phase, or set of phases. For example, if you know for sure you will be doing an EIM program, skip activity that is used to sell or position the organization (I still like to see a business case, even a small one).
- Focus on one element of EIM to do a detailed Road Map. If data quality is a large problem, do the phases through Architecture, but focus on rolling out and governing data quality.
- Use templates and acquired business models. Often specific industries already have a large amount of EIM policy predetermined via regulation.[2] These businesses tend to have standard models that are 80–90% common across all occurrences within an industry. So business EIM material can be transferred and reused from one organization to another. The potential gain in productivity from using a standard model on an integrated tool is significant over the life of an EIM program.

MAJOR DELIVERABLES FROM INITIATION

Getting started with an EIM program results in the following types of deliverables. Remember that you may not need them all depending on scope and relative information maturity.

- *EIM Program Design Plan (project plan)*—This is the plan to build the program. So we call it a project plan. It is best done using a formal tool like Microsoft Project™. There are basic project plan templates in the Appendices. This includes the standard project start-up tasks as well as the EIM-specific tasks.
- *EIM Vision and Scope*—One of the stages will require evaluation of the business model for your enterprise. Determine the business model scope and constraints; make sure you confirm if any business functions are off limits. For example, a pharmaceutical company may avoid placing RD under an EIM program. A manufacturer may determine that the data from line controllers is not to be incorporated. This deliverable also presents the notional vision of the EIM program—even at this early stage, it is good to lay out a high-level view of what EIM might look like for your organization. Use one of those presented in this book, or others from various publications as a starting point.
- *Definition of Enterprise and Mission of EIM*—This is the statement of scope, of what information assets EIM will manage. It is best framed in terms of business units, products, or brands—whatever those components are for your company. Then within those, frame the EIM scope in terms of content categories. If your business is highly regulated, you should seriously consider a scope statement that allows for a significant role for compliance. You also present the initial objectives/measurable success factors for EIM, a definition in very clear, measurable terms what success for the EIM program will look like.
- *Required Assessments*—List the types of assessments to be conducted, describe the general contents and goals of each, and determine how the data will be collected.
- *The EIM Team*—Define who are the members to do the day-to-day work.
- *The EIM Steering Body*—This defines the leaders, including sponsors and steering bodies.

THE EIM TEAM

When defining the EIM team, first and foremost follow the concept of convergence. This means business and IT areas provide staff. An ideal team is made up of personnel with a deep awareness of data issues and knowledge of the organization's culture. Typically this does not happen, but it is something to strive for. If you cannot acquire a blended team, then make sure there is a large proportion of business leaders on the EIM steering body and the EIM sponsor operates as high up the organization chart as practical.

> **OBSERVATION**
>
> My idea of heaven is having the EIM effort directly sponsored by an engaged CEO. This has happened one time in the 20 years or so we have been doing EIM and data management strategies. Additionally, the CEO met privately for lunch with EIM leadership on a regularly scheduled basis. It is no coincidence the EIM program rolled out smoother than others. While CEOs must always be careful not to appear to micromanage, strong sponsorship and presence at key meetings is invaluable.

Analyst Functions

Most EIM positions require the ability to collect and evaluate information and determine action. Business analysts and systems analysts are the best candidates. The analysts on the EIM team should be able to execute, or work with other personnel, on surveys and interpretation. They need to be able to review material, and identify and gather requirements and business goals and objectives. They must possess facilitation skills, and know how to run effective meetings.

Modeling and Artifact Functions

The development of the models and other artifacts requires personnel with the basic skills we look for in data modelers. The most important talent is the ability to present a concept in the abstract, then model and drive it toward a concrete expression of requirements. Data modelers do this by understanding the broad topics and subjects that define the overall content in the organization. They present the results in a model to achieve understanding and then drive the models to specific requirements of data elements or document types.

Most modelers have a title along the lines of data architect or data analyst. Not only can they draw the abstractions, but they also completely understand the need to collect the corporate DNA that goes along with the models. These are also the folks who can develop the Metrics and BIR Models.

EIM Program Manager(s)

Ideally, the EIM program manager, or day-to-day leader, is pulled from a business area. The primary requirements for this leader are strong influential leadership skills and respect and trust across the business. In many organizations, there is someone who has worked in several functional areas. This experience leads to a more balanced view of issues and conflicting priorities. To be clear, managers with little experience in IM or IT will require some training but they are better than an IT leader because of their business expertise.

An IT manager can lead EIM programs if they have respect and experience across the company. However, there has to be clear understanding that the EIM program is *not* an IT program. Even if it lives in the IT area, the EIM program manager must define a clear separation of duties. Remember, over time, the EIM program *will be telling IT what to do*, not vice versa.

EIM Leadership

EIM leadership consists of the EIM program manager and the various steering bodies. In small to mid-size organizations this will normally be a steering committee with the sponsor as chairperson, the EIM program manager, and key representatives from each major business function.

In larger organizations, there may be an EIM operating body in each business division, a steering committee, and even an executive committee. Make sure there is a clear definition of what each body is expected to do, and maximize the time participants make available to the EIM team.

ROUGH ESTIMATES

Use Table 17.1 for a *rough* guide as to the size of the required team and average duration based on the level of maturity and status of your EIM program. Team sizes are presented for the average team

Table 17.1 EIM Level of Effort/Team Size

Phase	Effort	EIM Program Scenario Numbers Scale: Small Typical Large								
		New			**Maintain**			**Restore**		
Initiation	Team size	2	3	4				2	3	4
	Duration (days)	7	10	15	See Sustaining— part of normal EIM processes			7	10	15
Assessment	Team size	3	5	6	2	3	4	2	4	5
	Duration	7	15	20	5	10	15	5	15	20
Alignment	Team size	3	5	6	2	3	4	2	4	5
	Duration	10	15	25	5	8	10	8	15	20
Vision	Team size	2	3	4	1	2	4	1	3	4
	Duration	7	10	15	2	3	5	5	8	12
Business Model	Team size	3	7	9	2	3	4	2	6	8
	Duration	10	15	25	5	10	15	8	15	20
Architecture	Team size	3	7	9	2	4	6	3	5	7
	Duration	7	15	25	4	10	15	5	15	20
Road Map	Team size	3	7	9	2	4	7	3	5	7
	Duration	7	10	20	4	10	15	7	10	20
Sustaining	Team size	5	10	15	1	2	2	3	5	4
	Duration	7	10	20	1	5	7	7	10	20
		Initial time activities only								

for typical organizations, for that specific phase, with a minimum number to the left, and a large-scope EIM effort presented to the right. If you are running phases or activities in parallel, the total EIM team size may be the sum of the parallel activities. Estimates do not include time for resources attending facilitated sessions, meetings, providing subject expertise, or reviewing deliverables.

The estimates are presented across the three planning scenarios mentioned in Chapter 16 and shown in Figure 16.3. They are summarized as follows:

1. You are starting from scratch. The entire EIM team is focused on a new program.
2. You have partial EIM, or your EIM program is under way and it is time for periodic maintenance. While part of the EIM team sustains the program, part of it "peels off" and checks for possible course adjustments.
3. You have EIM or subdisciplines, but it is stuck and you need to restore credibility. Part of the team sustains what is going on, but a goodly fraction of the team needs to assist in the reloading of the program.

Durations are based on review of historical work done by the author's teams over the years. Effort numbers for the maintenance scenario assume the program is viable or not threatened. Effort numbers for the restore scenario assume at least one subdiscipline of EIM is installed and the enterprise has some awareness and knowledge of IM.

There is no "rule of thumb" like a ratio of company revenue to team size. There needs to be at least one architect/modeler and two analysts to actually work through most activities. Scope of content assets, business areas, business risk areas, extent of required behavior changes, and the current state of IMM all contribute to the team size. If you are doing all content across many business functions in a multinational company, your team needs will be greater.

SUMMARY

The initiation of the EIM program should not only be a planning exercise, but it also should start to enlighten business and IT, and result in steps toward business acceptance of IAM. The road to IAM means looking hard at your organization's business directions. For some companies this may not be very handy. There are substantial benefits from the first few phases: alignment to IT, education of business leaders, statement of a future vision, and documentation of critical information categories. Even if the EIM program stops, there is sufficient material to hand off to a technical team to begin subdisciplines of EIM, such as MDM, data quality, or a data warehouse. The following chapters present the details to form the foundation for an EIM program development toolkit to achieve managing your data and content assets.

References

1. For the sake of space, I have assumed that there is some awareness or source for project start-up tasks that are common to all program design projects.
2. As of publication date examples are: The Data Model Resource Book Series by Len Silverston, Universal Meta Data Models by Marco and Jennings, Financial and Insurance Industry Models by IBM, and Universal Data Models by Embarcadero.

How to Read the Phase Chapters

18

Since we are focusing more on the "What to do" of EIM programs, our phases and activities will be broken down into a specific presentation format in the following chapters.

Locator—Each phase will be shown in reference to where it typically occurs in the overall approach. Think of it as the "you are here" arrow on the train station map. The activities will be shown as optional, mandatory, or conditional within the phase. The conditions affecting execution of an activity are mentioned within the approach narrative. Remember although the phases and activities appear at a certain position on the flow of EIM program effort, this is not a waterfall-type process. All of the phases are connected by living documents. Once EIM is up and running, the EIM team should consult and select whatever activities are required to accomplish modifications or expansion of the program.

Activity Summary Table—Each activity will be described within the same outline as shown in Table 18.1. The tasks are mirrored in the Appendices as well, and are expanded in the paragraph "Approach Consideration."

Business Benefit and Ramification—This paragraph will recap why the business needs to participate and execute these steps. The EIM process is designed to add value at all stages, even if the program were to be delayed at some point. Since the deliverables are accretive, every phase should add

Table 18.1	Activity Summary Outline
Objective	What am I trying to achieve? What is the goal or intended results?
Purpose	Why should I do it? Why the activity is important? This may be redundant with some earlier material directed at management, but it puts it all together in one place.
Inputs	What do I need to perform the step? What information is needed to execute the step; inputs from other steps?
Tasks	The tasks that complete the activity are listed.
Techniques	What will help me complete the process?
Tools	What technology is available to expedite this step?
Outputs	What is produced as a result of this step? Most steps contain examples or templates. Note—certain activity such as a data quality assessment or a data model creation is so well covered in other books that we *will not* present how to in this book. These are specialized processes for IM staff, and the use of the output is our focus vs. the creation of the output.
Outcome	How can I tell if I'm finished or ready to move to the next step? Guidelines to determine completeness of the step and readiness to continue to the next step are offered.

Making Enterprise Information Management (EIM) Work for Business. DOI: 10.1016/B978-0-12-375695-4.00018-7

something to the business. The earlier phases we present add value in terms of deeper understanding. The latter phases provide useful artifacts for project work.

Approach Consideration—Any scenario that may make the activity optional or alter its sequence is examined. We will also review if there are any differences between an EIM program that is new, established, or in trouble.

Sample Output—An example from the case studies may be supplied to show what the deliverable may look like. To save space we will not present examples of all outputs, only those that show where the activity fits into the larger view of the EIM processes, or is a unique work product contributing to the concept of IAM. There are templates for almost all major deliverables in the Appendices. There are types of output where we will refer to sources outside of this book.

Tips and CSFs—Where could we run into trouble? A business sponsor or program manager needs to know what to look for and what makes this activity end successfully. Many of these tips point out symptoms that indicate a problem in the EIM program or an obstacle to be overcome.

Assessments

The trouble with having an open mind, of course, is that people will insist on coming along and trying to put things in it.
Terry Pratchett

CONTENTS

Making Enterprise Information Management (EIM) Work for Business. DOI: 10.1016/B978-0-12-375695-4.00019-9

The assessment step gathers data about the perceptions around information and means an organization deploys to use data, and how the organization is positioned to carry out its day-to-day work while adopting the philosophy of IAM (Figure 19.1). The current state of an organization's information abilities, maturity, and content effectiveness is examined.

A series of assessment activities (Figure 19.2) review current capabilities across the following dimensions:

1. Organization—There are many aspects of the organization itself that will affect EIM and in turn be affected by EIM. This covers organization charts, distribution of staff, maturity of personnel related to information usage, and level of understanding of their data assets.
2. Alignment—This dimension addresses, foremost, the Business Alignment to the actual current state of IT. Are IT projects done within a managed portfolio, and is information a key consideration?
3. Operations—This dimension looks at the facilities that create and contain content. Whereas technology looks at the wire and pliers, operations looks at the usage of technology. Does the organization have operational processes and facilities in place to handle content efficiently? Are applications and systems processes heavy or data oriented?
4. Governance—The amount of enforcement, compliance, and application relative to information or information-related policy is reviewed. Is there oversight and enforcement of standards? Are there standards?
5. Technology—Does current technology adequately support information use and creation adequately?
6. Information—What is managed in terms of information? Is privacy and security a concern? Are there rules and models?

These criteria are fairly standard across IT assessments. We address these, however, relative to the assessment types below. We used to do one huge assessment across all six criteria, but found a single large questionnaire to be cumbersome when we had to make adjustments. For example, if our client provided resources to go out and do interviews, we had to redo everything, so extraneous questions were not asked. Then we were scrambling to reload the assessment. We also learned that *quantitative findings* accelerated the assessment process. Questionnaires and interviews were qualitative and very time consuming. Lastly, while we can certainly cover all we need to under these labels, certain areas within these criteria were actually more important to EIM, and it was easier to gather data within these topics (trial and error—we were not geniuses back then). We found that it was better to present assessments by the nature of the assessment vs. the criteria we had to assess. Table 19.1 shows how the basic IT criteria are addressed across the five assessments in our EIM process.

Table 19.1 comes in handy when you want to combine assessments, or perhaps define your own. Just remember that the shaded, large Xs mark intersections that are mandatory.

TIPS FOR SUCCESS

Interviews are the bane of EIM efforts. Earlier we presented a sidebar on them, and this is a continuation. Interviews collect subjective data. They have to be reviewed, analyzed, and typed up. You are taking unstructured information and attempting to create structured findings. If you are considering EIM and your team or your consultants head out with fresh blank notepads and a handful of questions, you are only assessing the mood of the organization as it is *today*. It also goes without saying that interviews are a method used by consultants to collect data, meet more executives, and deepen relationships. You may or may not be OK with that, but either way, there are better techniques to deploy *for this particular process*. There are interviews performed when doing EIM definition, but it is very important to use executive face time for confirmation, decisions, and direction, not data gathering.

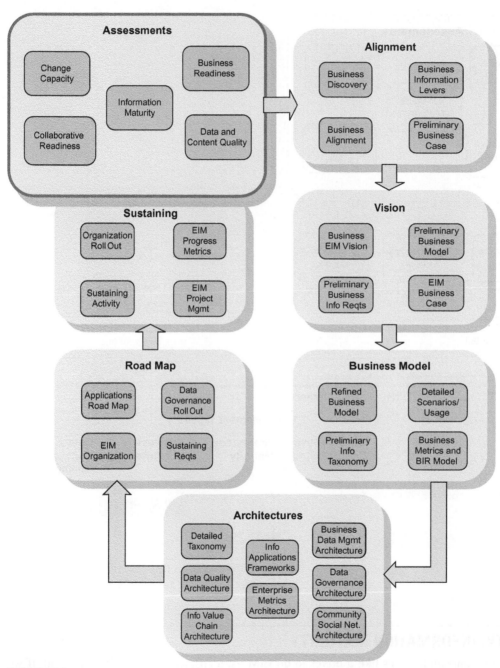

FIGURE 19.1

Assessment locator

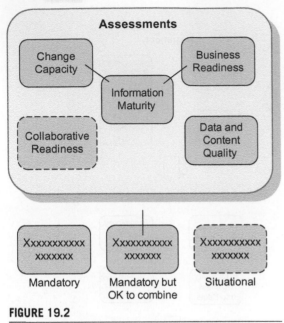

FIGURE 19.2

Assessment detail

Table 19.1 Assessment Criteria Cross Reference

	Assessment Types				
	Change Capacity	Collaborative Readiness	Information Maturity	Business Readiness	Data and Content Quality
Organization	X	X	X	X	
Alignment	X		X	X	X
Operations	X		X		X
Governance	X	X	X	X	X
Technology		X	X		X
Information	X	X	X	X	X

ACTIVITY: INFORMATION MATURITY

IMM of an organization seems like a driver to do EIM vs. a characteristic of EIM. After all, if we were "mature" we would not need EIM. It is a bit more involved than that. Anecdotal and hard evidence leads to the conclusion that organizations with a more proactive approach to information achieve better results. The key aspect of any discussion around maturity is during the early 21st century IT organizations began to see that there is a predictable maturity curve to climb around information production and usage. This in turn influences the definition of what the intended level of information maturity needs to be. There are definite stages of IMM along the way that can be described and measured.

While we review *how* the organization produces information and content, the main objective of this activity is to understand what the organization does with the content and information it produces. Usually this assessment is performed online over the company intranet. Questions focus on the relative impression management has regarding how well the company uses and manages data to its advantage. This includes use for decisions, communication, analysis, and critical functions such as R&D or compliance when the business requires these. Table 19.2 is a brief sample of some of the survey questions.

Table 19.2 IMM Sample Activity Summary					
		Disagree			Agree
	1	2	3	4	5
The enterprise has published principles on how we will view and handle data and information					
There are standards for how data is presented to all users and standards within IT for describing data					
There are policies for managing data that are published					
The data policies are understood and adhered to consistently					
There are rules for sharing and moving data in and out of the organization					
There is a widespread understanding of the importance of DQ					

Activity Summary (Table 19.3)

Table 19.3 Assessment Activity Summary	
Objective	Understand what the organization does with the content and information it produces. The focus is on the impressions and feelings business personnel have on how well the company uses and manages data to its advantage.
Purpose	Improving the leverage and quality of data and content is one reason the EIM program is considered and implemented. Besides identifying a current state, this activity provides the baseline for measuring progress toward future EIM effectiveness from an objective, qualitative standpoint.
Inputs	This activity requires development of survey style questions. Input would be a template from this book or similar process. Respondents must also be assured, and control in place, to maintain anonymity.
	If the EIM program is in place, this assessment can be reissued as part of ongoing measurement of EIM effectiveness, and will be initiated from the Sustaining phase.

(Continued)

Table 19.3 (Continued)	
Tasks	Determine scope of survey instrument Select or develop a maturity scale Identify all participants by name and group Orient respondents on importance and anonymity Agree on survey delivery (online, written, group focus) Review and modify maturity template Produce final form for delivery Deploy survey instrument Monitor online survey OR Distribute and monitor written version OR Prepare and deliver focus session(s) Collect and evaluate data Derive maturity score based on selected scale Collect existing standards, procedures, and policies for IM, info, resource utilization, prioritization, and controls and map to IMM scale Prepare findings for presentation.
Techniques	Survey respondents must be assured their answers are anonymous. There are three techniques, listed in order of preference: Online survey using intranet tool—most efficient means with highest response rates Focus groups, with groups segmented by management level—do *not* mix upper and lower management groups Written survey to be "check boxed"—this takes forever and response rates are low. Develop the IMM score with the team, and have the sponsor review and concur.
Tools	Online survey tools—most large companies have one licensed, or find one on the web, e.g., Survey Monkey™—use Excel to modify/develop the survey template.
Outputs	Survey results are evaluated and are usually produced in the form of charts or graphs A statement on the existence or lack of DG can be made Specific outliers or extreme results must be evaluated and addressed.
Outcome	IMM score and presentation delivered Results may include recommendations for next steps Sponsor concurs with findings, even if they are controversial.

Business Benefits and Ramifications

This activity provides an objective view of the level of sophistication in regards to information use. Often this survey will stand on its own to make a framing statement for the need for EIM. The results will provide valuable insight for developing the Road Map and ongoing EIM program metrics.

Approach Considerations

Most likely, the length of the survey will be of concern to your EIM leadership team. The sponsor will be concerned about alienating stakeholders this soon. Determining the scope of the instrument will be a function of determining what data you must collect for IMM, and whether or not you are combining this survey with another. The survey should take no more than 15 minutes in its online form or response rates will be too low to use.

The actual questions need to be very unambiguous. There will be a significant portion of responders that try to second-guess the survey. The full template provided in the Appendices has been adjusted to screen outliers. When we blend surveys we always throw in a few questions that have obvious answers to indicate possible attempts to influence the results.

Of course you want as many responses as possible. Respondents should represent, at minimum, middle and upper layers of management. I prefer to segregate the responses of various groups, as their answers are almost always very different. In addition there must be a mechanism to provide incentive to take the survey, as well as monitoring and follow-up processes to deal with laggards.

If the assessment is being done via facilitation or interviews, attempt to make the meeting as structured as possible. A group session should fill out the survey via a form, then tally and review the results. Interviews should cover a core set of questions in a survey format, that is, the interviewee offers a score. Also use the interview to collect personal impressions from interviewees. The population for interviews will be much smaller, so make sure the sponsor understands the IMM survey will be more anecdotal than statistical.

This activity is not considered optional, although it can be merged in with a Business Readiness and/or a Change Capacity assessment.

Sample Output

Table 19.2 shows a sample of some of the types of questions asked. All the surveys we use take this form of answer scale (called a Likert). We feel it provides a decent distribution regarding the answers and gets us closer to seeing how the organization really feels about how data and content is used.

Figure 19.3 shows two panels from the IMM results for Ubetcha. The Maturity scale ended up as a 1.8 (subjective based on concurrence with sponsor and executives).

During the Road Map and Sustaining phases, Ubetcha will need to determine where they want to end up on the scale they chose and how to remedy the perceptions revealed in the survey questions.

TIP FOR SUCCESS

Surveys have become a very popular means within organizations to measure just about everything. As a result, any attempt to survey may be met with suspicion or people may feel that they are not worth the investment in time. And depending on how survey results have been used in the past, you may also be surprised at how far you need to go to convince personnel they will remain anonymous. If the survey history in your organization makes it a poor choice for you, consider facilitated focus groups (conducted by individuals outside your organization, NOT your internal EIM team). It will take longer, but may lead to better results.

Time frames for this activity should average two to four weeks with the attention of a full-time resource from your EIM team and assistance from an internal survey group. Try your marketing or HR organizations for help. They usually do all kinds of surveys and are adept with them and they can help you with focus groups if you go that route. A short time frame is a success factor here. If there is a need to do focus groups, then assign two resources and get the groups processed within a month. Avoid the perception of "analysis paralysis." Remember there are people out there who will be looking for symptoms of the "same old IM project."

ACTIVITY: CHANGE CAPACITY

All organizations are unique in how they carry out their mission and activities, even within the same business arena or market. This set of behavior patterns or style of an organization represents its culture. Part of any culture is its capacity for change. Obviously, organizations vary as to how easily or rapidly they can accommodate changes. Therefore, the objective of this activity is to measure this

Question #	Percent Positive	Survey Question
26	49	I understand the key indicators that measure my organization's performance.
5	72	There are rules for sharing and moving data in and out of the company.
29	79	I use data analysis to make changes in my work processes to improve results.
21	85	My department has several databases, spreadsheets, or other data stores that we build and use to do reports.
28	94	I collect and analyze information related to my work.

- There is general belief that management understands the measures of organizational performance.

- Given the insurance regulatory environment, the strong positive response to question 5 is not surprising; however, it conflicts with general perceptions regarding DQ and controls.

- UIC management generally believes that it uses analysis to analyze and improve work processes.

- The high percent positive score for questions 21, 29, and 28 show that pervasive "shadow IT" may be exposing UIC to risks or higher costs.

- Question 28 indicates that most of middle management could be spending more time collecting and analyzing data than managing, and requires further review.

UIC Is Here

Level 1: Initial	Level 2: Repeatable	Level 3: Defined	Level 4: Managed	Level 5: Optimized
•Entrepreneurial •Individual •Fragmented •Chaotic •Idiosyncratic •Few users •Rules unknown •Variable quality •Costly	•Departmental •Consolidation •Reconciliation •Internally defined •Reactive •Local standards •Internal DQ •Specialist users •Local processes •Costly	•Integration •Enterprise view •Data accountability •Strategic alignment •Standards •Sharing and reuse •Centralized DQ •Planned and tracked •Wide data usage •Metadata mgmt •Common technology •Efficient	•Quantitative control •Closed loop •Low latency •Interactive •Unstructured data •Collaborative •Process efficiency and effectiveness •Built-in quality •Extended value chain •High availability	•Improvement and innovation •Real time •Extensive data mining •Knowledge base •Competitive intelligence •Data assets valued •Self-managing

FIGURE 19.3

IMM UIC

capacity for change and locate potential resistance points. If you do not do this, you risk missing vital information that will allow the EIM team to accommodate and leverage your culture, rather than fight it. In addition, the earlier the cultural issues are identified, the sooner any large obstacles will be recognized and addressed.

Activity Summary (Table 19.4)

Table 19.4	Change Capacity Activity Summary
Objective	Measure the capacity for the organization to change behaviors required for adapting IAM. Secondarily, identify potential resistance points.
Purpose	It is vital to assess the risk to EIM that will originate from culture change issues. The EIM program must be sustainable and cannot be made so without vital information that will allow the EIM team to accommodate and leverage the organization's culture. The results are used to adjust the Sustaining phase and will even influence the rollout of EIM projects and policies.
Inputs	Best practices indicate use of a standard change management process, which always includes an assessment step.
	The Sustaining phase may ask for this assessment to be revisited to measure how the organization is adapting to required changes.
Tasks[1]	Determine the formality of the assessment, that is, an informal structured meeting format or a formal survey instrument
	Determine the target audience
	Define the survey population or interviewees
	Define the approach—structured meeting, written, or online
	Administer the survey or conduct meetings
	Analyze and summarize findings
	Determine if additional investigation is required
	Leadership alignment
	Leadership commitment
	Determine what will be reported now vs. sent to the EIM team to use during subsequent phases.
Techniques	If the HR department has a change management team or organization development practitioners with change management expertise, utilize their skills.
	If time is short and informal, anecdotal exercise will be sufficient until the Sustaining phase.
	Another informal technique is to maintain the structured meeting questions as a check list, and review those with various groups as different personnel move in and out of the EIM effort.
Tools	Online survey tools—most large companies have one licensed, or find one on the web, e.g., Survey Monkey™—use Excel or Word to modify/develop the survey and questionnaire forms.
Outputs	The results may take the form of a report or presentation. Individual responses need to be held confidential within the EIM program, while aggregated results need to be widely communicated.
Outcome	The culture capacity assessment is complete when results are acknowledged and accepted by the executive team or sponsor.

[1]Nelson, K., & Aaron, S. (2005). The Change Management Pocket Guide: Tools for Managing Change *(Plan: Assess needs,* p. 12). Cincinnati, OH: Change Guides LLC.

Business Benefits and Ramifications

The data collected from this step will be used throughout the program design and for a long time after rollout. It provides an excellent baseline to measure EIM adoption as well.

Approach Considerations

This effort is strongly recommended. There really is no optional path—it has to be done. It can be done in two passes, a brief informal iteration now and then a detailed formal pass during the Road Map or Sustaining phase. The most common approach is to do a survey that is geared to reveal any glaring issues now, and then revisit the Change Capacity assessment during the Road Map and Sustaining phases.

Some organizations will resist any assessment of culture from an EIM (aka "technical") team. If the EIM team cannot overcome this obstacle, bury the most telling aspects of the Change Capacity instrument in the IMM survey.

The target audience is all management as well as knowledge workers or departmental analysts. The population to be surveyed needs to be segregated with results kept by whatever segments you choose. At minimum, segregate upper and middle management and all others.

This assessment is in the form of a formal survey and is best done online. If an online survey option is not available, we do focus groups. Given historically low response rates, the last resort is a form to be filled out. If the focus group or paper-form options are used, allow several weeks to get focus groups scheduled, and allow two weeks for forms to come back, but expect three weeks during which they actually keep showing up.

If there is a hint of sweeping changes, or resistance areas are already known (as in a prior attempt at IM failed in some way due to resistance), then a formal instrument is most likely mandatory.

Sample Output

A simple visual is the best means to present results. The UIC example shows a strong, but not insurmountable resistance to change (Figure 19.4).

TIP FOR SUCCESS

Often business or technology executives that have not engaged in formal business change programs will resist performing this step. It will seem "squishy." However, any root-cause analysis of the failures of large technology efforts over the decades shows the reoccurrence of a number of significant factors: poor communication, no alignment with the business on what is to be delivered, ineffective training, and lack of business sponsorship, to name a few. These are change management issues that have cost organizations millions of dollars in failed programs. If you want to do better with your EIM program, you *must* formally manage the changes required. The standard change management tasks used to support implementation of the EIM processes can be taken from any number of prominent OD industry sources or authors, including Prosci,[1] Change Guides,[2] LLC., John Kotter,[3] or Daryl Connor.[4] See the endnotes and bibliography for these sources. There is an *enormous* amount of material available for very little if any cost, and it is easily adapted to EIM.

ACTIVITY: BUSINESS READINESS

This assessment identifies whether the Business Alignment to IT is such that managed information would add value. Determining if the business' current state indicates a readiness for IAM can be difficult. Much of the (lack of) readiness of the business can stem from its information maturity level or

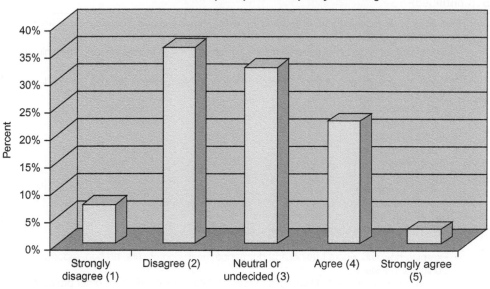

FIGURE 19.4

UIC Change Capacity

its culture. But we also need to look at usage of current data and information in alignment to business direction. Ideally you then blend these results with the IMM and Change Capacity.

Typically the EIM team will start to gather business goals and objectives, and then examine applications and business areas to determine if the business initiatives are well supported, or how they are supported by data. Often this assessment is done as a sort of justification for EIM. The business goals and objectives gathered here are refined in subsequent phases. If you do not do this assessment (e.g., the CEO says he already knows there is no alignment), then you will gather the goals and objectives in the Alignment phase.

Activity Summary (Table 19.5)

Table 19.5 Business Readiness Activity Summary	
Objective	Determine if current production and use of information is in line with business direction.
	Determine if the organization could increase value and achieve goals if some future state of EIM is attained.
	Determine if the enterprise has the capability to convey business direction and enable alignment with IAM.
Purpose	This assessment is done to start the business justification for EIM. In addition it starts to show where there are missed opportunities or excessive costs in the context of IM.

(Continued)

Table 19.5 (Continued)	
Inputs	This activity will require documentation of business direction, either provided to the team or from public sources.
	The IMM results could be of use if there are indications of little management communication about direction or willingness to share data.
Tasks	Determine specific expression of Readiness appropriate for the enterprise level of detail, does it include: 　Information 　Technology 　People/Organization 　Operations 　Alignment 　Governance 　Risk/Compliance Assess the availability of the information needed for analysis Gather data from all sources and review Record business strategies, goals, and objectives Examine decision-making maturity of the various forums or units Examine how and where business performance measuring occurs; ad hoc, reports, Business Intelligence Document the alignment of business to current data warehouse, BI, or other projects Determine if there is substantial reporting and analytics activity outside of IT and proposed future development Document project management processes and results Prepare Business Readiness presentation.
Techniques	Document review and analysis. Unless they are volunteering, avoid interviews to ask, "Where is the business going?" Use as much material as the executive team has for business direction. If access to this material is denied, use publicly available sources of data to derive business direction.
Tools	Excel or Word to manage questionnaires and findings.
Outputs	Outputs to the Alignment phase are the collected business goals and objectives.
	The management team needs to review, at least in a subjective way (see Figure 19.5), the current state of Business Readiness to use managed information.
	If the IMM survey has been done or is also being done, you can merge the two into one session to save executive time.
Outcome	You have a list of organization strategies, goals, and objectives. These are measurable, that is, there is some kind of metric that can be applied to the business directions.
	You have developed a list of the "data czars" in the organization, that is, those individuals with access to large amounts of data out of the oversight of IT or any kind of governance.
	You have findings that indicate how strongly business projects coordinate on an information basis, and how effectively the organization completes projects.

Business Benefits and Ramifications

If the business is sincere about IAM, they will want to provide direct input regarding the business direction to the EIM team. Many times as business leaders are sitting in a room reviewing the results, they will discern disparate initiatives and actually improve their strategic plans.

Approach Consideration

The level of detail sets the tone for this assessment. It can be a simple review of Business Alignment, or a deep dive into how well the business gets projects deployed. Identifying and analyzing the documents and findings can create some detective work, so a detailed version of this assessment could chew up some calendar time.

Perhaps the one layer of detail that has to be in all versions of this assessment is the documented business goals and objectives and the means employed to examine and report business performance. Any lack of Business Alignment will show up when business programs and projects are reviewed against the capacity to measure the programs and projects.

This activity can be combined with the IMM survey, where IMM surveys and the readiness aspect collects. A fraction of the time, the IMM, Change Capacity, and Business Readiness are combined by companies to provide a two- to three-week quick overview of current state. This is a good jump start and presell activity for EIM. And you can always iterate back for additional details, or pick up details in the Alignment, Road Map, and Sustaining phases.

If you have the aforementioned difficulty getting to material, for example, business leaders say "we will tell you what we want," you are off to a bad start. They are not internalizing what EIM means. Since the alignment details can be carried forward into the Alignment phase, it is perfectly acceptable to do a "guerilla" version of the business direction. Use public documents or generally available material like annual reports, management goals, budget projections, external wikis, financial publications, and trade publications. You bypass the "bad start" problem. If you get to doing detailed alignment then you are past the denial point. Worst-case scenario is to base the Readiness assessment on a round of interviews of executives and ask them "what they want" and "what is wrong." Don't turn down any invitations to talk EIM over with an executive, but remember interviews take a long time and are too subjective.

Sample Output

Figure 19.5 shows one method to present the alignment findings. It is more relevant to management if you place an indicator of severity, in this case black and gray lights.

TIP FOR SUCCESS

Again, if there is poor cooperation or little material to use, then IAM is not a priority. Focus on using EIM to improve data and content usage and cycle back at a later date to sell IAM. If the CIO has the accountability to "do EIM" but no authority, then gather business data through the optional channels mentioned above. The most important factor here is getting something that shows how the business is dealing with alignment and how it currently measures itself.

ACTIVITY: DATA AND CONTENT QUALITY ASSESSMENT

This activity will quantify the nature of the organizations' data usefulness challenges. Here we will identify business data and content issues. At this stage it is highly advisable to conduct a brief review of why these discussions are talking place, i.e., "our data stinks." However, we need to clarify exactly what "stinks" means. (Some organizations may be more elegant in their declaration, some less!)

Findings	Impact	Risk	Recommendation
Lack of business involvement in a business case or commitment to integrated data; there is no business sponsor evident.	Majority of projects are short term/tactical in nature and aren't predicated and aligned with long-term strategic objectives.	●	EIM program should focus on upper management sponsorship.
UIC personal lines does not have one source of business needs.	Not operating as one team. Limits the amount of enterprise solutions that can be deployed.	●	Finish the integration of cultures due to past M&A activities.
Current IM projects (BI) are not measured in terms of progress or contribution. "No time."	False sense of security—there is a LOT of effort to get numbers right the "next phase." Accountability is difficult to determine, as is degree of success.	●	EIM needs to establish overall sets of targets where value of project and data can be determined.
Lack of business involvement very evident during project meetings and review sessions. Business areas prefer to "go on their own."	No accountability or ability to discern who is delivering data. No oversight of data being spread out.	●	EIM steering committee needs to add or form subcommittee with more resistant business leaders
No approved business case/strategy for DW/BI projects. Most performance metrics are delivered from departmental systems. BI efforts supply data only.	Business and IT are not aligned on how best to leverage the company's information assets. UIC is not as competitive as it should be as a result.	●	(1) Develop a business-driven/aligned IAM strategy. (2) Establish a business sponsor and governance body that will provide oversight for the build-out and sustaining phases of IAM. (3) Secure the necessary financial/resource commitments for IAM initiatives after a business case is developed.
BI team is not tightly aligned with the business—doing one-off ad hoc files requests vs. a leveraged framework.	BI team has become an order taker and not a trusted partner with the business. This is not a strategic direction and is not best practice.	○	(1) Must develop two-way partnered relationship with the business on such things as communication, strategic planning, tactical projects, issue/risk mitigation, standards, and governance. (2) A DS manager should be assigned as the point person for each business unit needing information from the DS team. That individual should be routinely present at all business planning/operational sessions and should have standing meetings with key departmental stakeholders.
Buisness resources often cancel review meetings or walkthroughs.	Speaks to the lack of business alignment. Also, delays implementations and sacrifices the quality of deliverables—thereby creating postimplementation rework.	○	EIM needs to improve business alignment. Culture needs to change toward working together.
There are issues related to gathering good structured business requirements. Actual process used to collect requirements is unknown. The PMO manages project plans only.	End-state deliverables may not really meet the customers needs resulting in rework (efficiency/ROI issue). No opportunity to leverage current work, this will increase future development costs. There is no retention of knowledge learned.	○	Mgmt should have an overall EIM application strategy with high level information requirements.
The business tends to ask for reports vs. present a business need.	This hampers long-term effectiveness of information.	○	Business leaders need to participate in joint information sessions that cross departments. EIM needs to present findings and needs cross Functionality.

FIGURE 19.5

UIC Business Readiness

There are many techniques available to conduct this type of an assessment. This activity's execution depends heavily on prior information project efforts, as well as the current timing resource and data quality technology available to the EIM team. Often there is data quality profiling done, a formal set of exercise to discern data quality, but just as often the exercise needs to be anecdotal, due to constraints on time and resources.

Determining which techniques to use depends on available time, resources, and the existence of technology. Before you start, executives should look at a list of content and data characteristics and determine what they want to review. There are 12 possible dimensions to review (Table 19.6), but you need to also gain consensus on what is being measured from a business view.

- Regulatory risk—What are the possible costs? Have there already been issues?
- Errors and omissions—Has there been any loss of credibility or market presence?
- Costs of known data issue—What did the various issues related to "fat finger" errors and poor data management cost?

The characteristics listed above apply to all types of content, structured and nonstructured, and are often addressed in a discipline called "data quality." The information collected here can lead toward

Table 19.6 DQ Dimensions to DQ Cost Examples*

DQ Dimensions		Cost Characteristics and Examples		
Dimension	**Definition**	**Regulatory Risk**	**Errors and Omissions**	**Costs of Known Issues**
Data specifications	A measure of the existence, completeness, quality, and documentation of data standards, data models, business rules, metadata, and reference data.	Missing standards?	Misinterpretation creates safety issue	Inconsistency increases handling costs
Data integrity fundamentals	A measure of the existence, validity, structure, and content and other basic characteristics of the data.	Penalties for invalid data	Missing data lowers credibility	Poor coding results on overcharging
Duplication	A measure of unwanted duplication existing within or across systems for a particular field, record, or data set.	Privacy regulations violation	Double billing client	Conflicting answers
Accuracy	A measure of the correctness of the content of the data (which requires an authoritative source of reference to be identified and accessible).	Penalties for unproven results	Customers see wrong numbers	Higher rates from entering wrong address
Consistency and synchronization	A measure of the equivalence of information stored or used in various data stores, applications, and systems, and the processes for making data equivalent.	Penalties for inconsistent reports	Errors from failure to synchronize	Excess cost of synchronizing
Timeliness and availability	A measure of the degree to which data are current and available for use as specified and in the time frame in which they are expected.	Penalty for late report	Late data lowers credibility	Inaccurate responses to market conditions

(Continued)

Table 19.6 (Continued)

DQ Dimensions		Cost Characteristics and Examples		
Dimension	**Definition**	**Regulatory Risk**	**Errors and Omissions**	**Costs of Known Issues**
Ease-of-use and maintainability	A measure of the degree to which data can be accessed and used and the degree to which data can be updated, maintained, and managed.	Poor security fails audits	Loss of confidence after hacking	Cost of overrides and manual corrections
Data coverage	A measure of the availability and comprehensiveness of data compared to the total data universe or population of interest.	Overlook new regulators	Help desk can't see new user manual	Missed change in market conditions
Presentation quality	A measure of how information is presented to and collected from those who utilize it. Format and appearance support appropriate use of the information.	Misinterpretation slows approval	Omission loses contract	Can't parse out comment fields
Perception, relevance, and trust	A measure of the perception of and confidence in the quality of the data; the importance, value, and relevance of the data to the business needs.	Cost of additional audits	Reduction in shareholder value	Lost business
Data decay	A measure of the rate of negative change to the data.	Penalty for early destruction	Inadvertent insider info in e-mail	Lost sale from out-of-date catalog
Transactability	A measure of the degree to which data will produce the desired business transaction or outcome.	Penalties for insufficient reserves	Biggest customer gets competitor's statement	Wrong equipment installed

From McGilvray, D. (2008). Executing Data Quality Projects: Ten Steps to Quality Data and Trusted Information™. Burlington, MA: Morgan Kaufmann Publishers. Copyright 2008 Elsevier Inc. All rights reserved.

an ability to identify solid financial impact of poor IM, thereby reinforcing the EIM mind-set. We can also generate a "risk if we do not do this" statement. Typically, your organization already has a push or program for data quality. With IAM, data quality becomes a subdiscipline or function within EIM. Using the inventory analogy, data quality is similar to inventory control.

Activity Summary (Table 19.7)

Table 19.7 Data Quality

Objective	Quantify and/or qualify the nature of the organization's data usefulness challenges (aka DQ). This activity will identify current business data and content issues affecting usefulness of information.
Purpose	One of the core elements of EIM is managing the usefulness of data. DQ is mandatory for this element. As wonderful as you may think EIM is, it is better to do DQ without EIM, than EIM without DQ.

(Continued)

Table 19.7 (Continued)	
Inputs	Inputs from other activities might be recommended areas to profile. You may get these from the Business Alignment assessment or some anecdotal findings from IMM assessment.
Tasks	*The tasks here are very general and depend entirely on the level of detail you are permitted. Again, consult the excellent DQ books mentioned earlier in this book and found in the bibliography.* Identify data groups for assessment 　　Identify major groups for assessment 　　Compile inventory of known sources to analyze 　　Review source data issues 　　Identify known problems of low DQ 　　Prioritize areas to survey Establish DQ objectives and measures 　　Determine the specific assessment objectives or goals 　　Identify quality characteristics to be reviewed 　　Determine specific measures of the information 　　Determine the minimum DQ required for successful execution of the most significant process requiring the data Determine files or Processes to Assess 　　Identify location of data and content to assess 　　Determine measurement technique Identify data validation sources for accuracy assessment 　　Identify most authoritative source of data from which to assess the accuracy of data 　　Verify the accuracy of the surrogate source being considered Extract samples of data 　　Review source system files 　　Determine sampling technique (if any) for identified files 　　Extract samples of data Measure DQ 　　Analyze data for business rule conformance 　　Audit primary and secondary key cardinality 　　Audit domains and values 　　Map to quality criteria list 　　Identify cost of quality estimates Interpret and report DQ 　　Determine DQ issues root causes 　　Compile final DQ assessment report 　　Develop business impact statement for DQ 　　Deliver DQ assessment report.
Techniques	There are copious techniques for DQ, from interviews and reviewing issue logs (anecdotal) to complex algorithms (using a tool). If time is limited, techniques should be simple, and based on straightforward data collection. If a full data profiling is called for, a host of techniques will be used.
Tools	Simple efforts can use SQL to run queries, and Excel to contain results. Sophisticated efforts will use software from vendors who specialize in DQ.
Outputs	The minimum output is a statement of the relative level of DQ in terms of current issues, i.e., why can't the current level of DQ support intended use? At maximum, a report of the various data profile characteristics, financial impact, and remediation difficulty is developed. Any DG findings from the IMM survey can be enhanced.
Outcome	The outcomes of this step must be defined when it is started, since it can vary so much. You are done when the specific DQ exercises and reports are complete and turned into an assessment that is presented to business sponsors and accepted.

Business Benefits and Ramifications

At the risk of seeming glib, it is better to do data quality work and not do EIM, than to do EIM and not do data quality work. Some effort must be executed to assess data quality if you are at all serious about EIM. Data quality is a significant required element in IAM. Using the "hard asset" analogies, data quality is the equivalent of inventory control processes or material handling procedures. Without this, IAM cannot happen.

The business will benefit from understanding the costs of poor data quality, as well as the risk profile related to data quality. For example, if your enterprise is regulated, or privacy is a consideration in your business model, or there is an actuarial component to your model, you need to understand how your content and data can affect risk. The possibility of risk within content is a crucial driver to shaping the EIM program. The accessibility to data and content may seem like a technical issue at first. However, it is a major compliance component and affects Business activity. Therefore it is suitable to examine its influence in EIM at this point. The data quality elements of EIM are one of the risk mitigation mechanisms for IAM.

Approach Consideration

A Data Quality assessment is not an option. Even if you say it will not happen, it *will happen*. You cannot get very far into managing information in any way and not encounter data quality issues.

The only considerations for the approach is the level of detail to be done now vs. later, and the techniques that will be used to conduct the actual assessments. If no tools are available to perform a profiling, then the EIM team may choose to write queries against key data sets. No matter what level of detail or approach, there must be agreement on what is being measured and how the results are quantified.

If you have limited time when starting EIM, or you are positioning EIM to sell the program, use this as a tremendous opportunity to identify hard dollars impact of information *mis*management.

Sample Output

Farfel chose a middle ground, a quick two-week assessment based on some scans of primary data across five key areas of content. The content area included databases, document management, and collaborative facilities (SharePoint). Figure 19.6 shows (on a scale of 1–4) that there are issues, and the level of analysis was sufficient for Farfel to realize that data quality issues supported proceeding with the EIM program.

TIP FOR SUCCESS

Once a Data Quality assessment is started, the only real issues observed over time are "scope creep," as there is always something else to look for, and denial. Often findings are taken personally by constituents of the files or functions being reviewed. It may help to have the EIM leadership convey this is not a performance review.

ACTIVITY: COLLABORATIVE READINESS

A specific area of cultural readiness is the ability to collaborate. This activity measures amount of collaboration or other cooperative behaviors in existence. This may even include Facebook™-type constructs or even Twitter™ in some organizations. This assessment is important when content management, document management, and workflow are within the realm of the EIM team. Additionally, this assessment is handy if the Business Readiness assessment picked up on social networking as a

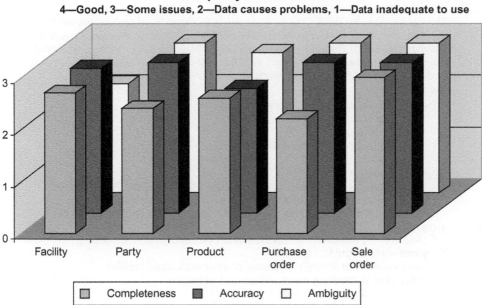

Data quality assessment—Farfel
4—Good, 3—Some issues, 2—Data causes problems, 1—Data inadequate to use

Completeness ☐ Accuracy ■ Ambiguity ☐

FIGURE 19.6

Data profile—Farfel

possible enabler of business goals. This assessment is usually done via examination of the technology available, its extent of deployment, and the usage. Additionally, a brief survey, similar to the Change Capacity, can be used to see if the organization even wants to collaborate.

This is not a trivial subject. As organizations become more sophisticated in the ability to reach across organizational boundaries, the need to leverage and manage the collaboration increases. In addition, there is an opportunity to improve how an enterprise makes decisions by instituting and managing collaborative and social technologies. There are several labels (ours is collaborative business intelligence or CBI) to the formal process of capturing and using the intelligence on *how* an organization interacts and responds to information. If anything like this is on the enterprise radar, then this assessment should be considered. Lastly, often companies have a situation where SharePoint or Lotus files are out of control. This assessment offers a chance to zero in on this issue.

Activity Summary (Table 19.8)

Table 19.8 Collaborative Readiness Activity Summary	
Objective	Determine the capability and/or the need for an organization to institute collaborative elements into the use of data and content.
Purpose	If there are elements such as workflow, document sharing (e.g., Notes, SharePoint), document management, and social networking-type facilities, then there are significant resources being used. These can present as much IAM opportunity as any database.

(Continued)

Table 19.8 (Continued)	
Inputs	Most of the time, the IMM, Change Capacity, or Business Readiness survey will trigger the need for this. When planning the entire Assessment phase, however, consider this activity beforehand. The will help with shaping the Readiness approach. Typical inputs are the questions related to cooperation, from the IMM or Change Capacity assessments, or determining that the business needs to consider workflow from the Readiness assessment.

Tasks	Determine assessment scope, does it include:
	    Web sites and content
	    Documents and sharing
	    Identifying existing communities of practice or interest
	    Workflow
	    Collaborative products
	    Contemporary facilities like instant messaging, texting, Twitter™, or Facebook™
	Determine scope of survey instrument
	Determine assessment approach—interviews, document review, or survey, or combination
	Collect existing standards, procedures, and policies for document sharing, workflow, internal wikis, blogs, etc. for review
	Collect inventory of SharePoint, Notes, or other work share facilities
	Identify all participants by name and group if necessary
	Orient respondents on importance and anonymity
	Identify interview of focus group participants if necessary
	Produce final form for delivery
	Deploy survey instrument
	Monitor online survey OR
	Distribute and monitor written version OR
	Prepare and deliver focus session(s)
	Collect and evaluate data from surveys, documents, and meetings
	Develop Collaborative Readiness statement based on predetermined scale
	Prepare findings for presentation.

Techniques	Interviews, surveys (online preferred), and facilitated sessions are techniques of choice.
Tools	On rare occasions large organizations may actually track work and content use through their intranet, and this data may be available. Otherwise Excel and Word are the tools in use here.
Outputs	The Readiness information from this is used to shape the EIM Vision, in that collaboration may be a new topic for many organizations. It can also shape the Business Model, since workflow can be altered, and the Architecture, since the facilities for collaboration may require modification or inclusion in EIM.
Outcome	This step is done when the assessment is reviewed and accepted by the EIM leadership.

Business Benefits and Ramifications

Collaborative communities often establish more efficient relationships that drive new business actions, as information and knowledge residing throughout the organization is optimized. The benefit of managing collaboration is that business areas, once fully engaged through these collaborative communities or mechanisms, can be measured and given feedback that they can use to improve not only the business but also their own work processes.

Table 19.9 Farfel Collaborative Assessment

Collaborative Assessment Results Summary

FarfelNet keeps the merchandiser in front of the desktop waiting for information, rather than in front of the supplier making the deal.
The catalog information is always one quarter old. During the holidays it is useless.
All merchandisers have their own "system" for managing suppliers, looking for trends, and maintaining catalog entries.
Representative FarfelNet survey responses:
  The overall organization of FarfelNet needs to be simplified. I find it very difficult to find presentations, brochures, etc. Navigating through the menu ultimately results in a search, and the search box most often results in no documents found.
  Very often I'm not able to find what I'm looking for or the relevant documents are not so immediately in evidence.
  Why do we use SharePoint? All we do is spread out old messes into new messes. We are wasting the potential for sharing.
  Also I find it hard to have to look at multiple web sites for competitors.
FarfelNet does not provide the productive work environment the Farfel merchandisers require to meet corporate objectives.

Approach Consideration

The existence of large amounts of Lotus Notes or SharePoint data may require a spin-off assessment, as many organizations wake up one day to find out they cannot control or afford anymore Notes and SharePoint sites. They tend to multiply like rodents. Otherwise this is a fairly straightforward assessment.

Sample Output

Table 19.9 shows some interview and survey results from Farfel. Farfel has one collaborative mechanism that was developed to support the merchandising area. It is a web site that allows access to merchandiser notes, proposals, supplier catalogs, and purchase orders for merchandise.

TIPS FOR SUCCESS

Understanding just what is being assessed can sometime be a challenge. Large organizations, like big companies or government agencies, have enormous amounts of content and many islands of local "knowledge stores." Blend this with the examination of current state, as well as there being a huge pressure to use more and more collaborative technologies, and scope becomes a problem. If there is a large amount of content in question, then make sure there is adequate time to conduct an effective Collaboration assessment, or spin off a project to add to the Road Map.

SUMMARY

The Assessment phase for EIM provides understanding and starts to seed the core data required to form the business-aligned architecture. The EIM team and more important the business sponsors will start to see the importance of building blocks like an aligned business model, data governance, and the role of culture.

The assessments need to be tailored for your situation, but some version of the key assessments of IMM, Change Capacity, and Data Quality *must* be done. It is fine to take a lighter approach due to time or other constraints, as long as the remainder of the EIM program development and sustaining activities incorporate the details. At some point you will address the details for the required assessments if you intend to treat data as an asset. Tailoring them means choosing when to assess, not if to assess.

The other assessment activities are optional and should be chosen based on business directions and circumstances.

References

1. Prosci is the recognized leader in change management research and the world's largest provider of change management products and training. Formed in 1994, Prosci has conducted longitudinal studies in the application of change management with more than 2000 organizations from 65 countries. Prosci sponsors the Change Management Learning Center at www.change-management.com. This online resource provides access to change management resources and research for more than 40,000 registered members. www.change-management.com

2. Change Guides, LLC: After writing the *Change Management Pocket Guide: Tools for Managing Change*, Stacy Aaron and Kate Nelson founded Change Guides LLC in the spring of 2005 to provide change management products and services to clients of all sizes, in all industries. Change Guides LLC is headquartered in Cincinnati, Ohio: www.changeguidesllc.com

3. John Kotter is a professor at the "http://en.wikipedia.org/wiki/Harvard_Business_School" \o "Harvard Business School" Harvard Business School and author, who is regarded as an authority on "http://en.wikipedia.org/wiki/Leadership" \o "Leadership" leadership and change. In particular, he discusses how the best organizations actually "do" change. Dr. Kotter has published numerous books including *Leading Change* (1996), which outlined an actionable, 8-step process for implementing successful transformations, and *The Heart of Change* (2002).

4. Daryl Connor is the author of the best-selling book, *Managing at the Speed of Change* (1992; revised 2006), and founder of Conner Partners, a consultancy with a long history of helping organizations address the human side of organizational change.

Alignment

20

To be thus enlightened is to remove the barriers between oneself and others.
Dogen

CONTENTS

As an EIM leader, business alignment appears conceptually simple; ask the business what it wants and then figure a way to fit it into EIM, right? But as pointed out earlier, business alignment is a frequently named barrier to success in IT. Often the business does not want to tell IT the business plan. IT portfolios still reflect specific initiatives and not an asset management mind-set even if the CIO is "in the loop"

Making Enterprise Information Management (EIM) Work for Business. DOI: 10.1016/B978-0-12-375695-4.00020-5

of business strategy, IT governance rarely embraces data governance. The attributions of benefits from a business initiative are rarely matched or posted to the IT project that enabled the initiative.

In the early years of the twenty-first century, CIOs began to get visibility to executive management, or report to the CEO. Business alignment should have decreased as a problem. But in many organizations, changing the reporting structure did not address the issue; the issue being *translation* of a business plan into a business EIM vision, and acceptance of IAM as more than a metaphor. Managing your content as an asset to the betterment of the entire enterprise, certainly requires connection to business direction. This phase of our process does just that. It takes business direction, and creates a view of where the value from IAM is derived. Stated differently, the Alignment phase develops the business view of how information and content will be used by the business to accomplish its goals.

Alignment refers to the direct linkage of IAM efforts to business strategies, and the measurement of information and knowledge projects against anticipated benefits. It is also an objective of the EIM program—aligned means that business needs are directly fulfilled by information and content management when called for. Alignment gives us the ability to tie an IM project to a specific business objective, and measure results against that objective. Alignment also flows through to the architecture and road map aspects of EIM. All EIM solutions, deliverables, and policies must originate somewhere in the business driver/goal/objective framework.

This phase collects and analyzes business objectives, goals, and drivers. All of these state how an organization is trying to improve itself, and are stated in terms relevant to the business area being described. Most methodologies and analysis systems have a hierarchy of goals, objectives, and so forth. We covered this ground in Chapter 8, but it is worth restating it here to ensure understanding. For this text, the hierarchy will be as follows:

- Drivers are industry- or market-inspired trends, usually stated in terms of a direction. These tend to be categories of business goals.
- Business goals are refinements of drivers, expressing the general trend in terms that indicate desired accomplishments within a time frame.
- Objectives are the specified, measurable criteria for achieving the goals and drivers.
- An example of a driver is customer intimacy. A goal would be improve customer retention, and the objective would be increase customer retention to 97% this fiscal year.

I know that any reader can present an example where these are reversed—goals are measurable, and objectives are from drivers. For the purposes of this book, we had to pick one hierarchy and stick with it.

Over the next few phases, the basic process is to decompose business drivers or goals into qualitative requirements based on business measures (metrics) and BIRs. Eventually, these are used to create data or parameters that suggest the type of architectures, support, and projects required to meet business needs. The driver/objectives hierarchy is applied to standard uses of information. Actions or process models, and detailed information requirements all derive from this essential process of Alignment.

The EIM program design is the culmination of effort anchored in the Alignment phase. Some business-visible elements of EIM originating here are:

- Processes that oversee information assets, such as data governance and data quality
- Definition of required business performance measurement-type projects
- Advanced workflow efforts

- Document and content management
- Refined and higher-value touch points with customers and other constituents
- New or refined business processes to meet business goals.

All of these will be tied to an overall philosophy and governance program that, while meeting business needs, ensures that data, information, and content in the enterprise is accounted for as a value-added asset, thereby maintaining effective returns in the investment in EIM.

Alignment supports the business case for IAM by ensuring that the benefits from information and content management remain anchored in business goals. There is a historical tendency for IM programs to become abstract. An added benefit of Alignment is that the EIM staff, usually made up of personnel from IT, are more focused on business issues vs. development of a "model," or an application.

This phase in EIM program development also needs to look into a value proposition, stated in the form of a mission statement or "elevator speech."

Part 1 told business leadership that a formal alignment of EIM and IAM philosophy to the business is mandatory. With a good alignment exercise, you can choose to target some of the subdisciplines of EIM to address business problems (like a data warehouse or data quality effort), while striving to attain the huge leverage provided by treating content as a true asset. Figure 20.1 shows where we are in the EIM cycle. This phase may occur at two different points in the EIM development process:

1. We are executing this phase to initiate the EIM program and align the new program to business, and in turn establish IAM as a philosophy to improve how information is used, thereby improving financial statements.
2. If EIM is under way, we are using this phase to refresh our awareness of the business, or perhaps find where in-stream information efforts are disconnected from the business.

Figure 20.2 shows we have four activities within this phase, and most of them have components that are mandatory.

The activities focus on a straightforward review of business strategic and tactical plans and decomposing those into enterprise information requirements. These requirements are stated in terms of how the business will actually use the content, and as a list of specific types of content that must be available to the business. Do not confuse this activity with the Business Readiness assessment. We use the same input, but instead of indicating a degree of misalignment (or not) we start to actually align EIM with the business.

ACTIVITY: BUSINESS DISCOVERY

The objective here is to complete (or start) gathering existing business plans and confirming existing objectives and goals. The Business Readiness assessment may have started this process. Again, strange as it seems, only half of our clients can reach to a shelf and pull down a cogent business plan. If this situation exists in your organization, or you have access to a high-level plan only, then the alternative collection technique applies here, i.e., public documents, internal plans, public web sites, trade journals, and so on. The difference between this activity and the Readiness assessment is we will take steps to add details to the business goals and objectives that will permit us to tie business needs to the future state vs. assess the current state. If the Readiness assessment provided access to business plan details, this activity is actually short.

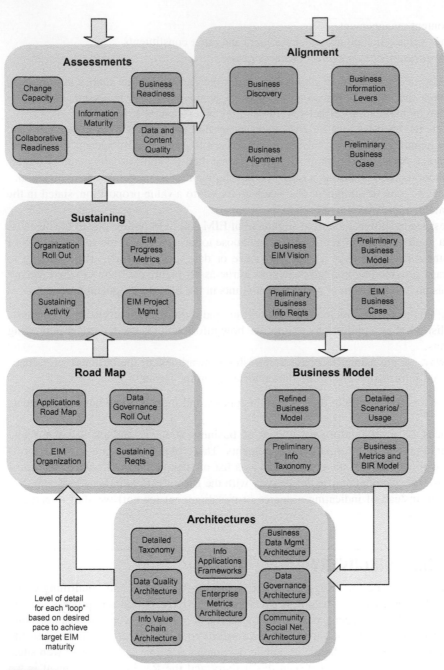

FIGURE 20.1

Where alignment occurs in the EIM process

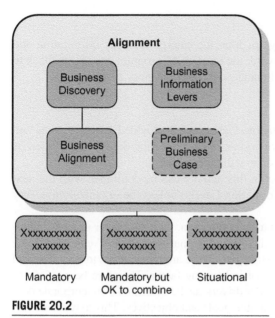

FIGURE 20.2

Activities within the Alignment phase

Activity Summary (Table 20.1)

Table 20.1 Business Discovery Activity	
Objective	Confirm business direction in terms of stated goals and objectives, then ensure there are measurable characteristics and a need to use data and content to meet the goals.
Purpose	If the assessment was light on business drivers, they need to be reinforced here. Otherwise, the business drivers need to be positioned in terms of a future state use of managed information.
Inputs	Business goal and objectives from the Assessment phase.
Tasks	Review business documents, earlier findings Develop a list of known business challenges, problems, and potential opportunities Turn challenges and opportunities into business directions Confirm future relevance of goals and objectives Confirm measures of goals and objectives Clarify possible EIM role in achieving business goals Ensure each goal or objective is measurable.
Techniques	Access to executives is very useful for the EIM sponsor or team. Often, this shortens this activity.
Tools	Either Excel for storing findings, or enterprise management tools, e.g., Systems Architect or Provision (if you have them).
Outputs	A list of business goals and objectives, with correlated metrics (or obvious content requirements).
Outcome	The EIM team produces a comprehensive list of business goals and objectives, which are reviewed and approved by the EIM sponsor or an executive group.

Business Benefits and Ramifications

This step captures, in business terms, the beginnings of how the enterprise needs information and content to achieve its objectives. From this point forward, the entire EIM program can be tied back to this list, ensuring that information assets are used and managed to meet business needs.

Approach Considerations

This activity should only take a day or so if the Readiness assessment provided baseline goals and objectives. If not, it may take a week or more. The longest aspect is reviewing documents (if there is no obvious business plan) and scheduling review sessions with executives.

From a project management perspective, the tasks in this activity can be combined with the next two activities (Business Alignment and Business Information Levers) unless the organization is very large, and you are examining multiple business units.

If you are using the "guerilla approach" to derive business direction, then remember to look outside your company at the business environment. It's also fair to say that "business drivers" can be a vague term. Most organizations have goals and objectives, or strategies. There are many layers to corporate and organizational strategies. Most list drivers as some sort of influencing factor. Therefore be cautious of semantics. A great deal of the time, goals, objectives, and/or drivers can be discerned from corporate documents. Just look for material that lists or implies measurable goals and objectives. This may take a few lunchtime sessions with peers, but a mildly facilitated discussion will enable a small group to derive a list of 10–15 good business goals. Make sure that you have these categorized in such a way that confirms you have enough. Use known challenges and problems to create some objectives. There should be items that if addressed would reduce risk, or drive good numbers to financial statements. There should also be items that reflect product or service changes, efficiency changes, or customer relationship improvement.

The main output for this activity is a matrix. The columns become the aforementioned drivers or strategies, goals and objectives.

Either way, there are several fundamental reasons for doing an analytical exercise for Business Discovery:

1. The ability to share data is not of prime interest to a CEO. It is lower costs, more revenue. If sharing data leads to those, fine; if not, don't bother leadership. Education through discovery forms a picture of using content to achieve results. Business and technology team members arrive at a common language.
2. Few EIM teams know enough about the business to replace executive insight—so other techniques are called for. But most executives have been interviewed into a stupor. Most of the time they appreciate the effort.
3. Business measures are objective, and we always end up with the same level of information that exhaustive interviews provide.

Sample Output

Here are two examples. Figure 20.3 is from Farfel. In the Farfel case, we assumed that there was not a lot of business strategy data lying around, and the executive team was struggling to pull a strategy together in light of a fierce business environment. So while there are objectives and targets for various areas, the strategy does not hang together very well. The EIM team placed the collected business statements and program objectives in a framework of business, process, and technology. Figure 20.3

Farfel Emporiums Summarized Goals

Driver	Goal	Documented Objectives	Measurable Attributes
Improve market share	Recover lead market share in category	Regain market share of 25%	Market share
	Increase top line sales across all categories and stores	Increase same-store-sales 15% over three years	Same-store-sales, forecasted vs. actual
Increase customer interactions	Improve customer experience	Increase visits per store from three to four per year	Store visits, market-basket return
		Improve service environment, highlight differences	Surveyed opinions
	Improve effectiveness of web site	Improve web site sales 15% without cannibalizing store sales	Percent sales from web site
		Integrate store and web site offerings	Frequency of assortment refresh. New products per season
	Increase repeat visits with more household awareness	Capture customer feedback, integrate findings into marketing	Store traffic
Product innovation	Offer an improved selection of products and services by channel	Beat competitors to market on new products	Time to market averages for specified product
		Implement the most appropriate and profitable product mix, with brand consistency and neighborhood variation	Same-store-sales, category product turns
	Maintain accurate merchandising processes	Improve procurement and store communications	Elimination of missed products or out of stocks
	Improve R&D to recognize new opportunities	Gain insight into Generation x, y buying patterns	Demographic, psychographic trends
Improve operational efficiency	Improve management of merchandise inventory assets	Reduce weeks of supply across appropriate product classes	Weeks of supply
		Improve cash flow and asset management to improve current ratios	Current ratio, inventory turns, and weeks of supply
	Identify business processes that can be improved to increase profits	Improve processes through more efficient collaboration	SG&A expenses, cycle times, division results
	Optimize store performance	Monitor and assist stores with declining performance of more than 3% gross sales decline	Same-store-sales, geographic and demographic sales potential
		Eliminate/relocate bottom 5% of stores	Same-store-sales, geographic and demographic sales potential
	Reduce SG&A	Reduce "shadow IT" to competitive or industry standard levels	Total cost of ownership for data usage, IT, and business areas

FIGURE 20.3

Farfel business drivers, goals, and measures

is an excerpt from a much larger document. Note the left to right progression from driver (based on team research in trade magazines) to a measure. Also note some of these focus on traditional data uses and others are aimed at problems like shadow IT and document management.

Ubetcha Insurance (UIC) had the advantage of a document that contained a business strategy. They also have the advantage of an industry that is regulated more than others, and can narrow down data requirements quickly. This is critical as your "vertical" industry will influence your IAM direction. Financial services, insurance, and banking are a long way down the road to a more thoroughly stated brand of IAM.

Table 20.2 shows the outcome of some of UIC's analysis.

Table 20.2 UIC Business Goals

Strategic Area	Goal/Objectives	Objectives	Measure/Requirement
Growth	Deliver continuous growth of 7% per year	Determine two new test markets by 20nn	Market size, activity
		Identify growth states and determine required investments	Investment per outlet, state, revenue potential
	Focus growth efforts on new UIC opportunities	Determine improvements in Internet sales, direct sales, and customer service areas	Channel activity
	Increase agency book of business to $1 billion by 20nn	Increase PIF productivity by 30–40%	Policy in force
		Institutionalize new agency office model geared to growth	Agency activity, sales
	Pursue cross-sell strategy	Work closely with UIC marketing on revised branding	Brand performance
		Execute on UIC-wide cross-sell initiatives	Sales by product
Products	Deliver products and services that meet or exceed the needs of existing and prospective policyholders	Develop new products that meet new customer needs	New product features determined
Pricing	Maintain acceptable pricing returns to support growth in all channels	Identify new pricing models	New pricing model
		Continuously enhance underwriting, pricing, loss adjusting capabilities	Pricing effectiveness, loss ratios
Efficiency	Ensure employees have tools and processes to be effective	Maintain current expense ratios within 2%	Expense ratio, employee productivity, employee effectiveness

---

TIP FOR SUCCESS

If executive attendance is skimpy (in other words, you are working under a mandate to "do EIM" and there was not a lot of thought put into this), then the results will be used to shape the EIM program. When you are questioned as to how you reached certain conclusions in terms of business needs and direction, you will have an audit trail. Continue to try and present your business findings. Sooner or later, an executive will notice and the EIM team will have management attention, since there is some serious strategy work going on without executive involvement. Of course the best success factor is to have that executive sponsorship and presence integrated into the EIM program as soon as possible.

ACTIVITY: BUSINESS INFORMATION LEVERS

Once a set of goals and objectives are developed, the next exercise is to cross the bridge from business driven to business aligned. We need to start to move toward a vision and business model. In other words, what is our enterprise like with IAM? Where does EIM fit into the current business? The technique is a two-stage analysis of business strategy in the context of using data and content.

This means we need to start to recognize Value levers, or broad areas where our business strategies are intended to achieve goals or objectives.

We also need to identify more specific actions, or Information levers, where the business will leverage data or content to meet measurable objectives. The Value levers are often used for executive presentations, the EIM Vision, and Preliminary Business Cases. They also "seed" the Information levers, and are usually buried in among the final list of Information levers. The Information levers are carried forward to help identify business benefits, new processes, new touch points for information, or additional business information requirements. They are important in developing information supply chain, or value chain presentation as well.

It is time to remember something we presented earlier: the *usage value* categories. They are repeated for reference in Table 20.3.

We need to align our goals, objectives, and drivers against these. There are other techniques for doing this, but I am presenting this one as it results in a more objective list of information

---

Table 20.3 Usage Value Redux

Usage Value Category	Data, Information, and Content Used to Improve or Achieve Goals Through
Processes	Improve cycle time, lower cost, improve quality
Competitive position	Capture competitive intelligence and differentiate yourself
Product	Create package and market unique, higher margin products
Asset/intellectual capital	Prolong leadership, embed knowledge into products and services
Enabler	Foster employee growth and empowerment
Risk	Manage risk of various types that threatens value by increasing liability

requirements. Other techniques entail interviews, and I would much rather ask executives to confirm the results of this exercise (they actually enjoy it) than ask them to fill it in via an interview.

If you do this activity in two stages, remember to base Value levers on strategies or drivers *only*. Table 7.1 contains an example of Value levers that corresponds with the sample output in Table 20.4. Often we do not need to do the Value levers, and can move straight to Information levers. We use Value levers when we need to better articulate business vision.

Activity Summary (Table 20.4)

Table 20.4 Information Levers Activity Summary	
Objective	Begin to establish a connection between business targets and the leverage of data and content to achieve the stated target (hence the name of the activity).
Purpose	Remember that the value of any asset is based on what we get from it when we use it. Data and content is not different. We need to start the process of answering the question, "What are we getting from the data and content?"
Inputs	You need the output from the Business Discovery activity—the drivers, goals, objectives list.

Tasks	Build the usage/value work sheets
	    Value lever sheet, if needed
	    Information lever sheet
	Schedule an internal EIM team meeting with selected subject experts
	Fill out the matrix, looking at each cell
	Review the results with business personnel external to the EIM team
	Modify, then present results to an executive or two, if they are available.

Techniques	Fill the matrix out in two passes—use EIM team members to do obvious ones, and then get a business SME to look at the others. Then take it to an executive or two for review. This exercise can take a week for several people if the list of objectives is long, as in a large organization.
Tools	Excel.
Outputs	A list of Information levers that present the conceptual means that the organization will use data and content to achieve objectives.
Outcome	A list of levers, which give a sense of vision and are oriented toward business needs, is complete, reviewed, and approved.

Business Benefits and Ramifications

We form a basis for a business-driven architecture and measurement of the value of our information assets. Even if the EIM effort were to stop at this point, the levers document can be used as a source document to be applied to any proposed IT project. An added benefit is this exercise always increases the support for EIM as business participants begin to see the benefits of a comprehensive view of information usage (remember fuel vs. lubricant?).

Approach Considerations

If you cannot get to an executive, review it with the EIM team. If they like it and can use it as input to later activities, move ahead.

You do not need to get every single business objective into this. There are too many in most companies, and they are not all needed. What are needed are the ones that visibly support business direction. One consideration we use is to time-box this, and go with a broad sampling of goals and objectives. When the levers start to repeat, or seem trivial, then we know we are too deep.

The basic technique is to facilitate a meeting where selected business personnel view strategy or driver against the usage categories. The goal is to make sure Information levers are tightly tied to a business objective. Frequently, we have attendees complete a phrase—"ACME company will use data/content to (insert the lever here) as a means to achieve (insert the goal here)." We then follow up by asking for more details about *how* the organization would react assuming the content was available to support performance, i.e., we get some details around any business processes that are affected. We also present basic business metrics that can be interpreted to trigger a specific lever. The answers are extracted, and that is what we call Information levers. But you can call them anything you want, and create a consolidated list for review by an executive group. That is all we do for now.

Even a smaller organization or an EIM effort gone underground can use this technique. Derive a smaller set of data and content usage. Just stay away from value or Information levers like:

- Inability to share information across the organization
- Multiple, inconsistent sources of data
- Lack of ability to generate reconcilable financial reports.

These are really requirements of some EIM element. These don't represent alignment with the business. These aren't even business requirements. They may *seem* like obvious "business" objectives if your organization is suffering information pain. If you incorporate these as objectives, you will have lost the opportunity to measure your value, and implementing data governance or other new policies will be very difficult.

Lastly, there may be initiatives or projects that are on the books, or in process. There are also most likely managers who can say, "I would use data to do X and Y if I had it now." This is an excellent place to capture these thoughts. Just find where they fit.

Lastly, make sure that EIM leadership and the EIM steering body or business leadership review the final list of levers. There may be something on the list that merits a protocol of keeping the findings confidential. We often come up with levers that mirror a "top secret" plan that is in the works.

OBSERVATION

It is a shame that many executives do not feel they have time to review this type of material. It is rich in content, and always generates creative conversations. When these are being done in "guerilla mode" (usually to improve an existing EIM situation), it is inevitable that someone "upstairs" will notice there is a bunch of people actually shaping this program and appearing like they will get something accomplished. Then you get their attention.

Sample Output

Table 20.5 represents UIC's Information levers. They are a refinement of the Value levers. Refer to Table 7.1. These documents can get large, so we left a lot out so it can be viewed. However, you will see the various phrases in this matrix appear in subsequent activities.

Table 20.5 UIC Information Levers

Strategic Area/ Driver	Goal	Objectives	BIR Requirement/ Metric	Information Levers/Preliminary Actions					
				Process	Competitive Weapon	Product	Asset/ Intellectual Capital	Enabler	Risk
Growth	Deliver continuous growth of 7% per year	Determine two new test markets by 20nn	Market size, activity		Identify new categories of customers		Target-specific products at new markets		
			Investment per outlet, state, revenue potential		Understand current customers, look for new regions with similar demographics				Identify profitable new markets, vs. new markets
		Execute on UIC-wide cross-sell initiatives	Sales by product	Identify cross-sell processes in multiple channels				Support channels with cross-selling	
Products	Get new product features marketed within one month of regulatory approval	Reduce new product deployment to one month	Reduce product data update time	Review and adjust product business activity					
Pricing	Improve underwriting efficiency	Reduce loss adjustment expense	Accurate loss adjustment expenses		Improve salvage agreements	Adjust product features	Understand value of customer of lifetime		Prequalify prospects and customers based on risk

---

TIP FOR SUCCESS

This exercise will most likely be well received. Do not be shy about asking to sit down with a division-level executive. If your sponsorship is adequate, this will not be an issue. Often, we will do a pro forma or notional version of the levers before we show it to executives. We will put industry trends with the Value levers as a thought starter. If you are in a restore mode for EIM, definitely have the EIM team do a pro forma version of these work products.

Once in a while, we will need to educate executives on the technique. Do not think they are slow to embrace the approach. They are being thorough. Remember, you are defining actions that someday may be in someone's performance goals.

ACTIVITY: BUSINESS ALIGNMENT

The objective of this activity is to take the results of the lever exercise and prepare a view of how the use of data assets will support business goals and programs. Since assets, if accounted for, have visibility (they can be seen and counted), we align the business to the levers and uses of content based on some type of lens to determine business value. This exercise is not rearranging the answers from the levers activity. The levers are used as "thought starters." As an EIM leader, you no doubt realize that the executive team is really interested in only three benefits—lower costs, more customers, or more revenue. This is not shortsighted. These are the three items that can directly affect a balance sheet or income statement. This activity looks to align the information use with this aspect of a business. Table 20.6 demonstrates the executive view of a few levers slotted into columns where financial results can be affected.

Table 20.6 Organizational Value and Information Use

	Organization Growth and Value from the Information View[1]			
	Visible Equity	**Intangible Assets (Stock Price Premium, or Higher Valuation)**		
		External Structure	**Internal Structure**	**Individual Competence**
	(Book value), tangible assets minus visible debt (author—and allowances for risks)	(Brands, customer, and supplier relations)	(The organization, management, legal structures, manual systems, attitudes, R&D, software)	(Education, experience)
Using content and data must increase value through ...	... adding to assets and equity while reducing liability	... increasing goodwill and market perception	... improving efficiencies	... improving our close relationship with our customers

[1]Sveiby, K. (1997). The New Organizational Wealth: Managing and Measuring Knowledge-based Assets. San Francisco, CA: Berrett-Koehler Publishers.

Lastly, this activity develops the mission statement or value proposition for EIM. At this juncture, you will be able to identify a connection between EIM and business value. The "elevator speech" analogy should be kept in mind.

Earlier (Chapter 5) we introduced material by Karl Sveiby, who wrote a seminal work in 1995 regarding the value of knowledge. It applies neatly to our concept of usage categories. When we run our levers through his model, an extension of Table 20.7, we will see something like Figure 20.3, Farfel's initial view of content value.

If incremental business value can be visibly demonstrated, a wide range of barriers to EIM program deployment and the changes required to adopt IAM will tumble down. If you require a business case, this lays an excellent foundation.

Activity Summary (Table 20.7)

Table 20.7	Business Alignment Activity Summary
Objective	Develop an auditable tie between Information levers and incremental change in business valuation.
	Present a business value statement, or mission statement of EIM.
Purpose	The EIM program will only succeed if the business can measure benefit. This exercise aligns levers with financial or market indicators.
Inputs	The results of the Levers and Discovery activities.
Tasks	Determine the business context to present levers
	Schedule facilitated session with business leaders or SMEs
	Capture business benefit results in the session, or refine results after presenting them
	Create value statements of interaction of data and business goals
	Publish results to the EIM team and/or steering committee.
Techniques	Facilitated session is best, but this can also be filled out by the team and confirmed, similar to the levers. The facilitated approach garners attention which is why it is preferred.
Tools	Excel, PowerPoint.
Outputs	A list of business benefits for input to a business case, or measurement during EIM program operation.
	A vision of how EIM may manifest itself starts to form.
Outcome	A list of business benefits that can be tied to some measure of financial return, that ideally has been reviewed by upper management.

Business Benefits and Ramifications

This step starts to display obvious business benefits, and is usually the activity that gets the attention of upper management. There will always be an upper management member of an EIM review body along the way. When the phrases "measuring business results, EIM, IT, and the balance sheet" are all used in the same sentence, you now have their attention. The mission statement and/or value proposition should provide an eloquent and brief statement of what EIM is going to do for the business.

Approach Considerations

The only creative challenge here is to select the correct "columns." If the Sveiby approach is not useful or relevant, for example, a government agency, then use other value or business criteria. Often we use the now ubiquitous market disciplines[1] like product, customer, efficiency. These are market drivers, but also directly impact financials.

Again, I prefer to do a notional version and then present it for confirmation, but allow the culture you work within to guide you. Either way, whether facilitated or one on one, the exercise of tying the levers to a financial view of the company is eye-opening.

If your EIM effort is in "restore" mode, you may want to dig up any areas where the current EIM-inspired (but floundering) efforts have added value. This is a great technique to *report* on EIM progress.

This activity is optional for one reason: certain organizations will not want the EIM team speculating on financial impacts. Again, this is a good sign. Very large organizations may want to do this (and the other levers activity) for discrete business units rather than the entire enterprise.

Sample Output (Table 20.8) (Figure 20.4)

Table 20.8 UIC Elevator Speech
Sample "elevator speech" developed for UBETCHA Insurance:
"UIC will manage information and content to support the business by improving balance sheets, managing risks, and enabling achievement of our goals."

TIP FOR SUCCESS

Again, senior leadership is good to have around to review this. It is also most advisable to be low key. While you are doing business alignment and reviewing business elements, it's good to remember that the EIM team is not who is running the business. Priorities change and markets fluctuate, so remember that the data used here is to make IAM work, and EIM effective and sustainable. You are not a high-end firm advising upper management on strategy.

Earlier I mentioned the "elevator speech." This is an excellent time to revisit it and see if it is holding up to your findings.

ACTIVITY: PRELIMINARY BUSINESS CASE

The last activity in the Alignment phase is to take a stab at a business case. This is an optional step, as you will visit this topic again during the Vision phase. If a business case is required, the objective of this activity is to start its development. They can take a long time and be onerous to develop, simply in terms of level of detail. This may be optional, but if there is rumbling at this point (e.g., someone says the EIM program is too new, far out, idealistic, and so on) then I highly recommend the preliminary case. There is no need for a detailed financial business case at this point. Just start to gather numbers and work on the case methodology.

The preferred approach is to take each lever, as well as each value/usage entry from the alignment step, relate it back to specific business objectives, and identify whatever benefit is evident.

Example of direct valuation increase due to information and knowledge

Increase value through....	Visible equity (book value), tangible assets minus visible debt (author and allowances for risks)	Intangible assets (stock price premium, or higher valuation)		
		External structure (Brands, customer, and supplier relations)	Internal structure (The organization, management, legal structures, manual systems, attitudes, R&D, software)	Individual competence (Education, experience)
Process Improve cycle time, lower cost, improve quality	...retention of customers increases sales and smooths inventory fluctuations	...high quality information in support of customer relations	...support of lower time to market for projects and products	...capture of experience and work patterns involved in collaborative intelligence
Competitive weapon Capture competitive intelligence and differentiate yourself	...sustaining brand and reputation leads to better supply chain partners	...awareness of brand strengths	...leverage of knowledge and experience to create more efficient structures	...measuring professional leverage and efficiency against the competition
Product Create package and market unique, higher margin products	...increase return on equity through new product growth	...support of products unique to clients	...support of R&D	...capture of product development experience
Asset/intellectual capital Prolong leadership, embed knowledge into products and services	...increase valuation through intellectual property embedded in products	...presence in services and products	...maintaining alignment of processes to market needs	...identification and archiving competence enhancing projects
Enabler Foster employee growth and empowerment	...improve earnings through efficiency	...knowledge information support that allows touchpoint decision making	...support of collaborative, cross-functional processes	...sharing of experience and knowledge collaboratively
Risk Manage risks, of various types, that threaten value by increasing liability	...reduce insurance premiums and contingent liabilities	...proactive assurance that external reports are accurate and in compliance	...ensuring compliance through audit trails and data lineage	...education of employees to risks induced through poor data quality

FIGURE 20.4

Farfel business valuation

For example, if we take a lever from Ubetcha Insurance, that of improving agents productivity, we can ask, "If this happens, what is the precise anticipated impact on financial statements?" Since we have an idea of processes and actions, we can either claim the whole amount or partial credit based on how much of the resulting business action may be directly enabled by good data. If agency growth was to contribute $10 million in new premiums, then we might see from our levers that good data and content would enable or help improve half of the business actions taken to grow the agent force. Then we can, pro forma, write down $5 million. Farfel feels it can improve equity through customer loyalty and product innovation. What would a financial analyst say in terms of stock price or retained earnings? Granted, this is early but the goal at this stage is NOT to develop an accurate forecast of business benefits; the goal is to "float a balloon" and gather data for whatever method we are going to use to demonstrate a financial business case.

Business leadership will usually permit assignation of benefits on a notional basis, and it is a great exercise to bring business SMEs together with the EIM team. This helps perform a reality check on how IAM is viewed from an importance or priority perspective, as well as levels of commitment and support.

Activity Summary (Table 20.9)

Table 20.9 Preliminary Business Case Detail	
Objective	This activity initializes and gathers preliminary data for development of the business case. In addition, we start to look for a financial methodology to present the case.
Purpose	If a formal business case is required, it is good to start here and iterate over a few phases as more is known about the ultimate shape or form EIM will take.
Inputs	Inputs are the results from Discovery, Alignment, and Levers.
Tasks	Determine required level of detail for the preliminary case Associate levers and business view with measurable goals and objectives Identify the financial changes planned if business goals and benefits are attained Associate a pro-form or notional financial benefit with each Information lever, or value statement Review benefits with a financial analyst, identify a method to show a return on the investment in EIM Review these preliminary results with the EIM steering body.
Techniques	EIM teams benefit from having a team member with a modest amount of financial acumen.
Tools	Excel to hold results and early calculations (if any).
Outputs	A view of business benefit as a result of EIM.
Outcome	The step establishes the predetermined level of detail for the preliminary business case.

Business Benefits and Ramifications

Business leadership will start to see two concepts forming:

1. EIM is a business program—and it seriously means to help the business achieve results
2. EIM will need to be measurable, and will most likely influence many business areas.

If this activity is not executed here, the Business Case in the Vision phase will achieve the same results.

Approach Considerations

If EIM is in place, revisiting the business case is a matter of reloading numbers and assumptions. While this is optional for forming the program, I would always look at the case at this step when making a pass though an existing EIM program. Is the effort is stalled? Is there resistance? The objectives and goals are handy and can be plugged in to your model.

If you are doing either an initial EIM program, or a major overhaul of EIM and related efforts, think about whether you need to support a vision and mission statement, and/or you need some early financial data. Starting the business case earlier provides time to address resistance to assembling hard data, or worth through the calculations with your financial team. Often this will be new territory for finance and the EIM team. Determining the financial methods and assigning benefits may require spreading the effort of a business case between this activity and the Business Case activity.

Sample Output

See Chapter 21, Business Case Activity, since it will reflect the same content as the preliminary version here.

TIP FOR SUCCESS

Since this is optional, it is important to note that by starting the business case here, you are acknowledging that it will be a large component of kicking off the EIM program and sustaining EIM. It may also mean that your culture is such that the business case will be reviewed closely. This gives naysayers a chance to shoot holes in the program. Make sure that there is backing from upper management on the notional nature of your data.

SUMMARY

This Alignment phase of the EIM process starts and maintains the core data required to ensure alignment and measure value.

The activities gather and confirm business direction, and apply a formal technique to identify opportunities for data and content to improve an organization. The results of this phase will permeate all other artifacts. While the activities can be compressed or adjusted, there must be some formal exercise to align business goals and business actions that leverage information. The higher you can raise the business visibility of these work products, the better. If your situation has minimal or skeptical business input, then proceed with alignment anyway, and seek out confirmation in subsequent phases of EIM.

Reference

1. Treacy, M., & Wiersema, F. (1995). *Discipline of Market Leaders*. Reading, MA: Addison-Wesley Publishing.

Vision for EIM

People deal too much with the negative, with what is wrong... Why not try and see positive things, to just touch those things and make them bloom?

Thich Nhat Hanh

CONTENTS

Once the business is in line with the leverage available from IAM and EIM programs, it is time to form a vision statement or an image that portrays EIM and IAM within the context of the enterprise. After a business statement of actions around content and data is available, i.e., from the Levers and Alignment activity, there is sufficient input to develop a vision. Vision means what a "day in the life" of an EIM-influenced enterprise looks like at some future point, as seen by the business (Figure 21.1).

Making Enterprise Information Management (EIM) Work for Business. DOI: 10.1016/B978-0-12-375695-4.00021-7

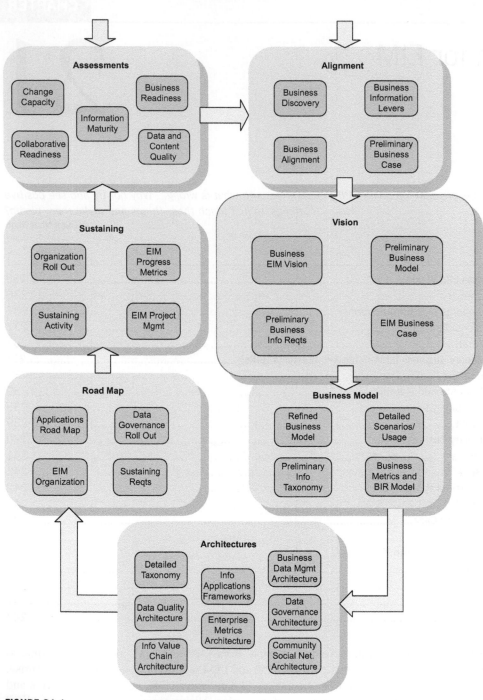

FIGURE 21.1

Vision phase as a component of the EIM process

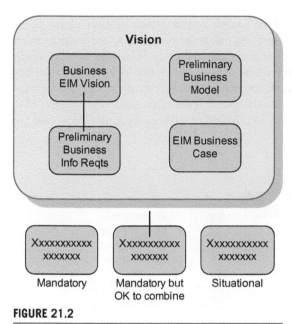

FIGURE 21.2

Vision activity detail

Vision is perhaps the most abused term in business, especially by consultants—everything is a vision. However, there is an important concept here that needs expressing. That concept is the "big picture" phenomena. When you do an EIM program, you will be asking the organization to change. People struggle to change without some view of the big picture. This vision of the future state helps individuals get comfortable with what's coming and that is your goal. What will a day in the life look like when EIM is working? What will be visible? How will behavior around data be different? What business goals will be more achievable?

Just like the levers and objectives, avoid "better decisions," or "better data quality" as a business vision statement. These are not business statements, have no relevance from a vision standpoint, and improperly position expectations.

The activities are simple and should not take long (Figure 21.2). Remember the Initiation step created a generic Vision for EIM. Most effort here will be delegated to staff to produce the Vision as a deliverable. We avoid defining a stated period for fulfilling the vision. It would be nice, but is also unrealistic at this juncture.

ACTIVITY: BUSINESS EIM VISION

Our objective is to develop a simple statement or picture of what EIM looks like. This is not always easy. There is a tendency to grab old "left to right" charts of data flowing from old systems to new ones. These are *not* visions of EIM. Visions can be one graphic or a strategic white paper. Determine what is best for your organization—at this point the most successful Visions are simple statements of principle and/or one page illustrations. They are ideal if they also suggest the value proposition that the EIM team is starting to formulate. Figure 21.3 in the sample output section of this chapter shows Farfel's initial vision. Figure 13.2 showed UIC's vision. At this point you want to see some connection between all of the talk about business support and the EIM program. You may have to reach ahead and offer pro forma EIM components to show where they would fit, but by now your team has an idea of what some of the larger components may be anyway. When you are underway and sustaining EIM, this phase is rarely revisited. You may revisit this phase if there is a need to restore the EIM program, or if you have done several aspects of EIM, like MDM and BI, as separate efforts, and are bringing them together.

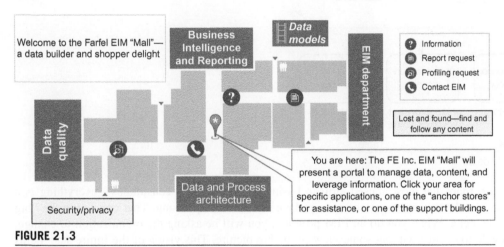

FIGURE 21.3

Farfel vision

Activity Summary (Table 21.1)

Table 21.1 Business EIM Vision Activity Summary	
Objective	Develop a simple statement or picture showing EIM within the context of your enterprise.
Purpose	A one-page view of EIM and how it fits day to day is invaluable in confirming direction at this point.
Inputs	Assessment results, business alignment, and the levers will allow one or two people to craft a visual or written statement of "day in the life" of EIM.
Tasks	Define the presentation style of the vision Acquire writer or artist if not on the team Iterate through several drafts of the vision Present and approve to EIM team and steering body.
Techniques	Creativity is invaluable. The best visions are symbolic via pictures or simple diagrams.
Tools	Drawing tools, Word, PowerPoint, Visio, etc.
Outputs	An easy to understand view of EIM and how it fits into the entire organization.
Outcome	The vision is presented and accepted by the EIM leadership.

Business Benefits and Ramifications

This activity starts to draw more business participants into the EIM program and increases understanding. Properly executed vision pictures can actually be galvanizing. The organization that the Farfel vision example is based on increased their comprehension and excitement for EIM by an order of magnitude.

Approach Considerations

This step can run in parallel with any other activity after Alignment. If there is sufficient excitement on EIM, it can even appear in the Road Map phase if not needed earlier. It may be revised after the Road Map phase in any case.

Avoid standard "information factory" material. These are the "left to right" flow chart illustrations that are common in information architecture and BI texts. These most certainly have a role and are a required illustration for the Road Map. But for now avoid any implication of technology frameworks.

Publishing the Vision will mean one of two approaches—the Vision is used as closely held selling collateral, or a wide-distribution material to present and educate on the big picture. Publishing should be in a format that allows it to be repeated and inserted in future material, e.g., a PowerPoint version. Often the Vision is used at first to sell the program internally, then forms the baseline for the eventual "big picture" chart.

Sample Output

Farfel decided, given the distinct lack of vision on EIM in the organization, to develop a prototype. This approach works very well (Figure 21.3).

TIP FOR SUCCESS

Once in a while someone will complain about time wasted doing "cartoons." The polite response is to delve more deeply into what specific issues they may have. You need to understand what these are so they can be addressed. Make sure that the purpose and importance of having the visual of the future is clearly understood. Getting active help from internal communications or marketing often results in a great image when creative minds come together, so look into assistance from these areas.

ACTIVITY: PRELIMINARY BUSINESS INFORMATION REQUIREMENTS (BIRS)

Certain organizations may want to lay out a "wish list" of required data and content. Like other preliminary work products, we have an opportunity to start a major artifact and acquire initial feedback. Collecting these requirements is a gathering exercise.

There is always a set of requests for content for web sites, data reports, or executive dashboards. There is also a large amount of information generated at the department level. This "shadow IT" may seem out of control, but remember there is often a valid need for a business area to create a data empire. This step will consolidate these needs with the prior findings and develop a detailed list of overall BIRs and/or metrics. Metrics are business requirements but they can be broken down into their component parts. BIRs are known requirements for data and content, and may or may not be associated with a metric, such as a web site, catalog, or safety manual. Sometimes the previous information levers we identified may be adequate for executives. Often cultures require a little more detail, such as a mention of broader categories of content. Examples are "online product catalog" or "consistent centralized customer data." Again these are various business views. In addition, the BIRs would also be a place to present an initial cut at priorities or constraints the business must place on content use.

Another technique often deployed at this point is to create a generic list of organization metrics or performance measures. If your company or unit is in an industry that is well known, e.g., finance, retail, banking, or government, then there are already enormous amounts of material and documentation of best practices, and basic lists of metrics. Many large vendors and consulting firms sell their own "vertical models" that contain predetermined sets of indicators, metrics, and subject areas.

Either way, the result of this exercise will be a list of specific items or requirements. Avoid trying to capture every single or presumed measurement or metric. Most organizations only have 200 or so indicators. Everything else is derived from these. Most companies swear they have 400–500 metrics. But you soon realize, for example, that order backlog by region and order backlog by product class is ONE metric—order backlog, with two views or dimensions, of looking at that metric.

Business events that create critical documents or processes that require crucial documentation, such as research or safety, should also be listed and their information (content) requirements recorded. *Associate all of the requirements with a business objective.* If this step is performed here, it will aid the team in a more precise calculation of a business case.

Ultimately, this activity (or the full Business Case activity) is not an activity of defining what the business wants; it is determining what the business *needs*.

Activity Summary (Table 21.2)

Table 21.2 Preliminary Business Information Requirements Activity Summary	
Objective	Develop a list of BIRs, including metrics and unstructured data.
Purpose	Develop the initial list of metrics and BIRs to allow leadership a view of what the business *needs* vs. hearing a list of what the business wants.
Inputs	The levers and early metrics from the objectives matrix. Also external models.

Tasks	Gather information levers and examine required content to enable them
	Gather measures for objectives and develop initial list of enterprise metrics
	Incorporate standard metric from your industry
	Look at value/info lever statements and extract any new categories of data or content required
	Examine significant business events and activities for content affecting risk—such as safety, regulated products, rate filings, etc.
	Examine backlogs of report requests, web site updates, and requisitions for external data
	Develop a classification scheme as to the origin of each requirement
	Refine alignment
	  Take BIRs coming from prior activity in EIM and verify the associated business goal/objective
	  Take BIRs that were uncovered in this activity and tie them to business goals/objectives
	Build a facility to hold and cross reference the BIRs
	Assign and organize findings by the classification scheme.

Techniques	Stay organized. Decide on a classification scheme that is relevant to your enterprise.
Tools	Make sure you have a good facility to manage these findings, e.g., systems architect, provision, and so on. If Excel is used make sure someone is good at managing Excel.
Outputs	Literally, a database of requirements that will help shape the EIM program.
Outcome	The EIM team has developed a list of data and content requirements that reflect the essential "information asset inventory classes" of your enterprise, and has tied these to business needs.

Business Benefits and Ramifications

Even if the EIM effort stopped here, the list of aligned requirements in the form of content and metrics has enormous value to all potential developers, requestors, and providers of information and data. There will be a significant awareness of the types of "information assets" you need to manage.

Approach Considerations

This effort needs to be time-constrained. It can go on forever if allowed. Best results are from focused efforts of one to three weeks and a subset of the EIM team matched to some SMEs; typically two to four depending on enterprise size.

The initial list of metrics is most likely available. Note that UIC even identified them in the Alignment example. Again standard industry metrics are available from many sources.

There may be requirements buried in your Value and Information levers. Major business transactions may also contain content requirements that are not evident from the levers exercise. Do not overlook the content that supports critical support processes, such as risk management or safety and inspections. Lastly, don't forget the current backlog of report and application requests.

For a large company this can become intimidating. For content associated with business events manage your analysis by following this guideline:

Will failure to manage this document or web page result in potential cost, loss of business, or compliance, civil or fiduciary risk?

Bump this question up against all major business events (new customer, orders, shipments, admissions, claims, scheduling, etc.). Also bump it up against critical support processes (research, clinical trial, procurement, heavy equipment maintenance, inventory, merchandising, allocations, actuarial, rate requests, etc.). Critical content requiring management will become evident.

The classification scheme for requirements serves to permit "auditability" and organization. List sources of the requirements, as well as category of content, such as metric, document, file.

While technically this could be optional (later steps can address BIRs), I strongly urge a preliminary step to develop an initial list that can be refined. It is simply more thorough. If you are pinched for time, then defer this to the next phase—Business Model. Both approaches work, I just like the additional pass. Often the political situation is such that leadership needs time to evaluate the requirements detail.

Sample Output

UIC used industry standard metrics to seed a list of requirements. So the definitions were already available. Table 21.3 is a brief excerpt from the UIC metrics list.

Farfel summarized all required data and content by classification. A brief sample is in Table 21.4. Definitions for metrics and BIRs were added in the Business Model phase.

TIP FOR SUCCESS

If you are finding yourself with huge lists of "required" reports or 500 metrics, the effort has gotten out of hand. You are looking for BIRs, not report specifications. The biggest likelihood of this problem results from an EIM team with a background of supporting reports, or business users who are looking for reports, not IAM. They will need to be restrained and/or educated. Remember, we need to identify business needs vs. wants.

Table 21.3 UIC BIRs

Metric	Definition
Claim recovery ratio	Percentage of claim losses recovered
Combined ratio	Ratio of loss expense to earned premiums
Household demographic count	Number of households in a specific market
Individual demographic count	Number of individuals in a specific market
Operating cost per feature	Overhead cost of managing policies allocated to policy features
Claim amount recovered	The amount of claim payment recovered from other insurers and third parties
Product profitability	The profitability of a product or bundle of products including losses and allocated expenses
Other BIR	
Claims adjusters file	Notes pictures and reports related to a claim
Policy illustrations	Hard copy legal documents representing the policy contract

Table 21.4 Farfel BIRs

Classification	Farfel BIR and Metrics Sample
Document/external	Demographic, psychographic trends
	Geographic and demographic sales potential
	Customer opinion
List	Out-of-stock products
	Product/item catalog
Metrics	Market share
	Current ratio
	Stock refresh frequency
	Percent sales from web site
	Same-store-sales
	Product turns
	SG&A expenses
	Store traffic
	Market-basket profitability
	Product time to market
	Weeks of supply
	New products per season
	Inventory turns
	Forecasted sales

ACTIVITY: PRELIMINARY BUSINESS MODEL

The abstract model from the Vision is not the only model we need. Given that we will be developing a program to manage information, we need to start to define how the organization relates to and uses the managed data and content, and how the data and content needs to be logically managed. This means we start the development of the EIM data, or information model, and some kind of process model.

We are not doing or plunging into elaborate months of model development. This is also a time-constrained activity. We only need to view the modeling, or abstraction of the assets being managed, to a conceptual level. In effect we are building a framework to hold together additional details that are soon to be developed. If we use the architecture and construction metaphor, we are doing the elevation version of the building plans, and a simple floor layout. The subsequent phase, Business Model, will add more detail to the data and process models.

This activity is optional because many organizations already have models. There may be enough IM in place to allow current models and mechanisms to be leveraged into the conceptual models required here.

The model is a means to communicate and understand enterprise needs. It is not the end product and *does not* require six months of detailed work. Most of the time we bring in a preexisting model from the same industry, or we have a client buy a model for their industry from a variety of sources. Even if a model is developed from scratch (they aren't), a good modeler can use the material gathered to date, and develop a conceptual view in no more than a few business days. For the rare occasion where a particular enterprise has no prior model, or is new and unique, then a data modeler (or two) will need a few weeks to establish an approved conceptual model.

The process model aspect is also optional. The levers and other findings have provided a set of possible business processes. These need to be defined at a high level and matched up to existing process models.

Activity Summary (Table 21.5)

Table 21.5 Preliminary Business Model Activity Summary	
Objective	Develop or refine existing abstractions of the business in the form of a data model and/or process model.
Purpose	This activity will provide a framework to add architectural detail later on. Also we now have a clear structure to define and confirm the enterprise content to be managed.
Inputs	The levers and BIRs will provide content for any data models. Also use existing models if available. The levers and usage/value statements and measures also provide process and business activity background to specify processes and data models.
Tasks	Gather existing artifacts, such as data or process models Determine level of detail to drive the preliminary models Define acceptable level of presentation for models, based on tools and current state Develop or refine a conceptual data model Develop or refine a process model reflecting known activities from levers and usage Incorporate results into existing tools or prepare for presentation and use in subsequent steps.
Techniques	Assistance from internal modelers, if not on the team, will expedite this effort.
Tools	Existing modeling tools, e.g., Erwin, BPWin, provision, or systems architect.
Outputs	Preliminary conceptual data model.
Outcome	The models produced are of sufficient detail to give the EIM team a sense of the required business data and process relationships. Management can review the models without confusion and understand how they represent the context and scope of EIM and what the business model will look like in the future.

Business Benefits and Ramifications

This activity presents an initial view to the business of the possibilities inherent in an IAM approach. The actions and models defined provide a refined view of how business goals can be satisfied through content and data anyway. Even if IAM is minimal in terms of the value part, better management of information assets can grow from this.

Approach Considerations

The data model is *not an option*. If it is not done now, it will be done later. Please do not interpret the need to be conceptual or deemphasize detail as a statement of flexibility. First, we are framing the organization and agreeing on context. No other tool does this as well. Second, we are moving toward some level of detail where a standard data model can be used to spring board many technical activities, and save a good deal of time and effort.

OBSERVATION

Far too often EIM or subdiscipline projects actually die at this point from being loved to death because of the data model. Historically, IT and particularly data management efforts placed a lot of emphasis on the model. They would be driven to minute levels of detail, or they would insist on so-called "enterprise-wide definitions" where every single data element has one unique meaning. For example, customer data can only mean "one thing." Experience proved this to be unrealistic. There needs to be a compromise between detail and relevance. The data model really does define the business incredibly well. Often data modelers learn more about a business in three weeks of modeling than a business executive who has been there for decades—I have witnessed this numerous times.

The EIM team will be most excited to resurrect old models, or start what they call "an enterprise version," which will be contrasted with nonintegrated project or application models.

This activity typically will run in parallel with other Vision activities and should take no more than three weeks if there is no model at all. This is a preliminary step, and again is used if the EIM team wants to present a preliminary version of key artifacts.

Presentation of actual data models gives me the willies. While there is no need to drag a businessperson through a primer in data modeling, they need to verify s*omething*. For data models, present a list of subjects and data entities with their definitions. Usually, this is adequate. From a business view, the lines and relationships in a data model are not really necessary at this time. Process models are best presented at a high or functional level. I have actually found that a walk through of any sort of model is often not necessary if the EIM sponsors feel that business needs are being met.

Sample Output

Farfel and UIC both did data models based on preexisting work merged into purchased or existing models. There are sufficient examples of data models in numerous texts to preclude the need to show extensive samples. A brief excerpt of UICs conceptual model is show in Figure 21.4. See Silverston and Agnew[1] or Hoberman[2] for excellent examples of models.

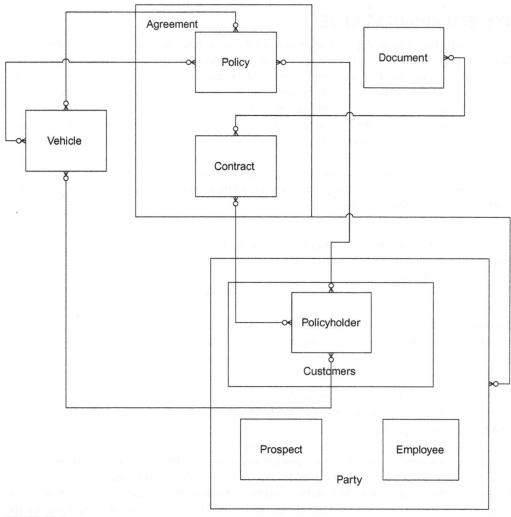

FIGURE 21.4

UIC model excerpt

TIP FOR SUCCESS

The data model at this point is NOT the final deliverable; it is merely a tool for better understanding of business context. Do not allow the EIM team to get carried away. On the other hand, this is a chance for your data architects to make sure they have a good representative enterprise model. Even if the sponsors are OK with no model review, use the opportunity to evolve the enterprise models.

ACTIVITY: EIM BUSINESS CASE

This last activity in the Vision step can consume a relatively large percentage of the EIM Vision phase. But the objective of this activity must be met: we need to quantify business benefits and align them in detail with the data and content we will be managing. In an organization where IT business cases have been abstract or nonexistent, just agreeing on how tangible the benefits are can consume a few hours of debate. Additionally, a finance department may be uncomfortable doing business cases with so-called "intangible assets." This is where your education skills will be required. Remember that for IAM, it *doesn't matter* if the asset tracked is intangible. Remember the analogy to electricity?

In Chapter 6 we talked about a "case for the case" and went over a set of concerns that this addresses. We need to quantify or qualify our response to these points in the business case; in other words, more detail. To review, they are:

- A perception that data and information initiatives fail all the time.
- A perception that spending on any "pure" IM projects is wasteful.
- Historical criticism of the IT area.
- Ongoing complaints that the IT data is not "correct"—so business areas need to create "correct" data.
- A growth of "stealth" or shadow IT in reaction to a poor perception of IT.
- Lists of projects where we "get it running with these shortcomings which we will fix later"—of course later never happens.

The business case must address these opinions head on but unlike in Chapter 6, a qualitative discussion will not work. So a suitable level of detail for the business case must be determined.

The Alignment phase produced, in essence, a list of opportunities. We may have even derived some financial numbers during the Preliminary Business Case activity. If management requires a full business case, we then need to process those numbers into a relevant business case. However, remember that the numbers we have are on the benefit side only. We also need to gather costs. Refer to Table 15.1 for the full equation of EIM benefits. And we have to determine the means of presentation and calculation. Are we going to do a financial case with predicted returns? What is the basis for the returns, a percentage of income or return on capital? So we need to determine the methodology of showing a return.

Over time, a return on an asset increases organizational value. The actual asset may decrease (depreciation on a machine), or increase (land value), or fluctuate (mineral assets in the ground). But if the asset is not reinforcing a balance sheet, or contributing to equity through usage, it would be eliminated. So as we prepare a business case, we need to also consider a pro forma presentation of changes in value. In some organizations that means retained earnings, or an increase in assets on a balance sheet. In other organizations, a *decrease* in risk may reduce liability, and thereby improve a balance sheet.

Once you have agreed on the nature of the case, and the components of the quantitative statements, the rest is "grinding it out."

Activity Summary (Table 21.6)

Table 21.6 Business Case Activity Summary	
Objective	Develop a clear business case for EIM, based on business drivers vs. historically thin justifications.
Purpose	A business case will create open debate on value and business alignment. This is important in getting upper management engaged in EIM.
	Asset management equals recognizing value. This process needs to begin at this time, so EIM can be based on an IAM value model, or on meeting business needs with a return on investment.
Inputs	All input is from Preliminary Business Case and Alignment activities.
Tasks	Fully understand and define business benefits
	Isolate information usage/value enablers and processes
	Identify/confirm business benefits that are possible—reduce the high-level numbers into benefits for specific instances of lever, value/usage, or process
	Describe specific benefits, costs, and/or "at risk"—look for risk across the three risk types—regulatory, civil, and financial
	Define relevant EIM benefit categories of risk management (regulatory, civil, etc.), business return, or business efficiency
	Identify potential cash flows.
	Examine current costs of IT and other information-related costs. We will revise the cost numbers in the Road Map phase.
	Apply the various financial benefits and the costs to whatever model we have selected.
Techniques	A simple financial model based on internal rates of return or similar measure is best. Stay away from headcount reduction unless that is the specific benefit called out in a business objective.
Tools	Excel.
Outputs	A concise statement of benefits in excess of potential costs and risk, with an indication of financial return.
Outcome	Management understands that there are benefits stemming from IM. The business case, as it stands, is sufficient to allow the EIM program to continue its development.

Business Benefits and Ramifications

After a business case is developed, the EIM team has a foundation for proving and sustaining the value of EIM. In addition, business accountabilities can be identified, progress can be measured, and buy-in sustained over the long term. The enterprise takes a huge step in understanding the value of information as an asset with this activity.

Approach Considerations

The activity summary in Table 21.6 lists tasks, but it is better we read the details of the activity outside of the table. The basic steps and outcomes are:

1. Fully understand and define business benefits—refine and present the benefits from the Alignment phase in terms of not only a perceived high-level number, but in terms of cash flow or earnings increase. If the preliminary case tentatively identified benefits, these must be confirmed.

2. Isolate information usage/value enablers—gather the levers and value/usage statements, and the processes we identified (if any) in the Preliminary Business Model we extracted earlier, and position them alongside the business goals and objectives to show WHERE this new managed content will help. (If you have a Preliminary Business Case this may already be done.)

3. Identify/confirm business benefits that are possible—reduce the high-level numbers into benefits for specific instances of lever, value/usage, or process.

4. Describe specific benefits, costs, and/or "at risk" quantifiers—perform a high-level consideration of possible risks and contrast them to the potential benefits. Also at this time examine those critical business events where we extracted content requirements and look for risk across the three risk types—regulatory, civil, and financial. Do not forget the costs from the data quality assessment as well.

5. Define relevant EIM benefit categories—place each one of the areas where you have discerned benefit into the following categories: risk management (regulatory, civil, etc.), business return, or business efficiency.

6. Identify potential cash flows—some of the benefits will actually demonstrate possible increase in cash flow. Isolate these in a list for the time being.

7. Examine current costs of IT and other information-related costs. Include all capital costs, depreciation, and overhead. Include cost of departmental end use databases, spreadsheets, and departmental "mini IT departments." This is a good beginning cost number. Why? If EIM is successful, the overall total cost of managing information assets must certainly not increase over the current investment unless there are new radical enablers in store we have not uncovered. So for the time being current outlay makes a good cost side. We will revise the cost numbers in the Road Map phase.

8. Apply the various financial benefits and the costs to whatever model we have selected.

Sample Output

Present the results in whatever format is palatable to the organization, but emphasize aspects of IAM.

A typical format is produced here as a guide. Both Farfel and Ubetcha have very different business case approaches, so here is a typical business case outline. Examples of their business cases are in Chapter 7 (Table 21.7).

OBSERVATION

We have never run into any client in the past 20 years of EIM work that could not produce a hard dollar number that proved an impact from poor data quality. For one client we even ran a few profiles pro bono to prove this point. The benefits are there.

TIP FOR SUCCESS

The EIM business case happens where data is used. This must be continually emphasized—don't forget there are challengers and naysayers out there. Stating a case with hard dollars will slow down early resistance. If an EIM program is already in place, the business case is updated. If EIM is struggling, a business case is redone. The preliminary activities (preliminary business requirements and preliminary business mode) tend to be done only on initial iterations of EIM programs.

Table 21.7 Business Case Outline	
Vision	Repeat the vision in terms of text and your "big picture" if you have one.
Methodology	Explain the quantitative approach being taken, and if it is notional.
Business alignment	State the various actions and/or scenarios EIM will enable. These can be stated as supporting specific business goals or strategies. Present the business view of financial opportunity from these strategies. Also present the process (or formula) by which EIM can claim some or all of these benefits. Even if you have to claim benefits on a notional (i.e., unofficial) basis, you are building the case for managing the information assets.
Risk statements	The business case is a vehicle to present how a venture will overcome risks and result in a return. If you do not talk about risks now you are not positioning yourself for success. Any other obstacles that are known need to be presented as well. It is possible an organization may not have the appetite for EIM, and will have to settle for a reduced version of IAM.
Costs of DQ	DQ is a risk area but is so significant it requires a separate discussion. As stated earlier, a large driver of EIM is dealing with DQ. Time permitting, you may even want to profile certain portions of the current data portfolio (if you haven't already) and demonstrate areas where there is risk and cost currently. Note I did not state "if you have areas of risk." All organizations that consider EIM to this point *have* DQ risk. If you did not have it, we would not have reached this stage.
Costs of missed opportunities	Highlight existing issues with data, reporting, poor content management, scary compliance issues, or high cost of ownership due to shadow IT. If these numbers are not apparent then invest the time to draw them out. List the business programs requiring some kind of managed data or content in order to be successful. There may be business actions and scenarios that cannot occur unless EIM happens, or may occur but not fulfill all expectations without EIM.
Presentation as a statement of value	When you present the business case, remember it is a business document. There can be no TLAs (Three Letter Acronyms), "technobabble," or exotic and abstract pictures. In addition, educate the audience on the essence of value.

SUMMARY

The Vision phase reinforces the reason for doing EIM. A vision of future is developed to convey a business perspective of the role of EIM. This is reinforced with the business case for EIM. Often the EIM team will need to execute a preliminary version of activities, such as starting to define BIRs and assembling the conceptual model of the business.

At the end of the Vision phase the EIM program has established or affirmed the reason for existence. Subsequent phases start to shape the actual program and further define the assets to be managed.

References

1. Silverston, L., & Agnew, P. (2009). *The Data Model Resource Book: Universal Patterns for Data Modeling.* Indianapolis, IN: Wiley Publishing, Inc.
2. Hoberman, S. (2009). *Data Modeling Made Simple* (2nd ed.). Bradley Beach, NJ: Technics Publications.

Business Model

22

Checking the results of a decision against its expectations shows executives what their strengths are, where they need to improve, and where they lack knowledge or information.

Peter Drucker

CONTENTS

Making Enterprise Information Management (EIM) Work for Business. DOI: 10.1016/B978-0-12-375695-4.00022-9

Upon completion of discovery and alignment, the resulting vision and business case need positioning against the existing Business Model to determine any necessary changes in business practices or the Business Model itself. We may have identified potential changes earlier during the Preliminary Business Model activity. The Business Model phase is where we both confirm and refine that result, or do the Business Model itself (and resulting impacts) (Figure 22.1). Often EIM will suggest that a business revise its external approach to suppliers, vendors, and distribution channels. For example, our case study insurance company (UBETCHA Insurance) has a problem with data quality from the field. If this data is poor because independent sales agents are entering junk, we may have to change how the agents are incented to achieve any improvement in data quality. This is no small task. Any businessperson can easily envision that there is a possibility to create major issues. It is best to identify these now.

In the real-life situation that UBETCHA is partially based on the organization was confronted with a tremendous issue. Their agents were asked to revise their treatment of data (via significant process changes) at the same time a major push was on to *process policies faster*. The result was a hostile agent force dealing with mixed signals delivered from two different business functions. That is why there is an activity available in this phase to drill into various scenarios where business processes may need to be detailed, reviewed, and better understood. Often there are new processes enabled by EIM. Other times, we uncover possible problems spots (Figure 22.2).

The actual data and content requirements to be managed are also further refined in this phase. Metrics and other BIRs are detailed in terms of definition and usage. Optionally, your organization can start to explore the taxonomy, or hierarchical arrangement of content areas, if content management and navigation are major elements of your EIM program.

ACTIVITY: REFINED BUSINESS MODEL

This step takes a brief but required interval to place the intended EIM architecture or blueprint up against the existing Business Model. The result needs to be acceptance of the implied changes by leadership or an adjustment to the EIM architecture. In terms of the architecture building metaphor, we are taking the initial view that the building meets required capabilities, can be built on the intended land, and won't irritate the neighbors. This activity is optional. It will operate in parallel with the other activities in this phase.

We refine the data model, and supplement it with additional findings from the Business Metrics and BIR activity. Many times the EIM effort will have material from internal process projects to access, or will be able to proceed with just taking the levers and usage elements, and defining some scenarios or use cases.

Often there are a large number of levers or usage statements. Since these all begin with verbs, they are fair game for a process model. And occasionally there are so many that we need to define new workflows or processes to determine how the organization will exploit all this organized managed data and content. We have had to create or re-define entire IVCs, including specification of all the various processes where business actions are supposed to turn data usage into hard returns. If you are proposing or considering serious internal workflow, content flow, or data processing changes to accommodate IAM, this step is worth a visit.

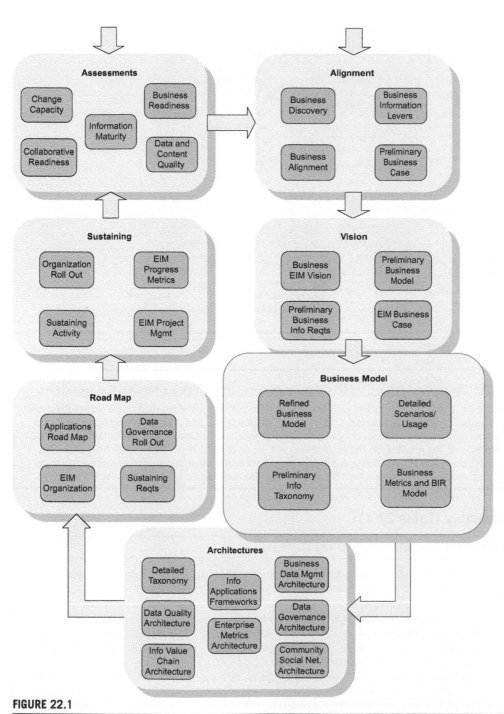

FIGURE 22.1

Business Model locator

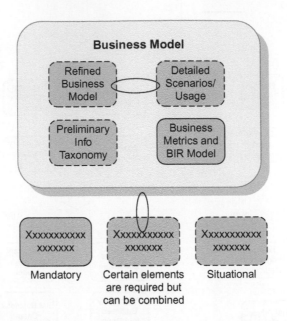

FIGURE 22.2

Business Model activity detail

What if all the people in your organization had access to any content data or information they wanted? Suppose it was all integrated, organized, and perfect in every aspect of quality and usefulness. Are your business areas able to state *now* what would be different? One more thing—they are not allowed to say "make better decisions." We want to know what the result of the better decisions will be. What will happen differently? What processes are improved? What are you actually doing with this managed stuff? And what is improved over the apparently "not so good decisions?" This is a *great* facilitation question. You may be surprised at how quiet the room gets.

Activity Summary (Table 22.1)

Table 22.1 Refined Business Model Activity Summary

Objective	Confirm preliminary findings for business process changes, and/or confirm a final definition of opportunities to alter processes or workflow to better leverage data and content.
	Define critical process or actions where the organization will achieve results or add value with specific application of managed data or content.
Purpose	Recipients of EIM program oversight will range across the entire enterprise. It is best not to blindside anyone with a new process or workflow. Altered processes will also influence the Architecture and Road Map work products.
Inputs	The Preliminary Business Process Model output, or the levers and BIRs will provide content for any data models. Also use existing data and process models. The Information levers and Usage and Value levers statements also provide process and business activity background to specify processes. These are all from the Vision and Alignment phases.

(Continued)

Table 22.1 (Continued)	
Tasks	Gather existing artifacts, such as data or process models if they do not already exist from the Preliminary activity
	Determine level of detail to drive the final Business Models
	Define acceptable level of presentation for models, based on tools and current state
	Develop or refine a conceptual data model from the metrics and/or BIR findings
	Schedule facilitated sessions to walk through the various levers and usage to identify business actions and possible new process models (new IVCs)
	(Trigger the Detailed Scenario/Usage Activity) to decompose the Value Chains to identify areas where new or revised business actions can occur using managed data
	Develop or refine Business Models reflecting known activities from levers and usage
	(and value chain results) from Detailed Scenario Activity.
	Incorporate results into existing tools or prepare for presentation and use in subsequent steps.
Techniques	Assistance from internal modelers, if not on the team, will expedite this effort. Also make sure to retain a conceptual view. Finally, if use cases are chosen, avoid detailed low-level use cases.
Tools	Existing modeling tools, e.g., Erwin, BPWin, provision, or systems architect.
Outputs	Refined conceptual data models.
	Refined activities, processes, or use cases of how the business can operate with managed data.
Outcome	The EIM team can identify specific area where there is opportunity to work more effectively, and use the managed content to business advantage. The data model provides a relevant platform to decompose meaning, data requirements, and reflect business rules.

Business Benefits and Ramifications

The business can answer, at least conceptually, how day-to-day activities will reflect where business benefits will happen, and what the managed data and content will look like. The EIM team can identify opportunities that require additional clarification. Or the EIM team will see possible situations where EIM directions and current processes create the need to manage changes in the organization more closely.

Approach Considerations

This activity can also be combined with the Detailed Scenario/Usage activity since they overlap. If there needs to be a lot of detail in the processes or a new value chain is defined, trigger the Detailed Scenario activity. It can also occur after the Metrics and BIR model is built, which will improve the data model content.

Usually, applicable business and data models are gathered from existing sources. If not, start with prepublished models for your industry. Determining the level of detail for the final EIM business model(s) will require discussion within the team. Whereas the preliminary models if addressed in the Vision phase were conceptual, the final models required to support EIM over the long haul will be more detailed. The typical level of detail required to get EIM started as a program is called a "logical" level model. Your data elements and their logical groupings are defined. A detailed model for physical implementation of databases is not required. Process models should also be at a level to capture and maintain the various information usage scenarios EIM will identify.

Table 22.2 Farfel Business Actions

	Information Usage as a Product—Build into Offerings				
Related Goal	**Levers**	**Possible Process or Scenarios of Information Use**			
Improve effectiveness of web site	Improve online ordering experience with access to order history	Provide means to enter preferences and profile purchase information (credit card, etc.)	Provide customers the ability to access complete order history to reorder or re-use part of an order	Store history and customer contact data	Enable repeat purchasing based on order history lookup	Provide customer with similar item offers
	Information Usage as a Process—Improve Cycle Times, Lower Costs				
Related Goal	**Levers**	**Possible Process or Scenarios of Information Use**			
Improve customer experience	Develop/supply customer profile/ score at POS touch points to offer promotions affinity cards, repeat purchase ease	Store history and customer contact data	Provide ability to access complete order history (in-store web access)	Evaluate histories to design offers and promotions	Offer promotions or affinity items at POS

Many organizations have disparate data models that were developed project by project. You have an opportunity to synthesize an enterprise logical model.

Ditto for process models. They should be logical, and can be synthesized or purchased. If for some reason you have no process models, then focus your process activities on the IVC activity, and plan a support project to develop a functional process model of the enterprise.

Either way, the models are important, as they support many elements of EIM, from the Enterprise DNA, specification of applications, to data lineage and maintaining your BIRs and metrics requirements. The models are vital tools, but they are not final products of EIM. Do not allow your EIM team to become model focused.

The IVCs are, once again, processes, or opportunities for processes, that use data and content to directly meet business goals. If there are enough information or value levers from the Alignment and Vision phases to attract management attention, or require management input, you may want to consider triggering the Detailed Scenarios/Usage activity.

Sample Output

Again, data models are easy to spot and a bit large to present with any relevance. Instead, we selected an example where Farfel levers decomposed into business activities. A refined version of Farfel processes was presented in Chapter 7. A sample of the spreadsheet linking possible actions to information use (levers) is shown later. The processes evolved into the value chain diagrams in Figures 10.6 and 10.7.

TIP FOR SUCCESS

Again, watch level of detail. It is not necessary to drive the models deeper and deeper in terms of details. Granted, there is value to this, but not for getting EIM started. It is a common error to have nothing happen until the "enterprise model" is done. If you have absolutely no detailed models and cannot acquire one, then I recommend a spin-off effort to continue with the development of the logical data model paralleling the Architecture phase. Presenting models merits consideration of the culture and level of leadership of EIM. It is perfectly OK to present a list of logically grouped data elements and their definitions. There is no need to drag a room full of management through Data Modeling 101. Have leadership delegate any detailed review tasks to subject matter experts.

At this point, an EIM leader who is not from IT will need to become familiar with the concept of meta data. The term enterprise DNA is more relevant and contextual to a business participant in EIM, but your EIM team will soon need to develop processes to manage meta data, and even specify tools to manage meta data.

ACTIVITY: BUSINESS METRICS AND BIR MODEL

We gathered an initial list of requirements in the Vision phase. This list needs the definition of what EIM will actually manage. The objective of this activity is to add some detail to these indicators and other information requirements to improve understanding, and position us for activities that will tie these business needs to the EIM architecture. For example, the flat world economy has created a huge demand on data interchange and global data movement. We often see companies at a loss when confronted with a situation where they have no "late night" computer time left to reconcile the daily activity and position data for usage the next morning. The results of this activity will prevent that type of occurrence in the future. In addition, we will develop an idea of the complexity of delivering content to authorized users. Finally, we produce a compendium or encyclopedia of documentation about the organization data landscape in terms of definitions and cross-references to use purposes and business actions. In short, we are continuing to define the "enterprise DNA"—how we *d*efine, *n*avigate, and *a*dminister our content. This was a term developed by Doug Laney at Meta Group to refine the concept of needing "data about your data."

Consequently, the metrics, indicators, and documents and other so-called unstructured content requirements are placed in a format (usually a spreadsheet) where we can start to add detail to the requirements, and qualify and quantify their characteristics. Table 22.2 shows an example from our insurance company. One huge advantage of this activity and the alignment techniques is the development of *agnostic* requirements. They reflect business needs vs. wants.

If the EIM program is up and running, this activity can be used to reflect new business or technology influences, for example, if a new line of business creates new metrics and BIRs, the EIM artifacts are updated then carried into the Architecture phase. A common reason to reexecute this activity is when business priorities change, and a new metric is required to measure performance.

Activity Summary (Table 22.3)

Table 22.3 Metrics and BIR Activity Summary

Objective	Document and cross-reference metrics and information requirements to business actions and predefined criteria.
Purpose	This activity forms a baseline and resources for architectural analysis, documentation, and identification of value-added projects. This required activity is a keystone for subsequent work.
Inputs	The Business Model, BIR, and Metrics material.
Tasks	Gather metrics and indicators
	Identify industry metrics
	Create measure sheets or records, one per measure, and/or BIR
	Determine level of review or walk through to verify/fill out the Metrics and BIR material
	Fill out template for workshops if required
	Confirm workshop sessions with predetermined stakeholders
	Hold workshops if required
	Refine business measurement model (add additional information) workshops
	Refine measurement criteria attributes (set up metric sheets/metric "database")
	Build BIR/Metric "database" from sheets
	Map conceptual data model subject areas to BIRs and Metrics to verify model relevance
	Optional—map measures to source systems where DQ may be a concern.
Techniques	Determine if SMEs can fill out sheets and collection of BIR or sessions are required. Determine if SMEs can fill out sheets and collect BIRs or if facilitated sessions are required. Remember sessions and explaining the Metrics and BIRs can be time consuming.
Tools	Excel.
Outputs	Metrics Model and "BIR catalog"—comprehensive listing and definition of core information and content requirements.
	Understanding completeness of what EIM will address.
Outcome	The catalog is complete to the point that all major indicators and critical data requirements can be identified. The conceptual data model is verified when mapped to the catalog as well.

Business Benefits and Ramifications

This deliverable (or something like it) is probably the most critical artifact the EIM team will develop and maintain. All relevant requirements that shape major elements of the EIM architecture are gathered and attributed with critical "meta" information, so the team can understand the nature of the requirements.

Approach Considerations

This is not optional. It will take two to four weeks for two to three EIM team members. Assigning a business SME will expedite the process. There will be facilitated sessions. Incorporating exiting documentation of metrics and information will also be useful. Once the metrics and BIRs are gathered, we create a database entry or spreadsheet for each requirement (Table 22.4).

After session or workshops to confirm metrics and BIR definitions, another activity takes place that starts a verification process or a self-check. Simply put, we need to make sure we are capturing everything. (This sounds more and more like accounting, doesn't it?) To do this the team and SMEs need to map data models to BIRs and Metrics to verify model relevance. Optionally, you can also map your metrics and BIRs to existing source systems where data quality concerns have been identified.

Each mapping exercise serves as a means to verify the team has captured as many requirements for EIM as possible.

Sample Output

Note we are now blending our business actions, drivers, and other requirements. We are not creating anything new; we are documenting what needs to be available. Table 22.4 represents *one metric requirements for UIC. There can be upward to 150–200 more of these artifacts, one for each metric, and/or BIR.*

Table 22.4 UIC Metric Entry

Measure Name	Premium Growth Rate
Description	The proportional indication of the growth (or decrease) of revenue for the current period in comparison with the previous period
Algorithm	[((Revenue current period/Revenue previous period)-1) × 100]
Objectives	Objectives from business plan or matrices Underwriting profitability Expense control and process improvement

Dimensions	Attributes used after the word "by" in a query or category to cross-reference
	  Time
	  Sales organization
	  Product
	  Geographic area
	  Demographic category
	  Policy types
	  Sales activity

Source	List possible data entities, subjects, or other sources required to produce this measure
	  Financial transaction
	  Policy

Business actions	Specific actions, events, or programs enabled by producing the measure, i.e., what is done with this measure, what decisions are made?
	  Analyze product volume sales
	  Analyze sales process performance
	  Analyze marketing process performance
	  Improve underwriting by uncovering new factors
	  Negotiate better presence via different deals to producers

Summarization	Known aggregation over time periods that need to be readily available for this metric, usually a time period like a month, etc. Not the same as dimension
	  Average
	  Monthly

Table 22.5 Farfel BIR Metric Mapping

Driver	Objectives	Goal	Metric/BIR	Data Entities/Content Categories								
				Product	Customer	Customer Profile	Store	Product Facility	Product Catalog	Promotion Activity	POS Sale	Web Content
Increase customer interactions	Increase visits per store from three to four per year	Improve customer experience	Store visits		x		x			x		
	Improve service environment, highlight differences		Market-basket return	x	x						x	
			Customer opinion			x						
	Improve web site sales 15% without cannibalizing store sales	Improve effectiveness of web site	Percent sales from web site	x								x
	Integrate store and web site offerings		Frequency of assortment refresh	x			x					
			New products per season	x								
			Product/item catalog	x					x			x

The Farfel example (Table 22.5) extends the BIRs and Metrics from our prior samples. Note we *added* some BIRs (in italics). This is not unusual when we start to map to a model. We add metrics, BIRs, sometime we even change the data model.

TIP FOR SUCCESS

This may be the first time the EIM team starts to hear "we do not have time for this, we will tell you what the requirements are." But the specific reason we developed the process in this activity was to avoid this discussion. You *must have* a set of architecture artifacts that represent the "E" in EIM, without business bias toward one party or another.

ACTIVITY: DETAILED SCENARIOS/USAGE

This activity is adjunct to the Business Model. It can be used in lieu of or as an enhancement. At this stage, the important step of asking your organization *what* it will do with information/data/content is answered in greater detail from a business viewpoint. If, for example, you have a lever that is "release new products," and you are OK dealing with the details as part of a project, you do not need this activity. Often we need to get into the details of *how* to get product X to market. If we need to do this, but do not need other aspects of the modeling efforts, then this activity is performed. This activity is called upon for specific iterations through the EIM process as a means to incorporate new opportunities or programs defined by the business. It is triggered by the Business Model activity or on a restore pass of the EIM program. It is not done unless an organization is pursuing business changes at significant touch points with customers, suppliers, etc., or has a nightmarish situation maintaining a particular subject area. The most frequent reason we have seen to do this activity is when a master data (MDM) or "gold copy" effort is under way. Often the entire IVC and data life cycle for creating and maintaining the master data subject, such as Customer or Item, is a candidate for new processes. Do not confuse this activity with IVC Architecture.

TIPS FOR SUCCESS

If you are doing MDM, do this activity. A lot of MDM projects head into the ditch when the project team realizes that the 20-year-old data entry process for Items has to change.

The objective here is to apply the levers to discrete business processes. Each lever can be used to lay out a scenario for what the business will look like, or how it will operate, when the EIM vision is fulfilled. The creation of high-level scenarios can be done based on the new architecture. Contrast these to the current state. The extent of changes will become obvious.

Organizations that are comfortable with the technique of "use cases" may find an opportunity to produce future state use cases.

If a Business Model is in hand and there are a number of processes or policies which have the potential of changing based on EIM, this activity serves to handle a spin-off effort that will define the details of the specific processes. We are not doing any process optimization or reengineering, rather we are highlighting and choosing to pursue process opportunities.

> **OBSERVATION**
>
> At this point, a reader (or some reader) will ask, "where is the gap analysis?" There is not one, but I owe an explanation. A gap analysis is a methodology to show the significance of a delta between a current state and a future state, used by consultants (internal or external) to show a problem and apply some kind of best practice to "close the gap." But we know there is a gap or we would not be here. Our future state is defined in the EIM program by definition. If the lingua franca of your company requires a "gap analysis," modify the Assessment phase by adding a very high-level vision based on best practices (out of this book or other literature) and contrasting the Assessment results.
>
> We have used use cases and simple flow diagrams for this activity and they are adequate to convey the results. This activity can be optional if there is already a process improvement or business modeling area in your organization. In that event use this as an opportunity to collaborate. Many companies have process areas that will fall over themselves to pitch in here.

Activity Summary (Table 22.6)

Table 22.6 Detailed Scenario Activity Summary	
Objective	Detailed definition of specific processes that will change and improve the business if IAM is in place.
	Recognition of new opportunities to push or pull new content into business areas.
Purpose	There is rarely an instance where an enterprise cannot create a very significant change in its Business Model if the enabling content is available.
Inputs	The output from the Business Model activity or a new opportunity outside of EIM that arises after EIM is in motion.
Tasks	Develop IVC from usage (business actions)
	Identify touch points where new managed content or data will touch, or be leveraged, by processes
	Map IVC processes to touch points
	Isolate the processes that create value or achieve the goal related to the originating action
	Isolate opportunities for improved efficiency, add to Business Case
	Evaluate enhancements and modifications to IVC
	Hold confirmation session for relevance of new processes
	Document New Business Models (Back to Business Model activity) as recommendations.
Techniques	Use cases, detailed process modeling.
Tools	Process modeling tools or enterprise design tools.
Outputs	Detailed opportunities to alter business processes achieving results through managed information.
	Enhancements to the business case.
Outcome	The selected actions are detailed and authorized as potential opportunity by business representatives.

Business Benefits and Ramifications

This activity can reinforce the EIM business case by demonstrating a process which is easier to grasp than "valuable information." In addition the EIM team has specific new processes that may be able to be built into projects that will reinforce, in a visible way, EIM value. Finally, changes in process entail Change Management activity and business areas will be glad to get an advance look at possible process changes.

Approach Considerations

If the Business Model requires a lot of detailed scenario development, it is best to use this activity and not interfere with other activities. The output from this will not be important until the Road Map and Sustaining activities—do not put this on a critical path.

This is a technique that requires familiarity with process modeling or use case. Even then, this is a different use of the technique, so I am going to supplement the task list. Let's review how we got here. We created the Farfel Information lever of "improve online experience." In other words, EIM will supply the right data so Farfel can supply a better experience online and increase web sales. Someone thought this was significant enough to ask the EIM team to add the details as to how this should work.

1. Develop IVC from business actions (see Business Model activity)—take the rough list of business actions that the levers may have implied, as we saw in Table 22.3. Turn these into a business process, or scenario, that will fulfill the lever. The swim lane format we show is popular but any process diagram will suffice.

2. Identify touch points where new managed content or data will touch, or be leveraged, by processes—within the new scenario or process model, some processes will be mundane. Like copy the customer profile. Others will actually create Business activity at crucial touch points, like "determine and offer promotions to customer." You want to isolate these processes that show promise of "moving the business needle."

3. Map IVC processes to touch points—take the isolated processes and match them up to any location in the business information life cycle where this process can be touched by customers, internal staff, decision-makers, or other stakeholders. In the example from Farfel, are there any other points where you can use "making order history available?"

4. Isolate the processes that create value or achieve the goal related to the originating action—again, identify the points where business improvement can happen. You may find other areas where this tiny bit of new value can be exploited.

5. Isolate opportunities for improved efficiency, add to business case—check if these touch points of new or improved value from information are in the business case. Are there new benefits? Are there performance metrics required to show the process is achieving a corporate objective? Did Farfel's business case account for using the order history action in other areas?

6. Document IVC alternatives if any—see if there is a better way to arrange all of the value-generating processes. In case of an MDM effort, you may have an entire new functional description of a Customer maintenance area. For Farfel, we may want to elevate the Order History action to a widely accessible object.

7. Review IVCs with SMEs—make sure you walk through the processes with a representative from business areas. It is a mistake to change around a business area and not have the affected parties along for the analysis.

8. Review IVC with EIM leadership and/or appropriate business leadership—once the various IVCs are vetted, it is time to see if management wants to get serious about them in the EIM program or wait for another day.

9. Conduct an IVC confirmation session to recommend IVCs to pursue or delay—the explicit goal of these sessions is to present the new opportunities to business leadership and get a direction and prioritization.

10. Hold a confirmation session for relevance of new processes—if a recommendation is made to proceed with a detailed revision or addition to business processes as a result of EIM, the impacted parties need to review the findings and recommendations.

11. Document New Business Models (back to Business Model activity) as recommendations—if you have gone this far, you now have a batch of new or modified processes. Time to update your models, so return to the Business Model activity.

Sample Output

NOTE that UIC supplied actions with the metric data sheet. UIC was OK with listing the possible actions and tackling the details later and did not execute this activity. Farfel took a run at some actions but associated them with the levers as well as the metrics and BIRs (Table 22.4).

The Farfel samples for this activity were already presented in Figures 7.6 and 7.7.

TIP FOR SUCCESS

The one area of concern is level of detail and amount of time to commit to this activity. Assuming you need to do this activity, how long do you allocate time and resources? We do not want to do business reengineering. On the other hand, an MDM project will look very silly when they turn the switch and no one knows how to add a new item to the catalog. Be certain to restrict this effort to business actions and levers that have originated in the Vision and Alignment phases.

ACTIVITY: PRELIMINARY INFORMATION TAXONOMY

Taxonomy is a hierarchical classification structure, such that it cascades from broad to specific or from parent to children. Scientists use taxonomy to organize chemicals and the animal kingdom. All organizations of any sort have several taxonomies. We use them as a means to organize large entities to manage them better. When you have taxonomy defined, content is easier to manage. It is like a bill of materials to classify, track, and maintain data and documents. For EIM we use the taxonomy in just this manner. The taxonomy provides a foundation to organize the enterprise DNA—the facility that describes how the organization looks from a data and content perspective. We started this DNA foundation in the Metrics and BIR model. We continue with this activity here. The objective of this activity is to develop an initial view of the taxonomies of major content areas, and then agree on how they are to be more fully described and characterized. In a subsequent activity in the Architecture phase we will complete the taxonomy for the EIA, the Data Governance Architecture, and the Community Social Network Architecture. For now we want to present the possible taxonomies within the enterprise and select some or all, and prepare them for final definition during the Architecture phase.

There are some characteristics of useful taxonomies we need to follow:

- Taxonomy is a hierarchical structure, we cannot allow networked structure for navigating content.
- Taxonomic categories are mutually exclusive and precise to avoid overlap and ambiguity; e.g., it is not possible to be both "animal" and "mineral."
- The taxonomic structure can have multiple independent categories or facets, and a content resource can (will likely) be assigned to more than one facet, e.g., to subject and to industry and to resource type.
- Taxonomies are independent of the type of content (although a content- or resource-type hierarchy is desirable). For example, key words can apply to any resource type, so that "data warehousing" topics may be presentations, white papers, or any other resource types. You would not have "data warehouse white papers" in a single hierarchy, but rather in two separate ones.
- While business context provides perspective, the taxonomy is independent of the organization structure (although an organization structure may be a valid hierarchy). See the example earlier— the same principle applies.

There are other rules, but we will apply them later. For now this is all the detail we require. Possible areas to look for taxonomies (some will sound familiar) are:

- Major business events that require content without formal structure, in addition to "row and column" data.
- Major subject areas such as:
  - Customer
  - Product
  - Services
  - Suppliers.

- Web content that interfaces with customers and other constituents.
- Internal documentation such as:
  - Safety manuals, operating manuals
  - EIM documentation—the "DNA" catalogs for IAM
  - Policies and procedures
  - Workflow and collaboration content
  - Compliance guidelines.

Activity Summary (Table 22.7)

Table 22.7 Preliminary Taxonomy Activity Summary	
Objective	Name the possible taxonomies with the enterprise, and determine which are to be detailed.
Purpose	Content management requires the ability to navigate and organize the content predictably. Taxonomies are simple structures for accomplishing this.
Inputs	The conceptual data model, other content identified by the Business Model, or Vision phases.
Tasks	List all possible content requiring a taxonomy Tie to business needs and/or actions and scenarios Determine relevance of those that support business needs Develop straw person categories for each candidate Schedule and prepare review sessions with SMEs Optimize across candidates Publish final list of recommended taxonomies.
Techniques	Keep it simple and fast, this is a preliminary look.
Tools	Standard taxonomies from public sources.
Outputs	List of taxonomy candidates approved for further detailing.
Outcome	List is approved and understood by EIM leadership.

Business Benefits and Ramifications

A taxonomy will leave either a good impression or a bad impression on users of managed content. If the taxonomy makes sense the EIM team will gain new support. Any organization with an Internet, intranet, internal Lotus Notes, or SharePoint will benefit from the taxonomy activities.

Approach Considerations

If there is little content management within the scope of EIM, this can be deferred until the Architecture phase. Remember—even if the EIM program will not be addressing the so-called "unstructured" aspect of content in the near future, it should still be considered when building the program. Always use common taxonomies if they are available. The Dublin Core, which was used for Farfel, is perhaps the most common publicly available offering.

Sample Output

The Architecture phase will show the final Farfel taxonomy example.

TIP FOR SUCCESS

EIM program leaders have to work hard during this activity to not confuse the EIM team or its sponsors. There is the potential to get carried away with this exercise. Usually, web developers can assist here, and may even have well-defined taxonomies already. Remember we are looking for an approved list in this preliminary step, not the entire definition. Using your Vision pictures as a means to demonstrate the taxonomy usage comes in handy. A poor taxonomy will result in excessive costs to maintain content or find information. If you are going to address taxonomy, it needs to be done seriously.

SUMMARY

This phase creates the business requirement for EIM. Major categories of content, expressed as metrics or BIRs, are defined. We refine how the BIRs and Metrics can support the business. Processes and resulting business actions for leveraging content are identified, and models built or modified to reflect the enterprise asset management perspective. We match data groups and elements to the requirements to ensure completeness and understanding of the scope of what EIM will manage. Optionally, we can go deeper into the process and design new workflows and even improve the business case. If we want, this activity provides a means to start to organize the navigation and definition of enterprise DNA, or metadata, via a first pass at enterprise taxonomies. The bridge to specifying the elements, Road Map, and rollout of EIM is stretching out to the other side of the valley. There is now a lot of material to use. The next phase, Architecture, will complete all of the major artifacts and allow us to define the EIM program elements.

Architecture Part 1

23

CONTENTS

Making Enterprise Information Management (EIM) Work for Business. DOI: 10.1016/B978-0-12-375695-4.00023-0

Architecture is an overused word. The reader is no doubt familiar with or has come in contact with "data architects," "solutions architects," and the ultimate-seeming "enterprise architects." Architecture is the name we give to developing the final abstraction of design from which we can build. It is a blueprint.

The blueprints for EIM are developed in this phase. Architectural components are designated, named, and justified. The EIM program definition undergoes full exploration of people frameworks, process frameworks, and technology frameworks. The actual building schedule and plan is the Road Map phase—which follows the Architecture phase. But this is the point you develop blueprints that deliver early results and still design the EIM program.

For an EIM program, the work products from this phase must present sufficiently understandable detail so that a team can build something that works and clearly contributes to the business. This is a phase you will also revisit. The blueprints developed and maintained here connect the EIM program to all other enterprise programs.

This phase uses all of the artifacts from the EIM program. Once the EIM Vision is clear, a Business Model is understood and maybe even some financial targets are designated, the detailed work begins.

This phase is the largest activity in terms of effort to design the EIM program (Figure 23.1). There is a great deal of analysis to choose and align a series of components. The Architecture phase will be the EIA. Even if you are planning on implementing only subdisciplines of EIM, this phase is necessary. Common principles and models are refined (or defined). A series of architectural elements are identified and assembled. The objective of this activity is to define the components necessary to carry out EIM, as well as how they interact in a specific organization. There are many generic elements that can be assembled. We need to nail down what the elements are for a unique enterprise.

As IM has matured, there has been some standardization to provide companies with great architectural resources. The Data Management Association or DAMA has produced a body of knowledge (DMBOK) that we will use.[1] This is of interest to a business program manager because there is a large cost savings available by:

1. Using standardized terminology among the various analysts and architects
2. Having a translation available for other terms.

There is no need to learn all of the elements within the DMBOK, but it is important to start to use common terms for the various parts of EIM. As we proceed, we are going to supply some business perspective about these components. Table 23.1 shows the various elements we will need to consider (in business terms) cross-referenced with the DMBOK[2] (when available).

The most difficult aspect of the EIA is determining this mix of component parts within the auditable design concept. It is easy for a consultant to tell you "you need X or Y." It is more involved to make sure your recommendation to do a certain type of framework can be tied to a business need.

The collective activities of the Architecture phase represent an analysis and design effort. This phase details each of the major architectural areas for EIM. They get more detailed treatment later, so for now let's understand the activities taking place, their interconnections, and how we can determine if we need to perform all the activities or set some aside. For nonstructured content, the EIM team will also develop a hierarchical definition of how all enterprise content fits together—more or less a card catalog for your enterprise. As explained in Chapter 22, this is called a taxonomy. Another mandatory product from this step is final documentation of your metrics, i.e., those measurements or

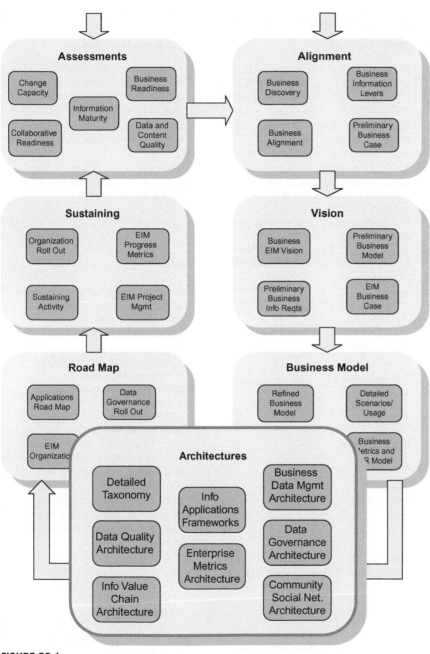

FIGURE 23.1

Architecture activity detail

Table 23.1 DMBOK/Business EIM Architecture Elements

Architecture Elements	DMBOK Definition	Business Descriptions
Analytics	BI procedures and techniques for exploration and analysis of data to discover and identify new and meaningful information and trends.	Features that allow sophisticated "drilling" and application of algorithms to rows and columns' data to identify trends and behavior.
Applications	Applications software functions and services implemented together to support one or more related business processes.	Collections of software functionality with a common business purpose.
Business intelligence	1. Query, analysis, and reporting activity by knowledge workers to monitor and understand the financial and operational health of the enterprise. 2. Query, analysis, and reporting processes and procedures. 3. A synonym for the BI environment. 4. The market segment for BI software tools.	Common label that applies to all types of reporting, scorecards, and data analysis capability.
Collaborative intelligence	Not in DMBOK.	Products and functions that permit sharing, common updating, and joint use of content and data without regard to department silos.
Collaborative business intelligence	Not in DMBOK.	The measuring and analysis of collaboration and managed workflows. Measures the performance of people vs. the organization. The term was trademarked in 2001 but is also used generically.
Collaborative technology	Not in DMBOK.	Class of software products that support workflow, social networking and sharing, and development of common content.
Data and content frameworks	Not in DMBOK.	A blueprint with the combination of design and structure allowing access to data, content, and use of BI.
Data governance	The exercise of authority, control, and shared decision making (planning, monitoring, and enforcement) over the management of data assets.	The organization and implementation of policies, procedures, structure, roles, and responsibilities which outline and enforce rules of engagement, decision rights, and accountabilities for the effective management of information assets.

(Continued)

Table 23.1 (Continued)

Architecture Elements	DMBOK Definition	Business Descriptions
Data models	A representation of the data describing real-world objects and the relationships between the objects, independent of any associated process. A data model includes the set of diagrams for each view along with the meta data defining each object in the model.	Representations of business topics and components in an abstract form to understand relationships. They are key to design of efficient EIM programs.
Data quality	The degree to which data is accurate, complete, timely, consistent with all requirements and business rules, and relevant for a given use.	A discipline that strives to ensure quality, integrity, and effectiveness of data and content.
Content management	The organizing, categorizing, and structuring of information resources, so that they can be stored, published, and reused in multiple ways. A content management system is used to collect, manage, and publish information content, storing the content either as components or whole documents, while maintaining the links between components. It may also provide for content revision control. Content management is a critical data management discipline for nontabular data found in text, graphics, images, video, and audio recordings.	Technology that creates and maintains "unstructured" content, web pages, documents, forms, etc. It ensures integrity, viability, and manages the risk involved with unstructured content.
Document management	The storage, inventory, and control of electronic and paper documents.	The storage, inventory, and control of electronic and paper documents.
Enterprise data architecture	Part of the complete enterprise architecture, including (1) an enterprise data model, and (2) the IVC analysis that identifies the linkages and alignment of the data model with enterprise views of business functions and processes, organizations, applications, and enterprise goals.	An element of EIM, managing the data models and IVCs and life cycles.
Information life cycle	Information supply chain—The flow of data across business processes (supply chain).	The river of data and content used by an enterprise, starting at its creation and ending in its removal.
Information management infrastructure	Not in DMBOK	The technology used to manage information assets.
Information management tools	Not in DMBOK	Technology used to manipulate, track, and develop information assets.
Information management organizations	Not in DMBOK	Departments, units, and teams arranged to support IAM.
Information value chain	The flow of data across processes in support of the enterprise's business value chain.	The series of processes and touch points where data and content use supports business goals.

(Continued)

Table 23.1 (Continued)

Architecture Elements	DMBOK Definition	Business Descriptions
Master data management	Processes that ensure that reference data is kept up to date and coordinated across an enterprise. The organization, management, and distribution of corporately adjudicated data with widespread use in the organization.	An authoritative, reliable foundation for data that is shared across many business functions, providing a single source of truth.
Meta data	Literally, "data about data"; data that defines and describes the characteristics of other data, used to improve both business and technical understanding of data and data-related processes.	The parameters and information required to allow an enterprise to define, navigate, and administer data and content. The documentation of enterprise "DNA."
Metrics	Measure—A unit of measurement used to quantify a characteristic or a quantified characteristic; the dimensions, capacity, or amount of something. Loosely used, a synonym for a metric. Metric—Unit of measure selected for use, used to monitor and control a process. A calculated value based on measurements used to monitor and control a process. Most metrics are ratios comparing one measurement to another.	Measurements of organization, market, or business performance.
Portals	A web site designed to be the "front door" through which a user accesses links to relevant sites. Typically, a portal site has a catalog of sites, a search engine, or both. A portal site may also offer e-mail and other services to entice people to use that site as the main point of entry or portal to the web.	Internet-based software to access multiple functions or applications.
Privacy	The state of being unavailable for observation.	The protection of personal or confidential data for customers or other key business parties.
Reference/code management	Reference data—Any data used to categorize other data, or for relating data to information beyond the boundaries of the enterprise.	The control over common values that describe specific domains, including standardized terms, code values, and cross-references to other unique identifiers.
Reporting	An automated business process or related functionality that provides a detailed, formal account of relevant or requested information.	The reading, organizing and display, or printing of data.
Security	The prevention of unauthorized access to a database and its data, and to applications that have authorized access to databases.	The functions and rules that manage and ensure content is accessed and updated by authorized parties.

(Continued)

Table 23.1 (Continued)

Architecture Elements	DMBOK Definition	Business Descriptions
Social networks	Not in DMBOK	Internet-based facilities where groups or individuals share data, thoughts, or content of common interest.
Standards	A model or example established by authority, custom, or general consent, used in measurement and comparison of quality, value, quantity, or extent.	Policies that specify appearance, handling, access, and use of data or content.
Taxonomy	1. In biology, the classification of living things according to their common characteristics. 2. In content management, a vocabulary (the list of terms in a dialect of an organization or community) organized into a hierarchy, generally to find terms easily.	A hierarchical description of an item, topic, or any other information for ease of navigation and searching.
Tools	Not in DMBOK	Nickname for the various software products that can be used to assist in EIM.
Workflow	A predefined sequence of activities that complete a process.	A discipline that manages and maintains efficient business processes.

indicators that are used to discern whether the organization is achieving its objectives. These can be listed and defined, or broken into further detail. Many of the areas below are treated in detail in other books and I have referred to several books where you can access those details. There is a required sequence to some of these steps, so they are presented in the appropriate order. We will present the Architecture phase in three sections, each of which can stand alone based on time frames, and level of maturity of the current IM environment.

The activities in this phase and the sequence in which we cover them are:

1. *Chapter 23*—Identification and design of the core content EIM will manage and the principles and standards required for managing information assets. This set of activities will always be performed initially and revisited.
   a. Enterprise Metrics Architecture
   b. Information Applications Frameworks
   c. Business Data (and Content) Management Architecture
2. *Chapter 24*—Design of the core EIM functions and processes for day-to-day IAM. In addition, the information life cycles to be governed are collected and confirmed.
   a. Data Governance Architecture
   b. IVC Architecture
   c. Data Quality Architecture

3. *Chapter 25*—Design the elements of EIM Architecture that manage unstructured assets.
   a. Enterprise Taxonomy
   b. Community/Social Network Architecture.

The EIM Architecture provides required context for the ways in which elements of enterprise data and content relate to each other. This is incredibly important in order to advance toward integrated management of information assets. If we extend our inventory metaphor, this is where we develop rules that tell us "If there are two items on this shelf, there can be only one item on that shelf" or "This type of item can only be stored in this type of container." There is also a great deal of detail generated that requires long-term management in its own right. This has been referred to as the enterprise DNA—the catalog or meta data that describes the elements and components of EIM and how they are interrelated.

Like any other blueprint, the work products here are the detailed design of a program which will be referred to again and again. It is important that the deliverables are not made exotic and mysterious. Far too often, an EIM effort stumbles or stops after the Architecture phase. There are a lot of boxes and arrows on large pieces of paper. The architects step back and are content. The business people nod and pretend to understand, because they are flummoxed. Then the team sets the pile of paper aside after they are told to "go get some low-hanging fruit—we need to see value." The architecture has failed to produce a blueprint the business embraces. The perception has become that implementing a real architecture takes too long and so before anything else happens, we need to go "look busy." In the more tangible world of construction and engineering, we always can hand over blueprints, and the digging and hammering starts. In addition, if there is a need to do the effort in stages, the stages are laid out after the ideal end blueprint is completed. IAM is no different, and the EIM program can be thought of as the architect's trailer in the corner of the large construction site. Little trailer, huge role. Business manager, remember when you lean hard on the IT staff to show something "we can use" and it is done in lieu (vs. as a short-term tactic) of a thought-out architecture, you are most certainly building a skyscraper without that little trailer in the corner.

It is essential that you time-box this phase, as it can drag on. It is perfectly fine to do enough "architecting" to establish principles, policies, and standards, dip into the Road Map phase and launch a project, *then* loop back to tidy up the Architecture steps. Just keep the projects within the defined architectures, policies, and rules.

Figure 23.2 shows which portion of Architecture we are covering in this chapter. All the activities are mandatory.

ACTIVITY: ENTERPRISE METRICS ARCHITECTURE

The first activity completes the analysis of the Metrics and BIRs and completes the definition of what core information assets must be managed. Rather than throw many ideas on a board and hash around with what kind of reporting and analysis mechanisms are required, or what capacity of plumbing is required, we apply a quantitative method. This approach evolved over many years of EIM work, and is a proven approach to discern how you will deliver data and content. It evolved as we saw far too many EIM-type projects go from a list of business problems to procuring technology without the appropriate details. This was due to two reasons.

1. CIOs or other technology executives see the benefit of the EIM-related effort, e.g., a data warehouse or master data project, but proceed without a business sponsor.

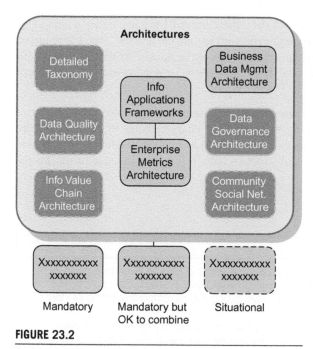

Architectures

- Detailed Taxonomy
- Info Applications Frameworks
- Business Data Mgmt Architecture
- Data Quality Architecture
- Enterprise Metrics Architecture
- Data Governance Architecture
- Info Value Chain Architecture
- Community Social Net. Architecture

Xxxxxxxxxxx xxxxxxx — Mandatory

Xxxxxxxxxxx xxxxxxx — Mandatory but OK to combine

Xxxxxxxxxxx xxxxxxx — Situational

FIGURE 23.2

Architecture component of the EIM development process

2. The guiding policies for technology selection were frequently based on blind adherence to a particular design philosophy or were influenced by a corporate standard that had no consideration of EIM-type projects. The procurement process became a political issue vs. a business issue.

Our firm keeps tabs on this particular foible, and we see at least 70% of EIM-related projects selecting tools and hardware before having *any* idea what the first application will look like or what measurable benefit it will bring. Obviously we require a better alignment to the business, so we need a step that can bridge us from business to technology requirements, yet maintain the auditable linkage between the two. Along the way, we discovered that many business requirements could be defined in terms of characteristics that guided our Road Map and technology decisions. This is the list of characteristics seen in Chapter 22. We now add more detail to the definition of the requirements.

The objective in expanding the Metrics and BIR model done earlier is to develop enough understanding of our requirements to guide the engineers in designing the frameworks that will hold, process, and manage our data and content. We add a great deal of detail for each identified metric *and* information requirement. We need to expand our description of these requirements beyond what they are and look at how we need to produce them.

This technique is objective by design. There are several reasons for this:

- Often, the information culture of an organization is such that there is an institutional expectation that business areas will get the data they demand. There must be physical location of the data in a storehouse unique to the department. (Heaven forbid if someone looks at how they come to their conclusions and that number at the bottom of the report.)

- While the business areas are asking for their own data, the current BI groups, either within IT or the business areas, focus on what kind of structure they want to manage and use. One group insists that smaller batches of data tied together by their dimensions are best, another wants to drop it all in a big "warehouse" and have users pursue data via a unique view, or window into the data, keeping all the dimensions centrally.

Each of the characteristics listed in Table 23.2 are significant shapers of the architecture and management policies around data assets. This activity will apply the characteristics to each Metric and BIR. You can use these characteristics for documents and content as well as traditional data. Again, even if you chose to address content without formal structure later, it is a solid practice to address the requirements to manage that content now.

Table 23.2 Metrics and BIR Characteristics		
1	Measurement volume	The estimated occurrences of this measure in terms of data required to support, or number of unique times this measure is generated over a specific time period. This indicates how much processing may have to occur to assemble this metric or store the results.
2	Granularity	The level of detail of the data required to support this metric. For example, a certain metric may require us to add up all of the activity from a web site. This is a lot of detail or granularity. Another may require us to multiply a weekly number by a factor. This is less granular.
3	"Historicity"	Historical requirements are considered in this characteristic. An occurrence of information that must be kept many years will need different management than one whose existence is fleeting.
4	Distribution	The extent to which the information will be used across an enterprise. Cross-functional and/or widely broadcast information generates a different set of management challenges.
5	Fact volatility	This characteristic is the frequency that information or content is added to or updated for the purpose of use in this metric or requirement.
6	Dimensional complexity	A statement is made as to the relative complexity of the ways we need to "slice" the metric, or index the document. Obviously, if a measure has many dimensions and some of them change over time, there is a complicated management issue. A document that must be cross-indexed or requires an enormous index section is also considered complicated.
7	Access type	The means of access to the content or metric is important to managing the asset. For example, will the information be accessed directly via a query, or rolled-off onto reports? Will we need to make an image available online?
8	Latency	The time from when the data is available to when it is required to be placed into our managed environment is called latency. Low latency, or a short time period, presents more complications in management and processing.
9	Source complexity	Often we need to get data from one place and process it so it ends up elsewhere. This characteristic defines the relative complexity of gathering and moving data into the managed framework.

(Continued)

Table 23.2 (Continued)

10	Frequency	We need to indicate how often the information is accessed for a particular measure or requirement. Do we need to get to the data often or infrequently? This characteristic is *different* from periodicity. Daily activity (the periods we want to view) may need to be viewed or accessed weekly (the frequency of use).
11	Response time	If we produce a requirement or metric, what is the desired time to respond to the production of the metric? How soon must the business react to the metric and take action, e.g., a response to a customer at a touch point? Again, a faster reaction requirement will cause us to build a different managed environment than one that has a slower response time.
12	Follow-up time	After a response is initiated, how long must there be before another party, if any, is to be contacted, or receive directions or resolution? In other words, you can respond quickly, but only be able to spend an hour on the event.
13	Persistency	This characteristic indicates the length of time data must be retained in the framework, and be usable. Contrast this with historicity which relates to historical storage. Persistent data needs to be accessible to be useful. Historical data can sit off in a vault and be recalled. Of course, if this particular metric or document has a high need for both, you have interesting management issues.
14	Availability	When should the information be available? One business day, 24 × 7? This characteristic indicates availability of the data access mechanism, not how fast you want to see it (that is latency).
15	Data quality	This characteristic is for applying any findings from DQ assessments or investigations to specific business needs. Alternatively, this also provides a means to insert a subjective awareness of data issues *in lieu of* a formal DQ investigation. This characteristic represents the degree of usefulness of the data *before* it is managed or received into the enterprise.

OBSERVATION

As an EIM leader, you will or have had the pleasure of exposing business partners to discussions around terms like: star schemas, dimensions, corporate information factories, or "data vaults." This is your ticket out of the noise. Let the business needs tell you the required method for structure, access, and delivery of data. All of the aforementioned approaches have great merit. However, you are responsible for focusing the team away from technical debates before you really need to pick one particular structure over another.

Note: A few of these characteristics defied a simple label—the ones in quotes are "invented" terms.

Metrics and Information Requirements Characteristics

The results from application of the characteristics described earlier are normally done with a relative score from a predefined set of values (Table 23.3). Each metric is scored across some or all of the 15 characterized in Table 23.2. The scores of all the metrics are then ranked, sorted, and analyzed.

A typical deliverable from this activity will feature several hundred metrics and equally as many documents, reports, or content types. The EIM team actually gets its own analytical database of sorts. We can examine the multitude of enterprise requirements across a range of characteristics. That is why we incorporate this activity first in the Architecture phase. Also, it's important to understand that this effort does not have to account for every single report or form. Imagine trying that with a huge multinational

Table 23.3 Characteristic Scores for EIM Metrics and BIRs

	EIM Metric and BIR Characteristics Score Sheet				
	Relative Complexity	1	2	3	4
Granularity—the level of detail required to support measurements, dimensions, and requirements	1–10	Aggregate over one year	Annual aggregate	Monthly aggregate	Item/entity aggregate>day
Fact volatility—the frequency that new data is ADDED or UPDATED for usage	1–10	Update>1x/yr	Update 1x/yr	Update 2–4x/yr	Update monthly
Dimensional complexity—the relative nature of how extensive and/or abstracted the various reporting dimensions are	1–10	Typical dimensions of month, year, etc. and no others	Easily understood dimensions, such as color, weight, etc.	Combinations of simple dimensions, i.e., weight and color need to be correlated	Dimensions become more than one or two layers deep in terms of taxonomy
Dimensional volatility—the frequency that dimensions change is ADDED TO, or UPDATED for BI uses	1–10	Dimension types and values are fixed, by regulation or tradition	Dimension types are fixed, and values change rarely, perhaps once every few years	Dimension types are fixed, but values change yearly	Dimension types may be added once in a few years, and dimension values change accordingly
"Historicity"—the extent to which historical reporting requirements are necessary	1–10	No history	Retain recent additions	Retain additions within fiscal year	Retain multiple years of additions
Latency—the time between when the data is available and when it is required to be placed into the framework	**10–1** Low latency is scored higher	Available within year	Available within quarter	Available within month	Available within week
Distribution—the extent to which the information will be used across an enterprise	1–10	Used only by department	Generated by department, limited sharing	Generated by divisions, widespread sharing by divisions	Generated by divisions, multiple department usage in divisions
Volume—relative amount of logical data required to meet all granularity, dimensional, and archival requirements	1–10	Less than 20 gb	20–50 gb	50–100 gb	100–300 gb

(Continued)

Table 23.3 (Continued)

5	6	7	8	9	10
Item/entity level	Line item/ header>day	Line item/ header by day. Document— archived files	Line item by header. Document— single copies	Line item (pass- seat)	Subline item
Update weekly	Update daily	Update 2x daily	Update>2x/ day	Near-time update	Real-time update
Dimensions can vary by subject values, e.g., customer profiles	Dimension values can change based on other dimensional values			Certain dimensions cannot be sourced, but can be derived from combinations of other dimensions	Certain dimensions do not exist
Dimension types will change, as well as new additions. Values will change within fiscal time frames	Dimension types change within fiscal periods. Dimension values change frequently, and old values must be retained	Dimension types change within periods, dimension values are dynamic enough to consider end-user maintenance of values	Dimension values change daily	Dimension values change near time	Real-time changes in dimensions as well as facts
Retain for year- over-year analysis	Retain for month-over- month analysis	Retain for week-over-week analysis	"As of date" within fiscal year	"As of date" over several years	"As of date" and period-over- period
Available two to four days	Available within 24 hours	Available 2x/day	Available>2 intervals/day	Near-time availability	Immediate xmt to DW
		Generated centrally, used by selected divisions	Generated centrally, used by multi divisions/ department	Wide usage across enterprise	Ubiquitous use by entire enterprise
300–500 gb	500–750 gb	750–1tb	1–3 tb	3–10 tb	Over 10 tb

(Continued)

Table 23.3 (Continued)

	Relative Complexity	1	2	3	4
		EIM Metric and BIR Characteristics Score Sheet			
Frequency—how often the information is accessed for a particular measure or requirement. Differs from volatility, e.g., daily activity is accessed weekly	1–10	1x per year	1x per quarter	2x per quarter	1x per month
Response time—how soon must the business react to the metric and take action, e.g., with customer or other touch point?	1–10	No required response to any touch point or stimulus	A response is required but there is no deadline	Response required within a fiscal year	Response required within a fiscal month
Follow-up time—the time desired to allocate to responding to a metric or stimulus, i.e., you can respond quickly, but only be able to spend an hour on the event	1–10	Follow-up has no cap on effort expended	Follow-up to resolve event can take up to a fiscal year	Follow-up to resolve event can take up to a fiscal month	Follow-up to resolve event can take up to a calendar week
Data quality—degree of usefulness or effectiveness of source data	1–10	Data is "clean"	Data is clean, but data controls are loose	Data is clean, but controls are loose, and sources are disparate	Some data may require fixing up some "fat finger" errors
Availability—when should information be available	1–10				During the business day
Persistency—the extent to which the data set remains stable	1–10	Data set never appended or updated	Data set appended to only when needed	Data set is appended to, but no updates	Data set is updated only as needed
Access type—mode of data access. For example, will the information be accessed directly, via query, or rolled-off onto reports?	1–10	Tab report	Control break report	Sorted breaks	Parameters and filters

(Continued)

Table 23.3 (Continued)

5	6	7	8	9	10
2x per month	Weekly	2x per week	Daily	2x per day	Many a day
Response required within a fiscal week	Response required within a fiscal day	Response required within a portion of a day	Response required within 90 minutes	Response required within 15–90 minutes	Immediate, real-time response required
Follow-up to resolve event must take between a day and a week	Follow-up to resolve event can only take a business day	The organization cannot afford to invest more than 1–23 hours	The organization cannot afford to spend more than an hour	The organization must be equipped to follow-up after a response within an hour	Response time and follow-up are the same—there is no time to make the touch point wait
Data may have correct values, but wrong context, (referential) 24 × 7	Data may have new values, or unknown domains	Domains have to be split up to create new values	Core subjects missing legitimate values (e.g., customer ID)	Beside domain and value issues, data must be reconciled to disparate sources	Data does not really exist in source systems, but needs to be staged for heuristic algorithms
Data set is updated periodically, but not refreshed	Data set must be refreshed monthly or on regular basis	Data set must be refreshed totally (reload)	Data set must be refreshed on demand	Data set must be refreshed daily for new use	Data set can be created and destroyed at will by user
Pivot table	Drill across	Ad hoc	Complex SQL	Need to subset data sets on fly	Need to create nonpersistent data sets

company. We need to examine the core indicators and core business events. Usually, there are enough items from these areas to provide sufficient detail for an accurate and relevant amount of analysis.

The EIM team will apply quantitative analysis to these findings. The predefined scores are gathered and analyzed. The next activity will translate these results into architecture, but the analysis and review of the analysis need to occur before declaring architectural elements.

Activity Summary (Table 23.4)

Table 23.4 Enterprise Metrics Architecture Activity Summary	
Objective	Develop the foundation that guides the derivation of the various elements that will make up the EIM Architecture. Develop the first view of how data and information will be accessed and managed.
Purpose	Capture the enterprise metrics and BIRs to create a foundation for capturing 80% of the data elements, dimensions, and content types required for most organizations.
Inputs	The Businesses Metrics and BIRs Model from the Business Model phase.
Tasks	Refine Business Metrics and BIRs if required Clarify industry metrics Determine characteristics to use (all 15 or subset). Create measure sheets or records, one per measure and/or BIR Determine level of review or walk through review results Identify participants Fill out template for workshops if required Confirm workshop sessions with predetermined stakeholders Hold workshops if required Add additional information to Metrics/BIR database Identify significant patterns and groups with the Metrics/BIR database Submit report of patterns and groups for verification Refine Metrics/BIR characteristics as required Prepare presentation of results of Metrics/BIR Architecture.
Techniques	We use a quantitative technique called affinity analysis. This technique examines all the occurrences of values in a set of data, and clusters them based on common characteristics.
Tools	There are tools that will provide clustering or affinity analysis, but they are clumsy with the data generated here. I wish I could say we have the perfect tool for this, but we can only suggest some downloaded macros from the Internet as well as the previously mentioned tools like system architect, which has crude capabilities. We tend to use Excel, a macro, and then our eyeballs to get logically meaningful groupings of requirements. We use the score sheet in Table 23.2 to rate the characteristics.
Outputs	All defined metrics and BIR characteristics are described or accounted for. There is an initial report of the various groupings and commonality between the enterprise requirements for information and content use. A database of some sort exists to hold and manage these findings.
Outcome	This activity is complete when the EIM team and EIM leadership have analyzed the requirements and feel they have enough data to justify choices of architectural elements. Usually, this means a level of detail in terms of all metrics and BIRs having their data sheets filled out, and resolution of all issues regarding metrics and BIR definition.

Business Benefits and Ramifications

The business now owns a very thorough documentation of metrics and information requirements. In addition the EIM team can now apply the concept of auditable design, and create a business-aligned EIM technical framework.

Approach Considerations

Start with trying to use all the characteristics offered here in the samples and templates. We have found it is easier to drop any that are not relevant to your enterprise once you start, than try and second-guess what might be useful. Produce work sheets, one for each metric, but add a page for metric or BIR characteristics (Table 23.5). If you are doing a full EIM effort, there may be a few hundred of these. Do not have one part of your team slog through these. Create a handful of EIM requirements

Table 23.5 Metric BIR Characteristics Sample

Characteristics	Metric Name – Premium Growth Rate Characteristic Description	Score
Measurement volume	The estimated occurrences of this measure in terms of data required to support, or number of unique times this measure is generated over a specific time period.	10
Granularity	The level of detail of the data required to support this metric.	9
Historicity	The extent of historical requirements in the metric or requirement.	10
Distribution	The extent to which the information will be used across an enterprise.	8
Fact volatility	The frequency that information or content is added to or updated for the purpose of use in this metric or requirement.	6
Dimensional complexity	The complexity of how we need to "slice" the metric, or index the document.	10
Access type	The means of access to the content or metric is important to managing the asset.	9
Latency	The time between when the data is available to and when it is required to be placed into our managed environment.	5
Source complexity	The relative complexity of gathering and moving data into the managed framework.	10
Frequency	Indicates how often the information is accessed for a particular measure or requirement. *Different* from periodicity.	8
Response time	The desired time to respond to the production of the metric or requirement.	4
Follow-up time	The time desired to allocate to responding to a metric or stimulus.	5
Persistency	The length of time data must be retained in the framework and be usable. Contrast this with historicity which relates to historical storage.	5
Availability	This indicates availability of the access mechanism, not how fast you want to see it (that is latency).	5
Data quality	This represents the degree of usefulness of the data *before* it is managed or received into the enterprise.	5

"SWAT" teams made up of EIM team analysts and SMEs. Give each team no more than 25 requirements. Orient them to the technique, send them out on Monday, and tell them to come back on Friday with the filled-out data.

Once the data is returned, it is entered into a spreadsheet or database, and analyzed. Other activities will actually do the analysis to determine technology needs or design an Application Framework. It is good practice to take a quick look at major patterns at this point and present them, so the other activities can develop a sense of what kind of additional analysis is required.

Metrics and BIRs are important to alignment. The measurements of the enterprise express whether goals and objectives are being met. A metric represents the details of a measurement that we can define in technical terms as well as business terms.

Sample Output

Table 23.5 shows the UIC sample of the relative scoring applied from Table 23.3 (1 being simple, 10 being challenging). Remember there are several hundred of these possible.

Once they are organized for ranking and analysis, the metrics and BIR characteristics data resembles Table 23.6. Note the Metrics and BIRs are sorted on granularity and latency. Even with this short sample, you can see how some requirements will require different management and handling frameworks than others.

The Farfel artifact shows the entry from the "database" of requirements (Figure 23.3).

TIP FOR SUCCESS

Over the years, we have experienced one or two behaviors that can cause the EIM team some concerns. First, when business SMEs participate in a metrics review to define if they need the metric fast or historically, etc., they will very often ask for maximum performance. For example, we have seen SMEs ask for real-time delivery of financial metrics when they have no need for them. When we ask for an explanation because there is no business goal tied to this request, it usually is explained by an answer along the lines of "it would be very cool to have it." This can mean either lack of attention to or understanding of the process, *or* missed business needs. Either way you will need to sit down and work through the issues. This can be time consuming, so be prepared to time-box this work or have some schedule flexibility.

The most notable success factor for this activity is to have several groups of cross-functional business SMEs (two–four in each group) plunge into defining the characteristics of the various metrics groups. If we have encountered one group that grumbled and complained of multiple algorithms, or having to focus on business needs vs. unjustified wants, we have had several other groups say this was the best analytical activity in which they have ever participated. They felt stepping back and considering how they *really* wanted to use information and measure their business to be very enlightening. Placing a time-box on the tasks also keeps the EIM team moving forward. This activity should be time-boxed to take no more than two weeks for *any size organization*.

If the BIRs contain documents, forms, or other content types that are not metrics, remember they can still have a characteristics sheet filled out. There may not be an algorithm to provide, but the other characteristics are equally useful and are evaluated in the same manner.

Table 23.6 UIC Metrics Sample Summary

Metric/BIR	Definition	BIR Volume	Granularity	Historicity	Distribution	Fact Volatility	Dimensional Complexity	Access Type	Latency	Source Complexity	Frequency	Response Time	Follow-up Time	Persistency	Availability	Data Quality
Combined ratio (metric)	Ratio of loss expense to earned premiums	10	9	10	8	6	10	9	5	10	8	4	5	5	5	5
Operating cost per feature (metric)	Overhead cost of managing policies allocated to policy features	10	9	10	8	6	9	9	5	10	10	4	6	6	5	5
Premium growth rate (metric)	The proportional indication of the growth (or decrease) of revenue from premiums	10	9	10	8	6	10	9	5	10	8	4	5	5	5	5
Product profitability (metric)	The profitability of a product or bundle of products including losses and allocated expenses	10	9	10	8	6	9	9	5	10	10	4	6	6	5	5
Claims adjusters file (BIR)	Notes, pictures, and reports related to a claim	9	8	7	4	6	4	3	9	8	6	8	7	9	8	8
Household demographic count (metric)	Number of households in a specific market	10	8	10	7	3	5	9	3	10	5	4	6	6	5	5
Individual demographic count (metric)	Number of individuals in a specific market	10	8	10	7	3	5	9	3	10	5	4	6	6	5	5
Claim amount recovered (metric)	The amount of claim payment recovered from other insurers and third parties	8	7	7	8	9	6	7	7	6	9	6	5	9	5	2
Claim recovery ratio (metric)	Percentage of claim losses recovered	8	7	7	8	9	6	7	6	6	8	5	5	9	5	2
Policy illustrations (BIR)	Hard copy legal documents representing the policy contract	5	7	7	5	5	6	4	5	3	4	7	7	8	7	9

ACTIVITY: INFORMATION APPLICATIONS FRAMEWORKS

There will be various applications, or collections of software with a function, that will come under the umbrella of EIM. Most common are applications like data warehouse, or BI. The EIM program sets the standard for how these applications will interact and what the portfolio of these applications will look like. This activity defines the required elements that will specify a framework to deliver data and content to the business applications with EIM. This is also where the EIM team can design their

Measurement	Definition	Unit of Measure	Calculation (formula)	Related Business Drivers	Related Business Goals	Subject Areas	Entities
Sales	Merch sales from all channels, service income	$$$'s	((Sales Units * price)+ residuals + commissions+service sku income) +/- (Prod comm fund adj) By contracted line, by units, by product line (Reported year over year)	Focus on Shareholder Return Enhance Customer Experience Product Innovation Improve Operational Efficiency	Improve returns on stores and under-performing products Reduce overhead and administrative costs Improve customer feedback Offer more profitable, attractive products	Activity Channel Facility Finance Party Product	Sale Order, Sale Order Line, Sale Order Channel, Sale Order Channel Role, Facility, Facility Type, Facility Role, Facility Role Type, Product, Product Category, Product Sale, Product Price, Payment, Period Type, Party, Party Role, Party Role Type

View By	Summary Levels	Report Freq	Access Freq	Access Type	Update Freq	Latency	Granularity	Periodicity	Historicity	Comp Period
Sku Product Hierarchy Contractor	SBU Nation Division Region District Store	Daily Weekly Monthly	Daily Weekly Monthly	Widespread, reports	Daily Weekly Monthly	Daily	Moderate for this metric	Week	10 years	Week to week Month to month TY/LY

FIGURE 23.3

Farfel metrics entry

"Corporate Information Factory"[3] or "Bus Architecture,"[4] or both if so inclined. We will identify and define master data, or reference data capabilities if there is a business's need to provide those frameworks as well.

We will be using the Metrics model, Data model, and any process-type work we have done, like the business actions or expanded levers. Analysis is performed to look for patterns. We defined many patterns in the prior activity, using the metrics to suggest batches of common requirements. These patterns point out the need to adapt the various architectural elements we require to the specific business challenges of the given situation. This is best explained via an example:

> An airline is an interesting business in that most of its operational decisions and many of its tactical, or managerial reports come from the same view of data, that of record of a passenger on a flight. One person, one seat, one flight "leg." Connecting to another city means another leg, hence another record. If we were developing the EIM program for this airline, we would examine the requirements expressed in our earlier work products. We would consider there are an enormous number of operational decisions (e.g., how many bags of pretzels or meals do we need?), as well as analytical decisions (is this leg profitable enough to provide more than pretzels?) based on the same data. Therefore, we must take into account building applications that access large amounts of data over a long period of time. The operational reports need to happen fast; the data must "be there." But the historical analysis can be done after a time and perhaps downstream from the hectic operational data. Therefore, we need a framework to provide operational reporting very fast *and* we also need a structure to provide historical analysis. And both structures need to contain granular data.

The Metrics/BIR model we developed tells us this. The business actions tell us what will be done with the reports, and the business goals tell us how much the business will benefit. So further analysis of the requirements groupings and business needs has pointed us in the direction of two common elements—a historical collection of detailed data we need to use for analysis, and perhaps higher performance structure for reporting. We can also identify the requirements for when and how much we need to move data from one area to another. Or from the operational ticket and reservation system to the reporting and analysis frameworks. Additionally, we have the details in the metrics and BIR characteristics to determine the nature of the file structures and even recommend the type of hardware and software to manage these applications.

OBSERVATION

All of this "stuff" really does fit together—it has to—because proposing something to the business such as IAM without being able to tie it all together and making it "auditable" is a rerun of the way it has been done for decades. Even if you are not going to delve into pro forma statements of information value, and only really need to get good results to support business drivers, all of this needs to tie together.

Analysis is performed to tell us how we will distribute data and content, how we will identify potential data issues, and where businesspeople can expect to have reliable, certified content. We will also be able to specify the rules for when and how business users can get to content for use within their areas, such as for product research, legal and compliance investigation, or actuarial analysis.

In addition, we will understand the kinds of control and facilities needed to ensure quality, so we will be examining where the "master" version of data will sit, where we desire certified sources to be placed, and how we want to maintain quality and integrity of content. We will also support controls (accuracy, privacy, and security) and compliance (think Sarbanes–Oxley) requirements.

Lastly, we will also address how all of our information assets will be moved around. Like our factory inventory metaphor, we will need to move material (data and content) from one work area to another. We may require special movement mechanisms or additional "wiring and plumbing." We will also be developing an idea of capacity and performance required to support the business. (It is useless to perform IAM if the IAM elements do not allow content to get where it needs to be in a timely manner.)

Activity Summary (Table 23.7)

Table 23.7 Information Applications Frameworks Activity Summary	
Objective	Identify and define the architecture elements of an EIM program that will deliver business applications.
Purpose	Produce a verifiable list of structures that need to be deployed over time. This allows for a more reasoned and accurate Road Map.
Inputs	The results of the Metrics Architecture step, as well as the various process and data models.
Tasks	Refine the analysis of Metrics/BIR
	Identify smaller grouping of requirements, and other characteristics deemed relevant:
	Time characteristics, latencies
	Other characteristics
	Specify reporting, BI, and analytics frameworks
	Generate spider charts or other graphic of framework characteristics
	Identify reporting BI framework elements (ODS, DW, DM, staging, etc.) from spiders
	Map Business and Information Requirements for and Analytic framework
	Develop framework presentation (spider charts)
	Identify reference and master data needs from DQ survey, BIRs, and dimensions
	Identify content management needs from BIRs and Business Model
	Isolate the dimensions from ALL Metric/BIRs
	List all dimensions and develop standard definitions
	Merge results of DQ assessment with applications and technology requirements
	Determine criteria to direct technical elements choices
	Consider possible unique requirements, e.g., for Privacy, Security, Encryption, Web click capture, Device Interface, external data
	Develop technology elements specification
	Perform information interface and sizing analysis (see MART technique)
	Identify gaps in current state technology
	Determine new technology requirements, existing technology to leverage, and technology to phase out
	Associate relevant technology categories with framework elements (technology classification; tools, data interchange, storage, content management, etc.)
	Determine criteria for technical elements
	Identify potential candidate software and services solution vendors
	Short list technology (time permitting, or if within EIM scope)
	Coordinate with Enterprise Architecture
	Diagram and document all architectural elements

(Continued)

Table 23.7 (Continued)	
Techniques	There is an alignment technique called MART analysis, M—Message, A—Aggregate, R—Replicate, T—Transform where we align business processes with the requirements to supply the processes with content and data in a timely and correct manner.
Tools	Again, the various enterprise architecture tools or Excel. Visio is preferred for the visual presentations.
Outputs	There is a robust set of deliverables:
	The initial list of application elements for EIM.
	The initial list of technical elements for EIM.
	List of and justification for specific data and content movement facilities.
	Merger of DQ requirements with the EIM architecture elements.
Outcome	The EIM team has completed the various work products, and presented the EIM Architecture elements, and the EIM leadership, as well as other constituents (like IT operations, compliance, and business areas) understand the nature of the proposed elements.

Business Benefits and Ramifications

The business areas will begin to see that elusive "something" they have been looking for since the EIM program started: there is now some evidence of what EIM will deliver. There are other support areas in the enterprise which will need to view this activity's results, as most organizations have architectural and technology standards that must be verified against the required elements for EIM.

Approach Considerations

The Metrics and BIR Architecture data and clusters and supporting models are ingredients in the soup that gets refined into architecture elements. These are not technology elements yet. We are specifying the types of applications the business will use. Applications have to be built or acquired, so this activity provides important support for the Road Map. At this point, you essentially have a collection of logically related batches of work. The Road Map will convert these into units of effort for deployment.

Depending on the complexity of your business and metrics model, you may have many groupings across the various characteristics. However, just being colocated does not mean that all of the metrics will exist in one type of application, or can be developed at the same time. The business members of the EIM team will need to look at the groups of requirements and ensure there is a common business direction.

Specific elements that may be defined include:

- Reporting, business performance management, and analytical application framework
- Management of "golden copy" of data also known as MDM
- Management of other reference items, such as codes (everything like state codes, sales regions, and product types)
- Management of those codes that are also important business dimensions, which are segments of the business you will want to sort and report by. (Sales *by* region, store profit *by* product class)
- Content where security, privacy, compliance, and regulation are of concern to the business
- Document management and workflow
- Text requiring the ability to be searched and analyzed
- Elements that will require data quality and data control consideration

- Business functional areas where the IVC recommends process improvements
- Business content integrity functions, like document destruction, data purging, backups, data retention, and archiving
- Requirements for sending data outside of the organization and bringing external data into the organization.

The EIM team will finalize the various types of frameworks and components, i.e., does the organization require "middleware" to connect databases? Is there a need to have "gold copies" of customer or product data? Are there significant needs to manage documents and workflow? Are the BI needs best served by a "single source of the truth" of some sort?

The EIM team starts by refining the Metrics and BIR Architecture output. After latency and granularity, other characteristics can be reviewed. Perhaps response and follow-up times are important, especially if the IVC work produced juicy new ways to use data at touch points.

Characteristics that affect the reading and usage are analyzed to determine the delivery frameworks for data and content, e.g., is there a data warehouse required? If you are revisiting this activity, you can use this step to verify the effectiveness of your current reporting and analysis environment. The output from this is usually produced in the form of a bar graph or plot. I prefer the radar plot, or "spider charts" as one client referred to them. Experimentation and analyzing the requirements by time period, latencies, and other characteristics deemed relevant are done using this technique. The EIM data architects will correlate the results of data movement (MART) or similar technique to design a framework to move and manage information. Similar steps are taken to identify required master data or reference data frameworks.

One of the specific business-aligned techniques we deploy is called MART. This mnemonic stands for:

M—Message; notification of a content change or business event across the various EIM applications
A—Aggregate; summarize, boil down, or otherwise move data to a higher abstraction, usually for reporting or managerial purposes
R—Replicate; move data and content as is, make a copy
T—Transform; alter or change content or data so it can be repurposed, such as converting from a code in an old system to a code in a new system, or performing a minor data quality operation for "cleanup" of a data error.

We take all of our business actions, IVCs steps, and/or processes we have defined (we can even use the original levers if time is short) and see how they need to acquire content and data or communicate with each other. An example is shown in Figure 23.4.

The EIM team will use the Metrics Architecture and MART analysis (and other techniques if desired) to develop a picture of how wide the pipes need to be and how fast the pumps must operate. Specific elements identified here may be facilities to:

- Synchronize data and content across the enterprise due to timing, or required redundancy
- Broadcast changes to critical data elements like reference and master data
- Clean up, or transform data so it can be used effectively further down the IVC
- Aggregate or restate data for historical use and management use.

There will be situations in some organizations where "plumbing" isn't fast enough and the proposed frameworks will need to look more like a circuit diagram, with a "main bus" that manages the coming

Determine nature of interactions between processes
To

From		Process A	Process B	Process C	Process D	Process E	Process F	Process G	Process H
	Process A		M, T	—	—	T	—	—	—
	Process B	M		R	M	—	—	—	—
	Process C	—	—		—	R	A	A	R
	Process D	—	A, T	—		—	—	—	—
	Process E	—	—	—	—		—	—	—
	Process F	R	R	R	—	T		—	R
	Process G	M	M	M, A	T	T	R		—
	Process H	R	R	T	T	T	T	—	

FIGURE 23.4

MART example

and going of business events. Technology-savvy EIM sponsors will recognize this as defining a need for service-oriented structures.

If the analysis of requirements indicates new technology needs, the EIM team is able to identify requirements and target specific brands and suppliers of technology at this point. If so inclined, they can develop lists of candidate suppliers and start procurement.

Sample Output

Here's an example from the case studies to show what the deliverable may look like. Rather than reproduce an artifact, it is more effective to show the flow from artifacts to framework (Figure 23.5).

I took Table 23.4 and produced a "spider chart" to show how the scores translate to a visual representation. Obviously, we would need to produce multiple charts based on our clustering (Figure 23.6).

TIPS FOR SUCCESS

If you are going through this for the first time, several enterprise constituents will most likely express concerns that must be addressed.

1. The enterprise will have technology standards or standard technology (two different concepts—same result). The EIM elements may conflict with the official or de facto standards.
2. There will be projects funded and under way that will reflect EIM elements. The business must decide the extent to which the EIM program influences work that is in progress. There will always be ragged edges here—in a large organization, there is no way to catch stuff that is "in flight" and draw it back into the governed EIM program.
3. There will be shadow IT areas that will begin about now to announce they are not going to relinquish (*insert their departmental product, tool, database, or reports here*), and will begin a process of complaining and/ or passive aggression. This is actually good news! First of all, you have their attention. Second, you have identified additional parties requiring EIM orientation and education. Lastly, they may have an EIM element in place that can actually be leveraged.

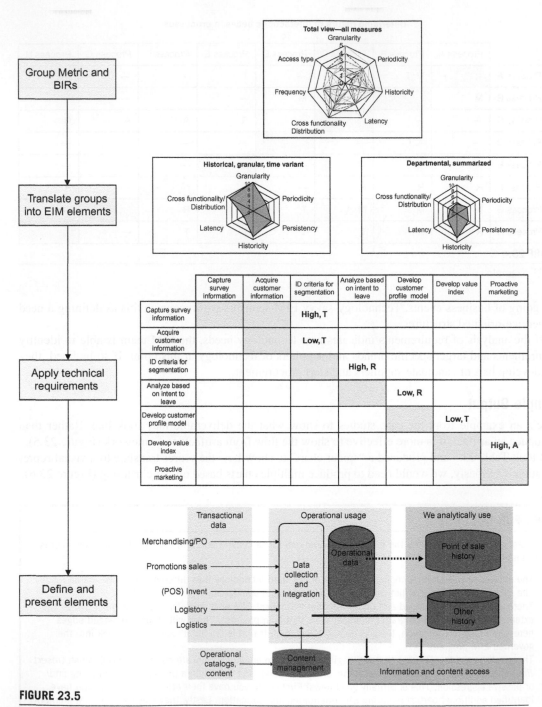

FIGURE 23.5

Farfel frameworks flow

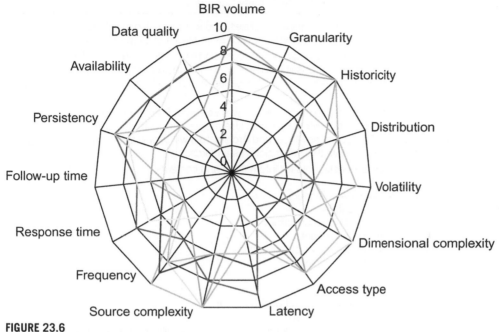

UIC EIM requirements characteristic summary

FIGURE 23.6

Ubetcha sample spider chart

ACTIVITY: BUSINESS DATA AND CONTENT MANAGEMENT ARCHITECTURE

At some point, all of the models and other elements we are defining need to come together to present a complete picture of EIM. This will include the nonarchitectural elements, like policies and procedures. Revisiting the definition of EIM helps us get our head around the scope of this activity:

> *EIM is the program that manages enterprise information assets to support the business and improve value. EIM manages the plans, policies, principles, frameworks, technologies, organizations, people, and processes in an enterprise toward the goal of maximizing the investment in data and content.*

As seen earlier, there are many elements in the EIM Architecture. We have many of the "tangible" architecture elements listed and justified at this point. This activity will blend in the required principles, policies, and structures, so the other elements are properly utilized and managed. The work products with principles and policies should not be underestimated or undervalued. The principles delivered here will anchor all EIM activity from now on.

Activity Summary (Table 23.8)

Table 23.8 Business Data (Content) Architecture Activity Summary	
Objective	Develop a verified list of required principles, policies, and standards, along with further refinement of the elements that will anchor the standards, such as models and support processes.
Purpose	The list of "tangible" elements like projects and technologies is only a partial list of what is to be managed. Effective EIM is not possible, however, without the accompanying policies and standards that will support governance, resolve issues, and set forth guidelines for business and technology staff.
Inputs	The results of the prior Architecture activities, as well as output from the Assessments, Alignment, Vision, and Business Model phases. Use assessment output to point to required principles and policy. The Business Model and Architecture will supply the elements requiring management and the elements that will maintain standards.

Tasks	List internal and external constituents for information and content
	    Identify IAM roles
	    Identify decision makers and readers
	    Identify updaters and clarifiers
	    Identify collaborators and communicators
	    Identify maintainers and engineers
	Define information and content user classifications
	Define preliminary list of EIM principles
	Refine data models
	Define information asset classes
	    Identify content types (structured and unstructured)
	    Identify categories within content types
	Associate information assets with candidate frameworks/applications from the prior activity
	Produce metric to entity mapping, BIR to entity mapping
	Complete data model, merge into logical data model if time permits
	Combine the data about Metrics and BIRs (the enterprise DNA) with the data and process models
	Ensure all dimensions exist in the data model and are defined
	Combine the data about Metrics and BIRs (the enterprise DNA) with the data and process models
	Define framework for enterprise DNA—start to call it meta data within the EIM team
	Develop summarized presentations of architectural elements
	Present and gain consensus on EIM Architecture elements.

Techniques	Do not derive information principles from scratch, there are copious sources that will save you time. There may be the need for some facilitated session within the EIM team to decompose principles into policies, and extract enterprise-specific principles and policies from generic sources.
Tools	There are standard lists for EIM principles and other required policy and procedure artifacts within the DMBOK and other sources (*DAMA Dictionary of Data Management*).
Outputs	An approved list of enterprise information principles and resulting policies. An initial list of standards, based on the models and architecture elements developed to date. Therefore, there will be data standards, code standards, applications, and DQ standards. Mapping of data models and metrics models to ensure completeness. Initial requirements for enterprise information asset "DNA"—meta data. Presentation of overall EIM Architecture.
Outcome	The outputs are completed, reviewed, and approved by EIM leadership.

Business Benefits and Ramifications

The enterprise can now view a comprehensive picture of the EIM Architecture and what will "touch" the business. In addition, the nonabstract programmatic aspects are now known, for example:

- Support technology is identified, so procurement cycles can begin
- Applications to manage data (like master data and codes), so the Road Map can incorporate these support applications and make sure that the business sees value
- Required policies and procedures to form the basis for designing Data Governance and the EIM organization.

Approach Considerations

This activity starts with a task for identifying constituents with potential impact on the development of the EIM program. This is important as more often than not, a company or organization has many different types of interactions with content and data, and as many different styles of human dynamics as there are people using data. The nature of the audience will reflect directly on the types of principles chosen, the standards specified, and the policies to be enforced. The various roles reflect the types of content policies that will be required to govern.

Principles are guidelines, usually stemming from a philosophy or belief. Most likely your principles will be divided between those that are business oriented and those more technology oriented. Your core list of information and content principles usually will start with these:

- Information is an asset.
- Information should be representative.
- Information should be authoritative.
- Information should be accurate.
- Information should be current.
- Information should be shared.
- Information should be secure.
- Information should be intelligible.
- Information should be cataloged.

Policies are consistent, repeatable statements and processes put into place to implement the agreed-upon guiding principles. They have to stem from an originating principle. For example, adopting data quality and data governance will be new processes, and not reactive audits. See Table 23.9 for a sample of a Farfel principle and related policies. Standards are a type of policy, and enforce appearance and usage. Examples are:

- Data standards—Definitions, formats, synonyms, glossary, dictionary
- Data model standards—Used by data modelers to convey meaning, rules, and relationships.

The EIM team identifies and classifies the various roles stakeholders will play in EIM. These roles will be important in determining the details for Data Governance, as well as identifying candidates for eventual training and orientation.

The preliminary principles are drawn from standard sources, but examine the stakeholders and principles and see if there are any possible nonstandard principles. For example, data accuracy is usually governed under a policy. But some organizations are so exposed to regulatory scrutiny that data accuracy may need to be a principle.

Last-minute updates to data models may be required based on review requirements and models to derive the frameworks. These need to be done now since the models from this point forward represent data and process standards.

The various types of content managed by EIM are described. This task not only identifies what structured and unstructured content are under the management of EIM, but also identifies where standards will be applied. For example, if the core subjects of UIC are claims, policies, and policyholders, the data model will represent data standards for these areas.

The EIM team should also map the requirements to data model, as a means to verify completeness. This will also position the team to specify projects in the next phases. Lastly, you will also have the material required for enterprise DNA. The mapping between models and requirements will serve to verify required completeness. You do not want undefined metrics, codes, or dimensions. Any discrete data elements that are defined at this point are significant in that they will be subject to principles, policies, and integration rules. There will always be data in an organization that is not important enough to worry about tracking as an asset. If it maps from a requirement, metric, or model at this point, however, it *is a managed asset that will be tracked.* The other term for DNA that is used is "meta data." The "meta data" is like the inventory tracking slip, or bar code. It is information about our information assets: where to find it, where it came from, who touched it last. I hesitated to use the term "meta data" until now, as the term has been overused and repurposed. And it falls into the "eye-rolling" category for businesspeople. However, you may want to use it if it is already out there in your company. Whatever you call it, most organizations will require a blend of acquired technology, home-grown software, and policy to meet the requirements of enterprise DNA. Remember enterprise DNA represents a business view of the functionality supplied by what is commonly called "meta data."

Sample Output—Farfel (Table 23.9)

Table 23.9 Sample Farfel Principle and Policy
Principle
• There will be a single authoritative source for customer data.
Rationale
• Improving our focus on customers requires easy access to accurate and consistent data that spans functional business units.
• Market pressures to retain customers.
• Information disseminated to the customer will be consistent.
• Common and consistent data is required to present Farfel customers with a single view of Farfel products and services.
• Costs associated with unnecessary movement and maintenance of redundant data will be eliminated.
• A single, clearly identified source of data will reduce access latency.

(Continued)

Table 23.9 (Continued)

Implications

- Business rules are required to manage and control customer data update.
- Capture data once and only once and validate at the point of capture.
- There will be a single source of authoritative data regarding customer satisfaction and loyalty for enterprise users, dealers, vendors, field personnel, and others.
- Establish clear points of data capture and business events resulting in data origination.
- Institute qualitative audits and integrity controls.
- Establish mechanisms and processes for capture and storage in the authoritative system of record.
- Identify application dependencies for use of the data and establish replication/propagation mechanisms to satisfy the dependencies.
- Establish data stewardship for customer data.
- IT and business unit data stewards must communicate and sponsor this effort.
- Customer data management policies must be defined.

Customer Data Policy

Root Principle

- There will be a single authoritative source for customer data.
- Business rule: Each functional area has its own "customer." Accepted terms, by function, are:
  - Ship-to customer
  - Bill-to customer
  - Prospect
  - Legal customer
  - A legal customer possibly has many ship-to customers
  - A legal customer possibly has many bill-to customers
  - A ship-to customer can have many bill-to customers (multiple shipments).
- Customer data is updated and captured in the customer relations area.
- The VP of customer relations is accountable for accuracy.
- All customer data entry personnel bear responsibility for data accuracy.

TIPS FOR SUCCESS

Typical challenges here are:

1. Too much material and a sense of being overwhelmed. There is a lot of data that is now being compiled and tracked. Often, the EIM team will want to place all of this material into a more organized facility, like a tool (if there is not one already). They will need to keep moving, struggle with spreadsheets, and add a Road Map project to get all of the EIM material organized. Stopping now would lose momentum. Just acknowledge that this is a known challenge, but it is all enterprise DNA and there will be a more formal facility at some point in the future.
2. There is a rush to get to an organization chart and a Road Map. Desired and required projects are becoming self-evident, as are the Data Governance and Data Quality functions. It is OK to be aggressive, and even allow the team to move into defining obvious sections of the Road Map, but remember there is still a level of engineering and rationale required so EIM is sustainable. You do not want a folder of projects without any of the supporting management or elements. You will end up back where you started.

It may sound trite, but establishing comprehension and getting approval is important. There will need to be some creative illustration of the EIM Architecture elements, how they are fitted together, and how they add value. The initial Vision depictions are often revisited and refined.

SUMMARY

These activities represent the core architecture tasks. At the end of these activities, the foundation is laid for what data and content is to be managed. The importance of managing the artifacts of EIM becomes apparent. Models, metrics, processes, and assessments all need to be accessible and navigable. Often, a picture of an architecture diagram is the only EIM artifact reviewed. The sequence and interaction of the tasks and artifacts will ensure the EIM recommendations are auditable and the recommendations are based on living documents which will add value in the future vs. sit on a shelf. Use of the living artifacts continues with the next set of Architecture activities.

References

1. DAMA. (2009). *The DAMA Body of Knowledge (DMBOK)* (1st ed.). Bradley Beach, NJ: Technics Publications.
2. DAMA. (2009). *DAMA Dictionary of Data Management* (1st ed.). Bradley Beach, NJ: Technics Publications.
3. Inmon W. H., Imhoff, C., & Sousa, R. (2000). *The Corporate Information Factory*. New York, NY: Wiley.
4. Kimball, R. (2002). *The Data Warehouse Toolkit* (2nd ed.). New York, NY: Wiley.

Architecture Part 2

The computer is a moron.
Peter Drucker

CONTENTS

The next activities reflect the procedural aspects of the EIM architecture. There are significant policies and processes to manage data. Many of them are in place in your organization as we speak, perhaps just poorly organized or ignored. We began to get an idea of these in the Enterprise Data Management activity, where we identified principles and policies. The Data Governance Architecture organizes how policies for data governance will be applied.

Business processes also receive attention. The IVC Architecture focuses on the information life cycle of the enterprise. If we addressed a series of detailed processes in the Detailed Scenarios activity then we have a series of IVC to incorporate into the EIA. This activity is recommended if the architecture element MDM is part of EIM, or we have to essentially reengineer the entire information

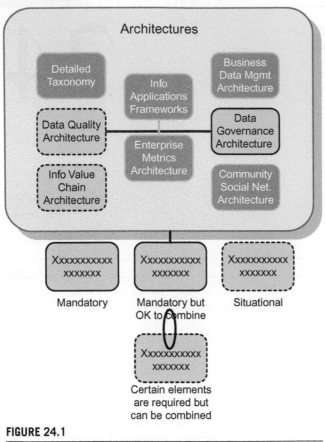

FIGURE 24.1

Architecture 2 activity detail

life cycle. An example is a financial services company that had 16 versions of customer identifiers; none of them in the least bit common. They acquired another corporation and discovered a half dozen more versions of customer ID. Few of the identifiers were consistent; most were of horrible quality even within their own applications, and the effort to clean up data quality, and remap and interface several hundred applications was downright intimidating. Not to mention uneconomical. The entire process of entering, managing, and using customer information had to be redone, as well as lay out the governance process, architecture elements, and Applications Road Map. Even if we did not do the Detailed Scenario activity, we may have to review information life cycles. Simply put, this activity is used to bring all of the IVCs, which are opportunities for process improvement, together and ensure the enterprise information life cycles reflect the new processes.

The Data Quality Architecture activity will use input from the Business Data Management Architecture. Data quality is significant enough that it often merits its own activity. There may be new processes and technology. Remember, data quality is a prime instigator for EIM; it is better to have data quality without EIM and impossible to have EIM without data quality. If for some reason you have a data quality program in place, then you can lightly visit or include this activity with the Business Data and Content Architecture step (Figure 24.1).

ACTIVITY: DATA GOVERNANCE ARCHITECTURE

From a business view, there is significant overlap between all of the seemingly new activity required to manage data and content assets. There are similar-looking models, and there is repeated talk of new policies and controls. And you will hear a continual concern on "how" the EIM program will tie all of the new disciplines together. That is the objective of this activity—specify the data governance component of EIM.

> Data governance is the organization and implementation of policies, procedures, structure, roles, and responsibilities which outline and enforce rules of engagement, decision rights, and accountabilities for the effective management of information assets.
>
> *John Ladley, Danette McGilvray, Anne-Marie Smith, and Gwen Thomas*

A few years ago, several other practitioners and I agreed on a standard definition for data governance.

The Data Governance Architecture being defined in this activity will incorporate the principles behind the enterprise IAM philosophy, the subsequent policies and procedures necessary to govern accordingly, and define the structures that will be required to ensure effective management of the data and content assets. The structures will include controls, compliance interfaces, and organizations and committees manage and enforce EIM policy, and resolve inevitable issues. The policies and procedures are principle based, and include the day-to-day activities to govern IAM. Table 24.1 shows the typical functions required for data governance. Another resource for data governance design and functionality is Gwen Thomas' book.[1]

As we said in Part 1, this is very similar to an audit function, except that the FASB and GAAP standards for organization information are specialized and do not apply (yet) to IAM. In this activity, we need to develop our own "audit standards" for the EIM data governance area. We will create our own GAIP™.[2]

An important consideration when developing a data governance framework is the structure of other oversight bodies in your organization. Is there a compliance area? Is there a legal department? Is there IT and finance auditors? Is there some sort of accepted data governance process already in place? These can be leveraged. In addition, you may uncover legal or compliance-based drivers that will smooth the acceptance of data governance in the organization. As one executive told one of our teams, "A letter from corporate counsel goes a long way toward changing data behavior."

Table 24.1 DG Baseline Functions

	Essential DG Functions
Governance leadership	Ensure effectiveness of leadership.
	Ensure compliance with standards.
	Ensure coordination of accountability.
	Measure DG effectiveness.
	Maintain perspectives of QA vs. QC.
	Maintain/promote awareness of DQ and data management functions.
	Resolve issues.
Plan	Develop privacy policy for data collection and use.
	Identify approach to DG.
	Identify areas requiring governance.
	Identify legal compliance areas.
	Clarify the nature of the changes DG will have.
	Identify key stakeholder groups and how they will be impacted by DG activity.
	Identify champions and sponsor(s).
	Understand the IM culture in which the change will occur.
	Classify resistance points.
Define	Establish data principles, policies, and standards.
	Define data meaning and business rules.
	Establish communications mechanism(s).
	Conduct promotion/information sessions.
	Confirm enterprise architecture principles with information principles.
	Plan education program (usually for middle management and up).
	Plan training (usually for middle management and below).
	Develop application code management requirements for reusability and consistency.
	Define enterprise MDM (policies, design, processes).
	Identify and define enterprise metadata management requirements.
	Identify corporate hierarchies and maintenance processes.
	Establish data stewardship council.
	Define steward and owner dimensions, DG organization.
	Define DQ and control processes.
	Define metadata usage and data lineage requirements.
	Establish data access and data control guidelines and requirements.
	Design and maintain metadata layer.
	Mediate and resolve conflicts pertaining to data.
Manage	Enforce data principles, policies, and standards.
	Refine DG roll-out strategy and metrics.
	Establish governance repository.
	Integrate the change management plan with the overall project plan.
	Secure data.

(Continued)

Table 24.1 (Continued)

	Essential DG Functions
	Implement business processes and systems for data privacy.
	Execute processes to support data privacy policy.
	Execute processes to support data access.
	Execute processes to support data controls.
	Implement regular metrics and measurement of DG implementation.
	Realign policies/practices and procedures to support, not contradict, the EIM area.
	Determine security requirements of enterprise data (includes privacy and access).
	Enforce use of integrated and managed data.
	Mediate and resolve conflicts pertaining to data.
Operate	Maintain policies for data collection and use (includes privacy, control, and data access).
	Enforce enterprise MDM (policies, design, processes).
	Enforce data principles, policies, and standards.
Sustain	Monitor and ensure that data usage adheres to privacy and regulatory requirements.
	Apply retention policy as described.

Activity Summary (Table 24.2)

Table 24.2 DG Activity Summary

Objective	Define the policy and functional details of the DG component of EIM.
Purpose	EIM must be proactive. Reactive EIM is a contradiction in terms. The DG must be defined with the adequate tools, organization, and procedures to allow it to function as a proactive, valuable component of EIM.
Inputs	The principles and policies from the EIM Management activity, assessment results, and Metrics Model are inputs. You will also benefit from the oversight and counsel of your legal or compliance department.
Tasks	Draft DG mission and vision statement
	Determine DG process to support business
	Identify processes to sustain key Business Measures or Metrics Model
	Define/support regulatory drivers
	Optional—work with finance and compliance and perform a pro forma "information risk forecast"
	Identify gaps in current state of data management
	Specify inadequate controls
	Specify privacy and security concerns
	Specify compliance and regulatory concerns
	Define baseline DG functions
	Identify DG detail processes if required
	Develop DG RACI
	Identify changes to SDLC processes

(Continued)

Table 24.2 (Continued)

	Design DG process details, deliverables, and documentation for SDLC integration touch points
	Identify preliminary accountability and ownership model
	Define desired roll-out schedule for DG
	Develop data steward/accountability identification approach
	Develop data stewards identification Draft template/matrix
	Define data steward roles/responsibilities
	"Identify data steward identification subject areas and prioritize them (e.g., customer)"
	Review and obtain approval of data stewards identification approach with EIM leadership
	Identify infrastructure technical components needed
	Identify requirements for enterprise data model standards and procedures
	Identify requirement for reference and code policies/procedures
	Determine desired IMM milestones for enterprise
	Develop DG management organization's vision and mission (optional)
	Identify governance issue resolution process
	Define data stewards' roles and responsibilities
	Review and obtain approval of data stewards
	Complete data stewards' identification
	Complete data stewards identification template for each subject area
	Identify DG oversight body(s)
	Conduct data stewards orientation
	Coordinate with HR and identified data steward(s) to revise data steward(s) performance goals and objectives
	Initiate EIM governance socialization
	Review current IMR guiding principles
	Present EIM DG functional model to business leadership
	Gain acceptance of DG in principle.
Techniques	There is a large amount of material on DG in the public domain. The bibliography lists some of these sources. The primary technique the team will use is the RACI technique to design the organization.
Tools	The DMBOK contains many aspects of DG, as well as several web sites, most particularly the DG Institute.[2] While not aligned with an educational institute the DG Institute is still a rich source of DG information.
Outputs	A functional design for DG. An organization chart and proposed DG organization, including the DG oversight group(s). A recommended series of target IMM levels. The accountabilities and responsibilities for ensuring IAM is occurring.
Outcome	EIM leadership has approved the recommendations for DG, and presented the DG recommendation to executive leadership. This is one of those steps where visibility to the executive level is required. At minimum you need acceptance in principle of the enterprise DG approach.

Business Benefits and Ramifications

If there were one activity that absolutely had to be chosen as a component of EIM or any of its sub-disciplines, it is this one. You could most likely manage to do some level of EIM without new technologies or data models, but you cannot do EIM without a governance mechanism. There is always a behavior change required when doing EIM at any level. Usually data governance is met with resistance where it is most needed. Even if data governance is widely embraced, it is still a new program with the same aspects as any other business program. We focus on data governance before other EIM Organization aspects, because data governance is so important and we need to establish these mechanisms before designing the rest of the EIM Organization.

Approach Considerations

There are many sources for basic data governance functions. One is included in Table 24.1. The main consideration is to determine those that do not apply or modifying them to fit your unique circumstances. Reviewing the Business Measures (or Metrics Model) will also serve as a "thought starter" for this. The EIM team can get a good idea of the various data and content elements that will require the most oversight.

Getting visibility now may be an issue with organization leadership. This stage is a month or so past the kickoff and excitement of EIM, meaning the program is under way and attention could be flagging. The information risk forecast is not so much a new deliverable as it is a restatement of where EIM fits into the organization.

The Assessments will have provided plenty of evidence about where data governance has been lacking. A *very important scenario* for reviewing the gaps in data governance as the Data Governance Architecture comes together is a company with widespread ERP applications, such as SAP or Oracle Financials. As mentioned in Part 1, EIM is not addressed by ERP software. There is no "EIM in a jar."

The RACI exercise for data governance is important, and will expend a large percentage of this activity. Each function must be reviewed across all EIM stakeholders, one at a time to determine:

- Responsibility—Does this party have a role in making the function happen?
- Accountability—Is this party the accountable position—i.e., "the buck stops here?"
- Consulted—Does the party have a contribution to make?
- Informed—Does the party need to be kept informed as to progress or measures of the function?

One function outside of actual governance that requires special attention is the IT applications/software development areas. Most of the time, modern application development areas have an SDLC that specifies the processes to get from idea to implemented system. Data governance will change the software development and other processes that touch data assets. Formal methodologies will most likely require a "data track" be added to the current project tasks and deliverables.

EIM will require modification of many other business processes to reflect the new policies regarding where and how data is captured and handled. If you are revisiting EIM due to weak acceptance or new challenges, this area almost certainly requires attention.

Once the RACI data, gaps, and functions are defined, the basic model of who participates in data governance and how it will happen can be brought together.

Governance is the body that will also impose standards on the various data and process models, and other artifacts that support EIM and EIM technologies. Often new controls and even document tracking software are required to improve governance.

> **OBSERVATION**
>
> The tasks for this activity mention data stewardship since it is a commonly used term. Please do not get hung up on this as a job title. While the idea of an appointed steward certainly is appealing and has merit, it still becomes set aside as a "special" function. We want *everyone* to be a data steward. I think the emphasis on special roles increases the culture change challenges, and prefer that new responsibilities and accountabilities are built into existing jobs and/or standard EIM job descriptions. The real purpose of this activity is to determine who has responsibilities and accountabilities as far as information assets are concerned.

There may need to be several types of committees specified as part of the data governance organization as well. These support oversight and issue resolution. Rob Seiner of TDAN has a simple structure that illustrates this, by defining three layers where data governance processes occur:[3]

1. Operational level—Applications development and business personnel directly interact and confront new policies. Data governance education and documentation provide the guidance here.
2. Tactical level—A middle management group oversees the day-to-day adoption of data governance and resolves issues from the operational level.
3. Strategic level—Normally called a data governance council, this level oversees policy and principles, and resolves issues that cannot be solved by the tactical level. They are the final voice for data governance (Figure 24.2).

As shown in our various examples, the data governance organization is not always a perfect fit to three levels. But this model is a good starting point.

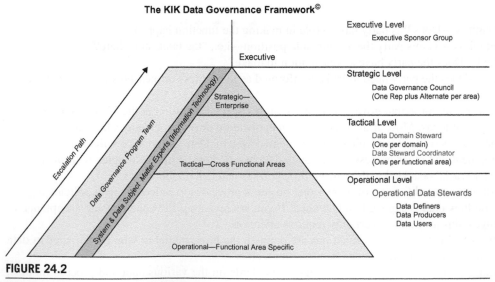

FIGURE 24.2

The KIK data governance framework
Copyright © 2007. Robert S. Selmer & KIK Consulting Services, LLC

Regardless of business style or enterprise type, data governance will be the underlying process to ensure IMM improves. This is one of the important metrics for EIM success. So make sure the EIM team develops a projection of where IMM needs to be over time to support EIM and IAM.

Sample Output

I chose several flavors of output to sample. Farfel needed a risk forecast. There was too much resistance as the EIM team neared the roll-out phases (Figure 24.3).

UIC did a very thorough job of evaluating where the various roles and responsibilities of EIM should be met. They summarized their RACI chart to show where accountability lies for various data governance functions (Table 24.3).

Information risk forecast outline

- Information asset opportunities area
    - Improved accuracy
    - Reduced redundancy
    - Improved integrity
    - Market knowledge
    - Support function data quality
    - Improved performance
    - Handling volume, velocity, and variety
    - Eliminated sources
    - Improved processes
    - Enriched content
    - Improved definitions and data lineage
- IAM risk environment
    - Regulatory environment
    - Civil risks
    - Financial risks
    - Data governance current state
    - IMM current state
    - Data quality impact

Information risk forecast scope

- Business Information Requirements (summarized)
    - Improved accessibility by users
    - Improved integration with business processes
    - Enhancements to existing business processes
    - Elimination of business processes
    - Improved relevance and timeliness
- Organizational scope
    - Internal content areas
    - Market environmental
    - Application portfolio
- Information asset management
    - IAM/data and content management
    - Business model management
    - Data interface considerations
    - Regulatory and legal issues
    - Data governance
    - Data quality
- Technologies
    - Content management and movement
    - Content and data access

FIGURE 24.3

Farfel information risk forecast

Table 24.3 UIC DG Accountability Chart

Responsible for the DG Function	Accurate Data Entry of Designated Operational Application	Accurate Data Entry of Enterprise Reference Data	Business Accountability of DQ of Designated Application or Subject Area	Identifying the Data Owner for a New or Changed Content or Data Item	Approving Requested Updates or Additions to Reference Data	Awareness of Importance of IAM in All Uses of Data and Content
Functional area manager/ director			X		X	X
Stakeholder	X					X
Executive sponsor				X		X
Data owner			X	X	X	X
Data steward	X	X			X	X
Data integrity analyst		X			X	X
Data architect		X			X	X
Application developer		X		X		X
Information producer		X		X		X
Knowledge worker, data entry	X			X		X

TIPS FOR SUCCESS

There are four areas where I would closely manage EIM team efforts during this activity.

1. Understand that you are not identifying just "stewards" in the dictionary sense of the word. First and foremost, you are identifying individuals who will be held accountable for the business role in EIM.
2. The RACI exercise is boring for many architectural thinkers. Do not let it bog you down. Dedicate a day, create some SWAT teams, and get it done. A full RACI chart is shown in the Road Map phase, EIM Organization activity. In addition, HR needs to become involved at this point because of the organizational design being developed within the team. As the EIM team is developing a proposed governance organization, EIM leadership should communicate this to HR. HR will also be involved during the Sustaining phase.
3. Start to educate upper management on data governance *now*. This means going over basic concepts and "day-in-the-life" scenarios, and having frequent short meetings with sponsoring executives. You must try and communicate as high up as possible. A common list of topics during a casual conversation with upper management might contain these topics:
   a. Review of the enterprise's definition of data governance
   b. Review of the data governance management structure
      i. Role of data governance sponsor
      ii. Role of lead data governance body

   c. Day in the life example scenario
      i. Data governance steering group meeting
         1. Review metrics on progress of activities to promote and sustain governance
         2. Resolve issue on format and location of new data element requested by product merchandising
            – Review refinements to principles and policies
         3. Review a new issue recorded when the EIM team rejected a request for marketing to develop a departmental database for campaign management instead of modifying and using the data already in place
         4. Review training material for next phase of governance rollout that will apply to the next release of the data warehouse
      ii. Data governance tactical team
         1. Derive lessons learned from prior month's crisis when a table was implemented without EIM review. Determine if punitive or remedial action is required.
4. Review proposed modifications to job descriptions with HR to increase accountability for data quality for managers in product development governance requiring executive buy-in. If maintaining visibility to executive leadership is difficult, consider tactics like these:
   a. Remind leadership that data governance is not a "project;" this is an important function for any organization in the twenty-first century in terms of compliance and risk management
   b. If you have worked with compliance or legal staff, ask them for representative opinions or examples
   c. Propose the review and action plan of the "information risk forecast" (see Figure 24.3) as the reason for the data governance review meeting.

ACTIVITY: INFORMATION VALUE CHAIN ARCHITECTURE

Data and content are born (created), used, modified, repurposed, and eventually they must die. There are those who want to hold onto every scrap of data a company has ever produced (actuaries and regulators). The lawyers in compliance want to keep data only until it is no longer legally required. Keeping data and content historically is a balancing act between economical usefulness and regulatory requirement and risk. There is always a conflict between having data around "just in case" and bearing the cost and risk of keeping it. It can cost a great deal to store files over time and even more to move information around the enterprise, sending it here, reporting it there, and updating it in a timely fashion.

At times even the identification of content is muddled, and we can have various bits of documents and files flying around, all indexed or keyed in a fashion that makes that occurrence "unique." However, we tend to mess these up over time with multiple versions of keys that may sound the same but point in different directions. In Figure 24.4 we see a simple example of how a series of business processes can use and leverage a common subject, in this case, claims. It seems simple unless each box where claims is used or altered has a different way of identifying a claim. At best, we will have confusion. At worst, we will be unable to count claims or accurately add up our liability to pay claims.

EIM will suggest new processes based on using well-managed data and content, e.g., the claims example. If we end up with a lot of processes and revised touch points, we most likely will be altering entire information life cycles of multiple data subjects. We touched on this earlier, but the most common occurrence of using this activity is when an enterprise decides to initiate one of the elements of EIM called master data. The concept of one golden copy is wonderful, but there usually ends up being a tangle of business processes that need correcting before the golden copy can be considered "golden." The IVC activity must occur when situations get severe enough that we cannot ensure the existing

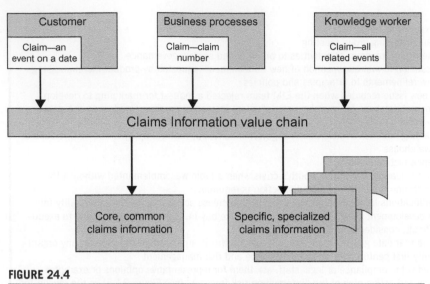

FIGURE 24.4

IVC example

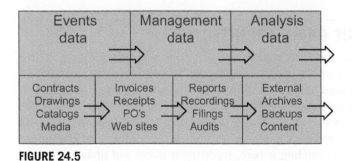

FIGURE 24.5

Consolidated IVCs

processes, or even the new business actions we have identified in the EIM program, will be able to operate the business without an overhaul of the methods and means of maintaining information. For a larger enterprise, you may even have multiple master data areas that can muddy the waters even more.

This activity uses a technique based on process optimization we call IVC analysis. We mentioned the IVC earlier (Chapters 10 and 21), in describing the "river" of content through organizations. Figure 24.5 results when we place all of the separate value chains together. We get a view of how content and data value moves through the organization. The "river" metaphor starts to look real.

To develop a managed information life cycle, special attention is paid to measures, volumes, and latency of information to ensure the combined IVCs are efficient. Developing the information flow details for the business processes that have been defined allows focus to fall on high-value processes.

We need information from prior steps to do this, Metrics/BIR Models and Taxonomy. We also need to consider the current state (from the Assessments) of IMM.

Activity Summary (Table 24.4)

Table 24.4 IVC Activity Summary	
Objective	You want to identify and optimize the processes that will acquire, use, improve the organization of, and then dispose of, data and content.
Purpose	There are many times when an EIM element will suggest or require process changes. Not just rules for usage and disposal, but how and when existing business areas interact with managed data vs. current processes which may be focused more on "local" data.
Inputs	This step requires all the output from prior Architecture and Business Model activities, including Metrics and Requirements Model, data models (for subject area), and business actions and objectives.

Tasks	Collect related information life cycle processes
	Collect current data life cycle rules for use and disposal
	    Conduct life cycle confirmation session
	    Data life cycle rules for use and disposal
	    Collect key processes/value that will use golden copies or candidate MDM areas or other content that will be managed under EIM
	Collect new business actions or processes suggested by Scenarios and Usage activity and Business Model activity
	Develop/Refine information life cycles to reflect new MDM and value chains from business actions and other sources
	Review Metrics and BIRs for cycle changes, volume challenges, DQ, or other characteristics that will affect processes
	Evaluate enhancements and modifications to information life cycle and value chains
	Document information life cycle alternatives
	Document changes to value chains based on life cycle constraints
	Review life cycles/value chains with SMEs, focus on regulatory constraints
	Review life cycles/value chain with EIM leadership and/or appropriate business leadership
	Conduct IVC confirmation session to recommend IVCs to pursue or delay.

Techniques	A thorough understanding of what an IVC means. See Chapter 21. Good process modeling techniques will help.
Tools	Process modeling tools or enterprise architecture tools.
Outputs	A series of process models that reflect optimized process business processes. Recommendations for, or refinement of, EIM elements like MDM or BI. Guideline for data life cycles.
Outcomes	The EIM team has presented and received approval to either explore, hold off, or not address the new processes. The EIM team has received acceptance of the content life cycle guidelines from compliance or other areas. The EIM elements have been modified or verified based on the output from this activity.

Business Benefits and Ramifications

Three decades of IM-type projects have revealed a core business fact: virtually all efforts involved in advancing the use of data or content will require business process changes; it's very rare that process change is not required. An EIM program that is being refreshed, or even is brand new, will probably be affected by this fact, and will need to ensure that business process aspects are considered.

Approach Considerations

The content to be processed is taken directly from the data models, Preliminary Taxonomy, or any other list of content or BIRs.

The actual modeling can be traditional data-flow diagrams, swim lanes, or any other technique that is acceptable. Just agree on *one* method beforehand. You will need to use SMEs or facilitated sessions. If there are a large number of business process opportunities, you may even want to consider doing a batch of preliminary processes, then selecting the ones deemed more important. Process modeling can be time consuming.

Once the basic versions are completed, they need to be optimized. This means interpreting the Metrics and Requirements data and mapping to the various characteristics. For example, a process to develop a cross-sell strategy for strategic customers may be perceived as an event to take place as soon as the large customer is known. But if the metrics and BIRs to support the processes are identified as being OK for a monthly provisioning, some clarification is in order.

Once the models are optimized, develop and conduct management-level presentations to review them, go over the benefits related to the new processes, and obtain recognition of the opportunity and guidance on how to proceed.

Sample Output

Figure 13.7 shows the Farfel value chain example. UIC felt that the Farfel-style optimization was unnecessary. Their issues were not in optimization so much as improving data quality and enabling the touch points. They used a swim lane format (Figure 24.6). High-priority touch points are highlighted.

TIPS FOR SUCCESS

Consuming too much time in process minutia is a risk of this activity. The goal is not to reengineer the company but look for legitimate areas where EIM can oversee usage, focus governance and other sustaining practices, and ensure the business achieves the desired targets.

The EIM team should time-box this effort, or split it into two passes, one high level and another for details on the higher-value processes. Otherwise it bogs down into a business process design effort and the information life cycle aspect is overlooked.

ACTIVITY: DATA QUALITY ARCHITECTURE

If the Assessment phase was anecdotal in treatment of Data Quality (it often is anecdotal to get started), we need to perform more investigation in this step. In large organizations, it is important to assess *how* data is insufficient. Is it just wrong values? Or are there correct values entered for the wrong circumstances? Are there processes that can be changed? Content, such as a form filled out for an order, is rarely able to be navigated at a later date to detect a trend. The objective of this activity is to determine the elements to correct, prevent, and repair data quality issues. During the Assessment phase, we may have done data profiling. Data-quality profiling measures the *effectiveness* of your content. Face it—you know that there is bad data. If not, you would not be reading this book! But you need to understand *in what ways* it is bad.

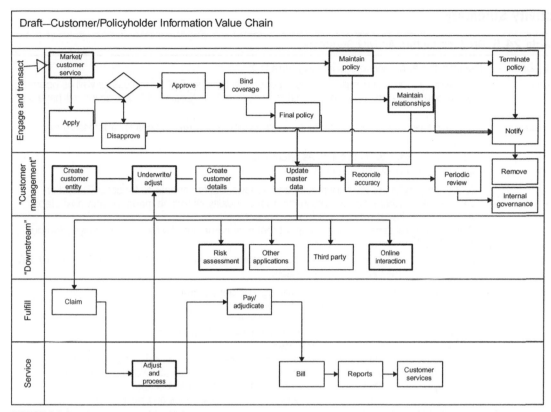

FIGURE 24.6

UIC combined IVC example

OBSERVATION

It is important to understand the following: data used to operate your day-to-day enterprise is rarely sufficient to support in-depth analytics. Businesspeople have a tendency to believe that if they were just handed all the operational data, they could do the sophisticated decision making that has been promised by BI for years. The ugly fact is, in 30 years of doing these types of efforts, I have rarely seen a transaction system with sufficient data quality or all the desired data to fully support downstream analytics.

Once we have an idea of the extent of data quality issues, the types of issues, and most importantly, the cost to the organization, we then derive the approach to correct and improve data quality through IAM. The Data Quality Architecture will produce the framework for technology to support data quality, processes to prevent and detect data quality problems, and the required types of governance (which will be fed to the Data Governance Activity) for oversight and compliance to data quality policies.

Two excellent sources for data quality investigation and remediation are Larry English and Danette McGilvray.[4]

Activity Summary

Table 24.5 DQ Architecture Activity Summary	
Objective	Develop the approach to ensure long-term DQ.
Purpose	DQ will have a profound impact and be a continual topic for EIM to address as well as operate. The organization also needs to see that moving from a discussion of DQ to action will have an impact.
Inputs	List of high-priority issues, root causes, and specific recommendations for addressing root causes.
	Output of DQ assessment results as reference.
	For business impact assessments:
	Business impact assessment results and specific recommendations for action based on results—e.g., where investments in information quality should be made, project next steps (output from *Step 4—Assess Business Impact*)
	Any learning related to business impact that may come out of a root-cause analysis (output from *Step 5—Identify Root Causes*).
Tasks	If no detailed profiling was done in the assessment, it must be done here—see Chapter 19, DQ assessment for the task list and approach.
	If there is a DQ approach in place or profiling was done in the Assessment, start here:
	Develop/document data controls approach
	Review data controls approach with EIM leadership
	Modify data controls approach with requested EIM leadership changes
	Review data control current processes
	Identify/review and document data controls current processes, deliverables, frequencies, etc.
	Identify/review and document data controls' current deliverables audience matrix (who receives what deliverables and what do they do differently because of them)
	Modify data lineage requirements based on industry trends and best practices
	Complete data controls' findings, observations, recommendations for document
	Finalize data controls for document for publishing and review
	Review data controls for document with EIM and IT leadership
	Modify data controls for document with EIM leadership revisions.
	Identify additional DQ tools (as required)
	Develop requirements for DQ tools and develop recommendation
	Review requirements for DQ tools with EIM leadership
	Evaluate and recommend DQ tools
	Acquire and install DQ audit tools
	Conduct required DQ tools training for DQ associates
	"Develop new DQ tools governance (policies, procedures, standards) for how Erie will use tools."
	Draft production DQ methodology (production data sources, audience, metrics, cycle time)
	Review production DQ methodology with EIM leadership and DG bodies.
	Draft source system DQ methodology (production data sources, audience, metrics, SLAs)
	Review source system DQ methodology with EIM leadership and DG bodies.
Techniques	Project planning will come in handy because each remediation approach will imply different project steps and tools. So the ability to quickly assess the extent of each approach to DQ is important.
	There are several "flavors" to remediate and ensure long-term DQ. Each of these implies benefits and trade-offs, so a cost benefit evaluation may be useful.

(Continued)

Table 24.5	(Continued)
Tools	The data profiling tools, if used in the assessment or here, will provide insight regarding the severity of issues and which remediation approaches are better.

Outputs	Specific action plans and recommendations for addressing root causes, preventing DQ issues, and correcting data errors (along with supporting documentation):
	    Improvement activities that do not require a project
	    Requirements for additional projects to support EIM and remediate DQ issues in the future.
	Personnel and organizations impacted by the plans and improvements.
	
	List of communication requirements for affected and impacted areas (for inclusion in the Sustaining phase).

Outcomes	EIM leadership and management have reviewed the DQ Architecture and approved the recommendations. The EIM team is aware of people, process, and technology impacts of the ongoing DQ element of EIM, and a list of communication requirements is available for the Sustaining phase.

Business Benefits and Ramifications

Ongoing data quality efforts will be one of the few areas where EIM may increase costs or alter investments in technology projects. That is why a cost benefit view may be required. There will also be implied procedural changes, organization changes, and new rules to follow.

Approach Considerations

The input from the Data Quality assessment will most likely point out several areas where data issues are caused by lack of controls, nonexistent edits, and no enforcement of existing standards.

Data controls are usually a surprise recommendation to management, as there is an assumption that the data is already under control. "After all, we close the books, right?" But there will be inaccuracies uncovered as data moves from one area to another or is repurposed. Remediation calls for new controls and edits.

Other data quality issues, where data is "wrong," can be the result of human, system, or external errors and handling. The mitigation will depend on the root causes of the data quality issues. Very often simple manual changes can be implemented immediately. The most common example is stopping the ability of a data entry operation to "override" an edit for the purposes of expediting a transaction.

Other root causes that the EIM team will present are missing data, missing documents, and document signatures, and there will be data the organization needs but that does not yet exist.

Whatever the root causes, mitigation approaches fall into four areas:

1. Fix the data issue "in place," i.e., correct it by typing over the proper value.
2. Automate data correction via a program that will correct data in place.
3. Clean up the data using a special tool that matches data to external values or uses algorithms to deduce correctness.
4. Eliminate the root cause at its source via process and system changes.

Once these approaches are identified and mapped to specific problems, then the data quality recommendations for production systems, mitigation projects, and manual process changes can be assembled. The EIM team can also determine if more technology is required. Service levels, impacts on processes, and people considerations are all folded into the data quality portion of the EIM architecture.

Sample Output

Figure 24.7 shows a summarized view of the data quality approaches for Farfel. The details of these types of approaches are best reviewed in the aforementioned books by English and McGilvray.

Farfel Data Quality Architecture

- Scope
  - Prioritized subject areas
  - Cleansing activity
  - Remediation activity
  - Data controls
  - Data quality subject areas
  - Tools
  - Implementation sequence rationale

Farfel Data Quality Architecture

- Prioritized subject areas
  - Cleanse vendor, stores, and sales data
  - Further profiling all subject areas to ascertain extent of required cleansing
- Cleansing activity
  - Assess and audit existing issues
  - Data transformation—When able and economical, correct data quality issues (e.g., Bill of Lading w/ all nines)
- Remediation activity
  - Identify and correct problems with data integrity (data content as well as metadata)
  - Establish "best practices" to correct data integrity problems in/at source through "root cause" analysis
  - Realign and cross walk purchased packages and ERP to enterprise data model

---

Farfel Data Quality Architecture

- Data controls
  - Develop alternative real-time balancing mechanisms to maintain data integrity/quality
  - Develop data management strategies to support SarbOx and Wall Street relationships
- Tools
  - Profiling and cleaning
  - Data movement incorporate data quality technology
    - Improve collection of POS data to safeguard against outages
    - Move all cleansing to occur against "raw" or source data
    - Install a data control layer data reduction due to data quality
- Implementation sequence rationale
  - Coordinate with business application projects
  - Deploy modified SDLC requirements phases ASAP before other phases of SDLC
    - Early detection of business application data implementation issues

---

FIGURE 24.7

Farfel data quality recommendation summary

TIPS FOR SUCCESS

If your enterprise has older applications or is large, you will have considerable opportunities for data and content cleanup. Please document thoroughly any content or data error where a cost or risk can be identified. The Data Quality Architecture will usually propose mitigation that carries with it some level of expense or even capital requirements. The cost benefit approach is the absolute strongest case to make for getting EIM off the ground via a data quality program.

The mitigation approaches will most likely impact people, either by altering a workflow or pointing out that their area is the owner of a problem. While this phase does not directly address these issues, documenting potential cultural challenges and even addressing a few of them informally can go a long way toward reducing resistance when EIM rolls out.

SUMMARY

Procedures are as important to EIM as diagrams and technology. The procedures are rooted in data governance, ensuring data quality, and maintain the information life cycle. The activity in this chapter serves to provide the "architecture" to specify and apply the process elements of EIM.

Data governance needs to define who is responsible for carrying out the processes and functions that oversee EIM. Data quality is the area that establishes how the organization will address data quality issues. Lastly, the overall information life cycles are a function of various business processes and current data movement.

References

1. Gwen, T. The Data Governance Institute web site, http://www.datagovernance.com/.
2. GAIP—Generally Accepted Information Principles for Information Asset Management, IMCue Solutions, 2009.
3. Seiner, R. S. (2007). KIK framework, *TDAN Newsletter*, July 2007.
4. Larry, E. (1999). *Improving Data Warehouse and Business Information Quality: Methods for Reducing Costs and Increasing Profits*. New York: John Wiley & Sons; McGilvray, D. (2008). *Executing Data Quality Projects: Ten Steps to Quality Data and Trusted Information (TM)*. Burlington, MA: Morgan Kaufmann.
5. McGilvray, D. (2008). *Executing Data Quality Projects: Ten Steps to Quality Data and Trusted Information (TM)*. Burlington, MA: Morgan Kaufmann (Chapter 3).

Architecture Part 3

*Knowledge has to be improved, challenged, and increased
constantly, or it vanishes.*
Peter Drucker

CONTENTS

The two activities detailed in this chapter are situational. They would apply if the organization will be incorporating content management, document management, workflow, collaboration, or social networking into the EIM program. If you are interested in doing one of these activities, there will usually be something in the other activity you will need to utilize (Figure 25.1).

Content management is the architectural element that will oversee web sites; EIM tends to be brought in when the content is dynamic, customer centric, and presents the full brand and image to the external world through the Internet. Content management is also relevant for inward facing sites, such as sales management, merchandising, or knowledge sharing.

Workflow and collaboration are relatively new to EIM programs but offer high returns. Managing and measuring how an organization gets work done will be significant in the twenty-first century. It requires an advanced view of EIM, but that should not prevent the EIM from considering these activities.

Making Enterprise Information Management (EIM) Work for Business. DOI: 10.1016/B978-0-12-375695-4.00025-4

319

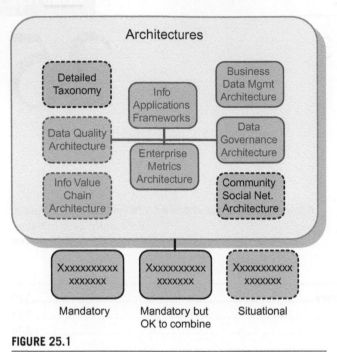

FIGURE 25.1

Architecture 3 activity detail

Newer technology as well as experience with facilities such as portals, blogs, wikis, Twitter™, and Facebook™ has provided a large number of options to explore. Social networking brings the capabilities of Facebook® and Twitter® to EIM. The actual use of a social networking type of tool does not originate in EIM per se. But the governance of the content and leverage of tools and content is leveraged is part of EIM. That's especially true if there is an external view of the organization via Twitter® or Facebook®.

ACTIVITY: COMMUNITY/SOCIAL NETWORK ARCHITECTURE

The objective of this activity is to address IAM aspects of content that are NOT in "rows and columns." This type of content, called "unstructured" content, includes things like e-mail, scanned forms, recorded media, text, and web pages. Most of our techniques, such as the Metrics Model, are adapted to this type of content as well as more structured "rows and columns" type data. There are still value chains for this content. Unlike an IVC that moves data downstream to a report or table in a department, content (and collaborative usage of data) moves out across multiple components of an organization, including external parties. This creates communities. For purposes of this book, communities refer to groups of common interest that may or may not cross business boundaries, but need

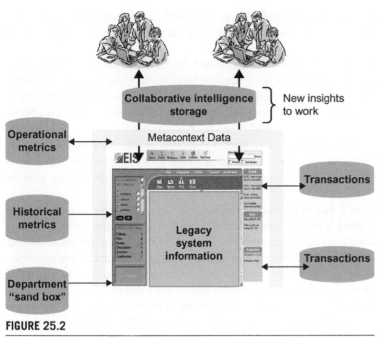

FIGURE 25.2

UIC example of collaborative intelligence

to share information and content. They may need to work collaboratively or may share common content for varied purposes.

Document management, workflow, and content management are three architectural elements that are most likely addressed in this step. Some organizations may also identify the need to "mash up" content from the Internet. A "mashup" is defined as a "web page or application that combines data or functionality from two or more external sources to create a new service."[1] They are used to combine content and data from many sources and present a broader picture of a situation or topic to a business user.

Another overlooked driver for EIM is measuring your own work. Every client we go to will at some point define a set of metrics that measure how they do their own work. Then they will wistfully place it low in priority since any technology capability to provide this has been immature into the early twenty-first century. But "mashups" and other uses of web-related technologies now enable an "inward look" at one's own processes. It behooves the enterprise to use this activity to determine if there are new elements that EIM can deploy to improve internal processes.

Figure 25.2 shows a prototype product done for UBETCHA. There are recently developed EIM elements that can be used to not only manage the assets (forms, documents, etc.) you use to do work, but you can also measure the actual work. If you deploy your data management or operational applications on an intranet, workflow and collaboration can be measured and analyzed by observing the various intranet activities and services. This area is called collaborative business intelligence or collaborative intelligence, and should be considered as a possible architectural element. The UBETCHA sample shows the intersection of event processing, performance metrics, workflow, and a variety of content.

Another driver for this activity is the expansion of Notes and SharePoint databases. Many companies have found that these collaborative facilities have become bloated dumping grounds for documents, and the redundancy costs far exceed any positive leverage from the content. Even if there is not a strong motivation to formally manage this content, remember it is still an asset. You are choosing not to manage it.

There is a lot of risk in memos and e-mails, as any state and federal regulators would be able to tell you. One has to only look at the evening news. I would not pass up the opportunity to at least define required elements and a framework for unstructured content management. Managing content risk is part of IAM.

We gave an example in Part 1 of a HR department creating a skills portal. The management of what people have produced and learned is an offshoot discipline of IAM. During the 1990s, this was called knowledge management. The practical instantiation of this concept occurs when an enterprise may see a need to implement facilities that will enable more cross-functional collaboration and sharing of content. Sharing of lessons learned, access to artifacts from prior projects, and management of complicated procedures where experience often creates modifications are common drivers for pursuing this EIM activity. There are many types of communities considered by twenty-first century organizations. Common drivers and goals that will trigger the need to formally build content management architecture are:

- Any business consideration or objective that includes customer interaction through web sites. For example:

  - Recipes that use your products
  - Downloadable user manuals or instructions
  - Online reporting of a problem or issue.
- Any facility where constituents can interact:

  - Warranty support
  - Work order assistance
  - Procurement and contracts
  - SharePoint or Notes sites

Any facility where employee collaboration and communication occurs on a network or intranet, e.g., instant messaging, large-scale manufacturing or building, and complicated transaction processing

- Text messaging
- Digitally recorded communications such as job site radio, ship-to-shore communication, cockpit voice recording.

While we group all of these into collaborative or social network technology, from an IAM viewpoint, we are deploying, conveying, and distributing *risk*. The benefits of collaborative technologies cannot be realized without managing the content-based risks. And that puts the generation and use of this type of content firmly into the realm of EIM.

Activity Summary (Table 25.1)

Table 25.1 Community Activity Detail/Social Network Architecture Activity Summary

Objective	Develop the approach and architecture for EIM to manage unstructured content such as e-mails, documents, web sites, and collaborative or social networking processes.
Purpose	This is an area that will offer many benefits and will have appeal to marketing and sales areas, but also can contain hidden risks. The purpose of the activity is to find the balancing mechanisms between widespread deployment and responsible management of the created and generated content.
Inputs	There may be business actions or levers that will point to collaborative processes. The Assessments may also have identified new areas, or the EIM team may need to identify candidates for this activity.

Tasks	Identify common collaborative processes from Scenarios and Business Model
	    Define subjects and content areas
	    Identify community functions
	    Identify collaborative processes
	    Refine new business processes alternatives
	    Develop design concept
	    Define required prototype areas
	Propose community design concepts (optional)
	Develop themes and develop storyboard standards
	Identify risks unique to collaborative facilities
	Identify user interface standards
	Identify collaborative technology
	    Define technical criteria
	    Develop vendor shortlist
	    Define strategy for content integration/management
	    Define development standards
	    Define technical architecture
	    Design standards for community look and feel and functionality
	    Identify/finalize content sources
	    Define structured and unstructured data requirements
	    Identify CRUD per content/data source
	    Identify associated IVCs and drivers
	    Identify content and data storage.

Techniques	The EIM team may not possess all the experience to understand this content area. Borrowing from the web maintenance or workflow areas will help.
Tools	There are limited tools to search out and inventory this content, given there is so much of it and it is pervasive. Normally, the results from the tasks are stored in traditional facilities like Word or Excel.
Outputs	The communities relevant to business goals will be defined. Content types requiring management will be listed, with mechanisms for content management defined. Risks unique to collaborative facilities will also be documented.
Outcomes	The EIM leadership has reviewed recommendations, and taken them to executive leadership for consideration. There may be further activity for the EIM program or it may be delayed.

Business Benefits and Ramifications

There is a tendency for organizations to think that typical web content or documents are not exposed to the same issues as financial or event data. Even if this activity results in a tabled recommendation, it is advisable to identify content types, sources, and benefit/risks examples. EIM, if viewed as a type of audit-based function, must exercise due diligence.

Often, the business will require education on the benefits from this activity. The recommendations developed here should keep the following common benefits in front of EIM sponsorship:

- Improved and new processes enabled through ability to view and collaborate with use of well-managed information.
- Identify best practices and increased productivity via monitoring of socially networked and collaborative activities and content.
- Reduced risk due to management and tracking of content.
- Secure extension of the enterprise out to constituents (e.g., customers and suppliers) to enable more effective interaction.

Approach Considerations

Collaborative processes will be visible in the Business Models or Scenarios. If the Assessment and Alignment phases have not addressed unstructured content or collaborative processes, you may want to schedule this activity for the periodic update of the EIM program. Community development and collaborative processes can form a significant subdiscipline of EIM. Two significant resources are books by Wenger and Saint-Onge.

There are many types of community and collaborative functions possible, but they break down into three basic areas:

1. Share content and collaborate within a defined group, such as sharing best practices, making workflow more efficient, or document templates.
2. Share and collaborate across groups, internal and external, such as sharing research findings between government agencies and medical providers.
3. Support service provisioning, such as user manuals through a web site, safety protocols in a plant, or workflow templates.

Within these groupings the EIM team will need to define the role of the community, responsibilities within the community, relevant content, define the content life cycle and associated value chains, and identify potential look and feel. Figure 25.3 shows the high-level definition of Farfel's communities.

Sample Output

TIPS FOR SUCCESS

There is a good angle and even business case for EIM in this area. The aforementioned growth of Notes and SharePoint becomes cumbersome. In the two years before this book was published, we ran across three large organizations investing in optimization and cleanup of these areas.

The collaborative and community aspect of EIM is not evident, but again, there is likely to be a business case lurking. If your organization has any component of your model where there are instructions, protocols, or guidelines that have to be published, then you have an asset requiring the same enterprise considerations as e-mail.

The social networking aspect of EIM may not seem evident to the EIM team. However, if your organization has a Twitter address, or blogs, or wiki, you are playing in this corner of the IAM universe.

ACTIVITY: ENTERPRISE TAXONOMY

If we did a preliminary taxonomy earlier, we will complete it now. Otherwise, if there is any hint of content management or workflow in the EIM scope, this step is mandatory. To review, a taxonomy is a hierarchical classification structure. A good example is the animal kingdom, represented by the picture in Figure 25.4. (We originally had a cartoon here, but were not given permission. Use your imagination as to what should be there.)

All organizations of any sort have several taxonomies. They need to be defined if there is any kind of navigation of unstructured data or content management. In a subsequent activity in this phase we will apply the taxonomy to the EIA, the Data Governance architecture, and the Community/Social Network architecture.

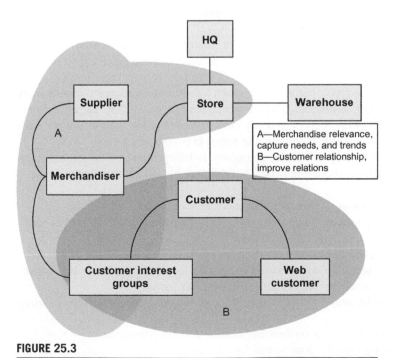

FIGURE 25.3

Farfel notional communities

FIGURE 25.4

Canis latrans is the taxonomic classification for coyote

Here are the earlier and the final guidelines for EIM-relevant taxonomy:

- Categories are mutually exclusive and precise to avoid overlap and ambiguity; for example, it is not possible to be both "animal" and "mineral."
- The taxonomic structure can have multiple independent categories or facets, and a content resource can (probably will) be assigned to more than one facet, e.g., to subject and to industry and to resource type.
- Taxonomies are independent of the type of content (although a content or resource-type hierarchy is advantageous). For example, key words can apply to any resource type, so that "data warehousing" topics may be presentations, white papers, and any other resource types. You would not have "data warehouse white papers" in a single hierarchy, but rather in two separate ones.
- While business context provides perspective, the taxonomy is independent of the organization structure (although an organization structure may be a valid hierarchy). See the earlier example— the same principle applies here.
- The taxonomy should not offer so many categories that users are overloaded with options.
- While there will be multiple levels in each hierarchy, aim for three to four levels so that users do not become frustrated navigating to where they want to be.
- Design the taxonomy with the goal that the top level of the taxonomy should be the most stable. This practice helps avoid user frustration which would occur with restructuring; however, changes should be expected at the lower levels to reflect changes in business focus.
- The lowest level of the taxonomy may be highly specific, e.g., a set of product offerings using proper names.
- The taxonomy must meet the needs of both content authors and content consumers.
- Rigorous user and content testing must be done to validate the taxonomy.
- Provide a category(s) along with search results so that users are properly oriented.

Activity Summary (Table 25.2)

Table 25.2 Taxonomy Activity Summary

Objective	Identify the appropriate taxonomy(s) that will enable navigation of enterprise content.
Purpose	If content management and collaboration are in the EIM scope, then the navigation and arrangement of content will be important. A formal exercise is required to ensure that content is arranged in such a way that navigation and maintenance is efficient.
Inputs	The results of the Collaboration activity, and a standard depiction of taxonomy relevant to your organization.
Tasks	List all possible content requiring a taxonomy Tie to business needs and/actions and scenarios Determine relevance of those that support business needs Develop straw person categories for each candidate Schedule and prepare review sessions with SMEs Develop validation process for final taxonomy Train/orient reviewing staff on taxonomy usage Test and verify taxonomy in facilitated meetings or via web development tools Align taxonomies with other elements of EIM architecture (what subjects, entities, etc.) Associate business direction with taxonomies Publish final list of taxonomies with business drivers.
Techniques	Take several types of data and content and fit them to a standard taxonomy. You will find out if the standard taxonomy is too abstract, and you can modify the taxonomy layers with terminology more appropriate to the organization.
Tools	There is a significant standard taxonomy guide called the Dublin Core. It is officially an open standard for enterprise DNA (metadata). We use it as the baseline for all work in this area. www.dublincore.org
Outputs	A set of taxonomies for navigation and administration of crucial enterprise DNA.
Outcome	The EIM team leaders have accepted the proposed taxonomies.

Business Benefits and Ramifications

It will be very difficult to allow for navigation to data and content and provide full searching and lineage without taxonomy. It has been done but the result is always content that cannot be found or excessive duplication of business content. This activity will lower long-term costs for content management.

Approach Considerations

Once the various candidates for content are lined up, matching the content to a known taxonomy provides the best means of presentation. Then the business needs and scenarios can be supplied to the content by viewing it through the lens of the taxonomy.

After taxonomy has been identified (it will take a few iterations), its usage must be matched to business drivers to ensure that creating a taxonomical structure will add value to the enterprise.

Sample Output

Table 25.3 is an example of a taxonomy from Farfel.

Table 25.3   Farfel Taxonomy Sample

Current Catalog Field	Element	Proposed Farfel Element	Definition
Title (Resource: title)	Title	Title	A name given to the content resource. Typically, a title will be a name by which the content is formally known
Index	Subject	Subject	The topic of the content of the resource. A subject may include key words, key phrases, or classification codes
Categories	Subject	Category	Similar to above

TIP FOR SUCCESS

There is a real potential to get carried away with this exercise. The EIM team may find themselves fascinated by this new kind of enterprise DNA. The team will need to time-box the activity and make sure the taxonomies are kept at a level of detail sufficient to navigate and support enterprise DNA.

SUMMARY

The EIA encompasses web site content, e-mails, manuals, and any other media that may be used by your organization. The EIM team needs to consider addressing these areas as part of the EIM program. You may just acknowledge their existence, and perhaps assess potential risk. The same goes for any type of content where collaboration or sharing of the content appears in business processes, or is being poorly managed, like SharePoint databases. Lastly, manual, safety protocols, and other documents where process or safety is involved need to be considered.

There are business benefits with managing these assets as part of EIM. Like any other element, there may not be an immediate need to roll out applications or consolidate content, but the asset management aspect of EIM means the financial aspects should be documented. Leadership needs to make a conscious decision on when and how to address this content.

Reference

1. Definition of "mashup" as found on Wikipedia. http://en.wikipedia.org/wiki/Mashup_(web_application_hybrid).

Road Map

26

Plans are only good intentions unless they immediately degenerate into hard work.
Peter Drucker

CONTENTS

The most common question I hear from EIM teams is "where do we start?" This is how the personnel responsible for implementing EIM or one of its components will view the program. "We all get the concepts, now how do we make it happen?" The devil is always in the details, and the EIM Road Map phase is where the details of "making it happen" are addressed. The Road Map phase is used at the beginning of an EIM program, of course, but is also revisited at regular intervals as long as the program is operating (Figures 26.1–26.3).

Making Enterprise Information Management (EIM) Work for Business. DOI: 10.1016/B978-0-12-375695-4.00026-6

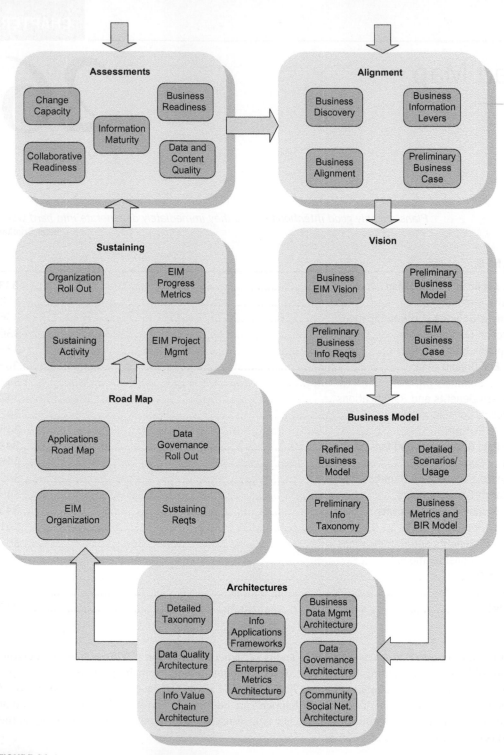

FIGURE 26.1

Road Map locator

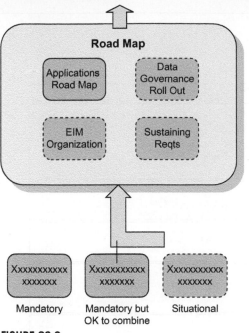

Road Map

- Applications Road Map
- Data Governance Roll Out
- EIM Organization
- Sustaining Reqts

Xxxxxxxxxxx xxxxxx — Mandatory

Xxxxxxxxxxx xxxxxx — Mandatory but OK to combine

Xxxxxxxxxxx xxxxxx — Situational

FIGURE 26.2

Road Map activity summary

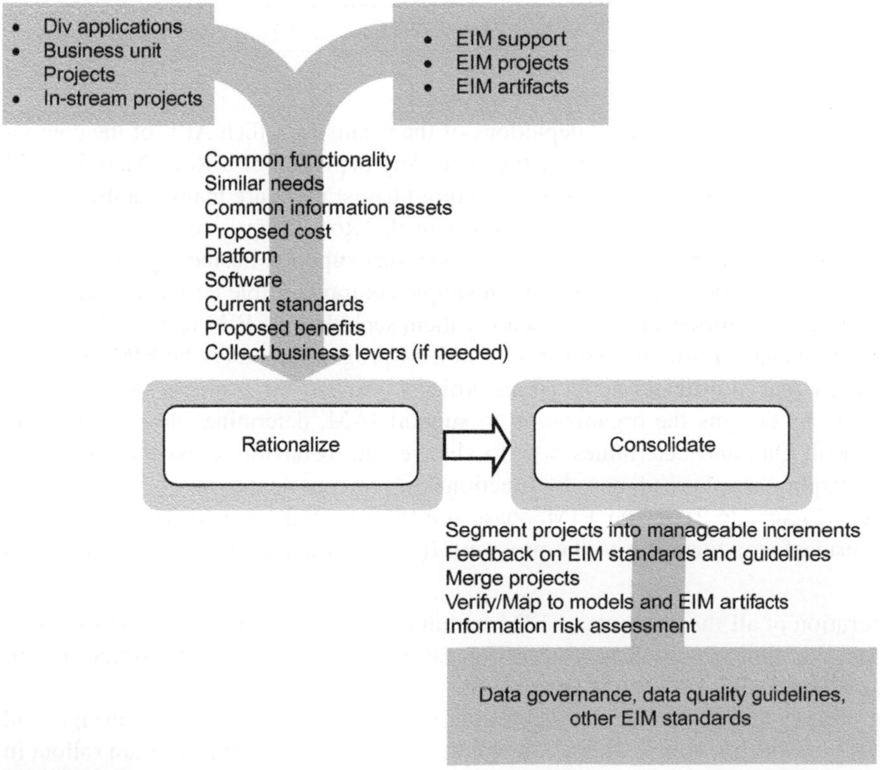

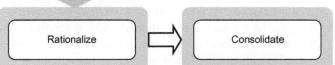

- Div applications
- Business unit Projects
- In-stream projects

- EIM support
- EIM projects
- EIM artifacts

Common functionality
Similar needs
Common information assets
Proposed cost
Platform
Software
Current standards
Proposed benefits
Collect business levers (if needed)

Rationalize → Consolidate

Segment projects into manageable increments
Feedback on EIM standards and guidelines
Merge projects
Verify/Map to models and EIM artifacts
Information risk assessment

Data governance, data quality guidelines, other EIM standards

FIGURE 26.3

Rationalization of Road Map

EIM Function	Planned EIM Projects	2007 1Q	2Q	3Q	4Q	2008 1Q	2Q	3Q	4Q	2009 1Q	2Q	3Q	4Q
Project Management and Business Applications	Project Preparation and Planning												
	Ongoing Project Management												
	Identify revised information projects												
	Identify coordination processes												
	Project A												
	Project B												
	Project C												
	Project D												
Change Management	EIM Change Planning Development												
	EIM Promotion												
	EIM Education												
	EIM Training												
Data Quality	Complete DQ Profiling												
	DQ support - Project B												
	DQ remediation - Project C												
	DQ support - Project D												
Data Governance	Enterprise Governance Roll Out												
	EIM Principles												
	EIM Policies - by project												
	EIM Procedures - by project												
	EIM Standards - by project												
Technology	Meta Data Management												
	Data Modeling Tool												
	Data Access Management												
	ETL / EAI Tool leverage												
	Repository / Catalog roll out												
	ETL / DQ coordination												
Data Management	Master Data for Item												
	BI / Reporting Framework												
	Enterprise Data Model												

FIGURE 26.4

EIM Road Map – Functional Orientation

The EIM Road Maps are multidimensional depictions of the means by which ALL of the components and elements of the EIM program will come together. Any depiction of a Road Map for EIM is much more than a Gantt chart with a few bars representing phases; there are many parallel events happening within the program. The most important aspect of the Road Map is to choreograph the interoperation and sequencing of EIM's many pieces in a way that supports business goals. Second, the Road Map needs to be boiled down and presented in simple comprehensible terms. The activities revolve around confirming the components and presenting them such that the EIM team and business leadership can comprehend and confirm the assembly of an EIM program. Finally, the EIM team will provide a roll-out strategy that coordinates applications projects (projects the business sees as "progress") and support projects, designs the organization to support IAM, determines how to integrate the Data Governance Roll Out, and determines how to change data behavior across the enterprise. Figures 26.4 and 26.5 display sample road maps by functional or project orientation.

The four activities (Figure 26.2) in the EIM phase are all required, even if you are repeating the phase in the form of an adjustment to the program. It is important to call out the Road Map objectives:

1. Show the interoperation of all the elements of EIM within the context of meeting business goals. Since these change over time, you will need to revisit all of the elements and determine if their roll-out plans are still relevant.
2. Present a roll-out strategy that is incremental and business aligned. Business strategic change, and during a periodic review of EIM this is where you would define a change in the program rollout in response to business changes.

EIM Project	Required EIM Functions	2008				2009			
		1Q	2Q	3Q	4Q	1Q	2Q	3Q	4Q
Customer Relations	Customer MDM								
	Customer data governance								
	Customer data quality								
	Customer management change pgm								
	Customer reporting								
Sales Performance	Sales data DQ								
	Sales Data Warehouse								
	Sale Data Governance								
	Sales department education								
	Sale department training								

FIGURE 26.5

EIM Road Map – Project Orientation

3. Identify the behavioral and organizational requirements to move the enterprise toward IAM. The team will define or modify what needs to be done to maintain the momentum of EIM.
4. Establish data governance—Data governance is one of the key success factors of EIM. Getting it started effectively and revisiting the function is mandatory.

There are four activities within this phase:

1. Applications Road Map—the identification and sequencing of the business, technology, and support projects required to manage and deliver data and content. Once EIM is established or has been attempted, the Road Map requires revisiting. When revisited, this activity focuses on resequencing or adjusting projects. Revisiting this activity can happen at any time, but at minimum I recommend this activity be revisited annually, given changes in the business environment or organization priorities.
2. EIM Organization—the design, or modification of the actual EIM area as well as other organization charts within the enterprise. This would include other IT organizations, content management, and web development, or business areas, such as order entry/client service areas that are touched by managed data and content.
3. Data Governance Roll Out—the initial events to institutionalize data governance occur here. Data governance functions will need to roll out before other aspects of EIM.
4. Sustaining Requirements—the cultural barriers and potential change management issues, enterprise constraints, measures of EIM value, and EIM Project Management are evaluated, and a plan to sustain the momentum and contribution of EIM is developed.

All four activities are mandatory during initial EIM design. Synthesizing, estimating, and researching various options can occupy a good portion of the EIM program's design. Therefore, if the EIM program creation has a time constraint, the activities here should be addressed as time-boxed, "level of effort" tasks.

ACTIVITY: APPLICATIONS ROAD MAP

The objective of this activity is to produce a deliverable that describes and sequences the incremental projects deployed by EIM. Projects, in the context of the EIM Road Map, are the discrete endeavors that deliver information assets, or create the facilities to support and manage information assets. They will have their own project plans and assigned teams. In other words, the EIM Road Map projects are where the work actually happens. They may take the form of a discrete effort to deliver content to a business user to support a business opportunity. The projects may also appear as add-ons to in prog-ress or near-term efforts where the new EIM policies would have an effect on the project approach.

Obviously, there is some complexity to deploying a large program. There will be two types of efforts that comprise the sequence of events:

1. Business projects—efforts that deliver businesses data, content, and capability are visible to busi-ness areas. These include:
   a. BI and reporting
   b. Master data
   c. Workflow/collaborative applications
   d. Risk management, fraud detection, safety programs
   e. Content integration, such as incorporating acquired data into internal applications
   f. Selling data, or revising products, services, and processes to incorporate improved information assets.
2. Support projects—applications that are required to manage data assets:
   a. Enterprise DNA or metadata facilities
   b. Activities to roll out and apply data governance
   c. Projects to position the enterprise to use managed data, such as new technology to manage documents or deploy analytics
   d. Projects for cleaning up areas of poor data quality.

The team will also need to determine what kind of road maps to present. For example, sometimes it is fine to show only the visible projects. Other times management will want to see all of the support projects that may be required, such as data quality cleanup, or installation of software. The EIM team may also create actual project plans for initial efforts so execution can begin immediately.

Consistent with one of the principles of our process, we still connect the projects being defined with business needs. Projects that are purely in support of EIM: technology procurement, data clean-up, and so forth, are also specified, but need to be coordinated with the business projects. There is one powerful reason for going to this level of coordination—within six months of embarking on EIM as a program, business needs will most likely change. The Road Map must be able to adapt to this change, meaning the interconnections of all of the various elements must be understood enough to allow for impact analysis and resequencing of effort.

Activity Summary (Table 26.1)

Table 26.1 Application Road Map Activity Summary	
Objective	Describe and sequence the various incremental projects to be deployed by EIM.
Purpose	There must be formal planning to coordinate business and nonbusiness efforts so EIM constantly contributes to the business. In addition, this activity will establish a plan that is easily adapted to changing business conditions.
Inputs	All output from all phases is likely to serve as possible input to this activity.

(Continued)

Table 26.1 (Continued)

Tasks	Identify business projects
	Create new/revise affinity groupings (mapping entities to measures, measures to business actions)
	Consider metrics and BIR groups
	Consider groups of data model to metrics or BIRs
	Consider groups of actions, levers, IVC, or scenarios to content
	Interpret groups and identify business projects
	Develop brief project descriptions
	Group/align business projects with business initiatives
	Associate relevant metrics, BIRs, IVC, etc., with respective projects
	Map project objectives to business drivers and information requirements
	Review preliminary project objectives and deliverables review
	Determine project constraints
	Prioritize and confirm projects
	Develop initial project roll-out strategy
	Review and confirm initial projects
	Develop iterative project abstracts
	Derive project plans
	Estimate project costs
	Identify support projects
	Review previous documentation for support projects
	Review MART and IVC data
	Review DQ architecture
	Review EIM architecture elements
	Review EIM data and content management elements
	Review DQ architecture
	Review technology recommendations
	List and describe support projects
	Develop general roll-out strategy
	Cross reference with business projects
	Determine critical path constraints
	Rationalize projects with IT portfolio and resources
	Design project presentation and Road Map presentation format
	Present to EIM leadership for approval
	Present to EIM sponsorship for approval.
Techniques	Affinity analysis is revisited and performed on the Road Map artifacts.
	Analysis of intersections and commonality within a matrix, similar to affinity analysis, will also aid in alignment and defining clusters of effort.
	Project planning techniques.
Tools	Any tools used to maintain the EIM artifacts will be used, as well as tools for affinity analysis and project planning.
	Visio or other drawing tools may be called in to develop the Road Map presentation.
Outputs	List and description of business projects.
	List and description of support projects.
	Detail project plans for the first few projects to roll out.
	Road Map visual depiction.
Outcome	EIM and business leadership conduct reviews, and understand and approve the project sequencing.

Business Benefits and Ramifications

This will be the first time many business constituents will perceive "real" work, as projects are tangible. This step also shows the need to be incremental. Given the nature of businesses and other organizations, the EIM program will need to be able to deal with changes in priorities. The ramifications to IT can be significant as EIM will influence existing applications plans. Business areas will also have a higher awareness of information (via IAM) and will be more proactive in terms of the structure and approach to projects, as opposed to submitting a request and backing away until it is completed.

Approach Considerations

The goal in defining business and support projects is to create manageable increments. Projects lasting for a year or two are totally unacceptable. The EIM program, while starting as a new function with a new philosophy (IAM), will implement projects iteratively; there can be no possibility of a big bang. "Big bang" projects fail at much higher rates, and the pressure of investing and delivering a large, visible effort invariably will overwhelm the ability of the organization to focus on the EIM projects.

Some sort of analytical exercise must occur to segment the EIM future state into "chunks" that can be delivered. Most of the time, this starts with an analytical exercise driven on finding the intersection between business need and the type of content required to meet that need. Then various initiatives to support that intersection are derived. For example, a company may need an application to manage workflow and complicated contract documents. This would be determined by the intersection of business needs and IAM capability.

In the Architecture phase we have matched metrics to data models to ensure completeness of our EIM architecture. We can also tie the business actions to these data models, and develop a presentation of where the metrics and BIRs tie this all together. All of these are techniques are used to discover what and how we can use IAM to increase value through incremental efforts.

Once the analysis is done, there will be adequate patterns and groups to allow the EIM team to segregate and bundle the artifacts of information into a project. The project needs two kinds of abstracts—a management summary that is 50 words or less, and a more detailed version for the eventual EIM team members who will be accountable for delivery. The detailed version will also present the related business objectives, metrics or BIRs, applicable data areas, and possible business processes, or scenarios that will be supported. In other words, we assemble a complete picture of the application delivered by the project.

The support projects are defined in a similar fashion, except we look at the artifacts containing technical, governance, and IAM-related elements. For example, the MART analysis may tell us we need transforming or messaging capabilities. If these do not exist, then we need a support project for procurement. If we have defined a need for reference data elements, we will need a project to design and roll out reference data. Often the Data Quality architecture will define a need for immediate remediation of data or content areas so they can be used in a business application. The data quality remediation efforts are also support projects. All of the support elements need to be affirmed and sequenced with correlating business projects. An example would be a business project to supply clean customer data to various touch points. In addition to the application to create and maintain the customer content, there will be subprojects to implement customer data quality cleanup and data governance policies for ongoing management of customer data assets.

The support projects are subordinate to the business needs. Far too often there is a project where the CIO acquires document management because someone says "we need it." As I've said repeatedly throughout this book, the subsequent misalignment to a specific problem results in an unfocused, failed project.

Once segments or work areas are identified, some sort of guiding body (e.g., an EIM steering committee) must meet and determine priorities: What business opportunities or needs are addressed first? This is never as easy as it sounds and often IT staff needs to leave the room while business leaders sort out their differences!

After prioritization, the remaining tasks are almost self-explanatory. The segments of work need to be reduced to discrete projects with associated project plans. This is a rationalization process that needs to map the proposed work to other efforts. For larger organizations this can be a significant task. Distributed IT areas will *always* have projects in the pipeline that overlap or challenge the IAM inspired efforts. The rationalization process serves to rein in competing efforts, bring in-stream projects under governance, and yet still allow work to proceed. Often a project started before or outside of EIM will be too far into development to be governed sensibly. But understanding which new projects will not be aligned with EIM will assist in ongoing planning for maintenance and enhancements. Figure 26.3 demonstrates the rationalization process.

Historically, EIM-type efforts fall into a trap of "infrastructure only" projects. IT tells the business area that they need to get the infrastructure up and running, then something will be delivered. This is a sign of nonalignment and a big mistake. My IT brethren may cry "foul" at this paragraph, but it is *not* good business to spend capital and/or increase expenses and not "move the needle." While EIM may require significant changes, it is not that complicated. But often IT departments act like they need to build the bridge before building the cars that will cross it. Humankind went to the moon *incrementally*. We need planning, good engineering, and solid principles that we stick to, i.e., the principles that:

- EIM must add to the business value all the time.
- EIM will roll out iteratively.

A project (in the context of effective EIM) is an effort that can be done in six to nine months. *Do not accept* one year plus efforts, OR "infrastructure only" projects as steps in the Road Map journey. Infrastructure is a supporting effort. Huge projects that "boil the ocean" are not successful. Think of the EIM program as a software company, and you are planning your major releases for your product, but must always add value to your clients, even with the first version or release.

The EIM team now starts to create project plans that can be executed. In our practice we call this "Monday morning preparation." What will you do next Monday when the consultants are gone? Detailed project plans can be developed for the most obvious candidates to be the initial projects, and the priorities will be based on business input. The list of discrete projects requires review one more time to determine if any project sequences turn out to be dependent on other projects. Some adjustment is always made at this point.

The sequencing and rollout is a function of the business efforts they need to support, the availability of current technology, procurement cycles, and critical path indications. Critical path indication means, as sometimes happens, that a business project cannot happen unless a certain support project is in place. When this happens the two must be bundled (remember no stand-alone technology projects) and redefined into manageable increments. For example, a business project will require a new source of content, or "scrubbed" data that will not be available until a support project is completed. These projects should be matched up as one "iteration."

Lastly, there might be business constraints on sequences. Priorities may call for Project A, but Project B is easier to do. This is a pure business decision, with the EIM team providing the ramifications of choosing a particular sequence of events to support the decisions.

Table 26.2 shows a sample template for this type of analysis. This matrix shows metric aligned to the data model, first as a simple cross-reference then after a clustering analysis. Other matrices such as business action or levers to metrics can also be developed.

You do not have to use these techniques. There are tools to assist as noted before. But you do need to ensure that any project you define can associate all of the relevant artifacts. Then you must document all of the relationships. Think of it this way—if you were the project manager for the first EIM project, would you not want all of the relevant material in one place?

For review and understanding the EIM team will need to develop more symbolic presentations than Gantt charts. In fact, save the Gantt chart for project managers.

The business will react more effectively to a different presentation.

Sample Output

See Chapter 13 for the Farfel and UIC Road Map pictures.

Table 26.2 shows a subset (the real matrix is much larger) of Farfel first aligning its data model to the metrics. The second pass results in a common requirement clustered about each other. These become the Road Map projects.

TIPS FOR SUCCESS

There will be a temptation to develop project details for more than a few projects. Don't get too far ahead.

Organizations often produce an annual list of projects or initiatives as part of their planning processes. When EIM is starting, this list of enterprise efforts needs to be mapped to the EIM project lists. There will often be overlaps. There will also be gaps in what EIM projects have planned to oversee, and what needs to be overseen.

Creativity must be applied to keep the units of effort within six to nine month time frames. For example, the metric groupings done for the architecture will have already pointed out batches of work. Align these against business needs and you will see that groups of metrics can be delivered to satisfy multiple business objectives. Since cost estimating will be necessary, the EIM team will want to dive deep into project details to get a firmer idea of cost. However, this level of detail is time consuming, and most likely, after the first two or three projects, the schedule or sequence will change. If management requires a longer horizon, just take the estimates of the first six to nine months' efforts and multiply over whatever (I recommend using three to five years) number of years. Since the EIM efforts are incremental you will have similar team sizes, and projects will tend to cluster around a certain investment level. Make sure you add whatever capital spending might be required for tools and technologies. Access to business leadership as well as clear, simple communication of the projects is critical. The first time this is all presented, there will be a temptation to show everything. For executive review, show only the 50-word abstracts. Make sure you have a one-page view of the entire Road Map deliverable. It must be abstracted to fit onto one page that can be seen from the back of the room. This is not a time to demonstrate how intricate the plans are.

ACTIVITY: EIM ORGANIZATION

The Road Map phase requires that we design the new EIM Organization. We actually started this when we designed the data governance (DG) aspect of EIM. However, there are more organizational considerations than data governance. Like data governance, there are a basic list of functions and roles to modify[1]

Table 26.2 Project Definition and Alignment Matrix

Farfel Metric to Entity—Sample Cluster—Initial Pass

Entity Metrics	Purchase Invoice	Purchase Order	Purchase Receipt	PO Sale	Product	Product Category	Product Catalog	Product Price	Product Sale	Retail Store	Online Order Pickup	Sales Type	Deduction	Payment	Period Type	Depreciation Schedule	Fixed Asset Maintenance	Fixed Asset Type	Maintenance Type	Demographic	Geographic	Party Geographic	Supplier	Merchandiser	Customer	Planogram Shelf/Location	Planogram Shelf Type
Contribution margin		x		x	D	D		x	x	x	x	D															
Warehouse inventory		x	x		x																				x	x	x
Gross sales		x		x	D	D		x	x	x	x	D													x		
Gross margin		x		x	x	D		x	x	x	x	D															
Inventory value	x	x	x	x	D	D	x	x	x	x	x	D															
On-time delivery		x				x	x																				
Reject rate		x			x	D	x																	x			
Return rate		x			D	D	x			x	x	D												x			
Stockouts		x			x	x	x																	x			
Store in-stock position		x	x		D	x	x																		x		
Back order rate																											
Weeks of supply		x			D	x				x	x	D												D			
Cost—labor		x				x								x	x									x			
Gross profit—$				x	x	D		x	x	x	x	D															
Gross profit—forecast accuracy				x	x	D		x	x	x	x	D															
Gross profit—plan accuracy				x	x	D		x	x	x	x	D															
Net profit—net variance				x	x	D		x	x	x	x	D															
Receipts—actual	x				D	D		x	x	x	x	D															
Receipts—to plan	x				D	D		x	x	x	x	D															
Cost—packing supplies	x																										
Costs—transportation	x																						x				
PO—approval tracking	D				x			x		x	x	D											x				
PO—lead time variance	x				D			x		x	x	D											x				
PO—price reduction	x				D			x		x	x	D											x				
PO—purchase price variance	x				D			x		x	x	D											x				
Sales			x	x	D	D		x	x	x	x	D		x	x								x		x		
Sales—plan accuracy				x	x	D		x	x	x	x	D			x										x		
Promotion—campaign effective				x	D	D		x	x	x	x	D												x	x		

(Continued)

Table 26.2 (Continued)

Farfel Metric to Entity—Sample Cluster—Initial Pass

Entity Metrics	Purchase Invoice	Purchase Order	Purchase Receipt	PO Sale	Product	Product Category	Product Catalog	Product Price	Product Sale	Retail Store	Online Order Pickup	Sales Type	Deduction	Payment	Period Type	Depreciation Schedule	Fixed Asset Maintenance	Fixed Asset	Fixed Asset Type	Maintenance Type	Demographic	Geographic	Party Geographic	Supplier	Merchandiser	Customer	Planogram Shelf/Location	Planogram Shelf Type
	Activity				**Product**					**Store**			**Finance**			**Fixed Asset**					**Party**						**P-gram**	
PO—approval tracking	X	X	D	X	X	X	D						X	X														
PO—lead time variance	X	X	D	D	X	X	X						X	X														
PO—price reduction	X	X	D	D	X	X	X	X					X	X														
PO—purchase price variance	X	X	D	D	X	X	X	X					X	X														
Receipts—actual	X	X	D	D	D	X	X											X										
Receipts—to plan	X	X	D	D	D	X	X											X										
Return rate	X	X	D	D	D	X	X						X	X				X										
Inventory value	X	X	D	X	D	X	X						X	X				X	X									
Weeks of supply	X	X	D	D	X		X						D	D				X	X	X								
Costs—transportation							X						X	X						X								
Cost—labor							X						X	X	X													
Warehouse inventory				X	D		X						X	X				X		X								
Store in-stock position				D	X		X						X	X	X			X		X								
On-time delivery				D	D		X						X	X	X	X		X										
Reject rate				X	D		X						X	X				X										
Stockouts				X	X		X											X										
Contribution margin	X	X	D	D	D	X	X	X	X																			
Gross sales margin	X	X	D	D	D	X	X	X	X	X																		
Gross margin	X	X	D	D	D	X	X	X	X	X																		
Gross profit—$	X	X	D	X	D	X	X	X	X	X	X																	
Gross profit—forecast accuracy	X	X	D	X	X	X	X	X	X		X																	
Gross profit—plan accuracy	X	X	D	X	D	X	X	X	X		X																	
Sales—plan accuracy	X	X	D	D	X	X	X	X	X																			
Promotion—campaign effective	X	X	D	D	X	X		X	X			X														X	X	
Sales	X	X	D	D	X	X		X	X			X															X	X
Back order rate	X	X	D	X	X	X																				X		
Net profit—net variance				X	X			X										X										
Cost—packing supplies							X																					

and adapt. Then an organization chart is developed, and a roll-out strategy determined. The rollout of the full organization occurs in the Sustaining phase.

The organizational design effort is a formal exercise, and uses traditional organizational design approaches. For example, a list of EIM functions is developed and usually put through a RACI analysis, which we also did for data governance.

R = Responsibility for the functions execution
A = Accountability for the functions execution
C = Consulted on the functions execution
 I = Informed about the functions execution

Organization charts are developed for the EIM area, as are lists of members for various committees. Lastly, job descriptions for any new roles and accountabilities are produced here. This includes other IT areas, or even business operational areas where managing data as an asset means a change in workflow or revised processes. The result is a firm view of where everyone will sit, what they are doing, and who is accountable.

Activity Summary (Table 26.3)

Table 26.3 EIM Organization Activity Summary	
Objective	Define the required organization charts, roles, responsibilities, and job descriptions necessary for managing information assets.
Purpose	The EIM program and IAM require new roles, or revision and improvement to previous roles in terms of handling information. The IT department will most likely get a revised organization chart.
Inputs	The DG architecture output, as well as standard templates for EIM functions.
Tasks	Identify EIM functions from templates 　　Verify EIM functions vs. DG 　　Isolate functions with regulatory relevance Incorporate gaps in current state of data management 　　Examine current data standards and policies Refine baseline EIM Organization function Identify EIM-affected business areas and new business functions Develop EIM RACI charts Develop draft organization charts Draft EIM Organization charter and mission statements Refine changes to SDLC processes for EIM Identify new job categories and positions Prepare new job descriptions Define desired roll-out schedule for EIM and business organizations Initiate EIM Organization socialization process 　　Review current EIM guiding principles 　　Present EIM functional model and organization charts to business leadership 　　Gain acceptance of EIM Organization in principle Submit job descriptions to HR for development.
Techniques	RACI analysis.

(Continued)

Table 26.3 (Continued)	
Tools	Excel for RACI.
	HR tools for job descriptions, Visio or PowerPoint for organization charts.
Outputs	Proposed EIM Organization chart.
	Revisions to business area organizations.
	Revised and new job descriptions.
Outcome	Approved representation of the EIM Organization.

Business Benefits and Ramifications

IAM will impart changes on business areas, and the sooner these are vetted, the better for the change process. A formal exercise permits the EIM team to show a business aligned plan vs. one based on moving bodies for accountability and visibility.

In addition, very often the EIM Organization is a recast of a standards body. This may or may not be appropriate for a given situation. There is high value in the RACI exercise in just having EIM team members talk through roles and responsibilities.

Approach Considerations

The templates to use are similar, but not the same as data governance functions. They are presented in Table 26.4. Where there is a perceived overlap or conflict, or just confusion with data governance, the EIM team should verify which functions belong where.

The Assessment phase may have indicated shortcomings in IM, and the functional list should be adjusted or checked to ensure any shortcomings in the current environment are addressed. Typical shortcomings that the new EIM Organization needs to address are:

- Conflicts in current data standards
- Absurd redundancy of content or data, via Note, SharePoint, or Access databases
- Failure to maintain standards
- Failure to follow standards
- Poor maintenance of current data dictionaries
- EIM functions spread across multiple IT areas.

Once a functional list has been determined, then build the RACI chart. Like data governance, this exercise can be time consuming, but it produces the best results. Unlike data governance organizations, the final EIM Organization chart will require some refining.

The final organization chart for EIM will be as much of a function of an organization's size and maturity as it will the RACI exercise. Factors that affect the final appearance of the EIM Organization(s) are:

- Span—how wide will the EIM Organization need to guide and govern? Megacorporations with many divisions or large government bodies will most likely require divisional levels of governance and standards as well as centralized versions. This is often called a federated organization model. Smaller organizations or organizations with a single service will be able to identify a more centralized EIM Organization.
- Authority—often, like span, organizations will need to restrict the authority of EIM in a division or segment, due to regulatory reasons, different levels of IMM, or market conditions.

Table 26.4 EIM Functions

Essential EIM Organization Functions, Excluding DG

Plan	Align data architecture with enterprise business strategy
	Establish priorities for information projects
	Understand goal for enterprise applications
	Understand Business Model
	Develop privacy policy for data collection and use
	Align information architecture with enterprise business strategy (revise scenarios, levers)
	Identify the key stakeholder groups and how they will be affected by EIM activity
	Understand the IM culture in which the change will occur
	Classify resistance points
	Assess Information Maturity
	Fund data systems
	Establish data technology infrastructure
Define	Confirm Enterprise architecture principles with information principles
	Develop concepts for designing interfaces to ensure gradual expansion of data management
	Define process for metrics maintenance
	Develop processes for enterprise information content and delivery (data models)
	Develop and establish enterprise metadata management environment
	Define IM usage metrics to determine effectiveness of IM
	Develop application code management requirements for reusability and consistency
	Define enterprise MDM (policies, design, processes)
	Identify and define enterprise metadata management requirements
	Identify corporate data hierarchies and maintenance processes
	Create and maintain the IM implementation plan (Road Map)
	Determine IM technology requirements and establish direction for IM technologies
	Establish DQ program
	Define IM roles and responsibilities
	Define IM organization structure
	Acquire and maintain appropriate skill sets to support IM
	Design and maintain metadata layer
	Define business requirements for information systems
Manage	Manage data architecture, models, and definitions
	Manage portfolio of information systems
	Refine Information architecture roll-out strategy and metrics
	Periodically establish priorities for IS projects; consider value drivers, and roles of process and applications areas
	Validate IM alignment with business and strategic planning
	Track industry trends in EIM and leverage if possible
	Develop other processes for EIM
	Manage data technical infrastructure
Operate	Ensure DQ and integration (by subject)

(Continued)

Table 26.4 (Continued)

	Essential EIM Organization Functions, Excluding DG
	Secure data
	Implement business processes and systems for data privacy
	Facilitate BI/ODS/DW design and maintenance (includes providing architecture and implementation)
	Execute processes to support data privacy policy
	Execute processes to support data access
	Execute processes to support data controls
	Realign policies/practices and procedures to clearly support the new IM and DG vision, not contradict it
	Develop customer/vendor/other subject area hierarchies
	Assess DQ (IS systems planning, implementation, and cycle production)
	Ensure business requirements are reflected in information requirements
	Create and maintain logical enterprise data model, including mappings and aliases
	Define data and business rules
	Create and maintain project logical data models, including mappings and aliases
	Maintain modifications to annual plans, budgets strategy, and portfolios
	Maintain scenarios within process models
	Maintain metrics—performance, process, financial
	Facilitate physical data models (technical database design)
	Evaluate and select IM technology
	Install and maintain IM technology
	Monitor and tune IM technology
	Identify and resolve IM technology problems
	Maintain and manage business rules repository
	Maintain accurate inventory of enterprise data management resources (interface to CMDB exists)
	Manage portfolio of information systems (applications and infrastructure components)
	Maintain metadata layer
	Develop and support application systems
	Design and maintain metadata layer
Sustain	Enable appropriate access to data
	Use data for analysis and data mining
	Provide guidance, education, assistance in support of data access
	Provide guidance, education, assistance in support of data usage
	Oversee data integration and transformation
	Maintain IM portal content
	Maintain alignment of IM across all organizations
	Ensure design of interfaces to new applications to ensure gradual expansion of data management
	Create and maintain logical enterprise data model for third-party applications including mappings and aliases
	Promote collaborative communities and communities of interest

- Visibility—political and cultural factors may require EIM to be more visible or less. While the EIM Organization chart may not necessarily look different, the visibility of the area may be adjusted by where EIM reports.
- Credibility—if the IT department has a horrible reputation you may want to consider keeping EIM out of IT altogether, and have it report through compliance or finance. Most likely there will be significant changes required within IT anyway in this situation, so a separation of duties is definitely in order.
- Geography—multinational organizations will require consideration of divergent or conflicting governments, languages, and time differences. Often technology will also be affected by location, so communications and sharing enterprise DNA may be affected.
- Brands/divisions/Business Model—companies with multiple brands and divisions may require separate EIM areas if the brands are very divergent. For example, a company that makes airplanes and also offers software services will require different or loosely affiliated EIM Organizations.
- IT style—if IT is outsourced, or is decentralized, the EIM Organization will need to adapt functions and roles to accommodate governing external entities, or entities with widely divergent technologies.
- Corporate culture—obviously, culture affects organizations, and EIM is not immune. For example, older and slower reacting organizations will require a different structure to administer IAM than a younger, more nimble company.

The EIM functions will also suggest changes to internal IT processes, in the same fashion that data governance did. But the EIM Organization effort will identify new positions or require revision of existing positions. These can be drafted at this time. Include any data governance positions before submission to HR.

Sample Output

The first sample is UIC's RACI. This is a small subset of the entire RACI (Table 26.5).

TIPS FOR SUCCESS

Data governance functions and EIM functions are often mixed into the same organization areas. This is not advisable. Some separation of duties is necessary for data governance to be able to objectively oversee EIM/IAM. Would you put the auditors of a bank inside the bank's finance department? Many organizations actually place data governance in the same area as compliance, and remove the function out of IT or the EIM area altogether. I also am not crazy about EIM reporting to a CIO. In a perfect world EIM is a separate function, like Finance or Marketing. Political reality rarely allows this to happen.

Consider using or consulting HR before submitting job descriptions. This business area can be nervous when someone else delves into human capital matters. In addition work with the CIO as there are usually other organizational agendas on the table. A common mistake to designing the EIM Organization is to ignore all of the influencing factors listed here. The most common EIM organization is arranged by functions. But in large organizations functional IAM gets lost in the difference between divisions, etc. In addition, other common mistakes are:

- Too much authority/work on one person—resource constraints end up having one person managing data and content as well as data movement, for example.
- Communication lines unsuitable for organizations—politics get in the way, and the EIM ends up in IT, with dotted lines everywhere.
- Totally hung up on stewardship and ownership terms—the EIM group is designed around stewards and owners, and lines of accountability and authority become blurred. Larger organizations will have *many* layers of "stewards." A best practice for EIM Organizations, in our practice, has become fewer individual "stewards" and more groups of stewards, with a cross-functional view of content usage.

Table 26.5 UIC RACI

	IM/DG Functions	CIO	Corporate Leadership	BI and Reporting	DG	Architecture and Standards	EIM Leadership	DG Business Leaders	Executive Officer/EVP	DG Committee	Applications	Culture Change
				EIM Department								
Plan	Align information architecture with enterprise business strategy (revise scenarios, levers)	I	I	C	C	R	A	I	C	—	—	I
	Establish priorities for information projects	—	I	C	C	C	A	—	C	C	—	—
	Understand goal for enterprise applications	A	C	C	—	C	A	—	C	C	—	A
	Understand Business Model (e.g., business channel)	A	A	—	—	R	R	—	C	C	—	—
	Develop privacy policy	R	A	—	—	—	C	C	—	—	—	—
	Identify approach to DG	R	C	—	R	C	R	A	I	C	—	C
	Identify areas requiring governance	—	—	—	R	C	C	A	I	R	—	—
	Identify legal compliance areas	—	A	—	—	—	—	—	A	—	—	—
	Identify the key stakeholder groups and how they will be impacted	—	—	—	R	C	R	R	—	—	—	A
	Identify champions and sponsor(s) of IM and DG	—	C	—	C	—	R	A	C	C	—	—
	Develop change management approach for IM and DG	—	—	—	—	—	R	C	C	C	—	A/R
	Fundamental data systems: IM and DG as well as IM projects like DW/BI	A	C	C	—	C	C	—	C	—	—	—
	Establish data technology infrastructure	A	—	C	—	—	C	—	—	—	—	—
Define	Establish data principles, policies, and standards	—	—	C	R	R	R	A	A	—	—	—
	Define data meaning and business rules	—	—	—	R	C	R	—	A	R	—	—
	Develop application code management requirements	—	—	R	—	R	A	—	—	C	—	—

Activity	R1	R2	R3	R4	R5	R6	R7	R8	R9	R10	R11	R12	R13
Define enterprise MDM (policies, design, processes)	I	I	C	—	I	C	A	—	C	—	R	—	I
Identify and define enterprise metadata management requirements	—	—	R	R	—	—	A	—	—	—	C	C	I
Identify corporate hierarchies and maintenance processes	R	A	—	—	—	—	—	—	—	—	R	—	I
Create and maintain the IM implementation plan (Road Map)	—	—	R	R	R	R	A	—	C	C	C	—	I
Determine IM technology requirements and establish direction for IM technologies	A	—	C	C	—	—	C	—	—	—	—	—	R
Refine DG council	C	A	—	R	R	—	C	R	C	—	—	C	R
Refine DQ program	—	—	—	R	R	—	R	A	—	—	R	—	—
Define IM roles and responsibilities	A	—	C	C	C	C	R	—	—	—	—	—	—
Consider change management road map	—	—	R	R	R	—	A	—	—	C	C	—	R
Prepare detailed change management plan, emphasis on rewards, resistance, and measurement	—	—	C	C	—	—	C	C	—	—	—	—	R/A
Define IM organization structure	A	C	R	R	R	R	R	—	—	—	—	—	C
Determine required education, training, skill sets required to ensure success	—	—	C	C	C	—	A	—	—	C	C	C	R
Acquire and maintain appropriate skill sets to support IM	—	—	R	R	R	—	A	C	—	—	—	—	C
Establish data access and data control guidelines and requirements	C	C	R	R	R	—	A	—	C	—	C	—	—
Design and maintain metadata layer	—	—	C	C	R	—	A	—	—	—	—	—	C
Mediate and resolve conflicts pertaining to data	R	R	R	R	R	A	R	A	R	R	R	R	C
Define business requirements for information systems	C	R	A	C	R	—	A	—	C	—	C	—	I

ACTIVITY: DATA GOVERNANCE ROLL OUT

Data Governance was designed in the Architecture step. Rolling out Data Governance is not an exercise in hanging up the "open for business" sign. Initial activity needs to be identified and planned.

The objective here is to develop and initiate an incremental strategy to deploy the policies and procedures for data governance, as well as indicate how the organization will mature along a defined timeline. Remember in the assessments we reviewed IMM. Assuming the enterprise wants to progress to a more mature level, the steps to get to that level are laid out.

There will be training and education needs. There will also need to be coordination with internal standards and methods teams. If you are touching unstructured content then the web developers, workflow, and document management areas will need to be engaged in the rollout.

The deliverable needs to be a business accepted view of the steps, time frames when data governance functions are activated and target maturity levels are established, and then the initial opening up of the data governance functions. A Gantt chart will work nicely here.

Activity Summary (Table 26.6)

Table 26.6	DG Roll Out Activity Summary
Objective	Define the roll-out strategy for DG. Initiate roll out of DG.
Purpose	EIM will ask the organization to achieve specified levels of IMM. The DG roll-out strategy ensures adequate governance at appropriate times.
Inputs	The output from the DG architecture activity.

Tasks	Refine DG organization (if EIM Organization indicated changes)
	     Refine governance bodies and committees
	     Refine DG charter
	     Confirm stewardship and ownership model if necessary
	     Define DG roll-out schedule
	     Refine roll out from DG architecture
	     Design DG metrics and reporting requirements
	     Confirm DG metrics reporting requirements
	     Identify DG metrics stakeholders and playmakers
	     Develop DG metrics requirements
	     Define metrics and collection mechanisms
	     Review DG metrics requirements with EIM leadership and obtain approval
	 Identify projects and stakeholders subject to standards and governance
	 Publish and review IAM principles
	 Review/revise modifications to SDLC and other IT processes
	 Roll out initial DG functions
	     Present initial road shows
	     Publish guidelines and principles
	     Implement DG policies/procedures orientation and training
	     Publish and implement SDLC integration documentation
	     Conduct DG audit processes training
	     Initiate DG audit processes
	     Define additional roll-out activity for the sustaining phase.

(Continued)

Table 26.6 (Continued)	
Techniques	Project planning techniques.
Tools	Project management tools.
Outputs	Revised DG roll-out plan.
	Initial roll-out activity, e.g., training, orientation.
Outcome	The DG area is in an active status, and initial DG activities are occurring.

Business Benefits and Ramifications

Data Governance must start before the other sustaining activities because the new projects being identified must be scrutinized for adherence to standards. In addition, a number of projects are certainly in process at your enterprise, and may or may not present EIM opportunity. These need to be reviewed and determined to move under the auspices of EIM or remain outside.

Approach Considerations

The first effort in this activity is to review the Data Governance Roll Out that was outlined during the Architecture phase. The EIM Organization and other activities may have created factors to alter the original roll-out perspective. Additionally, the data governance charter or even the stewardship models could require altering.

The revised Data Governance Roll Out schedule is based on moving out those functions that are absolutely required for the first EIM projects. The projects to be governed, the metrics to measure governance effectiveness, and the initial training and orientation for the governed projects are obviously required as projects are specified and rolled out. The data governance functions must be ready as soon as the Road Map phase is complete, as projects will be under way.

Lastly, the Sustaining phase will continue Data Governance Roll Out, and we need to revise the plan for implementing the other data governance functions.

TIPS FOR SUCCESS

This is actually a pretty benign activity, as those that are involved want to be there, and those that have other things to do, well, they are doing those other things.

One area to observe is reaction to the new auditing processes, and making sure the EIM team is not carried away with authority, and conversely, the projects being observed are not concealing activity from data governance.

ACTIVITY: SUSTAINING REQUIREMENTS

The last activity in the Road Map phase is the lead-in event to actual deployment of the EIM program. The objective is to identify the processes by which the EIM team, with support, will continue to operate the EIM program. Operating EIM means managing the program, measuring results, and overcoming any of the traditional obstacles that cause EIM programs to falter or fail. We call this sustaining vs. change management, because change management is only a part of this activity. We also need to look into metrics for monitoring EIM value, verify our organization is available in terms of resources, and a few other nuts and bolts items.

Earlier we stated that there will be obstacles, because IAM is "different" to most organizations. Different means change. EIM program success will depend heavily on managing the required changes in process, organization, and behavior. We need to understand who and how the resistance will occur. For example, we have surveyed IT departments where over half of the department was resistant to EIM and governance. (This is not an unusual finding.)

The EIM team will need to build or identify a formal team that will monitor change management. These often can come from the HR department.

Change management is a well-known discipline within the realm of managing human capital and organizational development. It is also a discipline that has been sorely lacking in the IT field, and especially around data governance and IAM. The nature and extent of change management needs to be determined in this activity. Most change management processes or methodologies feature three basic steps:

1. Plan—assess change needs and develop the approach to manage changes.
2. Do—launch the education, communication, training, and other tactics to transition people from one "state" of work to another.
3. Sustain—as the change event(s) continues, there must be mechanisms and structure put into place to ensure there is no reversion back to old ways.[2]

The Sustaining Requirements activity in the Road Map phase of our EIM program is the plan portion of change management.

OBSERVATION

After 20 plus years of EIM and related efforts, the root cause of all problems and failures of these types of projects is change management—*period*. If you do not manage the movement from the current state of behavior around information to the desired future state, regardless of whether it's full EIM or a subdiscipline like MDM, you will fail. This is *not* squishy HR stuff. Frankly, another reason we use the word *sustain* is to de-emphasize the change management process, and emphasize the result.

Our EIM process has given us some idea of the extent of change, via the Change Capacity and IMM assessments. We will need to develop a more specific analysis of the change impact on stakeholders. Based on the analysis of all affected parties, a set of responses to the findings are developed. Typical responses are:

- EIM communication plan
- EIM education plans (by type of stakeholder and degree of impact)
- Sponsorship expectations and guidelines
- Individual coaching plans for executives to enable them to effectively support the necessary changes

- Resistance management plan and tactics
- New process/policy alignment plan
- Organizational realignment plan: structure, roles.

All of the various areas in EIM and many business areas will touch or be touched by these responses. The final outcome of this activity is a detailed step-by-step plan for the various training, orientation, documentation, and reorganizing activities.

The team will develop the final outline of the Road Map itself, and describe the level of detail required for the particular enterprise.

Activity Summary (Table 26.7)

Table 26.7 Sustaining Requirements Activity Summary	
Objective	Identify the plan to address and manage changes required for IAM to be institutionalized, and adjust the Road Map to reflect consideration of change management requirements and organizational structure requirements.
Purpose	IAM equals change. EIM is also a program that requires measurement and monitoring. The requirements to sustain EIM need to be reviewed and approved.
Inputs	The Road Map activity outputs, as well as the assessments.

Tasks	Define EIM change management approach
	    Review assessments
	        Execute Change Capacity assessment if not done
	        Incorporate IMM results into Change Capacity
	        Prepare statement of change readiness
	    Identify change management resources
	    Identify mechanisms to *prepare* the organization for change
	        Define levels of communication required for specific stakeholders
	        Define mechanisms for delivering communication
	        Define level of involvement, specific actions, and tools for sponsor
	    Design tools to prepare the organization for change
	        Perform stakeholder analysis
	        Identify EIM stakeholders
	        Develop stakeholder analysis form
	        Complete stakeholder analysis
	        Review with EIM leadership
	    Determine levels of commitment for key stakeholders
	        Review results of stakeholder analysis
	        Determine action plan to address improving levels of stakeholder commitment
	    Develop sponsorship plan
	        Identify required sponsorship and right level of sponsor
	        Develop sponsor action plan
	    Develop communications plan
	        Identify audiences
	        Create messages and branding
	        Identify vehicles for communications
	        Define timing, frequencies, and delivery means
	        Review and approve communications plan

(Continued)

Table 26.7 (Continued)	
	Develop training plan
	Identify audiences
	Identify levels of training; orient, educate, train
	Identify vehicles for training
	Define timing, frequencies, and delivery means
	Review and approve training plan
	Develop resistance management plan
	Perform SWOT analysis
	Identify specific resistance profiles
	Develop responses to resistance
	Review and approve resistance management plan
	Develop change management plan
	Define specific activity schedule for change
	Design metrics and assessments to ensure change effectiveness
	Define WIIFM and consequences
	Define resources to fulfill change delivery
	Develop revised process/policy alignment plan: reviewing/updating existing policies and processes related to data governance and EIM
	Develop EIM management requirements
	Define EIM Organization Roll Out
	Revise EIM charter/mission if necessary
	Develop/refine EIM Organization positions
	Consolidate revised EIM tactics into change management plan
	Define/revise EIM rollout based on sustaining input.
Techniques	Assessment via survey if required.
	Change management assistance from HR.
Tools	Change management tool kit.
Outputs	Change management plan.
	EIM metrics.
	EIM organizations roll-out plan.
	DG rollout.
Outcome	EIM leadership approval of Sustaining Requirements.
	EIM sponsorship commitment known and confirmed.
	EIM effective change management strategy.

Business Benefits and Ramifications

The root cause of failure of EIM or similar programs is failure to proactively manage change, and develop a set of tasks to make sure the program will be sustained. Without some level of change management, data governance, data quality, or any other aspect of IAM requiring different behavior will not occur.

Approach Considerations

There are many change management processes available to review and use. All contain basically the same components and are effective when used appropriately. Key to EIM is to adopt an approach that:

- Focuses on resistance and motivation
- Offers some initial metrics for consideration
- Offers sample tools for additional assessments or facilitation of stakeholders and sponsors.

Stakeholder analysis should be done with selected EIM leadership and representatives from HR. The results must be confidential. After all, you will be identifying people in terms of their historical resistance to change, or delving into a review of human dynamics.

Communications and training plans are not lists of required PowerPoint slides. The various stakeholders will require different communication and training. Remember—education, training, and orientation are three concepts of the same thing. All serve the same goal—to keep the organization from reverting back.

Determining resistance is crucial. Like the stakeholder analysis, you will be sitting around a table talking about people. There are several means to classify resistance, and from an EIM view, you will need to classify between those that will be directly resistant, those that will be passive, and those who won't care. Direct resistance is, of course, the most controversial. However, there will need to be incentives for all types of resistance. An important principle of change management is to be able to answer the "What's in it for me?" (WIIFM) for all stakeholders.

At this point in the EIM program effort, resistance will be obvious. Most of the EIM team will be passionate as to the importance and value of EIM. Most business sponsors will be supportive, but will want to see some results in the near future. Most likely, a few business sponsors will begin to "hedge" a little if the political capital required begins to appear to be too much to invest, as this step will reveal the investment they need to make. Whatever happens, be calm. The initial reaction among the team will be "How can anyone possibly see this isn't a great program? Make them change or fire them!" However, resistance and hesitancy is *normal*. Take heart in the fact you have anticipated this and are planning the means to manage it.

Those of us doing EIM over many years are used to resistance in all forms, and there are few surprises. However, as someone who may be new, please bear this in mind: There will be resistance in the form of direct confrontation. Remember, many of the behaviors that IAM deems risky (e.g., departmental databases with mission critical data) are viewed as necessary and acceptable. Resistance management needs to start out as defining incentives, education on the benefits, and rationale for doing EIM, and in general a positive approach. Keep negative responses as a tool, but deploy them last.

There is a strong business case for formal efforts around change management. Table 26.8 shows some simple guidelines for justifying sustaining activities that are change management. IF you are having a problem getting change management incorporated into EIM, use this as an anchor to your pitch for change management.

The metrics for sustaining EIM take a variety of forms. Some were identified in Part 1. The categories for your measurement requirements are:

- Measure the success of EIM
- Metrics to indicate improvement in organization value due to EIM

Table 26.8 Justification for a Sustaining Program (Change Management)

Sustaining Program Benefit Profile

	Focus Areas for Sustaining Program		
Focus areas for business	Increase IMM	Maintain program Business Alignment	Roll-out organization
Mitigate risks	Reducing risk in data is an enterprise issue	Reduction of shadow IT "quick fix" mentality	Identify and mitigate resistance
Manage cost	Uncover opportunities for collaboration and efficient cooperation	Assess business benefits against framework costs and shadow IT elimination	Manage human capital costs from attrition/resistance
Achieve goals and opportunities	Increase analytical power of data	Identify gaps in business plans and information capabilities	DG manages costly project issues, ensures DQ accuracy in execution

- Metrics that report on the progress of utilization of data governance and EIM policies
- Metric measuring the effectiveness of change management programs and the rate of change adoption.

Sample Output

Table 26.9 is a sample stakeholder analysis guide.

TIPS FOR SUCCESS

EIM teams will benefit greatly from the help of an organizational development specialist to help define change management requirements and develop the plan.

Picking the right sponsor for EIM is absolutely essential. Per the Prosci Best Practices survey (2005, 2007, 2009), the right sponsor has been the most important success factor for any change effort. The right sponsor has the influence and political power to make things happen. Get that person on your side early on.

SUMMARY

For most organizations the Road Map deliverable is the first major output of an EIM program. It may be a road map that focuses on a subdiscipline, such as data warehouse or data quality. Either way, the incremental work of managing the information as an asset becomes real. This set of activities instructs the organization how to continue delivering necessary projects, but at the same time begins the transition to business management of information as an asset. If the information asset is to achieve reality in the sense we have presented in this book, all activities in this phase must be addressed.

The EIM team and IT will need to see the big picture of technology and business projects presented in a realistic, achievable timeline, data governance needs to be "switched on" in parallel with

Table 26.9 UIC Sample Stakeholder Analysis Guide

What Is a Stakeholder?	What Is Their Role?	How Will They React?	What Will Be Their Primary Concerns?	What Do We Need from Them?	How Should We Work with Them?
A stakeholder is any organization or person that: • Can influence the change • Is affected by the change. Stakeholders can be: • Individuals • Senior leaders • Groups of employees • Committees • Branch offices • Customers • Government or other regulatory agencies • Producers.	Identify each stakeholder's role or roles. Will this stakeholder: • Need to approve resources and/ or decide whether the change can proceed (a sponsor or gatekeeper)? • Need to change as a result of the effort (a target)? • Need to implement changes or convince others to change (an agent)? • React to or judge the success of effort? • Need to be an advocate of the effort (a champion)? • Perform work that can influence the success of the effort (a resource)?	How will the results of the effort be likely to impact the stakeholder? Will this stakeholder benefit or be adversely affected? Given the likely impact and historical behavior, how is this stakeholder likely to react? • Vocal, visible support? • Cooperative, quiet? • On the fence? • Say Ok but be obstructive or complain behind the scenes? • Express concerns vocally?	What are the primary concerns of this stakeholder? • What do they need or expect from the change? • What might influence whether they are supportive of the change? • What will this stakeholder need to feel informed, involved, prepared, or validated during the change? • What are the "red flags" or hot buttons for this stakeholder?	What do we need from this stakeholder? • Approval/resources • Visible support/ public endorsement • Access to them • Access to people on their team • Lack of interference with or blocking of the effort • Information • Task completion • Flexibility • Change in behavior.	Given what we know, how should we work with this stakeholder? • How will we prepare them for the change? • How will we communicate with them? • Do we need to learn more about their needs, concerns, or likely reaction? • Should they be part of the change team directly or indirectly involved (representative on team, solicit input, or provide regular feedback)?

the beginning of collecting the various EIM subdisciplines into one program. Finally, the process to implement the required behavior changes for managing data and content assets more formally are identified. The means to measure EIM success are designed, and will require creativity. The entire Road Map product must be presented clearly and reviewed with organization and EIM leadership.

Again, we do not need to spend a lot of money. Often the projects to be defined already exist. They are reorganized or relabeled for more efficient management and greater benefit to the business. But is it absolutely mandatory to develop a long range view of all of the activities that are touched by the EIM/IAM universe.

References

1. DAMA. (2009). *The DAMA Body of Knowledge (DMBOK)* (1st ed.). Bradley Beach, NJ: Technics Publications.
2. Nelson, K., & Aaron, S. (2005). *The Change Management Pocket Guide: Tools for Managing Change.* Cincinnati, OH: Change Guides LLC.

Sustaining EIM

CONTENTS

Making Enterprise Information Management (EIM) Work for Business. DOI: 10.1016/B978-0-12-375695-4.00027-8

Table 27.1 EIM Challenges and Responses

"You are slowing down my critical project"	The EIM team needs to prepare metrics to prove minimal or no impact
"Why can't I call (insert name here) and get a file downloaded like I used to?"	The EIM team needs to design education to convey the need to adhere to IAM policies
"We don't need more rules, we are doing it the way we always have since IT is never right"	The EIM team needs to build responses to resistance, through HR or other channels. There needs to be incentives to follow the new policies and accountabilities built into individual performance objectives
"How much is this costing us anyway?"	The EIM will need to indicate that the minimal incremental investment in EIM has value
"… but you said I own the data"	Clarify ownership and stewardship
"We are used to the data in that format"	That is OK—but the official version of the data will be from a different source

This phase covers the day-to-day operation of the EIM program. It will "operationalize" the requirements for sustaining EIM developed in the Road Map phase. This is the means by which the cultural obstacles that are barriers to IAM are managed. We also measure and report on the adoption of EIM and, if adjustments are required, trigger one of our other phases.

There are common concerns that will be heard as formal management of information is implemented, and you will need an appropriate response, similar to what is listed in Table 27.1. The Sustaining phase deals with the questions and the responses.

I have referred to doing components of EIM if the full EIM program does not take flight. For example, if an organization is too large for one EIM program, or so politically charged that formal EIM will take a while to roll out, then efforts like MDM and data warehouse will still be required. The Sustaining phase is the only phase out of the eight we have presented that should be done in all of its aspects, even if you are deploying only part of EIM, or a stand-alone feature.

The Sustaining phase is also the longest, as it never ends. Once EIM starts, diligence is required to keep it running. Even if you start EIM via a subdiscipline, or within a narrow portion of the organization, it will require sustaining activities to ensure ongoing value and growth (Figures 27.1 and 27.2).

Remember, your culture will almost certainly be a barrier. This is the first challenge to a sustainable program. Besides the cultural issues, there is the need to learn to run EIM. It is a new business program.

The extent of culture change needs to be addressed in the day-to-day operations of EIM. This includes rollout of new organization structures, planning to sustain and then actually sustaining the program, measuring and reporting value, and the ordinary management tasks.

Strong executive sponsorship is an essential factor for program success. Sometimes, you are lucky and compliance can mandate a level of governance due to regulation. (It is no coincidence that companies with high compliance requirements do IAM very well.) The EIM leader will need to rely on the strong sponsor many times during the first six months or more when the program is in operation. MDM creates culture change. Data warehouse creates culture change. Rule of thumb: *Any formal management of any portion of the content of an organization will require an organized effort to sustain the management of that portion.*

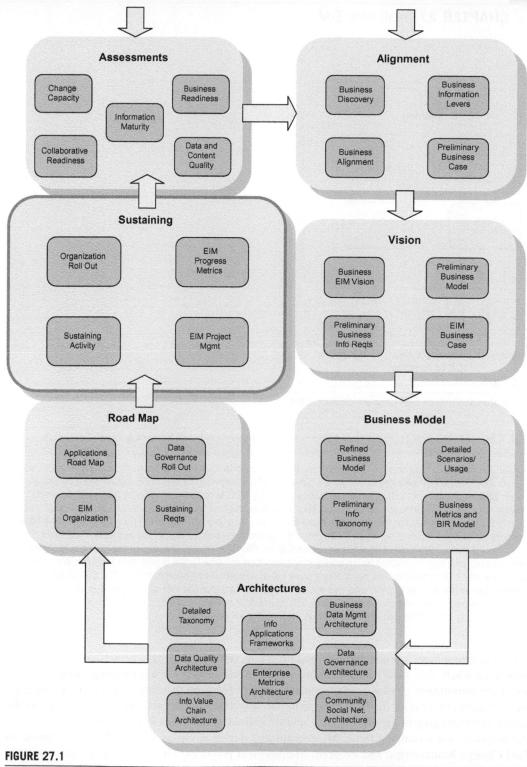

FIGURE 27.1

Sustaining locator

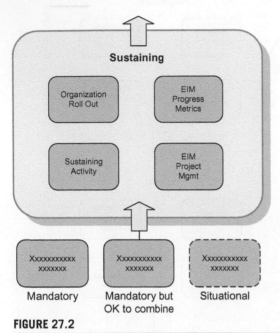

FIGURE 27.2

Sustaining components of EIM program development

> **OBSERVATION**
>
> Other features of the first few months will be confusion on job descriptions, a hesitancy to move away from old roles and responsibilities, and challenges to everyone's patience. While preparing for this book, I observed a company define an EIM effort, develop a thorough Road Map, and deploy an EIM department. Shortly afterward, business conditions required a reprioritization of the Road Map away from the first business projects and addressing of a new set of efforts. These efforts were defined in the Road Map—they were brought forward in priority. At the same time, the governance council received an issue. (Remember the governance council is the final authority—you don't want a lot going there.) While the EIM team was reloading its efforts, a VP (and member of the council) had gone outside the company and contracted for an emergency consultant to come fix the urgent data problem. Was it an act of resistance? Upon investigation, no. It was a short fall of education and internalization. The EIM program was still future "pie in the sky" to this VP, who had not connected the fact that the IAM philosophy was to be applied to every single business event and condition. It applied to operational as well as strategic efforts. When I visited them, I had to assure the entire EIM team this was normal. (I think the VP owes me lunch.)

The Sustaining phase is where most formal programs related to IM have ground to a halt, getting into situations where they have been unable to overcome resistance, or prove ongoing value.

Given the importance of change management, we will focus on that first and present a primer on change management activity for EIM. The material developed in that activity will also support the measuring and managing of various projects, and the rollout of the EIM Organization.

The activities for sustaining the EIM program and day-to-day running of EIM are all based on standard Change Management and Program Management practices. There is no rocket science here. But these activities are not trivial in terms of impact or contribution to success.

ACTIVITY: SUSTAINING ACTIVITY

Since we have assessments, and we have our requirements for Sustaining (from the Road Map phase), the objective for this activity is to develop the actual plan and products for sustaining EIM, and then start to actually implement and take the organization through the changes for EIM (or a subdiscipline). The objective is to develop the detailed plans to address resistance points, develop orientation and education materials, implement the various activities to facilitate changes in behaviors, and adjust processes.

This phase relies heavily on leveraging basic concepts of human dynamics and communications.

Human dynamics is the study of how human beings function individually and collectively.[1] In our case, we want to understand how humans react to EIM. A full-blown EIM program will expose many forms of human dynamics. Table 27.2 illustrates how various elements of EIM will affect human actions.

Different people will react differently, and the Sustaining mechanism will need to allow for the variety of responses.

Table 27.2 Human Dynamics

Human Dynamic Principles*		Elements of EIM (Not a Complete List)			
		Data Governance	BPM/BI/DW	Principles	Data Quality
Mental	Thinking Objectivity Vision Overview Structure Values	May welcome structure	May perceive loss of analytical abilities	May want more structure underneath the principles	May embrace rules enforcement
Emotional	Feeling Subjectivity Relationship Communication Organization Creative Imagination	May feel constrained by more discipline	May welcome collaborative data environment	May embrace better communications	May feel loss of flexibility or creativity
Physical	Making Doing Actualizing Sensory experience Practicality Systemic experience	May or may not seem practical	May resist loss of departmental Access databases	May perceive support of their view of common sense	May welcome more predictable data

*Seagal, S., & Horne, D. (1987). Human Dynamics—A Framework for Understanding People. Waltham, MA: Pegasus Communications.

Table 27.3 Effective Communications

Levels of Communication and Mechanisms for Communicating			
Face-to-face: meetings, interviews	Presentation: PowerPoint	Document: "Read and review the attached"	Casual: E-mails, tweets, voice mail
Level one ☺	☺	☺	☺
Level two ☺	☺	😐	☹
Level three ☺	😐	☹	☹
Level four ☺	☹	☹	☹

Communicating with the various stakeholders also requires consideration of the individual as well as the form of the message. Certain audiences for EIM will need to be aware of changes and new processes. Others will need to become intimately familiar. We use four basic levels of communications, and we always consider these against the various means available for communications. Not all stakeholder groups have to move through all levels of the process. In the twenty-first century, we can communicate in many ways, from face-to-face to 140 character digital bursts (tweets). All need to be carefully considered, with the right level of communications being attained with the right communication vehicle. Table 27.3 presents the four levels and the effectiveness of a variety of communication mechanisms. The four levels we use are:

Level one: The stakeholder has no real knowledge of the initiative and related projects. We do not want anyone remotely connected with EIM to remain at this level.

Level two: The majority of people in a stakeholder group are aware of EIM basics, know it means change, but do not comprehend the strategic significance or business reasons for IAM. Very few personnel touched by EIM can remain at this level and move through the change process. Only people who have to react to a specific instruction to change a specific action can remain here, such as an outsourced data entry clerk who merely uses a new screen or signs onto a new application.

Level three: The majority of a stakeholder group is aware of EIM/IAM meaning, and comprehend the meaning and need, but express concern on how their organization will operate and the effect on jobs and careers. The majority of stakeholders affected by EIM will be operating at this level, from programmers to business analysts to accountants.

Level four: Key stakeholder groups are aware of EIM, fully comprehend what IAM means, recognize and articulate the business benefits and impacts, and are fully committed. Obviously, we want management and leadership at this level.

This activity may revisit some surveys to confirm the styles of training, orientation, and communication required. Also, additional analysis of EIM participants and stakeholders will be done to tighten down specific responses to groups, or even individuals.

Activity Summary

There are numerous change management methodologies. Table 27.4 gives a generic presentation of activities required for EIM. For more details, refer to the bibliography at the end of this book.

Table 27.4 Sustaining Activity Summary

Objective	Define and implement the specific tools and actions required to ensure the required behavior changes for IAM.
Purpose	EIM requires change management. Without a formal process to assist people through the changes, the EIM program will fail.
Inputs	The assessments, plus a review of change-related findings that will inevitably crop up during the prior phases as different groups are brought into contact with EIM.
	The EIM and DG Organizations and architectures form Road Map and Architecture phases.
Tasks	Confirm affected stakeholders
	Confirm sponsor readiness
	Confirm "burning platform" or current state deficiencies
	Integrate the Sustaining activity with overall EIM Road Maps and project plans
	Identify new obstacles and constraints
	What issues need to be addressed and obstacles removed?
	How much stakeholder involvement will be needed?
	Define/modify roll-out strategy, select roll-out option by:
	EIM project
	EIM governed area
	EIM function or component
	EIM element
	Execute the change plan
	Activate training, communications, resistance management, etc.
	Develop materials for training, orientation, road shows, etc.
	Develop additional advocates if necessary
	Communicate short-term wins
	Communicate status and measurements of progress often to leadership
	Address problem areas aggressively
	Measure EIM change effectiveness
	Execute measurement surveys (if designed)
	Hold focus groups/interviews for feedback
	Realign impacted policies/practices and procedures to clearly support the new EIM Vision, not contradict it
	Update staff performance objectives and reward structures to reflect new accountabilities and compliance to new rules.
Techniques	Project planning, facilitations, Change Management experience, and clear communication and training mechanisms.
Tools	A variety of Change Management tools.
	Project Management.
	Communications vehicles—e-mail, web sites, PowerPoint.
Outputs	Design for Sustaining EIM.
	The EIM Sustaining activities.
	Feedback and adjustment over time of EIM activities.
	Responses to resistance and application of incentives.
Outcome	The organization adopts EIM/IAM. Sustaining EIM continues; there is no end point.

Business Benefits and Ramifications

We emphasized change management earlier. It is a requirement for EIM success. Without a formal effort to manage the transition from where EIM is to where it needs to be, you will fail.

Approach Considerations

The primary considerations for EIM change management are:

- *The sponsor*—The EIM sponsor must be visible and high ranking. If EIM lives in the IT organization, the sponsor *cannot* be the CIO.
- *The sustaining or change management team*—Initially, you will need a small (three to four is typical) group to develop the Sustaining plan and oversee its implementation. Over time, you will need a full time equivalent (FTE) to observe human dynamics and measure EIM effectiveness.

The various deliverables for EIM change are standard. Everyone doing any sort of EIM will require communication plans (review Table 27.5), training plans, and resistance management plans. There will always be resistance. There will always be the need to communicate and educate.

A new area to EIM or IT staff drafted into EIM will be the considerations of human dynamics. You cannot start a change effort by simply ordering everyone to behave differently. Outside of the military, few organizations can adapt that quickly. EIM especially cannot be done by fiat. Most likely, business users will feel betrayed or at minimum sense a contradiction. After all, they are told to do what it takes to get their jobs done, and that usually means doing their own IM. Now it is deemed unacceptable.

The key to altering behavior is to make sure that those who are affected by changes induced by IAM understand a few things:

1. *The big picture*—What does life look like after all of this is over?
2. *WIIFM*—What Is In It For Me—In other words, how is my situation better after I go through the discomfort of change? Why do I have to change from doing this all myself to waiting for help from someone else?
3. *Consequences*—While a perfect world will have everyone see the light, and immediately shift to IAM, in reality someone always digs in their heels. There must be both performance incentives and consequences for noncompliance. Unfortunately, I have often seen situations requiring some form of job action to reinforce the need for change.

As the Sustaining activity and Change Management tools are deployed, frequent measuring, feedback, and reporting of issues and progress are very important. This indicates sense.

Sample Output

Appendix H contains the outline for the Sustaining deliverables. Table 27.5 shows Farfels' communication plan.

TIP FOR SUCCESS

Once you have this activity under way, there will be a predictable level of complaining about training or orientation sessions. This is normal. The real success factor is getting to do this activity at all. Many organizations feel that change management is squishy, and many executives still feel that they can issue an order and everything will happen. Unless there is a huge crisis where everyone understands and feels simultaneous pain (which really is a highly compressed form of change management), issuing an order does not work. The success factor here is to make sure you execute a formal change management and sustaining plan, and then frequently report how well it is working.

Table 27.5 Farfel Communication Plan Example

Farfel Emporiums—EIM Sustaining Communications Plan

Date	Frequency	Event	Vehicle	Purpose	Key Messages	Audience	Sender	Developer	Review/Approval
Month/day/year	Once	Review of updated Farfel EIM communication approach and plan	Farfel EIM steering committee meeting	Inform	This is the approach we plan to take for communication for Farfel EIM. It will be linked to the new vision as the key enabler to achieve it. The plan is a living document that will be reviewed and updated frequently as projects come on line and work proceeds. Each project will have a similar plan	Farfel EIM steering team	—	—	—
Month/day/year	Once	Introduction and refinement of the Farfel EIM "elevator" speech	Farfel EIM management meeting	Marketing	Review of current elevator speech draft and refinement with input from the group. Discussion of what an elevator speech is, why it's important, and how it will be used	Farfel EIM management group	—	—	—
Month/day/year	Once	Message to organization about the wrap-up of the 90-day plan and next steps	E-mail	Marketing, inform	Announce receipt of the deliverable, discuss next steps, tell people there will be a kick-off meeting in a few weeks to provide more information	Farfel management team	—	—	—

(Continued)

Table 27.5 (Continued)

					Farfel Emporiums—EIM Sustaining Communications Plan				
Date	Frequency	Event	Vehicle	Purpose	Key Messages	Audience	Sender	Developer	Review/Approval
Month/day/year	Once	CEO meeting with Farfel leaders to set expectations for their support for Farfel EIM	Leadership team meeting	Marketing, inform	Reinforce key Farfel EIM messages and linkage to the Vision, establish expectations for support of Farfel EIM initiatives (including what happens if no support), key role of leaders in communicating the messages	Farfel leadership	—	—	—
Month/day/year	Once—become part of quarterly conference calls with linkage to Farfel EIM as a key enabler	Discussion with Farfel field leaders: Call with store managers	Conference call	Marketing, inform	Reinforcement of the key ideas (what, why) and next steps from the Vision introduction, restatement of ways to provide feedback, open dialogue with the organization (ask for questions ahead of time also), reiterate linkages to Farfel EIM	Farfel field managers	—	—	—
Month/day/year	Once	Farfel EIM kick-off meeting—combine with Vision announcement (see vision launch plan)	Town hall	Marketing, inform	Introduction to the next phases of Farfel EIM, how we got to where we are, where we go from here, why Farfel EIM is critical to Farfel's future success, what people can expect over the next few months, where to go to get additional information and ask questions, where to go to provide feedback	Farfel management team	—	Change team	—

Month/day/year	Once—become part of quarterly conference calls with linkage to Farfel EIM as a key enabler	Discussion with Farfel directors	Face-to-face discussion	Marketing, inform	Reinforcement of the key ideas (what, why) and next steps from the Vision introduction, restatement of ways to provide feedback, open dialogue with the organization (ask for questions ahead of time also), reiterate linkages to Farfel EIM	Farfel directors	—	Change team	—
Month/day/year	Once—become part of quarterly conference calls with reinforcement of Farfel EIM as key enabler of the new Vision	Follow-up Q&A with Farfel employees	Face-to-face discussion and conference call	Marketing, inform	Reinforcement of the key ideas (what, why) and next steps from the Farfel EIM introduction, restatement of ways to provide feedback, open dialogue with the organization (ask for questions ahead of time also), reiterate linkages to Farfel EIM	Farfel management team	—	Change team	—
Month/day/year	Periodically	Check-in to see if/how well messages are getting across	Pulse survey	Inform	Conduct periodic surveys to determine if messages related to Farfel EIM are coming through and being internalized by the organization	Farfel management team	—	Change team	—
Month/day/year	Quarterly	Ongoing town hall meetings with the entire organization to report on Farfel EIM progress. Should also include reinforcement of the Farfel Vision and Farfel EIM's link to it	Town hall	Marketing, inform, update	Progress to date on Farfel EIM, continued reinforcement of how it links to the Vision, tackle rumors, address questions, share feedback and success stories	Farfel management team	—	Change team	—

(Continued)

Table 27.5 (Continued)

				Farfel Emporiums—EIM Sustaining Communications Plan					
Date	Frequency	Event	Vehicle	Purpose	Key Messages	Audience	Sender	Developer	Review/Approval
TBD	Periodic	Employee meetings with leaders to discuss Farfel EIM. Leaders provided talking points, FAQs, and coaching in advance of meeting. Member of program team attends to provide support	Face-to-face	Marketing, inform, update	Opportunity for employees to meet with leaders to discuss questions and concerns about Farfel EIM. Chance to reinforce key messages, linkage to the vision, etc.	Selected employees	—	Change team	—
Month/ day/ year	Once	Overhaul of Farfel EIM web site	Intranet	Marketing, inform, update	Cleanup of current web page to reflect more up-to-date information and next steps. Add FAQs specific to Farfel EIM, make sure linkage to the new Vision is clear. Set up a "monthly message from CEO" section, set up a "leaders forum" section	Farfel management team	—	TBD	—
Ongoing	Biweekly (minimum)	Updates posted on the Farfel EIM web site	Intranet	Marketing, inform, update	Post new information on the web site: add to FAQs, progress reports, post new messages from CEO and other Farfel leaders. Monitor hits on page and look for ways to pull people into the web site	Farfel management team	—	Change team	—

As needed	Three to four times	E-mail to the organization: "Do you know what's happening with Farfel EIM today?"	E-mail	Marketing	A method to "pull" people into the Farfel EIM site. Message emphasizes new information on the site and reiterates the importance of staying abreast of what is happening with Farfel EIM	Farfel management team	—	Change team	—
Month/day/year	Monthly	Leadership team meeting	Farfel leadership	Inform, update	Farfel EIM becomes a repeating component of the agenda for these meetings. Discuss progress, reinforce key messages, expectations for leaders	Farfel leadership	—	Change team	—
Month/day/year	As needed	Updated marketing materials	Brochures, etc.	Marketing	Explanation to external partners of Farfel Emporiums' value proposition for them and how Farfel EIM will enable delivery of the value proposition —the WIIFM for producers and customers	Department heads, customers	—	Change team	—
Month/day/year	Once	Update to the Farfel web site	Internet	Marketing	Announcement of next steps with Farfel EIM, reference to the Farfel EIM web page, importance of Farfel EIM to achieving the Vision/Value proposition	Farfel management team	—	Change team	—

(Continued)

Table 27.5 (Continued)

			Farfel Emporiums—EIM Sustaining Communications Plan					
Date	Frequency	Event	Vehicle	Purpose	Key Messages	Audience	Sender	Developer	Review/Approval
TBD	Once	Update to the Farfel web site	Intranet	Marketing	Announcement of Farfel EIM and the new Vision, goals. Reinforcement of key messages: why now, why the right one for Farfel, support needed from the organization, what they can expect to hear going forward and when, why Farfel EIM is so important to Farfel's future, highlight Farfel EIM web site as place to go for information	Farfel management team	—	Change team	—
TBD	Quarterly	Update to the Farfel website	Intranet	Marketing	Farfel EIM "scorecard"—show progress on projects and goal achievement	Farfel management team (only accessible internally)	—	Change team	—
TBD	Quarterly	Cascade materials—talking points, slides, FAQs	Face-to-face meeting and discussion for managers with their employees	Marketing, inform, update	Reinforcement of key messages about Farfel EIM, progress, success stories. Materials will need to be updated at least quarterly to keep up with developments	Farfel leaders and managers	—	Change team	—

ACTIVITY: ORGANIZATIONAL ROLL OUT

This activity deploys the EIM Organization. New/revised job descriptions are activated, and new functions begin to execute. There may be recruiting, transferring, and retraining involved in getting the new EIM Organization started. In larger organizations, altering the organization charts and allocating staff to new job descriptions can be time consuming. Human resources will be a good friend to have at this point. Hopefully, they were engaged during the Road Map phase. If not, they need to be fully engaged now. Job descriptions, if not filled out earlier, must be completed.

There needs to be coordination between organizational deployment and the Sustaining Planning activity because there will be an immediate need for training and orientation of the EIM team. Ideally, the activity of preparation for training can begin even before the Road Map is complete. Either way, there is a definite need to train the new IM team on EIM and immediately orient management and leadership.

The sequence of the EIM Organization Roll Out is normally built around the Road Map, and the functionality that must be available as the Road Map unfolds. Since we have target levels of IMM defined (or should), the organization's behavior can be measured relative to IMM.

Activity Summary (Table 27.6)

Table 27.6 EIM Organization Activity Summary	
Objective	Deploy the EIM Organization.
Purpose	Provide a measurable managed deployment that is effective in terms of improving IMM, but does not result in idle employees or confusion of roles and responsibilities.
Inputs	Sustaining activities for training. The EIM Organization from the Road Map, and the EIM Road Map IMM targets.

Tasks	Complete new EIM team identification/socialization
	    Socialize EIM program and area to IT and compliance
	    Socialize new EIM manager
	    Identify and staff IM area
	    Establish physical location
	Review EIM charter(s)
	Present charters and EIM principles to new staff
	Present Sustaining activities and stakeholder analysis to EIM staff
	Orient executive team to EIM Organization (if not done in Sustaining activity)
	Schedule EIM team, committees, and executives for their orientation, training, or educations
	Align EIM team functions with Road Map projects
	Ensure estimates are understood and Project Management practices in place.

Techniques	Basic management and project management.
Tools	Project management tools.
Outputs	An operational effective EIM Organization. Understanding of the EIM team role to constituents.
Outcome	The EIM department is "official."

Business Benefits and Ramifications

Business areas will need to understand the role and begin to interact with the new EIM area as appropriate.

Approach Considerations

Coordinate this activity with the Sustaining activities. They cannot be combined, but should work closely together. Critical activities are the socialization and team building of new parts of the organization, and making sure the new teams and functions start to coalesce and work together.

Sample Output

Same as the organization charts shown in Part 1.

TIP FOR SUCCESS

Look for old loyalties to prior structures to crop up, or personnel more comfortable performing old duties in lieu of new ones. This applies for subdisciplines as well as global EIM. There may even be resistance to EIM from new team members. Finally, make sure that EIM is not a dumping ground for staff no one else wants. To address the resistance, make sure that the appropriate education and communication is occurring and that individuals understand and feel prepared for their new roles. The best CSF is to ensure that as roles change, individual accountabilities and performance objectives are realigned and incentive programs support the new direction. Without this, you have very little chance of success in changing behavior.

ACTIVITY: EIM PROGRESS METRICS

The purpose of this activity is to design and deploy a set of metrics for tracking and managing the EIM program. The requirements for metrics were defined in the Road Map phase. These are not metrics for measuring the Change Management portion of EIM, these are metrics for managing the effectiveness of EIM/IAM within the enterprise. However, it's important to note that these measures will help you gauge how well the organizational adoption of EIM/IAM is proceeding. There are several categories of metrics we need to design:

- Metrics to measure the success of sustaining EIM are identified and data collection methods defined. If you cannot report on the effects of EIM, then there is no defense when the complaints start.
- Metrics that at least notionally indicate improvement in organizational value due to EIM. These are divided into familiar sounding subgroups:
  - *Efficiency*—Are we improving the enterprise by making it leaner and more responsive?
  - *Return*—Is EIM increasing income or equity?
  - *Risk*—Are we reducing our reserves or insurance premiums as a result of EIM?
- Metrics that report on the progress of our EIM projects which are in flight. These are not metrics of project progress, these are metrics of utilization of Data Governance and Modeling functions, reviews of adherence to standards, and so forth.

Activity Summary (Table 27.7)

Table 27.7 EIM Progress Metrics Activity Summary	
Objective	Define and design measurements that report on the effectiveness of EIM and IAM.
Purpose	Present an ongoing businesses justification for EIM/IAM.
Inputs	The metric requirements from the Road Map phase.
Tasks	Define metrics requirements into categories of risk, return, efficiency
	Define metrics per the metrics model used in the Business Model phase
	Present metrics to EIM leadership for approval
	Deploy metrics collection and reporting in Alignment with the EIM Road Map
	Implement regular metrics and measurement of DG implementation
	Produce EIM effectiveness reports.
Techniques	Metrics model technique from the Business Model phase.
Tools	Excel, Enterprise Architecture tools.
Outputs	A set of metrics that are deployed and being used to report on effectiveness of EIM/IAM.
Outcome	These metrics are never really complete. As sophistication increases with EIM, we can develop a wider variety of metrics.

Business Benefits and Ramifications

The EIM metrics are required when resistance builds, or business priorities need to be reassessed. This is the only business-relevant manner to determine if EIM is working as expected.

Approach Considerations

Even though the definition and designing of the metrics is straightforward, collecting the data to produce the metrics is not. For example, some of the metrics rely on a count of knowledge workers. This is a derived number. Other metrics may require obtaining financial information that is not shared in detail. Make sure you can collect the data before you promise the metric.

Sample Output

The basic list of metrics that are offered to all enterprises appears in Table 28.1.

TIP FOR SUCCESS

If metrics are difficult to establish, do not give up. Use surveys or assessments to report on progress until the EIM environment produces enough data to allow for more quantitative metrics.

ACTIVITY: EIM PROGRAM MANAGEMENT

During the first few months after the EIM program goes "live," this activity serves to make sure that EIM projects are managed, sustaining activities take place, education and training occur on schedule, and issues are dealt with. As time goes on, this activity will monitor the functions of EIM, such as data governance, planning, applications assistance, and data quality remediation. Again, EIM is an ongoing experience. While there will be start-up considerations, the Sustaining phase is permanent.

Most of this activity is basic department/program management. Ideally, in a few years, this function and activity will be no different than any other strategic function. This is the ultimate goal. IAM is made endemic, and smoothly integrated into the daily ebb and flow of the enterprise.

Given that there is a lot of basic material on program management available from many sources, this activity section will focus *only* on EIM-specific activity and tasks.

Activity Summary (Table 27.8)

Table 27.8 EIM Management Activity Summary	
Objective	Manage the day-to-day EIM program.
Purpose	EIM is the same as any other program, and must adhere to a "going concern" principle, whereby it is operated as any other permanent enterprise function.
Inputs	All artifacts from all phases of EIM.
Tasks	Manage Road Map projects
	Report wins
	Interact with Change Management
	Ensure aggressive resolution of issues
	Manage EIM department functions
	Manage day-to-day operations
	Manage DQ
	Manage business data and content—oversight of the assets (databases, documents, content)
	Manage integrity and security—database administration and security
	Manage DQ
	Manage the IAM/EIM architecture elements
	Manage reassessments/EIM adjustments
	Manage data life cycles—acquisition, movement, purging
	Manage enterprise DNA (metadata), including EIM design and architecture artifacts
	Manage reference and master data
	Manage data and content usage (BI, reporting, catalogs, web sites)
	Manage tools and technologies
	Deploy and adjust EIM program
	Document metrics and EIM function performance
	Train and educate
	Implement tools and technology
	Promote and interact with change management
	Perform and review audits and service levels
	Interact with governing bodies
	Coordinate DG committees and councils
	Appoint and meet with major EIM project steering bodies
	Update executive EIM sponsorship
	Align EIM Project Management activity with existing IT practices
	Identify project templates
	Identify EIM project estimating tools
	Identify EIM tracking and accounting procedures for IT
	Forecast EIM project resources
	Utilize modified SDLC
	Interact with enterprise PMO (if one exists).

(Continued)

Table 27.8 (Continued)	
Techniques	Program and project management.
Tools	Project Management.
Outputs	The successful ongoing operation of EIM.
Outcome	This step is never finished—successful outcome means that EIM and EIM-related programs are sustainable, and IAM becomes part of organizational culture.

Business Benefits and Ramifications

Program operation has many deliverables, outcomes, and interactions. This is where the business absorbs and makes EIM part of any other business paradigm. EIM provides a new layer of project discipline. Projects will leverage common information and content areas and share common systems components. Note I said *will*, not *should*. A significant ramification to your enterprise will be a required alteration in the development and maintenance of your software applications.

TIP FOR SUCCESS

EIM programs or subdisciplines that mature to day-to-day operation must always make sure they are reporting progress. The value of IAM has to be reported continuously until it is woven into and accepted by the culture. Do no underestimate the value of "tooting our own horn."

Reference

1. Seagal, S., & Horne, D. (1997). *Human Dynamics* (1st ed.). Waltham, MA: Pegasus Communications.

Measuring EIM and the Value of Information

Management by objective works—if you know the objectives.
Ninety percent of the time you don't.
Peter Drucker

CONTENTS

Chapter 13 presented an overview of metrics and information value for EIM. This chapter will dive into the details of the metrics for measuring EIM success and progress. Specifically we will cover the meaning of the metric, its application, and how to collect the data.

In addition we will take a look at measuring the value of information. We cannot leave this book without going over some ideas on placing a value, even if it is a *faux* or unofficial value on the content portfolio.

METRICS FOR EIM

You cannot manage what you cannot measure. This obvious managerial creed has been neglected for too long in the IM area. Talking about an asset without the ability to measure the asset has made IT seem a bit out of touch with business. In fairness to IT, a lot of what we need to measure to demonstrate business seemed abstract. The abstraction, however, is a matter of perception. Anything can be measured.[1]

For example, we had a client who brought us in to assess why the BI team was not "up to the task." We mentioned this example in Chapter 2. Leadership was publicly critical of the IT area's support for reporting and data analysis. The so-called support environment was a data warehouse application used by only a few businesspeople. This was the first metric we reviewed that raised eyebrows. How can the environment in place be so ineffective if only a few people have experience with it? Therefore, while we assessed the staff and IMM, we also collected another bundle of metrics. Here is what we found:

- The existing "data warehouse" did have only a few users in one department, who extracted data and sent it to dozens of other users, unbeknownst to the BI team.
- The remainder of the business demanded, and got, hundreds (yes, hundreds) of extracted data sets which were loaded into departmental spreadsheets and Access databases, and almost all reporting and decisions were based on these local files.
- The total cost per knowledge worker, that is, the investment in hardware, software, labor, and fees to support this departmental analysis, was 30% higher than their competitors.
- Management received every single data element that could be provided, multiple times, every month. Every functional area has its own mini-IT staff, managing, moving, and reporting its own results.
- The conclusion we reached, and then had corroborated, was that the performance within the business area was simply poor. Too much time on moving data, too little time on making operational changes or making sound decisions.

Without using measurements, this company would have most likely continued to beat up its IT staff until they all left. (Turnover was already pretty high.)

For this chapter we have arranged the metrics by how they are used. Table 28.1 also lists how they are collected, provides a more detailed explanation (if required), and adds remarks on deploying

Table 28.1 EIM Metrics Master List

EIM Metrics	Definition	Collection
Measure effectiveness of DQ programs		
Counts of data occurrences that are in error	Report number of instances a specific field is stored incorrectly	Tool or programmed routine
Percentages of accuracy	Numerical values are not correct but are within some percentage	Tool or programmed routine
Financial impact of critical, albeit incorrect data elements		
Specific samples of fields in error and the financial errors contained, e.g.,	Fields where error created financial impact to organization	
Total premium at risk is $nnn because nn% of policies contain bad information		Tool or programmed routine
Percentage of e-mails with "at risk" comments, or contain potentially damaging information		Collected
Cost of bad catalog entries and poor content management due to lost online orders or returned product		Collected
Lost funding for government entities or contractors		Collected

(Continued)

Table 28.1 (Continued)

EIM Metrics	Definition	Collection
Loss of customer confidence due to errors		Collected
Loss of customers due to errors		Collected
DQ profile results—percentage of completion, accuracy, relevance	Predefined algorithms that organize data and content errors by categories	Tool or programmed routine
Annual DQ index	The year-over-year delta of DQ metrics and profile results combined as an index	Tool or programmed routine
Measure effectiveness of DG functions		
Counts of content by life-cycle stages (e.g., transactional, operational, decisional)	A content inventory of data or documents at various stages along the organizations information life cycle	Programmed routine
Document and data life-cycle times	The length of time content stays at one level of usage (e.g., an event or transaction) before it moves to another level of usage (e.g., managerial reporting); is content available when it needs to be, is it deleted when no longer of benefit?	Programmed routine
Information inventory change	Delta of actual information content inventory against maintained directory of content	Programmed routine
"Hits" or click counts on web-based tools	Report of counts of access to repositories, metadata, DNA tools, DG sites, collaborative sites, BI portals, or tools	Programmed routine
Application deployment to DG approvals ratio	Comparison or projects moved into production with projects DG has provided oversight	Collected
EIM approval and understanding	Feedback results from surveys of parties impacted by EIM	Collected
Usage of standard elements of EIM	Determines if standard elements and component of EIM being used, such as reference codes, master data	Programmed routine
Percentage of major data subjects that are "certified"	Sources or subject area that is governed, reviewed, and agreed upon as "sources of truth," e.g., number of customers stored in a customer master database and certified as accurate	Collected
Measure legal/compliance risks related to content		
Potential penalties per subject area	Total penalties possible related to a subject area, such as customer	Calculated
Loss of market/shareholder confidence	Estimate of reduction in equity if data causes loss of market confidence	Calculated
Litigation fees over time for data/ document regulatory noncompliance	Possible fees to defend organization against data-related claims	Calculated

(Continued)

Table 28.1 (Continued)

EIM Metrics	Definition	Collection
Cost per downtime event due to DQ (or other data-related issue)	Financial impact of data issues cause operations to cease	Calculated
Legal fees to defend privacy issues	Possible fees to defend organization against data-related claims	Calculated
The new risk of incarceration and cost to enterprise	"What if" vision assuming penalties and prosecution	Calculated
Measure financial risks related to content		
Credit exposure	Possible loss in credit portfolio due to data issues	Calculated
Liquidity	Possible reduction in liquid assets	Calculated
Operational costs	Possible increase in operational costs	Calculated
Call out specific shifts in reserves, retained earnings, goodwill	Possible changes based on data and content issues	Calculated
Equity/market value reduction	Possible reduction in equity if data causes loss of market confidence	Calculated
Measure contribution of EIM to business goals		
Operating income for year divided by number of knowledge workers[1]	Change in income divided by staff using data and content at touch points or analysis	Calculated
Relative value by subject area	Weighted score of subject area value based on perceptions of accuracy, relevance, DQ, and timeliness	Calculated
Measure EIM program performance		
Incentives and performance	Counts of activities or artifacts related to EIM performance	
Total count/amount of DG- or DQ-incentive rewards		Calculated
Attendance at orientation and training		Collected
Issues presented to steering committees		Collected
Performance reviews done with EIM targets included		Collected
Job descriptions revised with IAM accountability included		Collected
Performance targets achieved related to IAM		Calculated
Usage	Counts of use of data and content resources	
Number of users and access to single sources of truth		Collected
Reduction in departmental Access databases and spreadsheets		Collected

(Continued)

Table 28.1 (Continued)

EIM Metrics	Definition	Collection
BI use by user log on ID to track who is doing what		Collected
Measure efficiency of EIM		
Total cost of IT/party (customer, member, etc.)	Enterprise IT budget divided by total occurrences of a subject area	Calculated
DG/compliance divided by total income	Annual cost of DG and corporate compliance over income	Calculated
DG/compliance vs. risk reserves/ premiums	Annual cost of DG and corporate compliance over corporate risk numbers, either reserves or corporate insurance premiums	Calculated

[1]*Knowledge worker is defined as someone who uses information to make decisions and take actions that cause the fulfillment of objectives, and reads information. There are other definitions but this one suffices for this book.*

(if required). All of these metrics have been field tested. In many cases we collect the data and do the metric anyway, even if the enterprise has been lukewarm on measuring IAM.

FINANCIAL VALUATIONS

When you strip the abstractions aside, the financial valuation of information focuses on what portion of the balance sheet or income statement this new type of information is reported, and how it is calculated. The details of this require some understanding of financial management concepts, so we will first review the financial statement concepts before walking through the calculations.

Since many readers of this book may have a technical background, some accounting fundamentals need to be reviewed. If your intelligence is insulted, ignore the next section. If not, feel free to review the financial statement primer.

Accounting Primer

First, the balance sheet. A balance sheet is, in effect, a really big metric that reflects the overall value of an organization. The formula is assets = liabilities + equity. Traditionally liabilities are bad and assets and equity are good. ALL activities, events, and transactions in a business eventually are reflected on the balance sheet. It is called a balance sheet because the left side and right side of the equation *must* be equal.

The income statement is another metric-on-paper that provides a snapshot in time of the quality of financial activity, i.e., how good are we doing NOW? Its basic formula (very basic, as this will change greatly across industries) is sales minus cost of goods (or cost of sales). This gives you gross income. Then you deduct all those other expenses, like salaries, benefits, advertising, tuition reimbursement, the office party, etc., and that gives you net income. There is a lot more to financial statements than the above, but it will suffice for now.

Information on Financial Statements

Balance sheets can be enhanced with information through two approaches. One approach essentially states that the information you have appears on the balance sheet as an asset, but as an *intangible* asset. The calculations for this are still debated by the accounting types, but a strong case has been made, especially for mergers and acquisitions, that information and other intellectual content appear on the balance sheet. See Table 28.2 for the guidelines for doing this.

Similarly, there is a move now to audit *information portfolios* of organizations and assign a PV, or a value based on an implied interest rate. Calculations are weighted by relevance of information to

Table 28.2 GAAP/GAIP Relationship	
FASB Statement[1] Applicable	**Corresponding GAIP™ Principle and Rule**
Software Development	Value Principle: Development of Content Acquisition and Handling
25-2 Internal and external costs incurred to develop internal-use computer software during the application development stage shall be capitalized. [SOP 98-1, paragraph 21]	Internal and external costs incurred during the application development stage to develop internal-use software to manage, update, query, and convert or transform computer records, documents, web pages, websites catalogs, blogs, "wikis", emails, digital media, or other static digitally stored content shall be capitalized.
25-3 Costs to develop or obtain software that allows for access or conversion of old data by new systems shall also be capitalized. [SOP 98-1, paragraph 21]	Training and support costs for applications supporting digitally stored content shall be expensed.
25-4 Training costs are not internal-use software development costs and, if incurred during this stage, shall be expensed as incurred. [SOP 98-1, paragraph 21]	Non-applications development (such as departmental spreadsheets) that handles digital media and content shall be recognized as a separate expense category and expensed.
25-5 Data conversion costs, except as noted in paragraph 350-40-25-3, shall be expensed as incurred. [SOP 98-1, paragraph 22]	
Goodwill Recognition	Value Principle: Recognizing Maintenance
25-3 Costs of internally developing, maintaining, or restoring intangible assets (including goodwill) that are not specifically identifiable, that have indeterminate lives, or that are inherent in a continuing business and related to an entity as a whole, shall be recognized as an expense when incurred. [FAS 142, paragraph 10]	The costs of maintaining content or placing structures into place to restore content should be expensed, but tracked separately and allocated to content category and business unit.

(Continued)

Table 28.2 (Continued)

FASB Statement[1] Applicable	Corresponding GAIP™ Principle and Rule
Determining the Implied Fair Value of Goodwill	Value Principle: Determining the Implied Fair Value of Content
35-14 The implied fair value of goodwill shall be determined in the same manner as the amount of goodwill recognized in a business combination is determined. That is, an entity shall allocate the fair value of a reporting unit to all of the assets and liabilities of that unit (including any unrecognized intangible assets) as if the reporting unit had been acquired in a business combination and the fair value of the reporting unit was the price paid to acquire the reporting unit. [FAS 142, paragraph 21]	The implied value of an enterprise or operations content (Enterprise Content Value—ECV) shall be valued as though the entity was to be acquired, and the acquisition price was to reflect the fair value of the content of the acquired entity.
35-15 The relevant guidance in paragraphs 35–38 of FASB Statement 141, *Business Combinations*, before that Statement's 2007 revision, shall be used in determining how to allocate the fair value of a reporting unit to the assets and liabilities of that unit. Included in that allocation would be research and development assets that meet the criteria in paragraph 350-20-35-39, even if Subtopic 730-10 would require those assets to be written off to earnings when acquired. [FAS 142, paragraph 21]	Fair value of content is to include R&D and unamortized portions of trademarks and copyrights, websites catalogs, blogs, "wikis" as well as computer records, documents, web pages, emails, digital media, or other static digitally stored content.
35-16 The excess of the fair value of a reporting unit over the amounts assigned to its assets and liabilities is the implied fair value of goodwill. [FAS 142, paragraph 21]	Liability Principle: Reduce Value by Recognizing Potential Risk
35-1 Goodwill shall not be amortized. [FAS 142, paragraph 18] Instead, goodwill shall be tested for impairment at a level of reporting referred to as a **reporting unit**. [FAS 142, paragraph 18] (Paragraphs 350-20-35-33 through 35-46 provide guidance on determining reporting units.) [FAS 142, paragraph 18]	Liabilities inherent in enterprise content are to be considered and used to reduce any fair value calculation of content. Included in liabilities are pro forma risks due to regulatory shortcomings (e.g., privacy violations) failure to report consistently (e.g., the cost of corporate professional liability insurance) or potential lawsuits (e.g., from poor maintenance of user or safety manuals or misstatement of product ability). Enterprise content value (ECV) shall not be amortized, but will reflect the amortized amounts of capitalized software applications, hardware, and network equipment. The calculation of ECV is to consider the net effect of the relevance of all types of content to business operations, as well as the need to retrieve, acquire, move, and query all content throughout the organization (e.g., middle ware in addition to networks and servers).

[1]*All FASB statements are from the FASB Codification. Copyright September 2009.*

the business and are made against cash flow associated with business process or intellectual content. Similarly, IP is also valued by the PV of contracted revenue streams, such as a movie or book.

Wall Street focuses on the equity corner of the information balance sheet. In essence, the Wall Street types are examining how organizations manage their data and assigning a point or two to stock valuations. Eventually, this appears on the equity part of the balance sheet. This is indirect, but happening nonetheless.

Income statements should also see the effects from information projects, but in a more direct fashion. Essentially, the direct benefits of information projects should be calculated from a business perspective and be traceable to the "bottom line." "Better access to data" isn't making it to first base, let alone allowing a project to get started. But particular cash flow and benefits can be associated with the enabled business processes and content. Then reductions in expenses or increases in revenue can be tied back to information projects. Accountability for income statement changes is assigned and off you go.

All of the above are techniques currently deployed to somehow get the relevance of content or information stated. Usually, however, these are special situations, where IP is the main asset of an enterprise. Or a large software project has created a material change in income statements. Lastly, information is looked at as part of a merger or sale of an entity.

Basic Inventory Concepts

What if we do not have a special situation that has been addressed above? What if the normal day-to-day spending and benefits from using data and content need to be recognized? Do the Farfel retail or Ubetcha Insurance examples contain a driver for showing business value of data? Not really, but stating the pro forma value of the information assets is still an excellent tool to measure EIM effectiveness.

Doug Laney, a colleague of mine while we worked together at Meta Group, contributed heavily to the concepts in this section. Earlier this book touched on the economics of information. This chapter takes the consideration of value from a business case and extends it as a means of sustaining EIM. Doug and I delved into the means to actually measure the *value of data*.

The FASB sets out and maintains (at least in the United States) principles and guidelines for accounting. FASB bases these standards on a set of GAAP. FASB has addressed information several times, but not to the extent this book has implied. However, we want to accomplish two things in the next few pages:

1. That there is a relevant context to view information and content as an asset from an accounting standpoint, hence, we can measure it to develop a pro forma statement.
2. There is already enough in guidelines in current accounting literature for inventory valuation, and we can derive from these a set of GAIP™[2] that can serve as a foundation for managing and valuing an enterprise's managing data and content.

A cross-reference of asset accounting to information asset accounting is necessary. Table 28.2 cross-references selected existing FASB software and data guidelines with the GAIP™, and will suffice to point out if there is the organizational will; a fiscal view of information can be developed, if not reported. The entire FASB standards document cannot be reproduced here (it is 300 pages or so), but even the more general aspects of balance sheet accounting have applicable GAIP™.

Remember—the GAIPs are for notional reporting only—they are not intended for balance sheets. The GAIPs are inspired by the corresponding FASB statements and GAAP. *They are not official.* Refer to Table 28.4 for the list of GAIPs™.

On occasion we have been able to calculate a pro forma valuation of information and content. Execution of this technique should be done under the following scenarios:

- The EIM team has garnered the confidence of leadership and has matured to the point where the financial contribution of EIM is of interest.
- The EIM team is reviewing the EIM approach and has reached a point where leadership needs to see what the real perception of information is within the organization. This means the EIM team performs this exercise on its own as a means to garner support. We usually use a subjective valuation technique. This is a risky exercise, so check the balance in the political capital account before you go this way.

THE SUBJECTIVE VALUE TECHNIQUE

Table 28.3 will show the results of a sample valuation exercise. You may want to put your thumb on the page or mark it in some fashion so you can flip back and forth. We are doing a subjective assessment: "… reverse-engineering of information's financial value based on its direct or indirect use in generating revenue and reducing risk is tricky at best, but as illustrated can be accomplished. However, the real challenge comes in identifying and tracking the enterprise's inventory of information assets. The fluidity of raw materials and produced goods is glacial compared to the *velocity* of information throughout the layers of applications and databases throughout the organization. The *volume* of information managed by an organization also towers over its quantity of material inventory. And finally, the *variety* of forms information takes in its multitude of oft-redundant sources is much greater than the product and inventory mix of most organizations."[3] This technique is based on a premise that there exists in the organization a set of criteria that can be surveyed and will present a realistic and objective view of what kinds of data and content are valued by the business.

1. Select what assets to track—Extract (from your data model) a list of the major or critical subject areas, or topics of interest. Depending on the enterprise, this may or may not be every subject area. The example in Table 28.3 is a subset of UIC's total enterprise content. A short definition of the subject is included.
2. Determine value criteria—Select the relevant criteria, again unique by enterprise, that determine how data or information is perceived. In many cases there are common criteria, such as correctness or accuracy. Or latency may not be as important to one enterprise as another. Fluidity or volume may also be important.
3. Determine the value basis—Based on the enterprise, determine the basis for calculating value. Typically an income number or free cash is a good start. In the case of our example, UIC, we need to look at reserves and premium numbers.
4. Fill out sheet—Distribute or hold *individual meetings* to have business leaders fill out the matrix. The sample size for this technique does not have to be large. There is not a lot of differentiation once you get below functional or division heads. But do not fill this out in groups. Typically, one of the key findings is that the results are surprising.

Table 28.3 Subjective Value Example

Subject Area of Content or Data	Pro Forma Valuation of Data—Subjective Method										
	Top 10 Highest Values' Content Areas—Goodwill Basis										
	Relevance	Importance	Accuracy	Completeness	History	Volume	Volatility	Latency	Value Total	Weighted Value	Weighted Amount
	Relative importance to your job	Relative contribution to overall business success	Relative importance of accuracy of data to business success	Relative importance of all elements of this content being available	Relative importance of keeping history	Relative amount of events or transactions required to provide useful analysis	Relative effect of changing of values or instances	Relative importance of making this data or content available	Total of all scores	Content value total divided by total all values	Weighted value times the chosen asset basis (Goodwill) (000's)
Claim	5	5	5	4	5	4	4	5	37	7.505%	$157,606
Coverage	4	4	4	4	4	3	2	4	29	5.882%	$123,529
Household	4	3	4	3	4	4	3	4	29	5.882%	$123,529
Loss	4	4	4	4	5	4	4	4	33	6.694%	$140,568
Payment	4	4	4	4	5	4	4	3	32	6.491%	$136,308
Policy	5	5	5	5	4	3	5	4	36	7.302%	$153,347
Policyholder	4	3	4	4	4	3	4	4	30	6.085%	$127,789
Property	3	3	3	4	4	2	4	3	26	5.274%	$110,751
Underwriting	4	4	4	4	4	2	5	3	32	6.491%	$136,308
Reserves	3	3	4	4	5	2	5	3	29	5.882%	$123,529
Criteria total	61	64	61	60	71	54	60	62	493	100.000%	$2,100,000
Subjective value basis (000's)	Organization goodwill $2,100,000										

Table 28.4 Generally Accepted Information Principles™

Principle Name	Description	Remarks
Asset principle	Data and content of all types are assets. Data and content assets have all the characteristics of any other asset. Therefore, they should be managed, secured, and accounted for as other material or financial assets.	There is the concept that data assets do not deplete when "used," e.g., when I read data, it is still there for someone else to read. But this characteristic (that other assets do not have) actually pushes data and content toward requiring even more rigorous accounting, given the risks and costs of duplication and incorrect use. In addition, any debate that "data is not information" is meaningless in this context since business context is the only determinant. All content can be labeled as information, content, or data. All are *assets*.
Value principle	There is value in all data and content, based on its contribution to organizational business/operational objectives, its intrinsic marketability, and/or its contribution to the organization's goodwill (balance sheet) valuation. The value of information is reflective of its contribution to the organization's offset by the cost of maintenance and movement.	This principle acknowledges that there is value in the inventory of information and content within an organization, and that it requires an accounting.
Going concern principle	Data and content is not viewed as a temporary means to achieve results (or merely as a business by-product), but is critical to successful, ongoing business operations and management.	This principle recognizes the role of information as *fuel*, as opposed to the concept of information as a lubricant for business processes.
Due diligence principle	If a risk is known, it must be reported. If a risk is possible, it must be confirmed.	Concealing a potential liability just because it has "always been there" is as bad as not reporting unethical interactions with suppliers or banks.
Risk principle	There is risk associated with data and content. This risk must be formally recognized, either as a liability or through incurring costs to manage and reduce the inherent risk.	Risk management is a normal business function. In IT we manage risk with backup data sites. We do not recognize the risk associated with lost business or higher costs if we lose or mistreat data. We also overlook the considerable risk implied by content and data through inaccuracy and unauthorized use.
Quality principle	The meaning, accuracy, and life cycle of data and content can affect the financial status of an organization.	This principle acknowledges that DQ is important to business success, and is recognized as a high-level principle vs. a requirement for a specific project or initiative.

(Continued)

Table 28.4 (Continued)

Principle Name	Description	Remarks
Audit principle	The accuracy of data and content is subject to periodic audit by an independent body.	If DQ is an enterprise principle, it is therefore subject to verification.
Accountability principle	An organization must identify individuals who are ultimately accountable for data and content of all types.	Accountability means ultimate responsibility. Every type and occurrence of content must have a party designated that is ultimately accountable for management of the asset.
Liability principle	The risks in information means there is a financial liability inherent in all data or content, based on regulatory and ethical misuse or mismanagement.	This principle recognizes the need to account for contingent risk buried in data and content if you have not invested in a means to eliminate the risk.

5. Do the math—Tally the results by individual sheets as well as in aggregate. Usually you will see a wide range of priorities, which should not be news. But you will also see that certain subject areas where the "squeaky wheels" are demanding data are not the ones most relevant.
6. Allocate the value—Divide the aggregate scores by subject into the value basis. What you have is a subjective view of how information contributes to a view of organization value. If possible, contrast this to goodwill and the balance sheet values for capital spending in IT. The subjective value should come in between the two.

SUMMARY

Management and measurement go hand in hand. Managing information assets means some sort of metrics must exist. This chapter presented a list of metrics and ideas. There are many more metrics possible as there are information assets to measure.

There is a new realm of "information accounting" slowly developing that will remove information assets out of the realm of the abstract and fluffy accountability and place it into serious business context. (See Table 28.4 for the current list of GAIPs™ we use.) The need to produce proof of EIM effectiveness will create an expectation of measurement anyway. So there is really no intellectual excuse to avoid developing some type of proactive metrics and even a business valuation of information in an organization.

References

1. Hubbard, D. (2007). *How to Measure Anything*. Hoboken, NJ: John Wiley and Sons, Chapter 1, p. 3.
2. GAIP™. (2009). IMCue Solutions.
3. All FASB statements are from the FASB Codification. Copyright September 2009.

Down the Road

29

A common mistake that people make when trying to design something completely foolproof is to underestimate the ingenuity of complete fools.
Douglas Adams

CONTENTS

There will always be adjustments with EIM. Like any other established program or function, it must flex with changes in business climate. The artifacts and architectural elements are all based on business drivers, so flexibility is built in, but that does not mean the EIM components change by themselves. There needs to be recognition of events or changes (e.g., a merger, a new regulation) and then a formal effort to ensure sustainability of EIM. There is also the need to revisit the program and make ordinary adjustments. For example, if your EIM program is approached with a mind-set of minimal incremental cost increase, you want to ensure you are staying in the boundaries.

TIPS FOR SUCCESS

I cannot find words to express the depth of demoralization that starting EIM and not sustaining it causes among the involved parties. Within IT the "we told you so" contingent comes back into power as the EIM teams' ability to enforce governance declines. And even though it is irrational (and flat-out wrong), resistance to standards is

(Continued)

Making Enterprise Information Management (EIM) Work for Business. DOI: 10.1016/B978-0-12-375695-4.00029-1

> **TIPS FOR SUCCESS (Continued)**
>
> justified once again by the "get something done" mantra. Moreover, business sponsors, content owners, and stewards are disheartened and will move to refresh any lost political capital. Lastly, the executive team gets a black eye for rooting for a cause and then backing off. Again, if you want to do EIM in any of its flavors, it is a one-way valve. Going back to the old state is not really an option.
>
> Two processes or events come to light as the EIM program trundles forward. Business changes, technology updates, and cultural barriers all create the need to periodically refresh the Road Map. Second, IMM will improve. This results in new flavors of IAM, and possible new additions to the program. This chapter explains these two scenarios and covers the steps to modify the EIM program.

PERIODIC ROAD MAP REFRESH

Over the years, we have seen a common behavior where the elements and building blocks of EIM are in use: they run out of gas or fade into oblivion. Usually, normal business events divert the attention of EIM teams, then priorities change, and it is hard to get back to the "program." Culture barriers may become more difficult than anticipated, and the organization's will is diverted to other endeavors. Scheduling normal refreshing of the Road Map (and accompanying Sustaining Requirements) is required to maintain the EIM program energy. Chapters 13 and 14 presented the executive view of this activity. A normal planned visitation of the EIM strategy, without a change in business environment, means at minimum the EIM team needs to consider the Road Map from three major perspectives, Business Alignment, Sustaining Requirements, and Architecture Element changes.

Revisiting Business Alignment

At regular intervals (hopefully annually) or as required, the EIM team will get the go ahead to refresh the Road Map. The EIM team should be receiving feedback and metrics on program effectiveness. Business Alignment review is very important, as budget changes and Road Map priorities may be implied. The process to do this is no different than the initial process of aligning EIM to the business, just shorter. Often business directions become manifest in annual lists of "strategic projects" or "approved initiatives." The EIM team needs to review these as closely as broad announcements of direction and strategy. An overview of this is in Chapter 13.

Sustaining Requirements

After a period of time, battle lines will be drawn as to which areas are going to strongly resist EIM and those that will accommodate required behavior changes. You will also know if incentives are working (the WIIFM aspect). Lastly, part of EIM effectiveness is evaluation of feedback via a change management survey. The net result of these inputs will be revisions to the Sustaining plan. Specifically, you may have to revise:

- Communications
  - *Methods and events*—A common error is to stop having orientation events. Also broadcasts like newsletters or web sites are not kept up to date. Make sure that communication methods are received well, up to date, and relevant. It is perfectly OK to repeat sessions, in fact, it will be mandatory.

- *Branding*—Does the EIM still have a "brand" that is effective, i.e., does it invoke a feeling of a valid enterprise effort, or is the mere mention of EIM cause for raised eyebrows or squirming in seats? Modify the branding if necessary.
  - *Visibility of sponsorship*—Is your sponsor still "walking the talk?" Ensure that the sponsor still carries enough weight, and has been making the required appearances.
- Training
  - *Education*—If education is not working, revise the approach, or simply repeat the sessions. Often feigned ignorance is a form of passive resistance. Often, material needs to be modified to address different audiences, so there may well be multiple version of the same class.
  - *Orientation*—Orientation is *not* education. It serves only to inform areas that are not yet intimately involved with EIM. Make sure you are not orienting when you should be educating, or vice versa.
- Resistance interactions
  - *Revised WIIFM*—Revise incentives as needed, to reflect EIM success or address new forms of resistance.
  - *Disciplinary actions*—Sadly, any large enterprise will encounter individuals who require career-altering intervention. If this appears to be the case, incorporate HR into the revised Sustaining processes.
  - *One-on-one*—Do not hesitate to sit down across the table with managers or executives and talk through concerns and misunderstandings.

TIP FOR SUCCESS

Do not be demoralized when, after two or three sessions or multiple road shows, middle management still does not "get it." This is normal. Adult learning theory teaches us that it may take as many as six interactions for an adult to grasp a new concept. So be patient.

Architecture Element Changes

There will always be some sort of pressure to alter the technology or other elements in the EIM program. Business needs may require improved throughput due to volume of data. Or latency may have to decrease as an organization matures to go from once-a-month analysis to daily or even real-time reporting of business changes. It is not at all uncommon for an enterprise indicator to move from monthly to real-time requirements in the span of a year. Regulators may force a company to manage e-mail much sooner than planned. These are obvious changes, and will manifest in changes in Business Alignment and levers, as well as changes in the models.

Other elements will also need to change. If you have embarked upon designing IVCs as a means to understand business process changes, then there will be a continuous flow of new ideas as EIM matures information assets.

Finally, at some point social networking will appear as a challenge or opportunity. EIM must be alert for all the possible flows of social traffic. Table 29.1 illustrates this is not a single dimension challenge. EIM will need to consult with HR and compliance areas to develop policies on protocols, permissions, and use of these technologies.

The entire list for executing EIM phases and activities adjustment based on these three perspectives is shown in Table 29.2. Table 29.3 shows a more specialized list for adding new types of elements as EIM matures the organization.

Table 29.1 Social Traffic Directions

Social Network Considerations	
External communication and networking, outbound	Internal communications and networking, intra departmental
Example: Do we need to filter content if (for some reason) we allow Twitter™ on internal PCs?	Example: Is a Facebook™ metaphor appropriate for collaboration or is a more robust mechanism like SharePoint suitable?
External communications and networking, inbound	Internal communications and networking, inter departmental/business unit
Example: Does our business culture agree it is ethical to scan the web for consumer preferences?	Example: Can collaboration shorten cycle times to get products to market?

Table 29.2 EIM Refresh Activity Summary

EIM Program Refresh and Maintenance Activity Summary			
Phase	**Activity**	**Purpose**	**Output/Remarks**
Initiation	EIM Vision and Scope	Ensure changes have not affected EIM span	Revised Vision and Scope
	Definition of EIM and Mission	Ensure changes have not affected EIM Mission	Revised Mission; revisit with compliance area to check on new regulations or recent penalties
	EIM Specific Tasks	Revisit phases and call out required activities and deliverables	EIM refresh plan, note that activities will be combined and adjusted as required
	EIM Team	Adjust team if required	EIM Team
	EIM Steering Body	Adjust EIM leadership if required	EIM leadership
Assessments	Information Maturity/ Data and Content Quality/Business Readiness	Reassess IMM by applying EIM Metrics and reassessing other areas as required	If metrics are not regularly collected, then the ad hoc process begins to gather agreed-upon metrics for evaluation. Metrics need to be verified and checked for reasonableness and root-cause analysis done to determine cause of unexpected measurements. Metrics and reassessments are presented to EIM leadership
			Assuming root causes are determined, then a subteam should recommend additional EIM oversight, project modifications, or organization programs
Alignment	Business Discovery/ Business Alignment	Ensure business is receiving benefits, and incorporate adjustments to business plans	Business plan updates; also consider if *current* Road Map projects are making a contribution to EIM progress

(Continued)

Table 29.2 (Continued)

	EIM Program Refresh and Maintenance Activity Summary		
Phase	**Activity**	**Purpose**	**Output/Remarks**
	Business Information Levers	Look for new levers that may create need to revise or new EIM elements	Revised Information Levers
Vision	Preliminary BIR/ Preliminary Business Model	Determine if new business plans and/ or levers alter the BIR/ Business Model artifacts	Modified BIR/Business Model
Business Model	Refined Business Model/Business Metrics and BIR Model	Modify BIR and Metrics and data/process models as required	Refined BIR and Metrics Models; refined data and process models
	Detailed Scenarios/ Usage	Create and approve new IVC scenarios if required	New/refined scenarios and actions where managed content can add value
	Preliminary Information Taxonomy	Revisit or create taxonomy if unstructured content is coming underneath EIM activities	Revised/new taxonomy; as discussed earlier, often the taxonomy details and Content Management occur later in EIM programs' life
Architectures	Info Application Frameworks	Revise data and content life-cycle frameworks	Refined Application elements, e.g., MDM, reporting, BI, Document Management
	Business Data Management	Refine policies and procedures as needed	Refined policies and procedures; revise stewardship and accountability
	Data Governance Architecture	Revise Data Governance approach as needed	Revised DG processes or DG "style"
	Info Value Chain Architecture	Refined IVCs	Detailed use cases and scenarios for new levers
	Data Quality/Detailed Taxonomy/Enterprise Metrics/Community Social Network Architectures	Revise artifacts as required	Updated taxonomies, DQ processes, and redefined communities
Road Map	Applications Road Map	Reissue sequence, business, and supporting project definitions	Revised and approved Applications Road Map
	Sustaining requirements/EIM Organization/Data Governance Roll Out	Identify opportunities to modify Change Management and strengthen EIM program	Revised Change Management plan; revised EIM Organization and DG operations
Sustaining	Organization Roll Out/ Sustaining activity/ Data Governance Roll Out/EIM Project Management	Incorporate new Road Map and other changes into day-to-day activities	Refreshed EIM program

Table 29.3 New Elements to EIM

Phase	Activity	Purpose	Output/Remarks
Business Model	Detailed Scenarios/ Usage	Define nature of using "KM," unstructured content, and other concepts	Demonstrate to business areas the scenario promising the potential benefits
	BIR Model	List unstructured/ structured contents required to fulfill KM and other new scenarios	New BIR and content requirements—update the Metric/ BIR Models
	Preliminary Taxonomy	Assuming one is not available, develop the first pass	Preliminary Enterprise Taxonomy; it is perfectly OK to choose and modify a standard taxonomy (like Dublin Core)
Architectures	Community/Social Network Architecture	Specify collaborative/ knowledge communities	New communities and content usage
	Info Application Frameworks	Revise data and content life-cycle frameworks to include new content and ascribe meaning	Refined Application elements, e.g., Document Management, collaborative environments
	Business Data Management	Refine policies and procedures as needed	New content will require refined policies and procedures, and revised stewardship and accountability
	Data Governance Architecture	Revise Data Governance approach as needed	Revised DG processes for new content types
	Info Value Chain Architecture	Refined IVCs	Detailed use cases and scenarios for new content and related levers
	Detailed Taxonomy	Revise artifacts as required	Updated taxonomies
	Data Quality Architecture	Update processes to ensure controls and quality of content	Revise DQ approach

IMPROVEMENT IN IMM

The enterprise will get more comfortable with formerly managed data and content. This has happened many times since the mid-1990s when BI began to anchor itself in the mind-set of organizations. There is also an expectation now that there is always some degree of management of data in organizations that have been placed under severe regulatory scrutiny, e.g., brokerage and investments. Also new content will start to surface for EIM to manage, and terms like collaboration and "knowledge" will start to appear.

Very often some aspect of EIM (such as data quality) will have a better appeal than another, e.g., data governance. When this happens focus on the more appealing segment of the program. The minute data quality efforts demonstrate value you will also say "but data governance had a role in this as well."

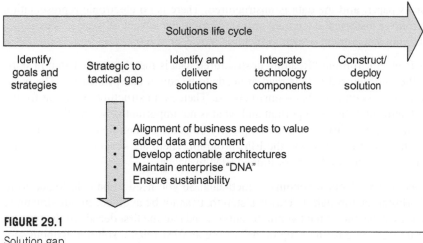

FIGURE 29.1

Solution gap

New Organization Behaviors

The attitude of business divisions will change the longer EIM is sustainable. At worse they will ask for their own copies of managed data (for performance reasons). Often, they will subliminally compete as to who does the best analysis, or who handles data more effectively. You will find that the convergence that we had to force will occur naturally. The mysterious gap between business needs and IT projects is closed (see Figure 29.1).

New Elements for EIM

The largest area of change will be the introduction of documents and other unstructured content to EIM. This will mean the EIM team will need to identify new technologies. It may also mean the EIM team itself will need to incorporate new staff that is trained on these technologies. The common error is to continue to separate robust content management from EIM—there will be an inevitable clash of architectures and standards. In addition, the enterprise will miss enormous opportunities to create communities that can leverage both kinds of content (structured and unstructured). This area goes beyond the obvious areas of e-mail and correspondence. It is challenging. Most enterprise content is in *this* category, not the "rows and columns" of data we spend so much time manipulating and storing. In his column on December 21, 2004, William McCrosky presents a nice view of the unstructured data spectrum.[1]

1. "The source document is paper, not electronic. Insurance, medical, and HR forms are often paper-based. Note that the data of interest, in this case, is reasonably structured. Its position on the source document can be spatially located.
2. The source document is structured—as in example 1—but it is already in an electronic form. A web technology such as XML may be used.
3. The source document is electronic, but the data of interest is not structured. E-mail and word processing documents fall into this category.

4. The source document is paper, and the data is unstructured. There is no electronic representation of the document—perhaps a historical document prepared before the advent of word processing.

5. The source is a "blob," not a document—such as pictures, voice, or video."

Another view comes from Bill Inmon: "Reading unstructured data is merely the first step in starting to filter it out. After the unstructured data is read, it needs to be edited and prioritized. The problem is that the unstructured data is exactly that—unstructured. There is no structure or format for the data; therefore, getting a handle on what is important and what is not important is no small feat."[2]

These two excerpts point out the difficulty and complexity on getting a handle on how to look at what is important within the new content facing the EIM program. There are several technology elements that must be considered, even by a business-trained EIM manager.

- *Enterprise DNA, or metadata*—Your taxonomy *is* metadata. So you need to be able to access it, navigate with it, and administer through it. This is a step that cannot be avoided. In our structured data world of the decades at the end of the twentieth century, and into the first decade of the twenty-first century, most of us were able to sneak up on delivering an EIM-related solution without substantial (if any) metadata. Unstructured content demands organized metadata.

- *Ontology*—A new big word with a simple meaning is ontology. It describes the rules and views of the taxonomy. Think of taxonomy as a hierarchical logical model, and the ontology more as logical tables or networks, like views into the taxonomy—crude but gets you there. Alternatively, an ontology is a way to organize taxonomies (and other expressions of data relationships "an ontology is a formal way to organize knowledge and terms). Typically, ontologies are represented as graphical relationships or networks, as opposed to taxonomies which are usually represented hierarchically."[3] An example would be to find cabernet in a query. The ontology would know that cabernet is a type of wine as well.

- *Content acquisition*—Regardless of how it is viewed and arranged, content is the "stuff" that is read.

- *Parse*—No matter what tool or approach, at some point, unstructured content will need to be chopped up into bits to be presented, summarized, or analyzed.

- *Tag or ascribe*—Content still needs to have meaning and context. Software called semantic engines combine taxonomy and ontology into an expression of context. Or to wax philosophical, "meaning" vs. definition. Whether the meaning is extracted out of the data and stored as structure, or the content is tagged in some meaningful way is irrelevant. All unstructured content needs to be examined and have some context assigned.

- *Management of unstructured content*—Like any other content to be managed, there are basic technology functions required, but they are made quirky due to the nature of the content.

- *Memory and storage*—Most likely unstructured content will occupy *lots* more disk and *lots* require more memory.

- *Community management*—If the EIM program has not addressed communities earlier, it is now mandatory. Content is useless unless it can be moved about and shared to fulfill a purpose. Determining who can collaborate, view, and share is a function of business needs, cross-functional process design, and regulatory governance.

- *Content management*—Loading, tracking, and storing with a good address, index, and viewing platform is mandatory. Your requirements may or may not go beyond the capability of some content management software.

- *View and use*—Invariably, you might say "there is a fact in this document" and another party will say "Fine—show me the document *and* the fact." Therefore, query tools and reporting will take on combining unstructured content with traditional "rows and columns."
- Do not forget to consider collaborative mechanisms such as SharePoint, or Wiki and Blog technology. All will produce content requiring oversight of value, cost, and management of risk.

Inevitably, the term KM will surface in the realm of IAM and especially when the unstructured content enters the picture. META group defined knowledge management as "… a discipline that promotes an integrated and collaborative approach to the process of information asset creation, capture, organization, access, and use. Information assets include databases, documents and, most importantly, the uncaptured, tacit expertise and experience resident in individual workers …" Most of this definition sounds like IAM, except for the whole tacit, uncaptured part. Except for a brief flurry between 1998 and 2004, KM is not a high-priority subdiscipline of IAM. There are certainly practical applications of "knowledge management," and in fact, the taxonomy presented for Farfel in our sample outputs is from the Dublin Core[4]—a KM taxonomy.

While this and the many other definitions of KM lead us to understand the concept, KM remains in the realm of "I'll tell you what it is when I see it" for many enterprises. Knowledge appears to be at the far end of some exotic value chains, i.e., we go from data to information to knowledge, but that, like other metaphors we have covered, doesn't do much to help us actually *manage* knowledge. The real perception is knowledge is perceived to live only between people's ears.

In reality, KM is different by organization. When KM begins to appear in the organization lexicon, the EIM team needs to consider what is meant by KM. Most of the time, what is perceived as a knowledge issue is a logistics issue, e.g., someone needed some information at some point in time and did not have it. We address that with IAM and the information scenarios and value chains. The real knowledge—the capture of tacit experience, or explicit conclusions to be viewed at a later date—is still missing.

What we can capture, and I suppose we can call it a form of KM, is *how* people are using information and content. We mentioned this earlier as "Collaborative Intelligence," or the measurement of how people work and collaborate. As this book is being developed, a range of new products are entering the business market with the ability to "observe" how data is gathered, assembled, and used. They all feature built-in metrics to report on workflow effectiveness. In this manner, we can see what, or who, is effective. Then we can train the remainder of the organization to act as the more effective individuals.

Regardless of the source of new elements, the EIM team needs to define what the real intent is when the term "knowledge management," "collaborative," or "workflow" appears. Then their activity should focus on the Taxonomy, Community/Social Network, and IVC activities.

Table 29.3 shows a short list of specialized activity for addressing the new elements of IAM.

SUMMARY

After the EIM program is up and running, you will be looking for some changes. The metrics from Chapter 28 may point out the need for adjustments, as will feedback from your EIM team or a change management team. Or it will be simply time to revisit the program, as with any other program, to ensure value, manage costs, and adjust budgets.

The entire enterprise will be moving from some old characteristics. Based on the last few chapters, the old to new state process will exhibit some or all of the following.

Old State

- Departmental IM, silos
- Project-level IM
- Limited enterprise visibility of architecture or models
- Proposals for and initial projects to integrate data, or centrally manage documents
- Some standard navigation or access for web or tools.

Middle Transition State

- Access to data and content standardized
- Data quality program under way
- New projects that avoid silo mentality
- Development of DNA and inventory of content
- Initial changes for information asset accountability: owners and stewardship.

New State

- Enterprise info visibility: Business measures, BIRs, architecture
- EIM looking at enterprise process models
- New content, knowledge, and collaboration are part of EIM
- Navigation standardized, communities defined
- Enterprise DNA (metadata) deployed
- Measurement of collaborative intelligence, workflow effectiveness
- Information accountability built into individual performance goals.

The EIM team needs to be aware of and plan to make changes in the program as the business matures and changes.

References

1. McCrosky, W. (2004, December). Unstructured data. *DM Review/Information Management Review*.
2. Inmon, W. H. (2004, December). *DM Review Magazine*.
3. Hoberman, S. (2008, May). Ontology and taxonomy design challenge. *Information Management Magazine*.
4. Definition and References for "Dublin Core" as found on Wikipedia: http://en.wikipedia.org/wiki/Dublin_Core.

Final Word

I may not have gone where I intended to go, but I think I have ended up where I intended to be.
Douglas Adams

CONTENTS

EIM BUILDING BLOCKS REDUX

Part 1 has its own summary chapter. Feel free to flip back and read it. There are three success factors and five concepts mentioned for leadership. They are good items to keep close.

This book has been pretty firm on the stance that all of your data and content is an asset (or liability) and you need to formally manage it. "Formal" means a suitable set of standards, policies, and governance to ensure that the business stays aligned with value-added use of data and content.

This chapter will wrap up Part 2. I assume you understand that IAM addresses all the categories of content an enterprise can use. The process in Part 2 sets up a process to design and maintain the asset management program. Besides addressing inhibitors to prior success with information projects, the EIM program strives to improve the business, as measured by the balance sheet or income statement.

Making Enterprise Information Management (EIM) Work for Business. DOI: 10.1016/B978-0-12-375695-4.00030-8

There are many books that address the elements of EIM. So we did not go into the details where someone else has already published advice. We focused on the program and the business benefits. To review Part 2, we will review the positive aspects provided by an EIM program. At some time, the EIM program will be challenged. Even if there is no challenge to the business viability of EIM, the various building blocks may give the impression of EIM being too encompassing but there are logical connections between EIM and all of the building blocks that contribute to EIM.

Business Model

EIM supports all aspects of the business. Where there is data or content, EIM is there. EIM does not change business strategy, it mirrors it. EIM strives to identify where data and content can improve business processes, and provide oversight of all content in the organization.

EIM needs to understand the Business Model to align with what the business needs to support business goals.

Data governance becomes part of the Business Model. It is not intrusive; it is a new business function.

EIM makes sure that business needs and the Business Model are respected, but change needs to happen.

Information Handling and Use

EIM ensures efficient, appropriate movement and access, and ensures efficiency and enabling of business processes. The incremental implementation, but global vision of the handling of information, is handled to ensure economical placement of content for right place and right time.

Information Life Cycle

Data has a life cycle that touches all parts of an enterprise, not just specific processes. While identifying opportunities to exploit data, EIM must also balance data risk and data leverage.

Applications

EIM ensures that there are no "local" EIM policies, only local applications. Business needs are met, but the mistakes and excessive costs of the past are avoided through oversight of applications development and information use. The Road Map phase supplies incremental applications that can add value but be managed with minimal risk.

There are no "technology projects" that cause loss of interest. There are business projects.

Technology

The EIM program coordinates with the Enterprise Architecture area to ensure technology supports the business and the technology investments are being aligned.

Organization

EIM is able to understand that all areas may be affected by EIM, but in a positive way. EIM helps design appropriate organizations and manage organizational changes incrementally, and helps organizations manage application changes for business areas. EIM also creates a new organization that ensures inventory management for data.

Compliance

EIM integrates legal, compliance, regulations, and data governance to provide deeper insight into the risk that is buried in data and content. Compliance areas can be leveraged to assist EIM and data governance.

Enterprise "DNA"

Managing information assets means oversight of the definitions, lineage, usage, and administration of the various assets covered by EIM. The EIM team will call the DNA metadata. The maintenance administration of good metadata ties the EIM Architecture together. Data governance ensures metadata is maintained and used.

Culture

EIM reveals to the enterprise how things get done in regards to data and content. While cultures must, to some extent, change, EIM attempts to leverage culture during the change process. The changes brought by EIM create resistance that must be managed.

Governance

The EIM program uses data governance to keep IT activity aligned with business needs. Data governance also provides for enforcing standards. Data governance creates rules for how and where data moves. Data governance is the compliance building block of EIM.

Managed Content

IAM states that all content is eligible. If your organization is balanced on information as fuel vs. lubricant, the EIM finds the correct mix of Information Maturity. EIM manages integration while doing the work that has to be done.

There is content in departments and remote offices. EIM manages this content as well to ensure the organization does not incur risk.

SUMMARY

I hope that this book has helped. Through examples, stories, or processes, there is hopefully something that anyone remotely connected with EIM can use. Remember, as long as EIM oversight is here, the increments can fit any situation.

Thank you for your time and attention. I hope it adds value in its usage the same way your organization will increase value through usage of its own data and content.

If there are any questions, thoughts, feedback, war stories, ideas, tips, or artifacts to share, let others know at http://www.eimforbusiness.com, and contribute to the blog or wiki.

Initiation Phase Summary and Work Products

This appendix provides the details for the Initiation phase, including activities, tasks, deliverables, references to sample output in the text, and relevant blank template(s).

INITIATION ACTIVITY WORK PRODUCT OVERVIEW (TABLE A.1)

Table A.1 Initiation Work Product Overview

Activity	Tasks	Outputs (Work Products)	Activity Deliverable
EIM Vision and Scope	Schedule scope and vision review session	EIM scope and vision session(s)	EIM vision and scope presentation
	Develop straw person vision and scope	Notional vision of EIM	
	Refine and finalize vision and scope	Business Model scope and constraints	
	Agree on definition of enterprise	Definition of enterprise	
	Identify source documents	Initial list of source documents and data	
Definition of EIM and Mission	Define IAM for enterprise	Definition of EIM/IAM philosophy	EIM definition and mission
	List possible EIM measures	EIM success measures	
	Develop EIM mission and value statement	EIM mission statement/value proposition	
	Develop straw person EIM definition	EIM definition	
	Build EIM elevator speech	EIM elevator speech	

(Continued)

Making Enterprise Information Management (EIM) Work for Business. DOI: 10.1016/B978-0-12-375695-4.0036-9

Table A.1 (Continued)

Activity	Tasks	Outputs (Work Products)	Activity Deliverable
EIM Specific Tasks	Review EIM phases for required activities and tasks	EIM program process tasks	EIM program design/restore plan
	Conduct SWOT analysis	EIM SWOT analysis	
	Define EIM tasks	EIM process activities and tasks	
Define Required Assessments	List recommended assessment and justification		EIM assessment approach
	Review assessments with EIM sponsor		
	Obtain approval and/or adjust assessment approach	Assessment list	
	Define final assessment list and adjust EIM tasks	Assessment task detail	
Standard Start-Up Tasks	Review enterprise methods	Standard enterprise project tasks	EIM program design/restore plan
	Incorporate enterprise project standards into EIM program development plans	EIM project library and resources	
EIM Team	List possible EIM team members	Nominate EIM team members	EIM team and stakeholder list
	Obtain team approval and commitment	Approved and oriented team members	
	List all EIM stakeholders and participants outside of team	Initial list of stakeholders and participants	
EIM Steering Body	Identify relevant leadership structure for enterprise EIM program	EIM steering structure	EIM leadership and roles
	Identify and appoint EIM sponsor	EIM executive sponsor	
	Identify and appoint EIM steering body	EIM executive steering body (if required)	
	Prepare EIM leader orientation material	EIM general steering body	
	Notify and orient EIM leadership	EIM role definition and orientation	

INITIATION TEMPLATES
Overall EIM Program Development Work Breakdown Structure (Table A.2)

Table A.2 EIM Program Development Work Breakdown Structure

Phase	Activity	Tasks
Initiation	EIM Vision and Scope	Schedule scope and vision review session Develop straw person vision and scope Refine and finalize vision and scope Agree on definition of enterprise Identify source documents
	Definition of EIM and Mission	Define IAM for enterprise List possible EIM measures Develop EIM mission and value statement Develop straw person EIM definition Build EIM elevator speech
	EIM Specific Tasks	Review EIM phases for required activities and tasks Conduct SWOT analysis Define EIM tasks
	Define Required Assessments	List recommended assessment and justification Review assessments with EIM sponsor Obtain approval and/or adjust assessment approach Define final assessment list and adjust EIM tasks
	Standard Start-Up Tasks	Review enterprise methods Incorporate enterprise project standards into EIM program development plans
	EIM Team	List possible EIM team members Obtain team approval and commitment List all EIM stakeholders and participants outside of team
	EIM Steering Body	Identify relevant leadership structure for enterprise EIM program Identify and appoint EIM sponsor Identify and appoint EIM steering body Prepare EIM leader orientation material Notify and orient EIM leadership
Assessment	Information Maturity	Determine scope of survey instrument Select or develop a maturity scale Identify all participants by name and group Orient respondents on importance and anonymity Agree on survey delivery (online, written, group focus) Review and modify maturity template Produce final form for delivery Deploy survey instrument Monitor online survey

(Continued)

Table A.2 (Continued)

Phase	Activity	Tasks
		Distribute and monitor written version
		Prepare and deliver focus session(s)
		Collect and evaluate data
		Derive maturity score based on selected scale
		Collect existing standards, procedures, and policies for information management, information, resource utilization, prioritization, and controls, and map to IMM scale
		Prepare findings for presentation
	Change Capacity	Determine the formality of the assessment. That is an informal structured meeting format, or a formal survey instrument
		Determine the target audience
		Define the survey population or interviewees
		Define the approach—e.g., structured meeting, written or online
		Administer the survey or conduct meetings
		Analyze and summarize findings
		Determine if additional investigation is required
		Determine leadership alignment to EIM
		Determine leadership commitment to EIM
		Determine what will be reported now vs. sent to the EIM team to use during subsequent phases
		Prepare Change Capacity report
	Business Readiness	Determine specific expression of Readiness appropriate for the enterprise level of detail, does it include:
		Information
		Technology
		People/organization
		Operations
		Alignment
		Governance
		Risk/compliance
		Assess the availability of the information needed for analysis
		Gather data from all source and review
		Record business strategies, goals, and objectives
		Examine decision-making maturity of the various forums or units
		Examine how and where business performance measuring occurs; ad hoc, reports, BI
		Document the alignment of business to current DW BI or other projects
		Determine if there is substantial reporting and analytics activity outside of IT and proposed future development
		Document project management processes and results
		Prepare Business Readiness presentation

Table A.2 (Continued)

Phase	Activity	Tasks
	Data Content and Quality	Identify data groups for assessment
		Identify major groups for assessment
		Compile inventory of known sources to analyze
		Review source data issues
		Identify known problems of low DQ
		Prioritize areas to survey
		Establish DQ objectives and measures
		Determine the specific assessment objectives or goals
		Identify quality characteristics to be reviewed
		Determine specific measures of the information
		Determine the minimum DQ required for successful execution of the most significant process requiring the data
		Determine files or processes to assess
		Identify location of data and content to assess
		Determine measurement technique
		Identify data validation sources for accuracy assessment
		Identify most authoritative source of data from which to access the accuracy of data
		Verify the accuracy of the surrogate source being considered
		Extract samples of data
		Review source system files
		Determine sampling technique (if any) for identified files
		Extract samples of data
		Measure DQ
		Analyze data for business rule conformance
		Audit primary and secondary key cardinality
		Audit domains and values
		Map to quality criteria list
		Identify cost of quality estimates
		Interpret and report DQ
		Determine root causes of DQ issues
		Compile final DQ assessment report
		Develop business impact statement for DQ
		Deliver DQ assessment report
	Collaborative Readiness	Determine assessment scope, e.g., does it include:
		Web sites and content
		Documents and sharing
		Identifying existing communities of practice or interest
		Workflow
		Collaborative products

(Continued)

Table A.2 (Continued)

Phase	Activity	Tasks
		Contemporary facilities like instant messaging, texting, Twitter™, or Facebook™
		Determine scope of survey instrument
		Determine assessment approach—interviews, document review, or survey, or combination
		Collect existing standards, procedures, and policies for document sharing, workflow, internal wikis, blogs, etc. for review
		Collect inventory of SharePoint, Notes, or other work-share facilities
		Identify all participants by name and group if necessary
		Orient respondents on importance and anonymity
		Identify interview of focus group participants if necessary
		Produce final form for delivery
		Deploy survey instrument
		Monitor online survey
		Distribute and monitor written version
		Prepare and deliver focus session(s)
		Collect and evaluate data from surveys, documents, and meetings
		Develop Collaborative Readiness statement based on predetermined scale
		Prepare findings for presentation
Alignment	Business Discovery	Review business documents, earlier findings
		Develop a list of known business challenges, problems, and potential opportunities
		Turn challenges and opportunities into business directions
		Confirm future relevance of goals and objectives
		Confirm measures of goals and objectives
		Clarify possible EIM role in achieving business goals
		Ensure each goal or objective is measurable
	Business Information Levers	Build the usage/value work sheets
		Value lever sheet, if needed
		Information lever sheet
		Schedule an internal EIM team meeting with selected subject experts
		Fill-out the matrix, looking at each cell
		Review the results with business personnel external to EIM team
		Modify, then present results to an executive or two, if they are available
	Business Alignment	Determine the business context to present levers
		Schedule facilitated session with business leaders or SMEs
		Capture business benefit results in the session, or refine results after presenting them
		Create value statements of interaction of data and business goals
		Publish results to the EIM team and/or steering committee

(Continued)

Table A.2 (Continued)

Phase	Activity	Tasks
	Preliminary Business Case	Determine required level of detail for the preliminary case
		Associate levers and business view with measurable goals and objectives
		Identity the financial changes planned if business goals and benefits are attained
		Associate a pro forma or notional financial benefit with each information lever, or value statement
		Review benefits with a financial analyst, identify a method to show an ROI in EIM
		Review these preliminary results with the EIM steering body
Vision	Business EIM Vision	Define the presentation style of the vision
		Acquire writer or artist if not on the team
		Iterate through several drafts of the vision
		Present and approve to EIM team and steering body
	Preliminary Business Information Requirements	Gather information levers and examine required content to enable them
		Gather measures for objectives and develop initial list of enterprise metrics
		Incorporate standard metric from your industry
		Look at value/information lever statements and extract any new categories of data or content required
		Examine significant business events and activities for content affecting risk—such as safety, regulated products, rate filings, and so on
		Examine backlogs of report requests, web site updates, and requisitions for external data
		Develop a classification scheme as to the origin of each requirement
		Refine alignment
		Take BIR coming from prior activity in EIM and verify the associated business goal/objective
		Take BIRs that were uncovered in this activity and tie them to business goals/objectives
		Build a facility to hold and cross-reference the BIRs
		Assign and organize findings by the classification scheme
	Preliminary Business Model	Gather existing artifacts, such as data or process models
		Determine level of detail to drive the Preliminary models
		Define acceptable level of presentation for models, based on tools and current state
		Develop or refine a conceptual data model
		Develop or refine a process model reflecting known activities from levers and usage

(Continued)

Table A.2 (Continued)

Phase	Activity	Tasks
		Incorporate results into existing tools or prepare for presentation and use in subsequent steps
	EIM Business Case	Fully understand and define business benefits
		Isolate information usage/value enablers and processes
		Identify/confirm business benefits that are possible—reduce the high-level numbers into benefits for specific instances of lever, value/usage or process
		Describe specific benefits, costs, and/or "at risk"—look for risk across the three risk types—regulatory, civil, and financial
		Define relevant EIM benefit categories risk management (e.g., regulatory, civil, and so on), business return, or business efficiency
		Identify potential cash flows
		Examine current costs of IT and other information-related costs (we will revise the cost numbers in the Road Map phase)
		Apply the various financial benefits and the costs to whatever model we have selected
Business Model	Refined Business Models	Gather existing artifacts, such as data or process models if they do not already exist from the Preliminary activity
		Determine level of detail to drive the final business models
		Define acceptable level of presentation for models, based on tools and current state
		Develop or refine a conceptual data model from the metrics and/or BIR findings
		Schedule facilitated sessions to walk through the various levers and usage to identify business actions and possible new process models (new IVCs)
		(Trigger the Detailed Scenario/Usage activity) to decompose the value chains to identify areas where new or revised business actions can occur using managed data
		Develop or refine Business Models reflecting known activities from levers and usage (and value chain results) from Detailed Scenario activity
		Incorporate results into existing tools or prepare for presentation and use in subsequent steps
	Business Metrics and BIR Model	Gather metrics and indicators
		Identify industry metrics (if not done yet)
		Create measure sheets or records, one per measure and/or BIR
		Determine level of review or walk-through to verify/fill out the metrics and BIR material
		Fill out template for workshops if required
		Confirm workshop sessions with predetermined stakeholders

(Continued)

Table A.2 (Continued)

Phase	Activity	Tasks
		Hold workshops if required
		Refine business measurement model (add additional information) workshops
		Refine measurement criteria attributes (set up metric sheets/metric "database")
		Build BIR/Metric "database" from sheets
		Map conceptual data model subject areas to BIRs and Metrics to verify model relevance
		Optional—map measures to source systems where DQ may be a concern
	Detailed Scenarios/ Usage	Develop IVC from usage (business actions)
		Identify touch points where new managed content or data will touch, or be leveraged, by processes
		Map IVC processes to touch points
		Isolate the processes that create value or achieve the goal related to the originating action
		Isolate opportunities for improved efficiency, add to Business Case
		Document IVC alternatives if any
		Review IVCs with SMEs
		Review IVC with EIM leadership and/or appropriate business leadership
		Conduct IVC confirmation session to recommend IVCs to pursue or delay
		Evaluate enhancements and modifications to existing IVC
		Hold confirmation session for relevance of new processes
		Document New Business Models (Back to Business Model activity) as recommendations
	Preliminary Information Taxonomy	List all possible content requiring a taxonomy
		Tie to business needs and/or actions and scenarios
		Determine relevance of taxonomy candidates to support business needs
		Develop straw person categories for each candidate
		Schedule and hold review sessions with SMEs
		Optimize across candidates
		Publish final list of recommended taxonomies
Architecture	Enterprise Metrics Architecture	Refine Business Metrics and BIRs if required
		Clarify industry metrics
		Determine characteristics to use (all 15 or subset). Create measure sheets or records, one per measure and/or BIR
		Determine level of review or walk-through review results
		Identify participants

(Continued)

Table A.2 (Continued)

Phase	Activity	Tasks
		Fill out template for workshops if required
		Confirm workshop sessions with predetermined stakeholders
		Hold workshops if required
		Add additional information to Metrics/BIR database
		Identify significant patterns and groups with the Metrics/BIR database
		Submit report of patterns and groups for verification
		Refine Metrics? BIR characteristics
		Prepare presentation of results of Metrics/BIR architecture
	Information Applications Framework	Refine the analysis of Metrics/BIR
		Identify smaller grouping of requirements, and other characteristics deemed relevant:
		Time characteristics, latencies
		Other characteristics
		Specify reporting, BI and analytic frameworks
		Generate spider charts or other graphic of framework characteristics
		Identify reporting BI framework elements (ODS, DW, DM, staging, etc.) from spiders
		Map BIRs and Metrics to BI and analytics framework
		Develop framework presentation (spider charts)
		Identify reference and master data needs from DQ survey, BIRs, and dimensions
		Identify content management needs from BIRs and Business Model
		Isolate the dimensions from ALL Metric/BIRs
		List all dimensions and develop standard definitions
		Merge results of DQ assessment with applications and technology requirements
		Determine criteria to direct technical elements choices
		Consider possible unique requirements, e.g., for privacy, security, encryption, web click capture, device interface, external data
		Develop technology elements specification
		Perform information interface and sizing analysis (see MART technique)
		Identify gaps in current-state technology
		Determine new technology requirements, existing technology to leverage, and technology to phase out
		Associate relevant technology categories with framework elements (technology classification: tools, data interchange, storage, content management, etc.)

(Continued)

Table A.2 (Continued)

Phase	Activity	Tasks
		Determine criteria for technical elements
		Identify potential candidate software and services solution vendors
		Short list technology (time permitting, or if within EIM scope)
		Coordinate with Enterprise Architecture
		Diagram and document all architectural elements
	Business Data Management Architecture	List internal and external constituents for information and content
		Identify IAM roles
		Identify decision makers and readers
		Identify updaters and clarifiers
		Identify collaborators and communicators
		Identify maintainers and engineers
		Define information and content user classifications
		Refine preliminary list of EIM principles
		Refine data models
		Define information asset classes
		Identify content types (structured and unstructured)
		Identify categories within content types
		Associate information assets with candidate frameworks/applications from the prior activity
		Produce metric to entity mapping, BIR to entity mapping
		Complete data model, merge into logical data model if time permits
		Complete incorporation of action, scenarios, and process into process models if time permits
		Ensure all dimensions exist in the data model and are defined
		Combine the data about Metrics and BIRs (the enterprise DNA) with the data and process models
		Define framework for enterprise DNA—start to call it meta data within the EIM team
		Develop summarized presentations of architectural elements
		Present and gain consensus on EIM Architecture elements
	Data Governance Architecture	Draft DG mission and vision statement
		Determine DG process to support business
		Identify processes to sustain key business measures or metrics model
		Define/support regulatory drivers
		Optional—work with finance and compliance and perform a pro forma "information risk forecast"
		Identify gaps in current state of data management
		Specify inadequate controls
		Specify privacy and security concerns

(Continued)

Table A.2 (Continued)

Phase	Activity	Tasks
		Specify compliance and regulatory concerns
		Incorporate Readiness findings
		Define baseline DG functions
		Identify DG detail processes if required
		Develop DG RACI
		Identify changes to SDLC processes
		Design DG process details, deliverables, documentation for SDLC integration touch points
		Identify preliminary accountability and ownership model
		Define desired roll out schedule for DG
		Define roll out of DG to support Road Map
		Develop data steward/accountability identification approach
		Develop data stewards identification, draft template/matrix
		Define data steward roles/responsibilities
		Identify data steward subject areas and prioritize them (e.g., customer)
		Review and obtain approval of data stewards identification approach with EIM leadership
		Identify infrastructure for technical components needed
		Identify requirements for enterprise data model standards and procedures
		Identify requirements for reference and code policies/procedures
		Determine desired IMM milestones for enterprise
		Develop DG management organization vision and mission (optional)
		Identify governance issue resolution process
		Define data stewards roles and responsibilities (use identified stewards list)
		Review and obtain approval of data stewards
		Complete data stewards identification
		Complete data stewards identification template for each subject area
		Identify DG oversight body(s)
		Conduct data stewards orientation
		Coordinate with HR and identified data steward(s) to revise data steward(s) performance goals and objectives
		Initiate EIM governance socialization
		Review current EIM guiding principles with leadership
		Present EIM DG functional model to business leadership
		Gain acceptance of DG in principle

(Continued)

Table A.2 (Continued)

Phase	Activity	Tasks
	Data Quality Architecture	Develop/document data controls approach
		Review/modify data controls approach with EIM leadership
		Identify/review and document data controls current processes, deliverables, frequencies, etc.
		Identify/review and document data controls current deliverables audience matrix (who receives what deliverables and what do they do differently because of them)
		Modify data lineage requirements based on industry trends and best practices
		Complete data controls findings, observations, recommendations, and document
		Review data controls for document with EIM and IT leadership
		Modify data controls for document with EIM leadership revisions
		Consolidate DQ causes and remediation
		Identify additional DQ tools (as required)
		Develop requirements for DQ tools and develop recommendation
		Review requirements for DQ tools with EIM leadership
		Evaluate and recommend DQ tools
		Develop new DQ tools governance (policies, procedures, standards)
		Draft production DQ methodology (produce data sources, audience, metrics, cycle time)
		Review production DQ methodology with EIM leadership and DG bodies
		Draft source system DQ methodology (produce data sources, audience, metrics, SLAs)
		Review source system DQ methodology with EIM leadership, DG bodies
	Information Value Chain Architecture	Collect related information life-cycle processes
		Collect current data life-cycle rules for use and disposal
		Conduct life-cycle confirmation session
		Data life-cycle rules for use and disposal
		Collect key processes/value that will use golden copies or candidate MDM areas or other content that will be managed under EIM
		Collect new business actions or processes suggested by Scenarios and Usage activity and Business Model activity
		Develop/refine information life cycles to reflect new MDM and value chains from business actions and other sources
		Review Metrics and BIRs for cycle changes, volume challenges, DQ, or other characteristics that will affect processes

(Continued)

Table A.2 (Continued)

Phase	Activity	Tasks
		Evaluate enhancements and modifications to information life cycle and value chains
		Document information life-cycle alternatives
		Document changes to value chains based on life-cycle constraints
		Review life cycles/value chains with SMEs, focus on regulatory constraints
		Review life cycles/value chain with EIM leadership and/or appropriate business leadership
		Conduct IVC confirmation session to recommend IVCs to pursue or delay
	Community Social Network Architecture	Identify common collaborative processes from Scenarios and Business Model
		Define subjects and content areas
		Identify community functions
		Identify collaborative processes
		Refine new business processes alternatives
		Develop design concept
		Define required prototype areas
		Propose community design concepts (optional)
		Develop themes and develop storyboard standards
		Identify risks unique to collaborative facilities
		Identify user interface standards
		Identify collaborative technology
		Define technical criteria
		Develop vendor shortlist
		Define strategy for content integration/management
		Define development standards
		Define technical architecture
		Design standards for community look and feel and functionality
		Identify/finalize content sources
		Define structured and unstructured data requirements
		Identify CRUD per content/data source
		Identify associated IVCs and drivers
		Identify content and data storage
	Detailed Taxonomy	List all possible content requiring a taxonomy
		Tie to business needs and/or actions and scenarios
		Determine relevance of those that support business needs
		Develop straw person categories for each candidate
		Schedule and prepare review and validation sessions with SMEs
		Train/orient reviewing staff on taxonomy usage

(Continued)

Table A.2 (Continued)

Phase	Activity	Tasks
		Test and verify taxonomy in facilitated meetings or via web development tools
		Align taxonomies with other elements of EIM architecture (what subjects, entities, etc.)
		Publish final list of taxonomies with business drivers
Road Map	Application Road Map	Identify business projects
		Create new/revise affinity groupings (mapping entities to measures, measures to business actions)
		Consider Metric and BIR groups
		Consider groups of data model to Metrics, or BIRs
		Consider groups of actions, levers, IVC, or scenarios to content
		Interpret groups and identify business projects
		Develop brief project descriptions
		Group/align business projects with business initiatives
		Associate relevant Metrics, BIRs, IVC, etc. with respective projects
		Map project objectives to business drivers and information requirements
		Review preliminary project objectives and deliverables
		Determine project constraints
		Prioritize and confirm projects
		Develop initial project Roll Out strategy
		Review and confirm initial projects
		Develop full project descriptions
		Derive project plans
		Estimate project cost
		Identify support projects
		Review previous documentation for support projects
		Review MART and IVC data
		Review DQ architecture
		Review EIM architecture elements
		Review EIM data and content management elements
		Review DQ architecture
		Review technology recommendations
		List and describe support projects
		Develop general Roll Out strategy
		Cross-reference with business projects
		Determine critical path constraints
		Rationalize projects with IT portfolio and resources
		Design project presentation and Road Map presentation format
		Present to EIM leadership for approval

(Continued)

Table A.2 (Continued)

Phase	Activity	Tasks
		Prepare detailed charters or initiation documents for first few projects
		Define general Roll Out strategy, select Roll Out option by:
		EIM project
		EIM governed area
		EIM function or component
		EIM element
		Present to EIM sponsorship for approval
	EIM Organization	Identify EIM functions from templates
		Verify EIM functions vs. DG
		Isolate functions with regulatory relevance
		Incorporate gaps in current state of data management
		Examine current data standards and policies
		Refine baseline EIM Organization function
		Identify EIM-affected business areas and new business functions
		Develop EIM RACI charts
		Develop draft organization charts
		Draft EIM Organization charter and mission statements
		Refine changes to SDLC processes for EIM
		Identify new job categories and positions
		Prepare new job descriptions
		Define Desired Roll Out schedule for EIM and business organizations
		Initiate EIM Organization socialization
		Review current EIM guiding principles
		Present EIM functional model and organization charts to business leadership
		Gain acceptance of EIM Organization in principle
		Submit job descriptions to HR for development
	Data Governance Roll Out	Refine DG organization (if EIM Organization indicated changes)
		Refine governance bodies and committees
		Refine DG charter
		Confirm data stewardship and ownership model if necessary
		Define DG Roll Out schedule
		Define Roll Out of DG to support Road Map
		Design DG metrics and reporting requirements
		Identify DG metrics stakeholders and playmakers
		Design metrics collection mechanisms
		Review DG metrics requirements with EIM leadership and obtain approval

(Continued)

Table A.2 (Continued)

Phase	Activity	Tasks
		Identify projects and stakeholders subject to standards and governance
		Publish and review IAM principles
		Review/revise modifications to SDLC and other IT processes
		Roll out initial DG functions
		Present initial road shops
		Publish guidelines and principles
		Implement DG policies/procedures orientation and training
		Publish and implement SDLC integration documentation
		Develop and conduct DG audit processes training
		Initiate DG audit processes
		Define additional Roll Out activity for the Sustaining phase
	Sustaining Requirement	Define EIM change management approach
		Review assessments
		Execute Change Capacity if not done
		Incorporate IMM results into Change Capacity
		Prepare statement of Change Readiness
		Identify change management resources
		Identify mechanisms to *prepare* the organization for change
		Define levels of communication required for specific stakeholders
		Define mechanisms for delivering communication
		Define level of involvement, specific actions, and tools for sponsor
		Design tools to prepare the organization for change
		Perform stakeholder analysis
		Identify EIM stakeholders
		Develop stakeholder analysis form
		Complete stakeholder analysis
		Review with EIM leadership
		Determine levels of commitment for key stakeholders
		Review results of stakeholder analysis
		Determine action plan to address improving levels of stakeholder commitment
		Develop sponsorship plan
		Identify required sponsorship and right level of sponsor
		Develop sponsor action plan
		Develop communications plan
		Identify audiences
		Create messages and branding
		Identify vehicles for communications
		Define timing, frequencies, and delivery means

Table A.2 (Continued)

Phase	Activity	Tasks
		Review and approval of communications plan
		Develop training plan
		Identify audiences
		Identify levels of training: orient, educate, train
		Identify vehicles for training
		Define timing, frequencies, and delivery means
		Review and approval of training plan
		Develop resistance management plan
		Perform SWOT analysis
		Identify specific resistance profiles
		Develop responses to resistance
		Review and approve resistance management plan
		Develop change management plan
		Define specific activity schedule for change
		Design metrics and assessments to ensure change effectiveness
		Define WIIFM and consequences
		Define resources to fulfill change delivery
		Develop revised process/policy alignment plan: reviewing/updating existing policies and processes related to DG and EIM
		Develop EIM management requirements
		Define EIM Organization Roll Out
		Revise EIM charter/mission if necessary
		Develop/refine EIM Organization positions
		Consolidate change tactics into change management plan
		Define/revise EIM Roll Out based on Sustaining input
Sustaining	Organization Roll Out	Complete new EIM team identification/socialization
		Socialize EIM program and area to IT and compliance
		Socialize new EIM manager
		Identify and staff IM area
		Establish physical location
		Review EIM charter(s)
		Present EIM charters and EIM principles to new staff
		Present Sustaining activities and stakeholder analysis to EIM staff
		Orient executive team to EIM Organization (if not done in Sustaining activity)
		Schedule EIM team, committees, and executives for their orientation, training, or educations
		Align EIM team functions with Road Map projects
		Ensure estimates are understood and project management practices in place

(Continued)

Table A.2 (Continued)

Phase	Activity	Tasks
	Sustaining (Change Management) activity	Confirm affected stakeholders Confirm sponsor readiness Confirm "burning platform" or current-state deficiencies Integrate the Sustaining activity with overall EIM Road Maps and project plans Identify new obstacles and constraints 　What issues need to be addressed and obstacles removed? 　How much stakeholder involvement will be needed? Define/modify Roll Out strategy, select Roll Out option by: 　EIM project 　EIM governed area 　EIM function or component 　EIM element Execute the change plan 　Activate training, communications, resistance management, etc. 　Develop materials for training, orientation, road shows, etc. 　Develop additional advocates if necessary 　Communicate short-term wins 　Communicate status and measurements of progress often to leadership 　Address problem areas aggressively Measure EIM change effectiveness 　Execute measurement surveys (if designed) 　Hold focus groups/interviews for feedback Realign impacted policies/practices and procedures to clearly support the new EIM vision, not contradict it Update staff performance objectives and reward structures to reflect new accountabilities and compliance to new rules
	EIM Program Metrics	Define metrics requirements into categories of risk, return, efficiency, DQ, DG Define metrics per the Metrics Model used in the Business Model phase Present metrics to EIM leadership for approval Deploy metrics collection and reporting in alignment with the EIM Road Map Implement regular metrics and measurement of DG implementation Produce EIM effectiveness reports
	EIM Project Management	Manage Road Map projects 　Report wins 　Interact with change management

(Continued)

Table A.2 (Continued)

Phase	Activity	Tasks
		Ensure aggressive resolution of issues
		Manage EIM department functions
		Manage day-to-day operations
		Manage DG
		Manage business data and content oversight of the assets (databases, documents, content)
		Manage integrity and security—database administration and security
		Manage DQ
		Manage the IAM/EIM architecture elements
		Manage reassessments/EIM adjustments
		Manage data life cycles—acquisition, movement, purging
		Manage enterprise DNA (metadata), including EIM design and architecture artifacts
		Manage reference and master data
		Manage data and content usage (BI, reporting, catalogs, web sites)
		Manage tools and technologies
		Deploy and adjust EIM
		Document metrics and EIM function performance
		Train and educate
		Implement EIM metrics tools and technology
		Promote and interact with change management
		Perform and review audits and service levels
		Interact with governing bodies
		DG committees and councils
		Appoint and meet with major project steering bodies
		Update executive EIM sponsorship
		Align EIM project management activity with existing IT practices
		Identify project templates
		Identify EIM project estimating tools
		Identify EIM tracking and accounting procedures for IT
		Forecast EIM project resources
		Utilize modified SDLC
		Interact with enterprise PMO (if one exists)
		Utilize modified SDLC
		Interact with enterprise PMO (if one exists)

Assessment Phase Summary and Work Products

This appendix provides the details for the Assessment phase, including activities, tasks, deliverables, and selected templates.

Initiation Activity Work Product Overview (Table B.1)

Table B.1 Assessment Work Product Overview

Activity	Tasks	Outputs (Work Products)	Activity Deliverable
Information Maturity	Determine scope of survey instrument	Survey audience/areas	IMM survey report
	Select or develop a maturity scale	Survey maturity scale	
	Identify all participants by name and group	Survey participants	
	Orient respondents on importance and anonymity	Survey orientation	
	Agree on survey delivery (online, written, group focus)	Survey delivery method	
	Review and modify maturity template	Approved survey contents	
	Produce final form for delivery	Final survey	
	Deploy survey instrument	Survey available	
	Monitor online survey	Managed survey data collected	
	Distribute and monitor written version	Managed survey data collected	
	Prepare and deliver focus session(s)	Managed survey data collected	
	Collect and evaluate data	Survey database	

(Continued)

Table B.1 (Continued)

Activity	Tasks	Outputs (Work Products)	Activity Deliverable
	Derive maturity score based on selected scale	Proposed IMM score	
	Collect existing standards, procedures, and policies for IM, info, resource utilization, prioritization, and controls and map to IMM scale	Mapped IMM to current state—gap analysis	
	Prepare findings for presentation	IMM survey presentation	
Change Capacity	Determine the formality of the assessment. That is an informal, structured meeting format, or a formal survey instrument	Change Capacity survey format	Change Capacity assessment report
	Determine the target audience	Change Capacity audience	
	Define the survey population or interviewees	Survey audience/areas	
	Define the approach—e.g., structured meeting, written, or online	Survey approach	
	Administer the survey or conduct meetings	Administered survey	
	Analyze and summarize findings	Survey database	
	Determine if additional investigation is required	Interview key individuals	
	Determine leadership alignment to EIM		
	Determine leadership commitment to EIM		
	Determine what will be reported now vs. sent to the EIM team to use during subsequent phases	"Need to know" findings	
	Prepare Change Capacity report	Change Capacity report	
Business Readiness	Determine specific expression of Readiness appropriate for the enterprise level of detail, does it include:	Readiness topics	Business Readiness report
	Information		
	Technology		
	People/organization		
	Operations		

(Continued)

Table B.1 (Continued)

Activity	Tasks	Outputs (Work Products)	Activity Deliverable
	Alignment		
	Governance		
	Risk/compliance		
	Assess the availability of the information needed for analysis	Collection method	
	Gather data from all sources and review	Business Readiness database	
	Record business strategies, goals, and objectives	Business strategy summary	
	Examine decision-making maturity of the various forums or units	Decision readiness	
	Examine how and where business performance measuring occurs: ad hoc, reports, BI	Business performance measurement methods	
	Document the alignment of business to current DW BI or other projects	Current state Business Alignment	
	Determine if there is substantial reporting and analytics activity outside of IT and proposed future development	Shadow IT and future Information projects	
	Document project management processes and results	Project management effectiveness	
	Prepare Business Readiness presentation	Business Readiness presentation	
Data and Content Quality	Identify data groups for assessment	DQ assessment subjects and known issues	DQ report
	Identify major groups for assessment		
	Compile inventory of known sources to analyze		
	Review source data issues		
	Identify known problems of low DQ		
	Prioritize areas to survey	Prioritized data groups report	
	Establish DQ objectives and measures	DQ survey objectives and measures	
	Determine the specific assessment objectives or goals		

(Continued)

Table B.1 (Continued)

Activity	Tasks	Outputs (Work Products)	Activity Deliverable
	Identify quality characteristics to be reviewed		
	Determine specific measures of the information		
	Determine the minimum DQ required for successful execution of the most significant process requiring the data		
	Determine files or processes to assess	List of target files within subject areas	
	Identify location of data and content to assess		
	Determine measurement technique		
	Identify data validation sources for accuracy assessment	Validation sources/methods	
	Identify most authoritative source of data from which to assess the accuracy of data		
	Verify the accuracy of the surrogate source being considered		
	Extract samples of data	Profile samples	
	Review source system files		
	Determine sampling technique (if any) for identified files		
	Measure DQ	Profile/examination results	
	Analyze data for business rule conformance		
	Audit primary and secondary key cardinality		
	Audit domains and values		
	Map to quality criteria list		
	Identify cost of quality estimates	Cost of DQ estimate	
	Interpret and report DQ	DQ root-cause analysis	
	Determine DQ issues root causes		
	Compile final DQ assessment report		
	Develop business impact statement for DQ		
	Deliver DQ assessment report	DQ assessment report	

(Continued)

Table B.1 (Continued)

Activity	Tasks	Outputs (Work Products)	Activity Deliverable

Collaborative Readiness	Determine assessment scope, e.g., does it include:
	  Web sites and content
	  Documents and sharing
	  Identifying existing communities of practice or interest
	  Workflow
	  Collaborative products
	  Contemporary facilities like Instant messaging, Texting, Twitter™, or Facebook™
		Collaborative Readiness assessment scope	Collaborative Readiness report

	Determine scope of survey instrument	Survey scope	
	Determine assessment approach—interviews, document review, or survey, or combination	Collaborative Readiness assess approach	
	Collect existing standards, procedures, and policies for document sharing, workflow, internal wikis, blogs, etc. for review	Assessment source material	
	Collect inventory of SharePoint, Notes, or other work-share facilities		
	Identify all participants by name and group if necessary	Collaborative Readiness survey participants	
	Orient respondents on importance and anonymity	Orientation for respondents	
	Identify interview of focus-group participants if necessary	Focus-group names	
	Produce final form for delivery	Final collaborative survey instrument	
	Deploy survey instrument	Executed survey	
	Monitor online survey		
	Distribute and monitor written version		
	Prepare and deliver focus session(s)		
	Collect and evaluate data from surveys, documents, and meetings	Collaborative Readiness survey database	
	Develop collaborative Readiness statement based on predetermined scale	Collaborative Readiness "score"	
	Prepare findings for presentation	Collaborative Readiness report	

Information Maturity Survey Template/Core Questions (Table B.2)

Table B.2 Information Maturity Survey Template

No.	Survey Questions	Strongly Disagree 1	Disagree 2	Neutral or Undecided 3	Agree 4	Strongly Agree 5
1	The enterprise has published principles on how we will view and handle data and information.					
2	There are standards for how data is presented to all users.					
3	There are policies for managing data that are published.					
4	The data policies are understood and adhered to consistently.					
5	There are rules for sharing and moving data in and out of the company.					
6	There is a widespread understanding of the importance of DQ.					
7	People are willing to be held accountable to a single standard of DQ.					
8	Data controls are adequate enough so we trust all numbers and information that are published.					
9	We can easily tie our need for information to specific business programs.					
10	Our transaction systems have all the data we need to do reporting.					
11	Data controls are adequate and we do not worry about regulatory issues due to data issues.					
12	My department owns the data we use; that is, we are responsible for using it accurately and correctly.					
13	The numbers my department reports to management are accurate.					
14	The reports we produce sometimes disagree with similar reports produced in other areas.					
15	The role of IT is to deliver data to me so I can analyze it and do all of my reports.					
16	We use different people to do analytics than generate reports.					

(Continued)

No.	Survey Questions	Strongly Disagree	Disagree	Neutral or Undecided	Agree	Strongly Agree
		1	**2**	**3**	**4**	**5**
17	We have too many things to do to take time for data standards.					
18	My company adapts quickly to changing business circumstances.					
19	We are good at data analysis—very few decisions are "gut."					
20	We cannot finish anything.					
21	My department has several databases, spreadsheets, or other data stores that we build and use to do reports.					
22	I have the knowledge available to me to meet my department's goals.					
23	If I have to, I gather the data we need regardless of guidance from IT and standards.					
24	My company operates on experience and gut feel.					
25	Knowledge is freely shared between members of my group and others no matter what functional area they come from.					
26	I understand the key indicators that measure my organization's performance.					
27	My company recognizes trends that signal obstacles or opportunities for company performance.					
28	I collect and analyze information related to my work.					
29	I use data analysis to make changes in my work processes to improve performance.					
30	There are standards within IT for describing data.					
31	My department has to do its own data collection since IT cannot deliver in a timely fashion.					
32	I have the knowledge available to me to help achieve company goals.					

Table B.2 (Continued)

Change Capacity Survey Template (Table B.3)

Table B.3 Change Capacity Survey Template

No.	Survey Questions	Strongly Disagree 1	Disagree 2	Neutral or Undecided 3	Agree 4	Strongly Agree 5
1	I understand the rationale for and the focus of the upcoming changes.					
2	Our senior leadership has communicated a clear and compelling reason for why change is critical to the organization's long-term success.					
3	People in the organization feel they can speak candidly to anyone, even if their views are contrary to leadership's.					
4	Previous changes in the organization have been well managed (i.e., we have a good track record of managing change).					
5	I am confident that I will have the opportunity to express my opinions and make suggestions about upcoming changes.					
6	I am confident that my opinions and suggestions will be given fair consideration.					
7	I am confident that barriers to success of the change will be identified quickly and addressed.					
8	Our senior leadership is aligned and committed to making the changes that will best position us for success.					
9	The way people think and act in my work unit will be compatible with the changes that are determined to be necessary.					
10	Although we haven't yet identified the specific changes that will be implemented, I trust that the organization will provide me with the resources needed to be successful in the future					
11	People throughout the organization understand the implications of the change for their areas of responsibility and feel that the change is urgently needed.					
12	I believe that by improving our business processes and technology, I will be able to make more valuable contributions to the organization in the future than I can today.					

(Continued)

Table B.3 (Continued)

No.	Survey Questions	Strongly Disagree 1	Disagree 2	Neutral or Undecided 3	Agree 4	Strongly Agree 5
13	I am confident that I will receive honest and accurate information about the change initiative and its impact.					
14	People throughout the organization feel that changes to our business processes are urgently needed.					
15	The risk and issues associated with the change have been identified in advance, and appropriate actions have been taken to reduce their impact.					
16	I am confident in my own ability to successfully implement any required changes that are identified.					
17	I am the type of person that naturally embraces work-related changes.					
18	I would be willing to function as a change advocate, helping my coworkers and business partners to embrace and implement the necessary changes.					
19	I believe that the organization will be even more successful in the future as a result of the changes.					
20	Our people have the skills, interest, and commitment to support the upcoming change initiatives.					
21	Communication regarding the changes is open, direct, and regular.					
22	Expected business results have been clearly identified up front, targets set, and measures established.					
	Open-ended questions					
23	What are the biggest challenges we face in making these changes?					
24	What have been the biggest contributors to the success or failure of other major change initiatives in which you have taken part?					
25	What are the organization's greatest strengths in addressing these kinds of changes?					
26	What are the best ways for us to provide support to you for the upcoming changes?					

Business Readiness Survey Template (Table B.4)

Table B.4 Business Readiness Assessment Survey Template

Business EIM Readiness Survey					
Domains	Topics	Exist	Documented	Applied	Outcome
Information management	**Data and Content Architecture**				
	Corporate data model				
	Corporate process model				
	Integrity and data controls				
	DQ program				
	DG program				
	Security considerations				
	Information access				
	Business champions/stakeholders				
	Data-sharing approach				
	Business users				
	External users (customers)				
	Parallel or competing efforts				
	Identified business benefits				
	Perceived barriers to success				
	Shadow IT				
	BI/DW strategy				
	Internal access				
	DW, ODS, etc.?				
	External access				
	IM budgeting				
	Alignment with business imperatives				
	IT master plan				
	DW/BI project funding				
	DW/BI budget amount				
	Project justification requirements				
Governance	**Data governance**				
	Principles				
	Standards				
	Policies				
	Decision-making process				
	Formal decision-making entities				
	Approval process				
	Standards and methods				
	Dispute resolution process				

(Continued)

Table B.4 (Continued)

Business EIM Readiness Survey					
Domains	**Topics**	**Exist**	**Documented**	**Applied**	**Outcome**
Technology	**IT/corporate governance**				
	Planning and control				
	Information architecture				
	Perceptions				
	Current systems environment				
	Source systems				
	Informational/decision support				
	Existence of documentation				
	Data access technology				
	LAN, WAN, Web				
	End-user access tools (reporting, query and analysis, data mining)				
	Data management technology				
	Extract and transformation				
	Data modeling				
	Metadata management				
	Middleware, service Layer				
	Content management				
	DW management, control, and usage				
	Technical Standards				
	Platforms (HW and OS)				
	Database platform				
	Application platform				
	Client workstation				
	Storage				
	Relational				
	Multidimensional				
	Statistics				
	Privacy, security				
	Infrastructure				
	E-mail				
People/ organization	**IT organization**				
	Centralized/decentralized				
	Alignment with business organization structure				
	Reporting relationships				
	Resource levels, budget adequacy				

(Continued)

Table B.4 (Continued)

	Business EIM Readiness Survey				
Domains	**Topics**	**Exist**	**Documented**	**Applied**	**Outcome**
	DW/BI teams structure				
	Roles and responsibilities (back end, front end)				
	Resource level				
	Business participation/shadow IT				
	DW/BI team interaction				
	Business units				
	DBA				
	Data administration				
	Information architect				
	IT infrastructure				
	Application development				
	Skills				
	Team background				
	Team business understanding				
	DW architecture knowledge				
	Extract and transformation				
	Data analysis for DSS				
	Technical competencies				
	Business user skills				
	DW training programs				
	Development process				
	Project management				
	Program management				
	Understanding of IM processes				
	Culture change process				
	Collaboration				
	Data sharing				
	Document/content sharing				
	Subject-matter experts				
	Collaboration technology				
	Tools				
	Administration				
Operations	**Service-level agreements**				
	Hours of availability				
	Performance				
	Help desk				
	Online help				
	Query consultation support				

(Continued)

Table B.4 (Continued)

Business EIM Readiness Survey					
Domains	**Topics**	**Exist**	**Documented**	**Applied**	**Outcome**
	DW operations management				
	Development/test/production acceptance				
	Configuration management				
	Data loading (times, controls)				
	Data usage monitoring				
	Query performance monitoring				
	Backup/recovery/restore				
	Capacity planning/scalability				
	DW configuration				
	Storage				
	Workload assumptions				
	IT sourcing/partnerships				
	DW development				
	Data center operations				
	Web				
Alignment	**Business drivers and strategy**				
	Business driver focus (e.g., customer, operational efficiency, product excellence)				
	Formal organizational process for translating business objectives to IT/IM projects				
	Existing informational support for decision making				
	Process for setting priorities				
	Cross-organizational business collaboration				
	Cross-organizational, objectives, measures, and vocabulary				
	External/regulatory considerations				
	Business requirements and process				
	Requirements gathering and transformation process				
	Measurement identification				
	Business scenarios				
	Anticipated categories of users				
	Skill levels				
	Data content responsibility				
	Current state usage/changes identified				

(Continued)

Table B.4 (Continued)

Business EIM Readiness Survey					
Domains	**Topics**	**Exist**	**Documented**	**Applied**	**Outcome**
Risk/ compliance	**Executive commitment**				
	Business sponsor				
	Business participants identified				
	DW project funding				
	Accountability				
	Risk assessments				
	Regulatory				
	Financial				
	Safety/civil				
	Corporate risk management				
	Compliance department				
	Management concerns				
	Inhibitors to risk management				
	CSFs for risk management				
	Privacy affects				

Alignment Phase Summary and Work Products

This appendix provides the details for alignment phase, including activities, tasks, deliverables, and selected templates.

Alignment Activity Work Product Overview (Table C.1)

Table C.1 Alignment Activity Detail

Activity	Tasks	Outputs (Work Products)	Activity Deliverable
Business Discovery	Review business documents, earlier findings	Collected documents	List of business goals and objectives, with obvious metrics
	Develop a list of known business challenges, problems, and potential opportunities	Business directions, goals, objectives	
	Turn challenges and opportunities into business directions		
	Confirm future relevance of goals and objectives	Goal/objective measures	
	Confirm measures of goals and objectives	Matrix of business goals and objectives	
	Clarify possible EIM role in achieving business goals	EIM role per goal	
	Ensure each goal or objective is measurable	Obvious measure or metric	
Business Information Levers	Build the usage/value work sheets	Value/Information lever work sheets	Value/Information levers
	Value lever sheet, if needed		
	Information lever sheet		

(Continued)

Making Enterprise Information Management (EIM) Work for Business. DOI: 10.1016/B978-0-12-375695-4.00038-2

Table C.1 (Continued)

Activity	Tasks	Outputs (Work Products)	Activity Deliverable
	Schedule an internal EIM team meeting with selected subject experts		
	Fill out the matrix, looking at each cell		
	Review the results with business personnel external to EIM team		
	Modify the present results to an executive (or two, if they are available)	A list of levers that present conceptual means that the organization will use data and content to achieve goals	
Business Alignment	Determine the business context to present levers	Organization context for Information levers	Business benefits with a data/content value context
	Schedule facilitated session with business leaders or subject matter experts	Business session for lever review	
	Capture business benefit results in the session, or refine results after presenting them	Revised levers and value statements	
	Create value statements of interaction of data and business goals	Value/Information lever statements	
	Publish results to the EIM team and/or steering committee	Business benefits from Value and Information levers	
Preliminary Business Case	Determine required level of detail for the preliminary case	Business case outline	Preliminary business case (optional)
	Associate levers and business view with measurable goals and objectives	Lever to benefit list	
	Identity the financial changes planned if business goals and benefits are attained	Financial targets	
	Associate a pro forma or notional financial benefit with each Information lever or value statement	Notional benefits	
	Review benefits with a financial analyst, identify a method to show a return on the investment in EIM	A view of business benefit as a result of EIM	
	Review these preliminary results with the EIM steering body	Reviewed benefits for EIM	

Alignment Matrix: Goals to Objectives Template (Table C.2)

Table C.2 Alignment Matrix Template

Strategic Area/ Driver	Business Strategy/Driver	Goal	Objectives	Business Measure

Alignment Matrix: Value Levers Template (Table C.3)

Table C.3 Value Levers

EXAMPLE OF DIRECT VALUE INCREASE (VALUE LEVERS) DUE TO INFORMATION

Increase value through*	CONTEXT External view or customer intimacy	CONTEXT Internal view or product innovation	CONTEXT Enabler of human resource, or efficiency
Process Improve cycle time, lower cost, improve quality			
Competitive weapon Capture competitive intelligence and differentiate yourself			
Product Create package and market unique, higher margin products			
Asset/intellectual capital Prolong leadership, embed knowledge into products and services			
Enabler Foster employee growth and empowerment			
Risk Manage risks, of various types, that threaten value by increasing liability			

*Categories from Veiby, Valuing Knowledge.

Alignment Matrix: Information Levers/Usage (Table C.4)

Table C.4 Information Levers/Usage

Strategic Area/Driver	Goal	Objectives	BIR/ Metric	Process	Competitive Weapon	Product	Asset/ Intellectual Capital	Enabler	Risk

Information Levers/Preliminary Actions

Vision Phase Summary and Work Products

D

This appendix provides the details for the Vision phase, including activities, tasks, and deliverables. It also includes a template for managing the BIRs.

Vision Activity Work Product Overview (Tables D.1 and D.2)

Table D.1 Vision Activity and Work Products

Activity	Tasks	Outputs (Work Products)	Activity Deliverable
Business EIM Vision	Define the presentation style of the vision	Revised vision prototype	Business Vision of EIM
	Acquire a writer or artist if not on the team Iterate through several drafts of the vision	Vision draft	
	Present and approve to EIM team and steering body	Approved Business Vision of EIM	
Preliminary BIRs	Gather Information levers and examine required content to enable them	Levers/content mapping	Preliminary BIRs
	Gather measures for objectives and develop initial list of enterprise metrics Incorporate standard metric from your industry	Initial metric and indicators list Initial metric and indicators list	
	Look at Value/Information lever statements and extract any new categories of data or content required	New content requirements	
	Examine significant business events and activities for content affecting risk—such as safety, regulated products, rate filings, etc.	Risk/content mapping	
	Examine backlogs of report requests, web site updates, and requisitions for external data	Current unfulfilled requirements	
	Develop a classification scheme as to the origin of each requirement Refine alignment	All requirements by classification Refined alignment	

(Continued)

Table D.1 (Continued)

Activity	Tasks	Outputs (Work Products)	Activity Deliverable
	Take BIR coming from prior activity in EIM and verify the associated business goal/objective		
	Take BIRs that were uncovered in this activity and tie them to business goals/objectives		
	Build a facility to hold and cross-reference the BIRs	BIR/Metrics management sheet	
	Assign and organize findings by the classification scheme	Final BIR report	
Preliminary Business Model	Gather existing artifacts, such as data or process models	Existing models	Preliminary Business Model(s): Conceptual data model business actions models
	Determine level of detail to drive the Preliminary models	Model constraints	
	Define acceptable level of presentation for models, based on tools and current state	Model presentation format	
	Develop or refine a conceptual data model	Preliminary conceptual model	
	Develop or refine a process model reflecting known activities from levers and usage Incorporate results into existing tools or prepare for presentation and use in subsequent steps		
EIM Business Case	Fully understand and define business benefits	EIM business benefits clarified	EIM Business Case—a concise statement of benefits in excess of potential costs and risk, with an indication of financial return
	Isolate information usage/value enablers and processes	Specific value statements	
	Identify/confirm business benefits that are possible—reduce the high-level numbers into benefits for specific instances of lever, value/usage, or process	Confirmed benefits	
	Describe specific benefits, costs, and/or "at risk"—look for risk across the three risk types—regulatory, civil, and financial		
	Define relevant EIM benefit categories risk management (e.g., regulatory, civil, and so on), business return, or business efficiency		
	Identify potential cash flows	Cash benefits	
	Examine current costs of IT and other information-related costs (we will revise the cost numbers in the Road Map phase)	Cost side of business case	
	Apply the various financial benefits and the costs to whatever model we have selected.	EIM Business Case	

Table D.2 Preliminary BIRs

EIM Preliminary Requirements					
Classification	**Preliminary BIR and Metrics Types (Samples)**	**Name/ Description**	**Planned/ New**	**Value Lever**	**Goal/ Objective**
Documents/external	Regulatory reports				
	Surveys				
	E-mail/correspondence				
Lists	Catalogs				
Metrics	Key indicators				
	Required—financial				
Documents/internal	Required—regulatory Safety manuals				
	Specifications/plans				
	Transactions/forms				
	Contracts				
	E-mail				

Business Model Phase Summary and Work Products

This appendix provides the details for the Business Model phase, including activities, tasks, deliverables, and a blank template to manage and track metrics and BIRs.

Business Model Work Product Overview (Table E.1)

Table E.1 Business Model Activity and Work Products

Activity	Tasks	Outputs (Work Products)	Activity Deliverable
Refined Business Model	Gather existing artifacts, such as data or process models if they do not already exist from the Preliminary activity	Current models	Refined data model
	Determine level of detail to drive the final business models	Refined conceptual data models	Refined process/action models
	Define acceptable level of presentation for models, based on tools and current state		
	Develop or refine a conceptual data model from the metrics and/or BIR findings		
	Schedule facilitated sessions to walk through the various levers and usage to identify business actions and possible new process models (new IVC)	Reviewed models	
	(Trigger the Detailed Scenario/Usage Activity) to decompose the value chains to identify areas where new or revised business actions can occur using managed data	Scenarios/usage for further analysis	

(Continued)

Table E.1 (Continued)

Activity	Tasks	Outputs (Work Products)	Activity Deliverable
	Develop or refine Business Models reflecting known activities from levers and usage (and value chain results) from Detailed Scenario activity	Refined activities, processes, or use cases of how the business can operate with managed data	
	Incorporate results into existing tools or prepare for presentation and use in subsequent steps	Refined Business Models	
Business Metrics and BIR Model	Gather metrics and indicators	Consolidated metrics and BIR list	Metrics Model and "BIR Catalog"—comprehensive listing and definition of core information and content requirements
	Identify industry metrics (if not done yet)	Standard or industry metrics	
	Create measure sheets or records, one per measure and/or BIR	Metrics/BIR data sheets	
	Determine level of review or walk through to verify/fill out the metrics and BIR material	Understanding of effort to fill out metric/BIR sheets	
	Fill out template for workshops if required	Workshop material	
	Confirm workshop sessions with predetermined stakeholders	Scheduled workshops	
	Hold workshops if required	Workshop results	
	Refine business measurement model (add additional information) workshops	Understanding completeness of what EIM will address	
	Refine measurement criteria attributes (set up metric sheets/ metric "database")	Metrics/BIR database formatted	
	Build BIR/Metric "database" from sheets	Updated metrics/BIR database	
	Map conceptual data model subject areas to BIRs and Metrics to verify model relevance	BIR/Metrics to data model cross-reference	
	Optional—map measures to source systems where DQ may be a concern	Metrics/BIRs to DQ issues cross-reference	
Detailed Scenarios/ Usage	Develop IVC from usage (business actions)	Extract process models with levers and other opportunities for using content and data	High-Value Scenarios and Usage—Detailed Scenario models of refined business actions and new processes and content usage

(Continued)

Table E.1 (Continued)

Activity	Tasks	Outputs (Work Products)	Activity Deliverable
	Identify touch points where new managed content or data will touch, or be leveraged, by processes	Possible value points for new processes	
	Map IVC processes to touch points	Intersection of opportunities and IVC processes	
	Isolate the processes that create value or achieve the goal related to the originating action	Detailed actions in business processes achieving results through managed information	
	Isolate opportunities for improved efficiency, add to Business Case	Enhancements to the Business Case	
	Document IVC alternatives if any	IVC opportunities to pursue	
	Review IVCs with SMEs		
	Review IVC with EIM leadership and/ or appropriate business leadership		
	Conduct IVC confirmation session to recommend IVCs to pursue or delay		
	Evaluate enhancements and modifications to existing IVC	List of new business processes for enhancement	
	Hold confirmation session for relevance of new processes	Reviewed improvement opportunities	
	Document New Business Models (Back to Business Model activity) as recommendations	Revised models	
Preliminary Information Taxonomy	List all possible content requiring a taxonomy	Content requiring navigation and tracking in a hierarchical fashion (e.g., web site)	Preliminary enterprise taxonomy(s)
	Tie to business needs and/or actions and scenarios	Content/business lever or objective cross-reference	
	Determine relevance of taxonomy candidates to support business needs	Prioritized taxonomy candidates	
	Develop straw person categories for each candidate	Draft taxonomies for review	
	Schedule and hold review sessions with SMEs	Taxonomy review material	
	Optimize across candidates	Optimized taxonomy list	
	Publish final list of recommended taxonomies	Optimized list of taxonomy candidates approved for further detailing	

Metrics and BIR Template (Table E.2)

Table E.2 Metrics and BIR Template

Metric name

Metric description

Metric algorithm
Describe HOW the metric is calculated

Related business objectives/goals

Objectives from business plan or matrices

1		
2		
3		
4		
5		

Related dimensions

Attributes used after the word "by" in a query

Dim 1		
Dim 2		
Dim 3		
Dim 4		
Dim 5		
Dim 6		
Dim 7		

Related entities

List subjects, entities, or other sources required to produce this measure

1		
2		
3		
4		
5		

(Continued)

Table E.2 (Continued)

Related business actions		
Specific actions, events, or programs enabled by producing the measure, i.e., what is done with this measure, what decisions are made?		
1		
2		
3		
4		
5		
6		
7		
Summarization level		
Known aggregations required to be readily available, usually a time period like a month, week. Not the same as dimension		
1		
2		
3		
4		
Metric name		
Characteristics	**Characteristic description**	Score
Measurement volume	The estimated occurrences of this measure in terms of rows of data required to produce, OR number of unique times this measure is generated over a time period	
Granularity	The level of detail required to support measurements and dimensions	
Historicity	The extent to which historical reporting requirements are necessary	
Distribution	The extent to which the information will be used across an enterprise	
Fact volatility	The frequency that information is ADDED TO, or UPDATED for BI uses	
Dimensional complexity	Relative complexity of the dimension in use, e.g., slowly changing, many dimensions	
Access type	Mode of data access, e.g., will the information be accessed directly, via query, or rolled off onto reports?	
Latency	The time between when the data is available to when is it required to be placed into the framework	
Source complexity	It defines relative complexity of gathering and moving data into the information framework	
Frequency	How often the information is accessed for a particular measure or requirement, differs from periodicity, e.g., daily activity is accessed weekly	

(Continued)

Table E.2 (Continued)

Response time	What is the desired time to respond to the production of the metric? How soon must the business react to the metric and take action, e.g., with customer or other touch point?	
Follow-up time	After a response is initiated, how long must there be before another party, if any, is to be contacted, or receive directions or resolution? The time desired to allocate to responding to a metric or stimulus, i.e., you can respond quickly, but only be able to spend an hour on the event	
Persistency	The length of time data must be retained in the framework. Also, the length of time the data stored is USEFUL	
Availability	When should the information be available? Business day, 24×7, etc.	
Data quality	The current degree of usefulness of the data	

Architectures Phase Summary and Work Products

This appendix provides the details for the Architectures phase, including activities, tasks, deliverables, and relevant blank template(s).

Architecture Work Product Overview (Table F.1)

Table F.1 Architecture Activity and Work Products

Activity	Tasks	Outputs (Work Products)	Activity Deliverable
Enterprise Metrics Architecture	Refine business metrics and BIRs if required	Refined metrics and BIR	Enterprise metrics and BIR architecture—all defined metrics and BIR characteristics are described or accounted for
	Clarify industry metrics	Business SME understands	
	Determine characteristics to use (all 15 or subset). Create measure sheets or records, one per measure and/or BIR	Completed metrics/BIR characteristics forms/database	
	Determine level of review or walk through review results	Metrics completion approach	
	Identify participants	Metrics architecture participants	
	Fill out template for workshops if required	Workshop material	
	Confirm workshop sessions with predetermined stakeholders	Workshop sessions	
	Hold workshops if required	Workshop results	
	Add additional information to Metrics/BIR database	Metrics database updated	
	Identify significant patterns and groups with the Metrics/BIR database	Initial report of the various groupings and commonality between the enterprise requirements	

(Continued)

Making Enterprise Information Management (EIM) Work for Business. DOI: 10.1016/B978-0-12-375695-4.00041-2

Table F.1 (Continued)

Activity	Tasks	Outputs (Work Products)	Activity Deliverable
	Submit report of patterns and groups for verification	Characteristics clusters or affinity analysis	
	Refine Metric/BIR characteristics as required	Corrected Metrics and BIRs	
	Prepare presentation of results of Metrics/BIR architecture	Metrics/BIR architecture	
Information Applications Framework	Refine the analysis of Metrics/BIR	Groups of BIR/Metrics by characteristics	Information applications framework
	Identify smaller grouping of requirements, and other characteristics deemed relevant		
	Time characteristics, latencies		
	Other characteristics		
	Specify reporting, BI, and analytics frameworks	BI/reporting framework elements	
	Generate spider charts or other graphic of framework characteristics		
	Identify reporting BI framework elements (ODS, DW, DM, staging, etc.) from spiders		
	Map, BIRs and Metrics to BI and analytics framework		
	Develop framework presentation (spider charts)	Spider charts for presentation	
	Identify reference and master data needs from DQ survey, BIRs, and Dimensions	Reference data groupings	
	Identify content management needs from BIRs and Business Model	Content management groups	
	Isolate the dimensions from ALL Metric/BIRs	Defined dimensions	
	List all dimensions and develop standard definitions		
	Merge results of DQ assessment with applications and technology requirements	DQ affect on groupings	
	Determine criteria to direct technical elements choices	Criteria for technology	

(Continued)

Table F.1 (Continued)

Activity	Tasks	Outputs (Work Products)	Activity Deliverable
	Consider possible unique requirements, e.g., for privacy, security, encryption, web click capture, device interface, external data		
	Develop technology elements specification		
	Perform information interface and sizing analysis (see MART technique)	MART results	
	Identify gaps in current state technology	Data movement gaps	
	Determine new technology requirements, existing technology to leverage, and technology to phase out	New technology requirements	
	Associate relevant technology categories with framework elements (technology classification, tools, data interchange, storage, content management, etc.)		
	Determine criteria for technical elements	The initial list of technical elements for EIM	
	Identify potential candidate software and services solution vendors	Justification and list of specific data and content movement facilities	
	Short list technology (time permitting, or if within EIM scope)	Merged DQ requirements with the EIM architecture elements	
	Coordinate with enterprise architecture		
	Diagram and document all architectural elements	Applications frameworks	
Business Data and Content Management Architecture	List internal and external constituents for information and content	EIM constituents	Business content and data management architecture
	Identify IAM roles	IAM roles	
	Identify decision–makers and readers		
	Identify updaters and clarifiers		
	Identify collaborators and communicators		

(Continued)

Table F.1 (Continued)

Activity	Tasks	Outputs (Work Products)	Activity Deliverable
	Identify maintainers and engineers		
	Define information and content user classifications	Types of content users	
	Refine preliminary list of EIM principles	EIM principles	
	Refine data models	Data models	
	Define information asset classes		
	Identify content types (structured and unstructured)	Content types	
	Identify categories within content types	Content categories, identification of information asset subgroups for management	
	Associate information assets with candidate frameworks/ applications from the prior activity	Framework/assets mapping	
	Produce metric to entity mapping, BIR to entity mapping	Information completeness verifications	
	Complete data model, merge into logical data model if time permits	Logical data models	
	Complete incorporation of action, scenarios, and process into process models if time permits	Process models	
	Ensure all dimensions exist in the data model and are defined	Verified dimensions	
	Combine the data about Metrics and BIRs (the enterprise DNA) with the data and process models	Unified models for IM	
	Define framework for enterprise DNA—start to call it meta data within the EIM team	Initial requirements for EIM asset "DNA"—meta data	
	Develop summarized presentations of architectural elements	Presentation of overall EIM architecture	
	Present and gain consensus on EIM architecture elements	EIM architecture approved	

(Continued)

Table F.1 (Continued)

Activity	Tasks	Outputs (Work Products)	Activity Deliverable
DG Architecture	Draft DG mission and vision statement	DG mission statement	DG architecture
	Determine DG process to support business	DG business support	
	Identify processes to sustain key business measures or metrics model	Metrics/BIR governance processes	
	Define/support regulatory drivers	Regulatory requirements for DG	
	Optional—work with finance and compliance and perform a pro forma "information risk forecast"	Information risk assessment	
	Identify gaps in current state of data management		
	Specify inadequate controls	Data control gaps	
	Specify privacy and security concerns	Privacy and security gaps	
	Specify compliance and regulatory concerns	Compliance gaps	
	Incorporate readiness findings	Readiness findings and gaps	
	Define baseline DG functions	Core DG functional model	
	Identify DG detail processes if required	DG process model	
	Develop DG RACI	DG RACI chart	
	Identify changes to SDLC processes	SDLC changes	
	Design DG process details, deliverables, documentation for SDLC integration touch points	SDLC modification details	
	Identify preliminary accountability and ownership model	Accountable personnel list	
	Define desired roll-out schedule for DG	DG roll-out schedule	
	Define rollout of DG to support road map		
	Develop data steward/ accountability identification approach		
	Develop data Stewards identification, draft template/ matrix	Draft list of data stewards	
	Define data steward roles/ responsibilities	Data steward roles and responsibilities	

Table F.1 (Continued)

Activity	Tasks	Outputs (Work Products)	Activity Deliverable
	Identify data steward identification subject areas and prioritize them (e.g., customer)	Stewardship areas	
	Review and obtain approval of data stewards identification approach with EIM leadership	Approved data stewardship approach	
	Identify infrastructure technical components needed	DG technology requirements	
	Identify requirements for enterprise data model standards and procedures	An initial list of standards, based on the models and architecture elements developed to date. Therefore, there will be data standards, code standards, applications, and data quality standards	
	Identify requirements for reference and code policies/procedures		
	Determine desired IMM milestones for enterprise	IMM schedule	
	Develop DG management organization vision and mission (optional)	DG mission and vision	
	Identify governance issue resolution process	DG issue resolution process	
	Define data stewards roles and responsibilities (use identified stewards list)	Data stewards positioned to participate in DG	
	Review and obtain approval of data stewards		
	Complete data stewards identification		
	Complete data stewards identification template for each subject area		
	Identify DG oversight body(s)		
	Conduct data stewards orientation		
	Coordinate with HR and identified data steward(s) to revise data steward's performance goals and objectives		

Table F.1 (Continued)

Activity	Tasks	Outputs (Work Products)	Activity Deliverable
	Initiate EIM governance socialization		
	Review current EIM guiding principles with leadership	Reviewed principles	
	Present EIM DG functional model to business leadership	DG model presentation	
	Gain acceptance of DG in principle	Approved DG architecture	
DQ Architecture	Develop/document data controls approach		DQ architecture
	Review/modify data controls approach with EIM leadership	Reviewed data controls	
	Identify/review and document data controls current processes, deliverables, frequencies, etc.	Data control current state	
	Identify/review and document data controls current deliverables audience matrix (who receives what deliverables and what do they do differently because of them)		
	Modify data lineage requirements based on industry trends and best practices	Data lineage requirements	
	Complete data controls findings, observations, recommendations, and document	Data control recommendations	
	Review data controls for document with EIM and IT leadership	Approved data controls	
	Modify data controls for document with EIM leadership revisions	Improvement activities that do not require a project	
	Consolidate DQ causes and remediation	DQ action plan and recommendations for preventing DQ issues and correcting data errors	
	Identify additional DQ tools (as required)	Requirements for additional projects to support EIM and remediate DQ issues in the future	

Table F.1 (Continued)

Activity	Tasks	Outputs (Work Products)	Activity Deliverable
	Develop requirements for DQ tools and develop recommendation	Personnel and organizations impacted by the plans and improvements	
	Review requirements for DQ tools with EIM leadership	List of communication requirements for affected and impacted areas (for inclusion in the Sustaining phase)	
	Evaluate and recommend DQ tools	DQ tools list	
	Develop new DQ tools governance (policies, procedures, standards)	DQ tool governance	
	Draft production DQ methodology (production data sources, audience, metrics, cycle time)	DQ methodology	
	Review production DQ methodology with EIM leadership and DG bodies		
	Draft source system DQ methodology (production data sources, audience, metrics, SLAs)		
	Review source system DQ methodology with EIM leadership, DG bodies		
IVC Architecture	Collect related information life-cycle processes	Current data life-cycle documentation	IVC architecture and refined information life cycles
	Collect current data life-cycle rules for use and disposal		
	Conduct life-cycle confirmation session	Data life-cycle regulations and policies	
	Collect key processes/value that will use golden copies or candidate of MDM areas or other content that will be managed under EIM	Relevant IVC process models	
	Collect new business actions or processes suggested by Scenarios and Usage activity and Business Model activity	Candidate IVC processes	

(Continued)

Table F.1 (Continued)

Activity	Tasks	Outputs (Work Products)	Activity Deliverable
	Develop/refine information life cycles to reflect new MDM and value chains from business actions and other sources	Optimized IVCs with high-value processes identified	
	Review Metrics and BIRs for cycle changes, volume challenges, DQ, or other characteristics that will affect processes	Refined IVCs	
	Evaluate enhancements and modifications to information life cycle and value chains	Approved IVCs	
	Document information life cycle alternatives	IVC alternatives	
	Document changes to value chains based on life-cycle constraints		
	Review life cycles/value chains with SMEs, focus on regulatory constraints	Reviewed IVCs	
	Review life cycles/value chain with EIM leadership and/or appropriate business leadership	Reviewed IVCs	
	Conduct IVC confirmation session to recommend IVCs to pursue or delay	Confirmed IVC direction	
Community Social Network Architecture	Identify common collaborative processes from Scenarios and Business Model		Community social net architecture
	Define subjects and content areas	Candidate content for collaboration	
	Identify community functions	Collaborative functions	
	Identify collaborative processes	Collaborative processes	
	Refine new business processes alternatives	Updated process models	
	Develop design concept	Collaboration concepts	
	Define required prototype areas	Prototype areas	
	Propose community design concepts (optional)	Community design concepts	
	Develop themes and develop storyboard standards	Collaborative storyboards	
	Identify risks unique to collaborative facilities	Statement of risk	

(Continued)

Table F.1 (Continued)

Activity	Tasks	Outputs (Work Products)	Activity Deliverable
	Identify user interface standards	Collaborative interface standards	
	Identify collaborative technology		
	Define technical criteria	Collaborative technology shortlist	
	Develop vendor shortlist		
	Define strategy for content integration/management	Content integration strategy	
	Define development standards		
	Define technical architecture		
	Design standards for community look, and feel and functionality		
	Identify/finalize content sources		
	Define structured and unstructured data requirements		
	Identify CRUD per content/data source		
	Identify associated IVCs and drivers		
	Identify content and data storage		
Detailed Taxonomy	List all possible content requiring a taxonomy	Taxonomy content list	Detailed enterprise taxonomy
	Tie to business needs and/or actions and scenarios	Business need/taxonomy support list	
	Determine relevance of those that support business needs	Business usage/taxonomy validation	
	Develop straw person categories for each candidate	Draft taxonomy levels	
	Schedule and prepare review and validation sessions with SMEs	Taxonomy review schedule	
	Train/orient reviewing staff on taxonomy usage	SMEs prepared to review taxonomy	
	Test and verify taxonomy in facilitated meetings or via web development tools	Verified taxonomy(s)	
	Align taxonomies with other elements of EIM architecture (what subjects, entities, etc.)	Aligned taxonomy to EIM architecture	
	Publish final list of taxonomies with business drivers	A set of taxonomies for navigation and administration of crucial enterprise DNA	

EIM BIR Metric Characteristic Score Sheet (Table F.2)

Table F.2 Metric and BIR Characteristic Score Sheet

	Relative Complexity	EIM Metric and BIR Characteristics Score Sheet									
		1	2	3	4	5	6	7	8	9	10
Granularity—the level of detail required to support measurements, dimensions, and requirements	1–10	Aggregate over 1 year	Annual aggregate	Monthly aggregate	Item/Entity aggregate > day	Item/entity level	Line item/ header > day	Line item/ header by day, document— archived files	Line item by header; document— single copies	Line item (pass–seat)	Subline item
Fact volatility— the frequency that new data is ADDED or UPDATED for usage	1–10	Update > 1x/yr	Update 1x/yr	Update 2–4x/yr	Update monthly	Update weekly	Update daily	Update 2x daily	Update > 2x/day	Near-time update	Real-time update
Dimensional complexity— the relative nature of how extensive and/ or abstracted the various reporting dimensions are necessary	1–10	Typical dimensions of month, year, etc., and no others	Easily understood dimensions, such as color, weight, etc.	Combinations of simple dimensions, i.e., weight and color need to be correlated	Dimensions become more than one or two layers deep in terms of taxonomy	Dimensions can vary by subject values, e.g., customer profiles	Dimension values can change based on other dimensional values			Certain dimensions cannot be sourced, but can be derived from combinations of other dimensions	Certain dimensions do not exist
Dimensional volatility—the frequency that dimensions change, are ADDED TO, or UPDATED for BI uses	1–10	Dimension types and values are fixed, by regulation or tradition	Dimension types are fixed, and values change rarely, perhaps once every few years	Dimension types are fixed, but values change yearly	Dimension types may be added once in a few years, and dimension values change accordingly	Dimension types will change, as well as new additions. Values will change within fiscal time frames	Dimension types change within fiscal periods. Dimension values change frequently, and old values must be retained	Dimension types change within periods, dimension values are dynamic enough to consider end-user maintenance of values	Dimension values change daily	Dimension values change near time	Real-time changes in dimensions as well as facts

(Continued)

Table F.2 (Continued)

EIM Metric and BIR Characteristics Score Sheet

	Relative Complexity	1	2	3	4	5	6	7	8	9	10
"Historicity"—the extent to which historical reporting requirements are necessary	1–10	No history	Retain recent additions	Retain additions within fiscal year	Retain multiple years of additions	Retain for year-over-year analysis	Retain for month-over-month analysis	Retain for week-over-week analysis	"As of date" within fiscal year	"As of date" over several years	"As of date" and period over period
Latency—the time between when the data is available to when it is required to be placed into the framework	10–1 Low latency is scored higher	Available within year	Available within quarter	Available within month	Available within week	Available two to four days	Available within 24 hours	Available 2x/day	Available > 2 intervals/day	Near-time availability	Immediate xmt to DW
Cross functionality/distribution—the extent to which the information will be used across an enterprise	1–10	Used only by department	Generated by department, limited sharing	Generated by division, widespread sharing by division	Generated division, multiple department usage in division			Generated centrally, used by selected division	Generated centrally, used by multidivision/department	Wide usage across enterprise	Ubiquitous use by entire enterprise
Volume—relative amount of logical data required to meet all granularity, dimensional, and archival requirements	1–10	Less than 20gb	20–50gb	50–100gb	100–300gb	300–500gb	500–750gb	7501tb	1–3tb	3–10tb	Over 10tb
Frequency—how often the information is accessed for a particular measure or requirement differs from volatility, e.g., daily activity is accessed weekly	1–10	1 x per year	1 x per quarter	2 x per quarter	1 x per month	2 x per month	Weekly	2 x per week	Daily	2 x per day	Many a day

Attribute	1–10										
Response time—how soon must the business react to the metric and take action, e.g., with customer or other touch point?	1–10	No required response to any touch point or stimulus	A response is required but there is no deadline	Response required within a fiscal year	Response required within a fiscal month	Response required within a fiscal week	Response required within a fiscal day	Response required within a portion of a day	Response required within 90 minutes	Response required within 15–90 minutes	Immediate, real-time response required
Follow-up time—the time desired to allocate to responding to a metric or stimulus, i.e., you can respond quickly, but only be able to spend an hour on the event	1–10	Follow-up has no cap on effort expended	Follow-up to resolve event can take up to a fiscal year	Follow-up to resolve event can take up to a fiscal month	Follow-up to resolve event can take up to a calendar week	Follow-up to resolve event must take between a day and a week	Follow-up to resolve event can only take a business day	The organization cannot afford to invest more than 1–23 hours	The organization cannot afford to spend more than an hour	The organization must be equipped to follow up after a response within an hour	Response time and follow-up are the same—there is no time to make the touch point wait
Data quality—degree of usefulness or effectiveness of source data	1–10	Data is "clean"	Data is clean, but data controls are loose	Data is clean, but controls are loose, and sources are disparate	Some data may require fixing up some "fat finger" errors	Data may have correct values, but wrong context (referential)	Data may have new values, or unknown domains	Domains have to be split up to create new values	Core subjects missing legitimate values (e.g., customer id)	Beside domain and value issues, data must be reconciled to disparate sources	Data does not really exist in source systems, but needs to be staged for heuristic algorithms
Availability—when should information be available	1–10				During the business day	24 × 7					
Persistency—the extent to which the data set remains stable	1–10	Data set never appended or updated	Data set appended to only when needed	Data set is appended to, but no updates	Data set is updated only as needed	Data set is updated periodically, but not refreshed	Data set must be refreshed monthly or on regular basis	Data set must be refreshed totally (reload)	Data set must be refreshed on demand	Data set must be refreshed daily for new use	Data set can be created and destroyed at will by user
Access type—mode of data access, e.g., will the information be accessed directly, via query, or rolled off onto reports?	1–10	Tab report	Control break report	Sorted breaks	Parameters and filters	Pivot table	Drill across	Ad hoc	Complex SQL	Need to subset data sets on fly	Need to create nonpersistent data sets

Table and values are from IMEdge™ Copyright 2007 IMCue LLC.

MART Analysis Templates

Analyze the nature of the data/information flow between locations or processes in the IVC (Table F.3).

Table F.3 MART Matrix

Determine nature of interactions between processes

To

From	Process A	Process B	Process C	Process D	Process E	Process F	Process G	Process H
Process A								
Process B								
Process C								
Process D			---					
Process E								
Process F								
Process G								
Process H								

Determine types of usage by subject area

	Subject A	Subject B	Subject C	Subject D	Subject E	Subject F	Subject G	Subject H
Operational								
Managerial								
Analytical								
Distributed								
Central								
External								
Internal								

M = Message or low-latency event
A = Aggregation or a roll-up calculation
R = Replication or copy
T = Transformation or value changes or format altered

Road Map Phase Summary and Work Products

This appendix provides the details for the Road Map phase, including activities, tasks, work products, and deliverables. Templates for Sustaining requirements, the Road Map outline, and sequencing of EIM projects are shown.

Road Map Work Product Overview (Table G.1)

Table G.1 Road Map Activity and Work Products

Activity	Tasks	Outputs (Work Products)	Activity Deliverable
Application Road Map	Identify business projects		EIM application road map
	Create new/revised affinity groupings (mapping entities to measures, measures to business actions)	Grouping of common benefit or information asset usage	
	Consider Metric and BIR groups		
	Consider groups of data model to metrics, or BIRs		
	Consider groups of actions, levers, IVC, or scenarios to content		
	Interpret groups and identify business projects	Working names for initial projects	
	Develop brief project descriptions	Initial project descriptions	
	Group/Align business projects with business initiatives	Matched projects to associated business needs or other enterprise programs	
	Associate relevant metrics, BIRs, IVC, etc. with respective projects	Project/requirement list	
	Map project objectives to business drivers and info requirements	Business-driven project objectives	
	Review preliminary project objectives and deliverables	Reasonableness check for projects	

(Continued)

Table G.1 (Continued)

Activity	Tasks	Outputs (Work Products)	Activity Deliverable
	Determine project constraints	Associated constraints to projects	
	Prioritize and confirm projects	Adjusted projects prioritized	
	Develop initial project roll-out strategy	List and description of business projects	
	Review and confirm initial projects		
	Develop full project descriptions		
	Derive project plans		
	Estimate project cost		
	Identify support projects	List and description of support projects, e.g., DQ projects, technology projects	
	Review previous documentation for support projects		
	Review MART and IVC data		
	Review DQ Architecture		
	Review EIM Architecture elements		
	Review EIM data and content management elements		
	Review DQ Architecture		
	Review technology recommendations		
	List and describe support projects	Support project roll-out plan	
	Develop general roll-out strategy		
	Cross-reference with business projects		
	Determine critical path constraints		
	Rationalize projects with IT portfolio and resources		
	Design project presentation and Road Map presentation format	Road Map visual depiction	
	Present to EIM leadership for approval	Approval for business review	
	Present to EIM sponsorship for approval	Approved Road Map and projects	
EIM Organization	Identify EIM functions from templates	EIM function list	EIM organization chart and descriptions
	Verify EIM functions vs. DG		
	Isolate functions with regulatory relevance		

(Continued)

Table G.1 (Continued)

Activity	Tasks	Outputs (Work Products)	Activity Deliverable
	Incorporate gaps in current state of data management	Refined EIM functions	
	Examine current data standards and policies		
	Refine baseline EIM Organization function		
	Identify EIM-affected business areas and new business functions	Business impact report	
	Develop EIM RACI charts	EIM Organization RACI analysis	
	Develop draft organization charts	EIM Organization chart	
	Draft EIM Organization charter and mission statements	EIM charter and mission	
	Refine changes to SDLC processes for EIM	SDLC change requirements	
	Identify new job categories and positions	New position list	
	Prepare new job descriptions	EIM job descriptions	
	Define desired roll-out schedule for EIM and business organizations	EIM Organization roll out schedule	
	Initiate EIM Organization socialization	EIM socialization sessions	
	Review current EIM guiding principles		
	Present EIM functional model and organization charts to business leadership		
	Gain acceptance of EIM Organization in principle		
	Submit job descriptions to HR for development	Approved job descriptions	
DG Rollout	Refine DG organization (if EIM Organization indicated changes)	Refined DG organization design	Implemented DG area
	Refine governance bodies and committees		
	Refine DG charter		
	Confirm data stewardship and ownership model if necessary		
	Define DG roll-out schedule	DG roll-out schedule	
	Define rollout of DG to support Road Map		

(Continued)

Table G.1 (Continued)

Activity	Tasks	Outputs (Work Products)	Activity Deliverable
	Design DG metrics and reporting requirements		
	Identify DG metrics stakeholders and playmakers		
	Design metrics collection mechanisms		
	Review DG metrics requirements with EIM leadership and obtain approval		
	Identify projects and stakeholders subject to standards and governance	List of initial subjects for orientation to DG	
	Publish and review IAM principles		
	Review/revise modifications to SDLC and other IT processes		
	Roll out initial DG functions	Active DG area	
	Present initial road shops		
	Publish guidelines and principles		
	Implement DG policies/ procedures orientation and training		
	Publish and implement SDLC integration documentation		
	Develop and conduct DG audit processes training		
	Initiate DG audit processes		
	Define additional roll-out activity for the Sustaining phase	DG Sustaining Requirements	
Sustaining Requirement	Define EIM change management approach		Sustaining requirements and change management plan
	Review assessments	Change readiness report	
	Execute Change Capacity if not done		
	Incorporate IMM results into Change Capacity		
	Prepare statement of change readiness		
	Identify change management resources	Change management team	

(Continued)

Table G.1 (Continued)

Activity	Tasks	Outputs (Work Products)	Activity Deliverable
	Identify mechanisms to *prepare* the organization for change	Specific mechanisms and actions for change management	
	Define levels of communication required for specific stakeholders		
	Define mechanisms for delivering communication		
	Define level of involvement, specific actions, and tools for sponsor		
	Design tools to prepare the organization for change		
	Perform stakeholder analysis	Stakeholder analysis	
	Identify EIM stakeholders		
	Develop stakeholder analysis form		
	Complete stakeholder analysis		
	Review with EIM leadership		
	Determine levels of commitment for key stakeholders		
	Review results of stakeholder analysis		
	Determine action plan to address improving levels of stakeholder commitment		
	Develop sponsorship plan	Sponsorship plan and orientation	
	Identify required sponsorship and right level of sponsor		
	Develop sponsor action plan		
	Develop communications plan	Communication plan for EIM	
	Identify audiences		
	Create messages and branding		
	Identify vehicles for communications		
	Define timing, frequencies, and delivery means		
	Review and approval of communications plan		
	Develop training plan	Training plan for EIM	
	Identify audiences		
	Identify levels of training: orient, educate, and train		

(Continued)

Table G.1 (Continued)

Activity	Tasks	Outputs (Work Products)	Activity Deliverable
	Identify vehicles for training		
	Define timing, frequencies, and delivery means		
	Review and approval of training plan		
	Develop resistance management plan	Resistance plan	
	Perform SWOT analysis		
	Identify specific resistance profiles		
	Develop responses to resistance		
	Review and approve resistance management plan		
	Identify and design change measures and assessments	EIM change management metrics	
	Develop change management plan		
	Define specific activity schedule for change	Change management schedule (IMM timetable)	
	Design metrics and assessments to ensure change effectiveness	EIM change management metrics	
	Define WIIFM and consequences	WIIFM, incentives	
	Define resources to fulfill change delivery	Enhanced change management team	
	Develop revised process/policy alignment plan: reviewing/updating existing policies and processes related to DG and EIM	Revised policies affected by governance	
	Develop EIM management requirements	Day-to-day EIM management requirements	
	Define EIM Organization roll out		
	Revise EIM charter/mission if necessary		
	Develop/refine EIM Organization positions		
	Consolidate change tactics into change management plan	Change management plan	
	Define/revise EIM roll out based on sustaining input	EIM Organizations roll out plan	

Table G.2 is to be used as a means to identify what needs to be presented in Sustaining requirements. For example, Farfel and UIC are entirely different due to internal politics, applications portfolio, and business models. The cells that are filled in are examples of types of requirements.

Table G.2 Generic Sustaining Requirements Development Template

EIM Building Block	Develop Sustaining Requirements for EIM – Template/Example					
	Training/Orientation Needs	Communication Needs	Stakeholder Analysis/Role	Sustaining Risk/Resistance	WIIFM	Organization Rollout
Business Model	Convey current state issues due to poor EIM; Convey changes in business model	Periodic report of EIM progress measures	Change agents	Business risk, financial impact		
Information handling and use	New latencies, analytical uses, and content management	Roll-out sequence	Leverage departmental expertise	Shadow IT growth	DQ incentives	Roll-out sequence
Information life cycle	New IVC, touch point enabling	Measures of progress, roll-out sequence	Internal and external facing	Ensure use of new processes	DQ incentives	
Applications	Revised methods, standards	Reinforcement of reasons	Identify CIO role; ERP/package support	Monitor applications and individuals	Revise performance goals	Roll-out sequence; New BI/ reporting structures
Technology	New interfaces; Role of ERP packages	Reinforcement of reasons; EIM portal	Privacy/security changes		Revise performance goals	Roll-out sequence
Organization	Walk the talk	Web site/EIM portal		Human capital loss	Revised performance goals	Roll-out sequence

(Continued)

Table G.2 (Continued)

| EIM Building Block | Training/Orientation Needs | Develop Sustaining Requirements for EIM — Template/Example | | | | |
		Communication Needs	Stakeholder Analysis/Role	Sustaining Risk/Resistance	WIIFM	Organization Rollout
Executive team	Orientation road show	Quarterly summary	Walk the talk	Verify buy-in		Verify buy-in
	EIM basics	EIM Metrics report	Maintain priority of program	Time issues	Design incentives	
	Sustaining plan orientation	Issues summary	Design incentives	Consultative approach		
	DG processes	Sustaining updates	Visible support	Seek opinions		
	DQ basics	Improvement to IMM		Brief, concise meetings		
Management	Orientation road show	Monthly summary	Walk the talk	Specific resistance	Design incentives	
	EIM basics	EIM Metrics report	Visible support	Face-to-face meetings		
	DG processes	Issue status	Codesign new processes	Measure resistance		
	DQ basics	Improvement to IMM	Demonstrate new processes			
	Sustaining orientation					
DG committees	Orientation road show	Quarterly summary	Walk the talk	Proactively seek resistors	Frequent checkup	
	EIM basics	Issues summary	Visible support			
	DQ basics	DG metrics	Timely resolution of issues			
Functional business areas	Orientation road show	Monthly summary	Walk the talk		Proactively seek resistors	
	EIM basics	Improvement to IMM	Codesign new processes		Seek opinions	

External parties	DQ basics; Sustaining plan orientation	Learn new processes, standards	Demonstrate new processes; Visible support	Seek opinions	Revise SLAs	
Applications developers	Orientation road show; DG processes; SDLC changes; Advanced EIM	Monthly summary	Walk the talk; Visible support		Proactively seek resistors	Proactively seek resistors
Operations	Orientation road show; DQ basics	Monthly summary	Walk the talk		Proactively seek resistors	Proactively seek resistors
Compliance	Orientation road show	Monthly summary	Support new processes and governance	Regulatory interface	Seek opinions	Coordinate with compliance processes
Enterprise "DNA"	EIM basics; DG processes; Train business and IT	EIM Metrics report; Quarterly updates			Incentives to use	
Culture	Change management team	Corporate communications role	Update stakeholder analysis	Find leverage points in current culture	Ensure concept is sold	Roll-out sequence
Governance	Extensive orientation and training to DG	Monthly web site	By individual through middle management		Incentives to use; disincentives for abuse	Roll-out sequence
Managed content	New standards, rules, principles, and policies	Measurement of progress	All touch points identified	All touch points identified	Incentives to use; disincentives for abuse	Interface with DQ rollout

EIM Road Map and Applications Description Outline Template (Tables G.3 and G.4)

Table G.3 Road Map/Application Project Deliverable Outline

1. EIM program development approach
    1.1 Objectives of EIM program
    1.2 EIM scope
    1.3 EIM Business Vision
    1.4 EIM Road Map visuals
    1.5 EIM Architecture visuals
2. Business Case
    2.1 Business drivers and goals
    2.2 EIM value levers
    2.3 EIM Information Levers
3. Target EIM Content and Data Management Architecture
    3.1 Subject areas and data models
    3.2 Information value chain(s)
    3.3 Revisions to business processes
    3.4 BI analytics/data access framework
    3.5 Taxonomies
    3.6 DQ standards and architecture
    3.7 Master data areas
    3.8 Reference data approach
    3.9 EIM Organization chart
4. EIM Organization and governance
    4.1 DG Architecture
    4.2 DG approach
    4.3 Data principles
    4.4 Data policies
    4.5 Governance repository
5. Technology solutions
    5.1 Technology categories
        Middleware
        Hardware
        Data movement
        Metadata/DNA
        Data access/BI
    5.2 Category short lists/recommendations
6. EIM implementation
    6.1 Infrastructure and business application projects

(Continued)

Table G.3 (Continued)

    6.1.1 Project derivation
        Segmentation and alignment
           Prioritization factors
           Business segments
           Community definitions
           Technology segments
           Support segments
    6.1.2 Business objectives/project alignment
    6.1.3 Project abstracts
        Infrastructure projects
           Interfaces
           Hardware
           Software
           Middleware/services
           Intranet/portals
           Collaboration/Social Networking
           Revised security/privacy
        Support projects
           Discovery
           Codes
           Migrations
           Cleanups
  6.2 Business application projects detailed specifications
    6.2.1 Project A
        1. Project overview
           1.1 Project description
           1.2 Project business benefits
           1.3 Project context
           1.4 Project goals and objectives
           1.5 Project derivation
        2. Organization/processes impact
        3. Governance interface
           3.1 Guiding principles
           3.2 Procedures and standards
        4. Technology
        5. Change management
        6. Implementation plan
           6.1 Implementation considerations

(Continued)

Table G.3 (Continued)

Table G.4 Road Map Sequencing Matrix

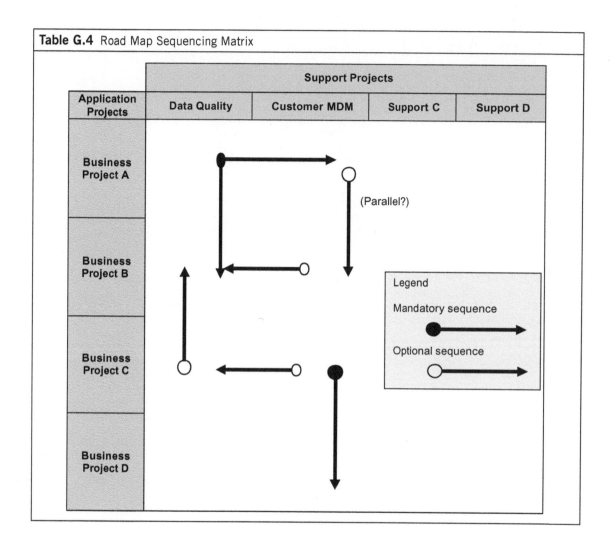

Sustaining Phase Summary and Work Products

This appendix provides the details for the Sustaining phase. A template presenting generic training needs and a generic change management plan is provided for reference.

Sustaining Work Product Overview (Table H.1)

Table H.1 Sustaining Phase Activities and Work Products

Activity	Tasks	Outputs (Work Products)	Activity Deliverable
Organization Roll Out	Complete new EIM team identification/socialization		EIM organization in place
	Socialize EIM program and area to IT and compliance	Understanding of the EIM team role to constituents	
	Socialize new EIM manager	An operational effective EIM Organization	
	Identify and staff IM area	EIM staffed	
	Establish physical location	EIM department	
	Review EIM charter(s)	EIM charter	
	Present EIM charters and EIM principles to new staff	Oriented staff	
	Present Sustaining Activities and stakeholder analysis to EIM staff		
	Orient executive team to EIM Organization (if not done in Sustaining Activity)	Oriented executive team	
	Schedule EIM team, committees, and executives for their orientation, training, or education	Training and orientation events	
	Align EIM team functions with Road Map projects	EIM managing projects	
	Ensure estimates are understood and project management practices in place		

(Continued)

Making Enterprise Information Management (EIM) Work for Business. DOI: 10.1016/B978-0-12-375695-4.00043-6

Table H.1 (Continued)

Activity	Tasks	Outputs (Work Products)	Activity Deliverable
Sustaining (change management) Activity	Confirm affected stakeholders	Stakeholders contacted and aware	Change management activities and sustaining plan deployed
	Confirm sponsor readiness	Sponsor ready	
	Confirm "burning platform" or current state deficiencies	Defined current state	
	Integrate the Sustaining Activity with overall EIM Road Maps and project plans	Defined current state	
	Identify new obstacles and constraints	Remediation to resistance approach	
	What issues need to be addressed and obstacles removed?	Feedback and adjustment over time of EIM activities	
	How much stakeholder involvement will be needed?	Responses to resistance and application of incentives	
	Define/modify roll-out strategy, select roll-out option by:	Modified EIM rollout	
	EIM project		
	EIM-governed area		
	EIM function or component		
	EIM element		
	Execute the change plan		
	Activate training, communications, resistance management, etc.	EIM change management execution	
	Develop materials for training, orientation, road shows, etc.		
	Develop additional advocates if necessary		
	Communicate short-term wins		
	Communicate status and measurements of progress often to leadership		
	Address problem areas aggressively		
	Measure EIM change effectiveness		
	Execute measurement surveys (if designed)	EIM effectiveness surveys	
	Hold focus groups/interviews for feedback	Surveyed feedback	
	Realign impacted policies/practices and procedures to clearly support the new EIM Vision, not contradict it	Confirmed alignment of policy	

(Continued)

Table H.1 (Continued)

Activity	Tasks	Outputs (Work Products)	Activity Deliverable
	Update staff performance objectives and reward structures to reflect new accountabilities and compliance to new rules	Remediation to resistance approach	
EIM Program Metrics	Define metrics requirements into categories of risk, return, efficiency, DQ, DG	EIM Metrics definitions	EIM metrics
	Define metrics per the Metrics Model used in the Business Model phase	Metric Model of EIM Metrics	
	Present metrics to EIM leadership for approval	Metrics presentation	
	Deploy metrics collection and reporting in alignment with the EIM Road Map	A set of metrics that are deployed and being used to report on effectiveness of EIM/IAM	
	Implement regular metrics and measurement of DG implementation	DG metrics	
	Produce EIM effectiveness reports	EIM Management report on effectiveness	

EIM Management	Manage Road Map projects
	    Report wins
	    Interact with change management
	    Ensure aggressive resolution of issues
		Road Map progress	EIM program status

	Manage EIM department functions
	    Manage day-to-day operations
	        Manage DG
	        Manage business data and content—oversight of the assets (databases, documents, content)
	        Manage integrity and security—database administration and security
	        Manage DQ
	        Manage the IAM/EIM architecture elements
	        Manage reassessments/EIM adjustments
	        Manage data life cycles—acquisition, movement, and purging
		The ongoing operation of EIM	

Table H.1 (Continued)

Activity	Tasks	Outputs (Work Products)	Activity Deliverable
	Manage enterprise DNA (metadata), including EIM design and architecture artifacts		
	Manage reference and master data		
	Manage data and content usage (BI, reporting, catalogs, web sites)		
	Manage tools and technologies		
	Deploy and adjust EIM	EIM deployment stages	
	Document metrics and EIM function performance		
	Train and educate		
	Implement EIM Metrics tools and technology		
	Promote and interact with change management		
	Perform and review audits and service levels		
	Interact with governing bodies		
	DG committees and councils		
	Appoint and meet with major project steering bodies		
	Update executive EIM sponsorship		
	Align EIM Project Management activity with existing IT practices	EIM Project Management	
	Identify project templates		
	Identify EIM project-estimating tools		
	Identify EIM tracking and accounting procedures for IT		
	Forecast EIM project resources		
	Utilize modified SDLC		
	Interact with enterprise PMO (if one exists)		
	Utilize modified SDLC		
	Interact with enterprise PMO (if one exists)		

Generic Training Needs Assessment

Remember, all stakeholders will need some kind of orientation or training (Table H.2).

Table H.2 Generic Training Needs Template

Training Needs Assessment Template		
Question	**Response**	**Source**
Project scope		
What is the overall scope of the implementation?		
Are there any other software or company business drivers that might affect the implementation?		
What level of understanding is there about the changes that will arrive soon?		
What are the timelines and key milestones?		
End users		
How many end users will require training?		
How many users per department and function?		
List the job titles of the end users and provide a brief description of each title		
How many in each area are heavy users (use significant functionality on a regular basis) and light users (mainly look at reports or use minimal functionality)? Which shifts do they work?		
What are the languages and language skills of the users?		
What is the geographic distribution of the end users? List the location and number of end users by department.		
Are job descriptions for the end users readily available? Where? Do they describe current or future state job roles/responsibilities?		
Training infrastructure		
Which organization(s) is responsible for employee education and training? What is this organization's role in supporting the implementation?		
What types of employee education and training programs are currently offered (e.g., operations, computer literacy, etc.) and by whom? Include internal and external programs. Obtain a copy of the curriculum, including a list of trainers, target audiences, locations, and a schedule for each course.		
How is a new hire trained today?		
What type of training is most commonly used (i.e., paper-based, computer-based training, self-paced, and classroom)?		
What company standards already exist for training materials and online systems?		
Have any past training projects been particularly effective/ineffective? Explain why.		
Facilities		
List the training facilities available for end-user training.		
Who is responsible for planning and overseeing the details of the training facilities? Training delivery?		
What is the seating capacity at each training facility?		
How many workstations are there at each training facility?		
How far in advance do you need to book your facilities?		
Describe any scheduling limitations that may exist for training?		
Is there a reproduction department or other facility available to support duplication of training materials?		

(Continued)

Table H.2 (Continued)

Training Needs Assessment Template		
Question	**Response**	**Source**

Resources

Who are the sponsors of the training effort?

Are there any training resources dedicated to the implementation? If so, how many?

Who will manage the training program?

Who will schedule the training?

Who will customize the training materials and create the exercises?

What resources are available for materials production (i.e., printing, binding, etc.)?

When will the training resources join the project team?

Who are the key SMEs? What are their individual areas of expertise?

What is the availability of the core team to support the trainers?

Who will review and/or approve the key end-user education and training deliverables?

Have you identified trainers? Who are they? What are their areas of expertise?

Technology

What type of workstations do you have? Operating system, processor, memory, hard drive disk space, CD-ROM drive, VGA, or higher resolution–pointing device

What type of servers do the computers run on at the training facilities? Are there dedicated servers?

Type of connection from training facilities to the project server—LAN/WAN?

Do training workstations have access to the intranet/Internet?

Are there projectors and screens in the classrooms? What types?

Are there printers in the classrooms? Are they shared? What types?

Web-based learning and performance support

If you have an intranet, will it be integrated with the web-based learning and performance support?

What type of connectivity do you have?

What type of server software do you have?

What type of web server software is running?

How much server disk space do you have?

What type of information needs to get from the web site to the training database?

Do you have a webmaster/technical resource that understands and manages hardware, connectivity?

If you do not have a webmaster/technical resource, can you outsource this function? Do you have the budget to do this?

Do you have a web content and migration strategy?

Do you have someone to update and publish web content?

Do you have a web-authoring package?

Do you have people skilled at using your web-authoring package?

Is there a web graphics artist in house?

Does your company use a standard browser?

Have you used web-based training before?

Is there a standard web-based training product that your company uses (CBT Systems, Asymetrix)?

Generic Change Management Plan Template (Table H.3)

Table H.3 Generic Change Management Plan Reference Template

Generic Change Management Plan Template (See Bibliography for Other Sources) Planning for Change (Sustaining Requirements in Road Map Phase)
Define change management approach: conducted in conjunction with the change management program team
Assess the size and nature of the change
Conduct organizational impact analysis: type of change, degree of change (incremental vs. dramatic), individuals impacted, time frame
Determine degree of change planning required based on impact analysis (the bigger the change, the more complete the plan)
Review CM program governance requirements
Review project objectives and requirements
Identify stakeholder groups impacted by the proposed changes — internal and external
Identify potential issue areas: resistance, work overload, apparent skill gaps
Conduct stakeholder analysis
Conduct analysis for each stakeholder group
Determine degree of impact to each stakeholder group: low, medium, high
Determine what roles each stakeholder group will need to play
Assess what concerns each group may have and how each group is likely to react to the changes
Conduct a stakeholder commitment assessment and incorporate results into the stakeholder analysis
Determine what is needed from each group
Determine how best to work with each group
Conduct change Readiness assessment with stakeholder groups
Analyze results of the Readiness assessment and note areas of concern
Develop approach to address areas of concern
Develop/deliver project sponsorship model
Assess sponsor and business lead capabilities to manage change
Educate sponsor and business lead on roles/responsibilities
Educate sponsor and business lead on change, as needed
Develop plan to engage leaders as part of sponsorship for the change
Create periodic meeting schedule: biweekly, monthly, quarterly
Consider using forums that already exist
Clarify and communicate leadership accountabilities as part of the change
Address resistance when it occurs
Develop detailed project change management plan
Develop communications plan
Identify the audiences for the change, both internal to the impacted organization and externally in the remainder of surety
Executive and business leaders, mid-level managers and supervisors, frontline employees

(Continued)

Table H.3 (Continued)

Generic Change Management Plan Template (See Bibliography for Other Sources)
Planning for Change (Sustaining Requirements in Road Map Phase)

    Identify and develop key messages
      Review key messages for the cornerstone program
      Develop unique messages for each audience based on change impact to them
      Customize messages where needed based on results of stakeholder analysis
    Determine content timing, packaging, delivery method, frequency, and sender
    Consider "who" should deliver message, for each key message
    Review communication plan with sponsor, business lead, project manager, and CM program team
  Develop training needs assessment
    Identify and document necessary skill and/or behavior changes required to support the change and assess current gaps
    Identify stakeholders that require training
    Conduct a needs assessment and gap analysis for each
    Document requirements for training development
  Develop resistance management plan
    Review results of Readiness assessments
    Define what resistance may look like
    Define a strategy for managing resistance
    Review the resistance management approach with the primary sponsor
    Communicate the resistance management plan to leaders in the stakeholder organizations
  Develop measurement plan
    Identify which measurement categories and tools to use
    Customize selected tools to project needs
    Collect measurements based on project roll-out schedule
Managing change
CM project execution
  Integrate CM plan activities with overall project plan
    Track progress of tasks
    Evaluate results, resolve issues, and adjust plans as required
  Develop implementation checklist
    Develop list of all work that must be completed prior to implementation
    Review list with project team, project sponsor, and business lead
    Make sure that all tasks are accounted for and completed
    Create action plan to address those items not completed
  Develop staff transition plan—requires HR involvement
    Identify jobs that may require movement of people
    Identify type of change
    Identify new skills required
    Identify individuals impacted (HR)
    Identify actions by individual (HR)
    Identify communication messages for individuals and the broader organization

(Continued)

Table H.3 (Continued)

Generic Change Management Plan Template (See Bibliography for Other Sources)
Planning for Change (Sustaining Requirements in Road Map Phase)

Collect and analyze feedback—to be handled centrally by the CM program team
    Identify feedback collection tools and process based on overall program approach
    Collect feedback from the organization: pre-change, during change, after implementation
    Analyze feedback and compliance data
    Develop action plans to address issue areas
Conduct training needs assessment
    Identify the individuals to provide information and list those names in the source column of the needs assessment tool
    Conduct interviews
    Document findings in the assessment and conduct any required follow-up
Diagnose gaps and manage resistance
    Identify root causes of resistance
    Develop corrective actions
    Provide information to sponsor and leaders to manage change
Identify early wins
    Communicate and celebrate successes
Sustaining change
CM project follow-up
    Develop organizational alignment action plan
        Customize the tool to the project situation you are in: eliminate areas of the action plan that are irrelevant and add those that may be needed
        Facilitate a discussion with the appropriate individuals to assess existing systems and structures using the template work sheet
        Identify areas where current infrastructure may need to be modified to sustain the change objectives
        Validate the data and gain alignment with HR and the appropriate stakeholder groups
        Add the action steps to the detailed change management plan and execute the steps during implementation
    Develop the change integration checklist
        Define the audience for conducting the change integration checklist
        Could be a random sample or the entire organization
        Determine the best means to conduct the survey: electronic, facilitated meetings, Excel spreadsheet, etc.
        Analyze the results and identify common themes
        Report findings to sponsors and stakeholders as appropriate
        Develop action plans to address gaps
        Conduct the survey again in 90–120 days to determine progress
    Conduct after-action review of the change management process
        Select participants: project team and stakeholder
        Conduct meeting
        Capture and reuse lessons learned from change process

EIM Topics Bibliography

Ariyachandra, T., Fuller, C., & Watson, H. J. (2004, December 1). *Data warehouse governance: Best practices at Blue Cross and Blue Shield of North Carolina*. Volume 38, Issue 3, pages 435–450, Netherlands, Elsevier B.V., Decision Support Systems. (Digital) HTML (http://www.sciencedirect.com/science/article/B6V8S–49NOFPB-2/2/ceb73b462b193a5c56f4070ebc5178fc).

Boddie, J. (1993). *The information asset*. Upper Saddle River, NJ: Prentice-Hall (Yourdon Press Computing Series).

Brackett, M. (1994). *Data sharing using a common data architecture*. New York: John Wiley & Sons.

Bryce, M., & Bryce, T. (1988). *The IRM revolution: Blueprint for the 21st century*. M. Bryce Associates.

Cook, M. (1996). *Building enterprise information architectures*. Upper Saddle River, NJ: Prentice Hall (Foreword by John Zachman).

Chisholm, M. (2000). *Managing reference data in enterprise databases*. San Francisco, CA: Morgan Kaufmann. See review at http://www.tdan.com/book030.htm and web site supporting the book at http://www.refdataportal.com/.

DAMA Chicago Standards Committee. (1999). *Guidelines for implementing data resource management* (3rd ed.). DAMA International Publication #1 (Available from DAMA International).

Davenport, T. H., & Harris, J. G. (2007). *Competing on analytics*. Boston, MA: Harvard Business School Press.

English, L. (1999). *Improving data warehouse and business information quality: Methods for reducing costs and increasing profits*. New York: John Wiley & Sons.

Inmon, W. H. (1993). *Data architecture: The information paradigm*. New York: John Wiley & Sons.

Kerr, J. M. (1991). *The IRM imperative*. New York: Wiley Professional Computing.

Loshin, D. (2008 28). *Master data management*. Burlington, Morgan Kaufman. The MK/OMG Press (Paperback).

McGilvray, D. (2008). *Executing data quality projects: Ten steps to quality data and trusted information*. Burlington, MA: Morgan Kaufman.

Newton, J. J., & Wahl, D. (Eds.), (1993). *Manual for data administration*. Washington, DC: GPO, NIST Special Publications 500-208.

Redman, T. C. (2008). *Data driven: Profiting from your most important business asset*. Boston, MA: Harvard Business Press.

Reid, R., Fraser-King, G., & Schwaderer, W. D. (2007). *Data lifecycles: Managing data for strategic advantage*. London, John Wiley & Sons, Ltd.

Silverston, L., & Agnew, P. (2009). *The data model resource book: Universal patterns for data modeling*. Indianapolis, IN: Wiley Publishing, Inc.

Simsion, G., Witt, G. (2004, November 4). *Data modeling essentials* (3rd ed.). San Fransisco, Morgan Kaufman.

Thomas, G. (2006). *Alpha males and data disasters: The case for data governance*. Orlando, FL: Brass Cannon Press.

Thorp, J. (2003). Fujitsu Consulting's Center for Strategic Leadership. *The information paradox* (Rev. ed.). Ryerson, Canada: McGraw-Hill.

Index

Printed and bound by CPI Group (UK) Ltd, Croydon, CR0 4YY

03/10/2024

01040319-0005